PRODUCT LIABILITY IN COMPARATIVE PERSPECTIVE

This book examines the law of product liability from a comparative perspective. With the European Directive on Product Liability enacted over twenty years ago, this publication analyses the state of product liability in a number of key jurisdictions including both Western European countries and new Member States. Account is also taken of recent developments further afield, including the United States and Japan. Distinguished contributors, including a high court judge, European Commission official, leading litigators and academics, provide individual country reports and a number of integrated comparative studies. The book is designed for practical use by legal practitioners, academics, students and others interested in the area of contract, tort, civil procedure and multi-party litigation. In particular, practitioners will find the country reports an essential reference point.

DUNCAN FAIRGRIEVE is Director of the Tort Law Centre at the British Institute of International and Comparative Law, and is also Maître de Conférences at Sciences Po, Paris. He is a qualified French avocat and practises in the fields of product liability and commercial litigation in Paris.

PRODUCT LIABILITY IN COMPARATIVE PERSPECTIVE

Edited by

DUNCAN FAIRGRIEVE

CAMBRIDGE
UNIVERSITY PRESS

CAMBRIDGE UNIVERSITY PRESS
Cambridge, New York, Melbourne, Madrid, Cape Town, Singapore,
São Paulo, Delhi, Dubai, Tokyo, Mexico City

Cambridge University Press
The Edinburgh Building, Cambridge CB2 8RU, UK

Published in the United States of America by Cambridge University Press, New York

www.cambridge.org
Information on this title: www.cambridge.org/9780521847230

First published 2005

A catalogue record for this publication is available from the British Library

Library of Congress Cataloging in Publication data
Product liability in comparative perspective / edited by Duncan Fairgrieve.
p. cm.
Includes bibliographical references and index.
ISBN 13: 978 0 521 84723 0
ISBN 10: 0 521 84723 0 (hbk)
1. Products liability – European Union countries. 2. Products liability. I. Fairgrieve, Duncan.
KJE1630.P76 2005
346.2403'8 – dc22 2005046367

ISBN 978-0-521-84723-0 Hardback

CONTENTS

FIGURES

FOREWORD

This is an extraordinary book, in which I am honoured to be included, and which I am even more privileged to be able to introduce. It contains contributions from an array of the leading thinkers in the field of product liability; and it provides substantial food (non-standard, and certainly not defective) for thought for practitioners, academics and students alike. The British Institute of International and Comparative Law has been in the forefront of debate in the field of product liability, organising conferences from which no self-respecting practitioner or academic in the area could afford to be absent, and now, after 'rounding-up all the usual suspects', producing this totally riveting book.

As the judge in the Hepatitis C litigation, I had the opportunity of climbing a steep learning curve, supervised by Counsel, but educated by leading academics not only from the United Kingdom, but from Europe and of course Australia. Now they are all collected together in one place. They may not agree (either with each other, or – even! – with the Hepatitis C judgment) but, taken together, their views constitute the corpus of present thinking, and it makes a stimulating and enlightening read.

SIR MICHAEL BURTON

CONTRIBUTORS

HIS HONOUR JUDGE MICHAEL BROOKE QC.

MR JUSTICE BURTON, High Court Judge; President of the Employment Appeal Tribunal; Chairman of the Central Arbitration Committee.

PROFESSOR DR CEES C. VAN DAM, Professorial Fellow in European Tort Law and Director of the Regulation Forum, British Institute of International and Comparative Law.

DR DUNCAN FAIRGRIEVE, Fellow, British Institute of International and Comparative Law; *Maître de Conférences*, L'Institut d'Etudes Politiques de Paris; Avocat à la Cour, Paris.

IAN FORRESTER QC, White and Case LLP.

LUIS GONZÁLEZ VAQUÉ, Advisor, DG MARKT, European Commission.

CHRISTOPHER HODGES, Partner, CMS Cameron McKenna.

PROFESSOR GERAINT HOWELLS, Professor of Law, Lancaster University and Barrister, Gough Square Chambers.

STEFAN LENZE, Visiting Fellow, the British Institute of International and Comparative Law.

PROFESSOR MIQUEL MARTÍN-CASALS, Professor of Civil Law, Observatory of European and Comparative Private Law, University of Girona (Spain).

PROFESSOR MARK MILDRED, Professor of Litigation, Nottingham Trent University.

DR LUKE NOTTAGE, Senior Lecturer, University of Sydney Law Faculty.

DR ELEONORA RAJNERI, Researcher in Private Law at the Faculty of Economics of the Università del Piemonte Orientale.

DR MAGDALENA SENGAYEN, Research Officer in Product Liability and Regulatory Issues, Centre for Socio-Legal Studies, Oxford University.

PROFESSOR JANE STAPLETON, Research Professor, Australian National University; Ernest E. Smith Professor of Law, University of Texas; Commonwealth Fellow, British Institute of International and Comparative Law.

PROFESSOR DR HANS CLAUDIUS TASCHNER, Former Head of Unit, European Commission.

DR SIMON TAYLOR, *Maître de Conférences*, Université Paris 7 Denis Diderot.

NICHOLAS UNDERHILL QC, Fountain Court Chambers.

PREFACE

The aim of this book is to examine the law of product liability from a comparative law standpoint. It is now ten years since the publication of *Comparative Product Liability*, edited by Professor C. J. Miller and published by the British Institute of International and Comparative Law in association with the United Kingdom National Committee for Comparative Law. The time was thus ripe to examine the topic again.

The origin of this book is a research project undertaken by the Tort Law Centre at the British Institute of International and Comparative Law. Many of the contributions to the book have emerged from the Institute's work on product liability, whilst other chapters were originally presented by their authors at Institute events.

It is also appropriate to mention here the role of the Product Liability Forum, which, as well as generously supporting the work of the Institute in this area, has provided a stimulating arena for discussion of product liability issues.

Many thanks also to the staff of Cambridge University Press who have overseen the production process.

The Law is as stated on 1 March 2004.

DUNCAN FAIRGRIEVE

1

Introduction

DUNCAN FAIRGRIEVE AND LUIS GONZÁLEZ VAQUÉ

Product liability and overlapping interests

The essence of product liability is the apportionment of the risks inherent in the modern mass production of consumer goods. A choice must be made as to who should bear these risks: the victim, the state or the manufacturer?

Despite this apparent simplicity, the law of product liability is indeed a complex one, lying as it does on the overlap of a series of different matrices. In terms of substantive law, the law of contract and the law of tort make up one layer of rules, with oft-conflicting concepts and approaches. To this, a supranational stratum has been added. The European Directive on Product Liability has brought an important dimension of European Community law,[1] with the introduction of terms often alien to the national systems, such as 'putting into circulation' or 'defect', as well as the technical debates over competence and levels of harmonisation brought about by the European legislation. The law of product liability is further complexified due to the superposition of a myriad of other domestic rules stemming from the broader legal framework of consumer law, procedures governing damages claims, and, in some scenarios, the application of notions of public law.[2]

This complex legal framework must also be set within the broader policy debate. The framing of product liability regulation has been underpinned by a stark debate with conflicting viewpoints, on occasion

Any opinions expressed in this piece or mistakes made are those of the authors personally, and do not represent the views of the Commission.

[1] Council Directive of 25 July 1985 on the approximation of the laws, regulations and administrative provisions of the Member States concerning liability for defective products (85/374/EEC), OJL 210.

[2] See e.g. Conseil d'Etat, 3 March 2004 (State liability for failure to take preventive measures to reduce risks of work-related asbestos exposure). The text of this judgment and analysis of the decision may be found on the BIICL Product Liability Database, which may be accessed at www.biicl.org.

characterised as a struggle of consumer versus industry. Avoiding such oversimplification, account must nonetheless be taken of the important macro debate about how the varied interests of the victim, the producer, the insurer, the distributor *et al.*, should be correctly accommodated within the architecture of product liability regulation. At the core of any system for civil liability is the concern for the correct provision of compensation. There is however a recognition that in framing the law in this area, account must be taken of broader considerations, including the availability of alternative means of financial support such as insurance payments and social security awards, broader societal concerns about the function of the tort system, as well as the rights of the defendants, a consideration referred to in the contribution by Christopher Hodges as 'commercial continuity'.[3]

The European Directive and harmonisation

The factors which led to the intervention of the European legislator in this area of the law are significant.[4] Under a broad consumer-protection agenda, the Commission's attention settled on civil liability, with reform of the European-wide product liability at the forefront. Underpinning the development of the Directive were the parallel but distinct concerns of, on the one hand, the US-influenced review of commercial sale and supply of goods, and, on the other, the potent impact of the European-wide thalidomide drug tragedy in the 1960s and the inadequate response of traditional contract (warranty) and tort law to the plight of the victims.[5]

After protracted negotiations at a supranational level, partly due to the conflicting policy considerations described above, the European Product Liability Directive was eventually adopted.[6] The Directive was introduced as an internal market measure under Article 100 of the Treaty, which concerns the harmonisation of laws directly affecting the establishment of the common market. Nonetheless, there has been a good deal of debate whether the measure should correctly be perceived as an internal market or rather as a consumer protection initiative. In the contributions to this

[3] See chapter 11.
[4] Generally, see J. Stapleton, *Product Liability* (London: Butterworths, 1994) chapter 3.
[5] Ibid.
[6] Council Directive of 25 July 1985 on the approximation of the laws, regulations and administrative provisions of the Member States concerning liability for defective products (85/374/EEC), OJL 210.

book, we shall see that the European Court of Justice seems to have preferred the internal market argument. As a result, it has been decided that the Directive was intended to effect a 'complete' and not 'minimum' harmonisation.[7] As a consequence, Member States cannot increase consumer protection other than in areas where this was provided for expressly by the Directive.

A series of obstacles to this goal of maximum harmonisation remain. As a consequence of political compromises, Member States were presented with a menu of options and add-ons under the Directive, covering the development risks defence, the exclusion of primary agricultural produce and game[8] and a ceiling on personal injury damages. Moreover, many of the concepts in the Directive are left undefined, such as the crucial notion of 'putting into circulation'.[9] Even where a definition is given, the margin for manoeuvre in interpretation can be large.[10] Thus the core notion of 'defect' of a product is defined as when a product does not 'provide the safety which a person is entitled to expect'.[11]

Crucially, under the Directive, various key elements of a product liability action are simply left to domestic law, including areas as fundamental as causation, remoteness of damage, standard of proof, contributory acts, assessment of damages, procedure and rules of discovery. Over and above these areas specifically left outwith the Directive, Article 13 of the Directive leaves open the possibility of a co-existence of product liability systems. We shall see that these parallel systems play an important role in countries such as France (where the innovative *Cour de Cassation* case law on no-fault liability can be considered markedly pro-claimant),[12] and Germany (where the thalidomide tragedy resulted in a statutory no-fault regime for liability in pharmaceutical cases).[13]

[7] See Case C-183/00 *Gonzalez Sanchez v Medicina Asturiana SA* [2002] ECR I–3901; Case C-52/00 *Commission v France* [2002] ECR I-3827.

[8] Subsequently amended: Directive 99/34 OJ 1999 L 141/20.

[9] See Articles 6, 7 and 11 of the Directive. Under the French provisions, a further gloss is thus given on the notion of 'put into circulation', as follows: 'A product is put into circulation when the producer has voluntarily parted with it. A product is put into circulation only once' (Article 1386–5 of the Civil Code).

[10] Note also that linguistic variations have themselves engendered further divergences. The differing interpretation of the Article 9(b) exclusion of the first 500 euros of property damage between a lower-limit cut-off point or a non-claimable insurance-style 'excess' are examined in the contributions to this book.

[11] See Article 6 of the Directive.

[12] See chapter 5 on product liability in France.

[13] See chapter 6 on product liability in Germany.

Clearly, given these potential divergences, it is crucial to compare and contrast the national courts' stances in order to assess the success of the objective of unification. We turn thus to the role of comparative law.

Product liability: why compare?

Comparative law is increasingly recognised as an essential reference point for judicial decision-making. Whilst the English courts have long been open to considering how legal problems are solved in other jurisdictions, and in tort cases the courts have even showed an interest in looking further afield than common law jurisdictions,[14] the recent case of *Fairchild v Glenhaven Funeral Services Ltd* has further reinforced this trend. In his judgment, Lord Bingham conducted a comparative law survey on a point of causation and declared that:

> Development of the law in this country cannot of course depend on a head-count of decisions and codes adopted in other countries around the world, often against a background of different rules and traditions. The law must be developed coherently, in accordance with principle, so as to serve, even-handedly, the ends of justice. If, however, a decision is given in this country which offends one's basic sense of justice, and if consideration of international sources suggests that a different and more acceptable decision would be given in most other jurisdictions, whatever their legal tradition, this must prompt anxious review of the decision in question. In a shrinking world . . . there must be some virtue in uniformity of outcome whatever the diversity of approach in reaching that outcome.[15]

The growing use of comparative law poses a challenge to judges and counsel. It is recognised that scholarship also has an important role to play in making comparative material available in a systematic manner. The role of comparative law in the judicial process is subject to increasing scrutiny, covering topics as diverse as the relevance and weight of comparative law arguments, to the practical aspects of how to present those arguments to a court or the accessibility of source materials.[16]

[14] See e.g. *McFarlane v Tayside Health Board* [2000] 2 AC 59, 73 and 80–1; *Henderson v Merrett Syndicates* [1995] 2 AC 145, 184; *White v Jones* [1995] 2 AC 207, 263.

[15] [2002] UKHL 22, para 32. Lord Rodgers also observed that '[t]he Commonwealth cases were supplemented, at your Lordships' suggestion, by a certain amount of material describing the position in European legal systems . . . The material provides a check, from outside the common law world, that the problem identified in these appeals is genuine and is one that requires to be remedied' (para 165).

[16] See generally Guy Canivet, Mads Andenas and Duncan Fairgrieve, *Comparative Law before the Courts* (London: BIICL, 2004).

Comparative law has a particularly important role to play in the development of European Community law. For, unless there is an exchange of judgments of national courts on the application of Community law, then any goal of harmonisation becomes illusory. Harmonisation cannot solely be achieved simply through legislative initiative. It must also be fostered by means of debate between the legal communities of the Member States, and an exchange of the decisions applying and interpreting that primary legislation.

This comes to the fore in the application of the Product Liability Directive. The potential role for comparative law, as well as the challenges that it poses, are well illustrated in the seminal product liability case of *A v National Blood Authority*,[17] in which Mr Justice Burton drew extensively upon comparative law as a core aspect of his decision-making.[18] His Lordship opined that:

> I have had the great benefit of detailed submissions in writing, and some ten days of exegesis and argument orally in opening and closing by leading counsel, just on the law, including authorities and academic writings from France, Germany, Spain, Portugal, Sweden, Denmark, Belgium, Italy, Holland, Australia and the United States, as well as the United Kingdom and the European Court.

It is thus clear that the harmonisation effort does not end with the mere implementation of the Product Liability Directive. The success of the enterprise is likely to depend upon the harmonised *interpretation* of the provisions by the national courts. It is hoped that in some way this publication, as well as the Product Liability Database developed by the British Institute,[19] will participate in this laudable endeavour of achieving 'a higher and consistent level of consumer protection throughout the Community'.

Contents of the book

There have been a number of learned publications examining European product liability in comparative perspective.[20] Any comparative study of

[17] [2001] 3 All ER 289; [2001] Lloyd's Rep Med 187.
[18] For detailed discussion, see chapter 2.
[19] For more details of the BIICL Product Liability Database, see www.biicl.org.
[20] See e.g. P. Kelly and R. Altree (eds.), *European Product Liability* (London: Butterworths, 1992); G. Howells, *Comparative Product Liability* (Dartmouth: Ashgate, 1993); A. Geddes, *Product and Service Liability in the EEC* (London: Sweet and Maxwell, 1992); D. Campbell and C. Campbell (eds.), *International Product Liability* (London: LLP, 1993); C. Hodges (ed.), *Product Liability: European Laws and Practice* (London: Sweet and Maxwell, 1993).

product liability can at best give a snapshot of the law at a given time, as the legal provisions and decisions constantly develop. However, the time is clearly ripe for a re-evaluation of the present state of the law through an examination of the reception of the European Directive in a number of European countries, both long-standing Member States as well as New Member countries.

The contributions to the book are divided between a series of discrete reports on the state of product liability in individual countries, and contributions which examine the issues from a horizontal approach, analysing developments from a European perspective or presenting and comparing approaches in different legal systems or across a region.

In the first part of the book, 'Country reports', accounts are given of the legislation and case law on product liability in individual countries. Much of this analysis is concerned with the way in which the European norm has been integrated into the national legal systems, raising issues governing the reception of an external legal notion into a pre-existing national system. The reception of the Directive is illustrated in a representative series of Member States, encompassing both common law and civil law countries, including England, France, Italy, and Spain. Commencing with a rich comparative law analysis by the protagonists (counsel and judge) in the English case of *A v National Blood Authority*,[21] undoubtedly the leading judicial analysis of product liability provisions in any of the Member States,[22] contributions then follow covering developments in Continental systems.

A number of common themes can be identified in the contributions in this section. First, and unsurprisingly, the theme of harmonisation underpins many of the contributions. The authors thus undertake an assessment of the way in which the national systems have received the new European norm, the way in which the substantive law has been transformed, and how far the process of harmonisation has been achieved.

Second, and linked to the first, the contributions highlight the growing importance in the Member States of the taking into account of solutions adopted in other systems. A cross-fertilisation of judicial solutions is recognised as increasingly important. This is most strikingly evident in the aforementioned English case of *A v National Blood Authority*.[23] Over and above this, Professor Cees van Dam explains how the Dutch Supreme Court DES case has attracted international interest.[24] Nonetheless, it is

[21] [2001] 3 All ER 289; [2001] Lloyd's Rep Med 187.
[22] For detailed analysis of this case, see chapter 2.
[23] [2001] 3 All ER 289; [2001] Lloyd's Rep Med 187.
[24] See chapter 7.

clear that much remains to be done to enhance this comparative law exchange. The methodology for facilitating and encouraging this process is a point that is developed in other contributions.[25]

Third, and in contrast with these initial themes, it is important to note that in the various Member States, there is evidence of a continuing vitality of the parallel regimes of liability. This is partly due to substantive reasons, where the pre-existing systems in some respects offer more favourable solutions (see for instance Italy and France),[26] and partly due to inertia created by lack of familiarity with the new regime.

Fourth, it is clear from the contributions that difficulties of interpretation continue to prevail. This is well-illustrated in the detailed analysis of Professor Martín-Casals,[27] who analyses the Spanish cases with a fine-tooth comb, and observes that whilst the court decisions show that the judges are grappling with the issues, there has nonetheless been a number of judgments which are ambiguous or equivocal on crucial issues under the Directive. The European judiciary are thus undergoing a compulsory education in the thinking underpinning the Directive, in respect of which the learning curve is steep![28]

Fifth, on a similar theme, many of the contributions highlight the recurring theme of the problem of access to justice, which is left outside the scope of the Directive. The small number of cases under the Directive across Europe is attributed in part by Dr Rajneri in her paper on Italy to the difficulty,[29] as contrasted with the US, in funding the development of products claims. This concern underlines the importance of the procedural environment on the successful assertion of substantive rights, a factor which has been highlighted by studies undertaken into the operation of the Directive.[30]

In the final contribution in this section, Professor Howells traces the English case law on the notion of defect.[31] Beyond the substantive law, his contribution examines the way in which the English product liability decisions make a case study for the development of European private law. This piece thus provides a bridge between the country report section and the further contributions, which take a more lateral perspective.

[25] See in particular chapter 8, 'Defect in English law – lessons for the harmonisation of European product liability' by Professor Geraint Howells.

[26] Respectively chapters 4 and 5. [27] See chapter 3.

[28] See the words of Mr Justice Burton in the Foreword to this book.

[29] See chapter 4.

[30] See Lovells, *Product Liability in the European Union: a report for the European Commission, February 2003*, Markt/2001/11/D.

[31] See chapter 8.

Moving beyond the country-based analyses, Part II, 'European influences', adopts a horizontal approach to the topic, analysing the way in which the concepts in the European norm have been applied and developed across the Member States.

Professor Dr Hans Claudius Taschner provides an authoritative opening to this part.[32] As the person most closely associated with the genesis and drafting of the Directive, he expands his views on the current state of the harmonisation process in uncompromising fashion. He highlights three recurrent themes: the debate over the standard of liability arising from the Directive, the ceiling on the amount of damages and the vexed question of the development risks defence.

The issue of the development risks defence is then taken up in some detail by Mark Mildred, combining the viewpoint of a practitioner and academic.[33] This is a timely contribution at a point where the very existence of the defence is currently under review by the European Commission, and an important report into the economic effects of the defence has been undertaken.[34]

In his paper, Christopher Hodges points out that the picture across Europe in relation to the substantive law on liability contains a number of variations and that certain decisions fragment the appearance of harmonisation.[35] This complex situation is accentuated by divergences in the areas of access to justice, litigation procedure and levels of compensation.

As a conclusion to this part, Professor Howells analyses the harmonisation debate from a supranational and Member State perspective.[36] Using the central concepts of defect and the development risks defence to show that constructive steps need to be taken to clarify key elements of the Directive in order to facilitate the harmonisation process, Professor Howells makes the important point that harmonisation can only be advanced if cross-border dialogues are encouraged and enhanced. He thus makes

[32] See chapter 9. [33] See chapter 10.

[34] The Report of the Fondazione Roselli was submitted in June 2004. The overriding conclusion of the Report was that the economic impact of removing the development risks defence would be significant and therefore the defence should not be removed. In the report, it is argued that the removal of the development risks defence from the Directive would lead to a decrease in product variety, radical innovation by producers and basic research into new products. Insurance costs would also rise and in some cases risks would become uninsurable. The report recommends however that the Commission create a compensation fund at an EU level as a means for guaranteeing protection from product development risks.

[35] See chapter 11. [36] See chapter 12.

a powerful plea for the creation of common communication structures, such as the development of case law databases.[37]

Part III, 'Comparing systems', brings together a series of papers comparing products legislation and cases across a number of different jurisdictions.

Simon Taylor analyses two very different legal systems, England and France.[38] Taking these countries as representatives of the civil law and common law legal families, Dr Taylor's analysis is a case study in the effect of the harmonising goal of the Directive. Dr Taylor notes that despite the objective of maximal harmonisation, there still appears to be considerable divergence in both systems, due in large part to the continuing co-existence of, and, in France, the preference for, pre-existing parallel liability systems.

The European theme is continued in the contribution of Magdalena Sengayen which touches upon a topic largely unexplored in Western academic writing, that of the product liability laws in Central Europe, namely Poland, the Czech Republic and Hungary.[39] This is a crucial subject both in practical terms, due to the developing economic importance of the New Member economies, and in conceptual terms, due to the impact of enlargement on the broader harmonisation process. Dr Sengayen develops the argument that while the substantive provisions of the Directive are not likely to cause an upheaval in Central Europe as product liability provisions have never been considerably different from those in Western Europe, the surrounding context of institutional and procedural basis of the Central European product liability regimes is indeed undergoing a profound transformation.

In the two final chapters of this book, the focus of analysis shifts beyond Europe to analyse developments further afield. Professor Jane Stapleton, the leading authority on product liability, examines and compares developments within the US and Europe, taking as a focus the increasingly controversial topic of pathogenically infected products, such as bacterial and viral infection of products, and diseases such as Creutzfeldt-Jakob Disease (CJD).[40] Dr Luke Nottage examines the impact of the principles underpinning the European Directive in Japan.[41]

For ease of use, the text of the European Directive on Product Liability is included in an Appendix to this book.

[37] See footnote 19 above. [38] See chapter 13. [39] See chapter 14.
[40] See chapter 15. [41] See chapter 16.

PART I

Country reports

2

The use of comparative law in *A & Others v National Blood Authority*[1]

MICHAEL BROOKE QC AND
IAN FORRESTER QC

Introduction

The editor of this publication has invited two of the claimants' advocates instructed in an important case presenting both comparative law and Community law questions to describe how the case came to judicial attention, and the legal and factual challenges presented by arguing broad principle-driven doctrines before an English court during a trial lasting forty-nine court days. We represented 112 individuals who were infected with hepatitis C as a result of blood transfusions in England. This chapter, written with the consent of the claimants' solicitors, is extended with a postscript by counsel for the defendant and completed by an afterword from the trial judge. The claimants were successful, but it was a 'close-run thing'.

The problem of contaminated blood transfusions is not new to medicine or to litigation, especially in the United States. The United Kingdom avoided the excesses of the United States by having a non-commercial blood-bank system. The claimants had certainly been injured but it was questionable whether they had a good cause of action under conventional negligence principles. It is intrinsically difficult to establish liability on the part of a public authority performing a valuable public service. A case based on negligence would need to demonstrate considerable levels of breach of duty. While the HIV Haemophiliac Litigation ('HHL')[2] in England was brought to an acceptable conclusion for the plaintiffs infected with HIV from blood products, the difficulty of pursuing such a case in negligence against government departments and agencies raising

[1] *A & Others v NBA* [2001] 3 All ER 289; [2001] Lloyd's Rep Med 187. Hereafter references to the reported judgment will be by paragraph number thus: para.

[2] Where the plaintiffs' cause of action was negligence.

arguments of immunity and 'non-justiciability' and at the very least challenging the plaintiffs to establish 'Wednesbury negligence'[3] were only too daunting.

For the victims of infection with the hepatitis C virus through blood transfusions a case based on Community law appeared more promising, precisely because it was intended to remove the need to prove negligence or knowledge on the part of the blood authorities. However, as of the late 1990s, although the EU Product Liability Directive[4] had been in force for some fifteen years (and had been under discussion for years before that) it had been little commented upon by courts in the UK or indeed elsewhere in the Common Market. The Newcastle solicitors who represented the majority of the potential claimants had already instructed barristers specialising in common law clinical negligence and product liability to review their clients' chances. One was also a member of the Paris Bar, with a network of professional colleagues and professional acquaintances in France and elsewhere. Counsel advised the potential claimants they had a sustainable case under the Consumer Protection Act 1987 ('CPA') upon the basis that blood infected with hepatitis C virus was defective upon a proper construction of the CPA.

The point being novel and not straightforward the Legal Aid Board authorised the solicitors to seek a second opinion from further counsel, based in Brussels, a member of a London chambers, working with colleagues of different nationalities.

The latter's opinion on the application of the Directive was first sought in 1997. In March 1997, he gave the opinion that it was reasonable to presume that patients and others would expect to receive uncontaminated blood in a transfusion, and would correspondingly regard as 'defective' blood which might infect them with a serious illness. As we will describe further below, the Directive presented a number of questions: would the public at large be entitled to regard as 'defective' a blood transfusion which might transmit hepatitis C, and would the various defences contemplated by the Directive avail the defendant blood authority? On this basis, questions of whether the potential defendants had followed good practice with respect to epidemiological probabilities appeared relevant not so much for

[3] For non-English lawyers, liability of the public authority by reason of its manifestly gross or unreasonable misconduct.

[4] Council Directive 85/374/EEC on the approximation of the laws, regulations and administrative provisions of the Member States concerning liability for defective products.

whether the blood was defective under the Directive but rather whether a defence might be available based upon the patient's acceptance of the risk or the defendant's unawareness of the risk. The opinion noted that there were surprisingly few judicial decisions applying the Directive, although there was a large quantity of material commenting on the proposal to have a Directive, the dangers and uncertainties of the Directive and its implications for domestic product liability law. Particular attention in counsel's opinion was given to the writings of the European Commission official charged with drafting the Directive who, from the early 1970s, had been responsible for shepherding the proposal through the process of intergovernmental and intra-institutional negotiation to a conclusion in the form of the promulgation of Directive 85/374/EEC.

The two leading counsel thus separately reached the conclusion that an action based upon the Directive would indeed have a reasonable prospect of success. A number of supplementary opinions were dispatched, on the strength of which the solicitors were able to persuade the legal aid authorities in England that the case was maintainable. (The Scottish legal aid authorities apparently rejected a parallel claim for help in Scotland, on the grounds that the case was not winnable.)

The medicine

It is necessary to give a brief outline of what the scientific case was about. Hepatitis is an inflammation of the liver, which can be caused by various viral infections. Once the hepatitis A virus and the hepatitis B virus had been identified in the early 1970s, it was then appreciated that post-blood-transfusion viral hepatitis continued to occur due to infection with other (as yet unidentified) viruses and NonA NonB Hepatitis (NANBH) was the description applied to this viral hepatitis. It was particularly noted because people were regularly seen to develop symptoms of hepatitis after receiving blood transfusions. At first, there was no direct screening test to identify donors as carrying the virus, but there were practical procedures for excluding blood from donors at increased risk of carrying the virus. These were called 'surrogate' tests and the most useful one was to carry out a blood test to check the levels of an enzyme produced in the liver (ALT). High levels of ALT in the blood were suggestive that the person might have some abnormality of liver function, and one possible cause for this was that the donor was a carrier of the NANBH virus. This surrogate testing of blood donors had been routine in Germany since the 1960s;

it was made routine in the USA in 1986 and in France by 1988. Routine ALT screening of blood donors was considered in the UK but was never introduced.

In May 1988 came a breakthrough when the Chiron Corporation of America announced the identification of the hepatitis C virus and the development of a prototype screening test. The first version of the test (the Ortho Elisa) became commercially available in late 1989 (when a licence for the export of the test from the USA was first obtained) and it was soon used in programmes for the routine screening of blood donors in Japan and in France. In May 1990 the US Food and Drugs Administration (FDA) gave approval for use of this test within the USA and so it went into routine use for screening there, as well as in a number of other countries.

There were concerns about the accuracy of this 'first generation' test, both as to its sensitivity (not detecting all it should, i.e. false negatives) and its specificity (detecting those it should not, i.e. false positives). A further concern was the lack of a confirmatory or supplementary test to verify positive results and identify some of the false positives. Nevertheless the relevant Department of Health committee (UK Advisory Committee on Virological Safety of Blood: ACVSB) advised, in principle, as early as November 1989 that the Ortho Elisa should be used for routine screening subject to three conditions.[5] In May 1990 a confirmatory test (RIBA 1) became available. In July and November 1990 the ACVSB recommended that screening of blood donors should be started, subject to the holding of various trials. Second generation Elisa tests became available by April 1991. Routine screening of blood for hepatitis C was introduced throughout England and Wales on 1 September 1991.

NANBH had been a proxy in the HIV Haemophiliac Litigation (HHL) for the AIDS virus emerging in the 1980s, the argument being that the precautions, which could and should by then have been taken against the contamination of blood products with NANBH, would also have avoided their contamination with the yet to be identified HIV.[6]

Near the end of the HHL, Mr Justice Ognall allowed the plaintiffs' lawyers to act in the forthcoming Hepatitis Litigation, using the knowledge acquired when acting in the HHL, particularly resulting from the disclosure provided by the various defendants. In the Hepatitis Litigation NANBH, no longer the proxy, was the target itself.

[5] Satisfactory pilot tests, FDA approval and availability of a confirmatory test.

[6] The keystone of the argument was the Scottish decision by the House of Lords in *Hughes v Lord Advocate* [1963] AC 837.

The English legal principles

The Product Liability Directive (1985/374) came into effect on 25 July 1985 after a very lengthy process of drafting, lobbying, discussion and negotiation, including intergovernmental and parliamentary discussion. The UK[7] implemented the Directive by passing the Consumer Protection Act 1987, which came into effect on 1 March 1988. A claimant's cause of action under the CPA is made out where *Damage* is caused to the *Claimant* by a *Defect* in a *Product* taken to have been *Produced* by the *Defendant*.[8] Section 4(1)(e) of the CPA provides that a defendant may escape liability by showing:

> That the state of scientific and technical knowledge at the relevant time was not such that a producer of products of the same description as the product in question might be expected to have discovered the defect if it had existed in his products while they were under his control.

The litigation therefore turned on the rights of patients infected due to transfusions after 1 March 1988.

Most[9] of the claimants in the Hepatitis Litigation relied on the CPA cause of action, although argument in the litigation essentially focused on the Directive, whose words, by common consent, prevailed in case of doubt, and it is that cause of action which is the subject of Mr Justice Burton's judgment in *A & Others v NBA*.

Preparation of the case

The Directive is framed in the civil law tradition, expressed very tersely with questions of general principle set forth in a few words. The fifty[10] days in court turned on the proper construction[11] of fewer than one hundred words. A respectable case could be made that the reasonable expectation of the public at large should reflect the intrinsic characteristics of transfused blood in a bag: having come from another person's body, it could not fail to contain the qualities of the blood of the donor. It would be strange, the

[7] One of the early states to do so.
[8] I.e. the producer or the own brander or the importer or the supplier unable to identify the producer.
[9] There were a small number relying on clinical negligence.
[10] Forty-nine days trying the case and one day delivering the reserved judgment.
[11] Legal argument as to that proper construction took place on no fewer than thirteen days in the course of the trial.

defendants would say, if liability could exist despite the defendants having taken every, or every reasonable, or every practical, precaution against the transmission of contaminated blood. If it were proved that no method (or no sufficiently reliable method) existed of catching infective bags of blood, was the ordinary citizen entitled to hope that the transfusion service would never deliver an infective bag of blood? Could society regard as 'defective' what science could not prevent?

Setting the purpose of the legislation in context would be essential. The preparations fell into different categories: (i) research on German civil law under Article 823 of the *Burgerliches Gesetzbuch* (*BGB*, the German Civil Code) until the adoption of the Directive; (ii) gathering *travaux préparatoires*; (iii) consulting the now-retired drafter of the Directive; (iv) research in other EC Member States and in the United States concerning relevant writings and judicial experience; (v) carrying out research at the Max Planck Institute; and (vi) collecting all language versions of the legislation and selecting those portions of other authorities in foreign languages which required translation in whole or in part into English.

German law

The *Bundesgerichtshof* (*BGH*, Germany's supreme civil court) rendered a series of judgments from 1956 concerning product liability. In each case, undoubted injury was done due to the failure of a product: the fork of a bicycle broke and injured the rider; a mineral water bottle exploded, injuring a child; a consignment of vaccine infected a flock of chickens with fowl pest. In each case, the supplier said that the product had been manufactured according to the highest possible standards, under the strictest conditions of supervision, and with all due diligence. In the 1956 case, the *BGH* found for the manufacturer, stating that the injury was one of the *Lebensrisiko*, one of the risks of life, and that without demonstrable fault on the part of the manufacturer, the victim could not be compensated. The victim almost always would lack the capacity to show how the fault had occurred (particularly without a doctrine like *res ipsa loquitur*), and anyway the manufacturer could show it had done all in its power to prevent rogue products reaching the market. The climate of opinion changed in the late 1960s/early 1970s due to the thalidomide tragedy (*Contergan* was its name in Germany) when children were born with unforeseen defects, and was further influenced by the legal consequences of compensating victims of the crash of a Turkish aircraft in Paris in 1974 because of a badly designed cargo-hold door. The *BGH* decided to reverse its previous positions and found for the claimant in an exploding mineral water bottle case in 1995. Translations of these judgments (which are by English standards quite brief) were prepared; and copies of the relevant portions of the *BGB* were compiled both in German and in English translation.

Travaux préparatoires

The Secretary General of the European Council was requested to furnish copies of the *travaux préparatoires* from the Council's archives pertinent to the drafting, review, modification and final adoption of the Directive. After some weeks, the Secretariat General supplied a large mass of documents dating back to the earliest days (late 1960s, early 1970s) when notions of a European Directive on product liability were first canvassed. Included were memoranda prepared within the context of a Council of Europe experts' committee, the first working drafts of a possible Directive prepared within the Commission, submissions by a wide range of parties concerning the merits of the draft Directive, and, most interestingly, the minutes of the many meetings of the EU Council Working Group at which the proposed Directive moved through its successive stages to final adoption in 1985. Most of the latter documents were in French and indicated the identities and theories of the Member States requesting particular modifications during the drafting process. The *travaux préparatoires* could be relied on, the Claimants thought, to demonstrate that most of the arguments to be considered in the litigation had been reviewed and debated extensively during the drafting process; quite how far they would be useful was uncertain.

Consulting the retired draftsman of the directive[12]

Commission officials generally rotate between positions every three to five years. The Product Liability Directive was so controversial and so sensitive that the official in question had the rare privilege of seeing it through from initial conception in about 1970 to ultimate adoption by the Council in 1985. He had written an excellent book in German on the subject[13] and was a teacher of law at German universities. He quite relished the opportunity to see how a case concerning the Directive was prepared and was happy

[12] Professor Doctor Hans Claudius Taschner.

[13] *Produkthaftungsgesetz und EG-Produkthaftungsrichtlinie* (München, 1990).

to give his personal comments on the history of the Directive, and a statement was framed recording his recollection of its drafting. There was debate between opposing counsel concerning the admissibility of such testimony, since part of it would consist of recording familiar institutional and procedural facts about how directives are drafted, revised, debated and adopted. Community law (it was said) is a matter for argument, not evidence. The learned doctor could not testify to the proposition that a former Commission official considered the Directive should be interpreted in a particular way, but his insights were plainly useful to a full understanding of the history and the purposes of the Directive. After discussion with the Bench and between counsel, it was agreed that he would not submit testimony and that the procedural history to which he could speak would be adopted as part of the submissions by the claimants on the history of the Directive.

Research in other EC Member States and in the United States concerning relevant writings and judicial experience

As already noted, although the implications of the adoption of the Directive had been widely debated, and indeed colourfully debated, actual decisions applying the Directive appeared to be rare. Judgments in all civil law countries are brief by comparison to English standards. The reasoning of the French *Cour de cassation* may be one short sentence, a phenomenon that has so far survived scrutiny by the European Court of Human Rights. There is generally speaking no principle of *stare decisis* in civil law jurisdictions, although the significance of that difference can be exaggerated.

It was therefore decided to research the implementation of the Directive in France, Spain, the Netherlands, Belgium, Italy and Portugal. Accordingly, friendly members of the bar in those countries were consulted and requested to report on significant academic writing or judicial decisions concerning the Directive, particularly in the context of medical practice. It turned out that there was a remarkable dearth of judicial authority and a moderate level of academic commentary during the period after the adoption of the Directive. Two cases had reached the European Court, one of which had been decided. One lower court judgment emerged: a district court in the Netherlands made a finding partially favourable to the claimants and partially unfavourable (that the blood was a defective product but that the hospital could not be blamed for having delivered it to the patient, since the defect could not have been screened out). There were a number of French cases reflecting more the distinctive and painful history of contaminated blood in France than the Directive in particular. Apart from the German cases before the *Landgericht*, *Oberlandesgericht* and *Bundesgerichtshof*, referred to above, there were few other judgments of obvious relevance, but the academic commentary was fairly copious, and would in due course be relied upon both in argument and in the judgment. The professional colleagues in other countries were extremely interested and helpful in suggesting lines of approach and relevant sources of academic literature.

Advice on the American experience was sought from an American friend, Professor Shael Herman, who taught at the Tulane University of Louisiana and at the Sorbonne. He synthesised the complex and inconsistent American history of how blood transfusion infection cases have been handled judicially and legislatively.

Carrying out research at the Max Planck Institute

Academic writing is a stronger source of legal authority in the civil law tradition than in England. In the absence of judgments of higher courts (with the notable exception of Germany) it was necessary to review the available literature. For this purpose, the best-equipped law library in Europe was the Max Planck Institute in Hamburg. The Institute staff were hospitable and welcoming. Works from a number of authors of different nationalities in German, Swedish, Spanish, Italian, Portuguese and English were consulted. One curiosity was that Belgian authors wrote on German law, German authors wrote on French law, and Australian authors wrote on English and Australian law. The claimants were thus able to produce at least twenty-five books and articles published outside the UK relevant to the fundamental questions presented by the litigation: Was blood capable of being regarded as a product? Was it the reasonable expectation of the public that a blood transfusion would not contain hepatitis C virus? Was the public entitled to regard as defective a contaminated transfusion? What was the relevance of the precautions which could in theory be taken or had in fact been taken? Did it make a difference if the unwanted characteristics of the transfused blood were incapable of being eliminated by skill and diligence? What was the relevance of the prescribing doctor's knowledge of the risk of infection? Of what relevance was the so-called 'state-of-the-art defence'? Was the public entitled to have an expectation about the quality of transfused blood which was technically unattainable in the circumstances?

Collecting all language versions of the legislation and preparing translations of other material

The parties were greatly helped by the fact that the judge having the conduct of the litigation, Mr Justice Burton, was known to speak French comfortably and, as it turned out, other European languages very adequately. It was not necessary to go to the expense of preparing translations of all the material in various foreign languages. This was particularly convenient as to French, the language of most of the *travaux préparatoires*. However, translations of the entirety of two of the judgments of the *BGH* were prepared, as well as translations of the Arnhem district court judgment and Swedish *travaux préparatoires* which accompanied the promulgation in Swedish law of the Directive. The full texts of the academic commentators relied upon were made available and translations prepared of sentences or paragraphs which seemed particularly relevant. (All counsel spoke French, and some spoke moderate German and Italian.)

The request for a reference in 1999

In October 1999, the claimants invited the judge to make a preliminary reference to the European Court of Justice on a number of questions as to the true and proper construction to be placed on the Directive. This application was rejected. His order indicated that he felt the request was premature in that it was not yet certain what questions would turn out to be the relevant ones. A year later the trial started before the same judge. By then the scene had been set for a very full comparative analysis of how the Directive should be construed and applied to the facts relating to the claimants' infection through blood transfusions with the hepatitis C virus.

The non-issues

Three points of general importance hovered in the wings of the trial but did not in the end arise for decision. They are worth mentioning in passing and may crop up in future cases.

Product

On the generic pleadings the claimants' allegation that blood and blood products were 'products' within the meaning of the CPA was not admitted by the defendant. The defendant's position on the pleadings had support from one of the leading academic writers in the field, Professor Jane Stapleton in *Product Liability*,[14] but in the event it was conceded by the time of trial that blood and blood products were 'products'.

Producer

The defendant admitted that it was responsible for the liabilities of its predecessors in the National Blood Transfusion Service and the Bio Products Laboratory[15] and in effect accepted that they were the producers within the meaning of the CPA. During the course of the trial it was submitted by the defendant that in approaching the question of the consumer's legitimate expectation as to the safety of blood, the court should put in the defendant's favour the fact that, unlike a purely commercial producer, the defendant had no alternative but to continue supplying blood to hospitals and patients, as a service to society. Burton J rejected this argument in paragraph 42 of his judgment: noting that the defendants did not put forward a defence under Art. 7(d) '*that the defect is due to compliance of the product with mandatory regulations issued by the public authorities*', he concluded that there was no necessary reason why a public authority or a non-profit-making organisation should be in any different position from a commercial undertaking if the product is unsafe. He also noted that that was the opinion expressed by the Advocate General (Colomer) in the '*Danish Kidney Case*'.[16] This was before the ECJ gave its judgment in the case[17] on various questions referred to it by the Højesteret (Danish Supreme Court).

Consumer Protection Act versus Directive

There are significant differences between the wording not merely of Article 7(e) and section 4(1)(e) CPA but also between Article 6 and

[14] Published by Butterworths, London, 1994. Professor Stapleton is Research Professor, Research School of Social Sciences, Australian National University, Ernest E. Smith Professor, University of Texas School of Law, Commonwealth Fellow, British Institute of International and Comparative Law and Academic Associate, Fountain Court.

[15] The Regional Health Authorities and the Central Blood Laboratories Authority.

[16] *Henning Veedfald v Århus Amstkommune* Case C-203/99, para. 27.

[17] Holding that Art 7(c) ('. . . *the product was neither manufactured by him for sale or any form of distribution for economic purpose nor manufactured or distributed by him in the course of his business*') did not furnish a defence where the defective product is used in the course of a medical service financed entirely from public funds and for which the patient is not required to pay any consideration. The Court also addresses some interesting questions directed to whether the damage suffered in the case (loss of a harvested kidney through contamination prior to transplant into the plaintiff) was within Article 9 of the Directive.

section 3 in the definition of defect. The differences between Article 7(e) and section 4(1)(e) were considered by the European Court of Justice in the enforcement proceedings brought by the Commission against the UK[18] to challenge the adequacy of the UK's implementation of the Directive. As the pleadings developed, a pattern emerged of the claimants sticking resolutely to the wording of the Directive, while the defendant stuck to the wording of the CPA. By the time of the trial, however, it was accepted on both sides that the dominant provision was the Directive and that insofar as the CPA's wording differed from the wording of the Directive, the CPA should not be construed differently from the Directive. As Burton J said: '. . . and consequently the practical course was to go straight to the fount, the Directive itself'.[19] The clash of the statutes, feared by the Commission in its challenge to the UK's implementation of the Directive and an issue on our pleadings,[20] did not in fact take place, although a great deal of time was spent analysing *Commission v UK*, in at least three language versions.

The core issues

The two fundamental issues were:

a. Is the infection of blood with hepatitis C virus a defect within the meaning of Article 6?
b. If so, was the state of scientific and technical knowledge such that the existence of the defect could not be discovered as provided by Article 7(e)?

Article 6 (1) provides: 'A product is defective when it does not provide the safety which a person is entitled to expect, taking all the circumstances into account, including:

i. the presentation of the product;
ii. the use to which it could reasonably be expected that the product would be put;
iii. the time when the product was put into circulation'

[18] *Commission v UK* Case C-300/95 [1997] All ER (EC) 481. [19] Para. 2.

[20] Despite the terms of section 1(1) CPA: 'This Part [of the Act] shall have effect for the purpose of making such provision as is necessary in order to comply with the product liability Directive and shall be construed accordingly.'

The main points of common ground were:[21]

a. That liability under the CPA is 'defect-based' not 'fault-based' (Recitals 2 and 6 of the Directive).
b. That the question to be resolved is the degree or level of safety or safeness which persons generally are entitled to expect.
c. The expectation is that of the public at large.
d. The expectation is not the *actual* expectation of persons generally, but what they are *entitled* to expect. 'Legitimate expectation' became the common formulation of the expectation, which was consistent with other language versions of the Directive, e.g. '. . . *la sécurité à laquelle on peut légitimement s'attendre . . .*'
e. The court decides what the public is entitled to expect.

Against that common background, a. The claimants' primary case on defect was that:

i. The legitimate expectation of people generally throughout the relevant period[22] was that transfused blood would not infect patients with hepatitis C.
ii. The conduct of the producer is irrelevant and questions of avoidability of the defect, practicability of its avoidance and economic feasibility thereof are all irrelevant.

b. The defendant's case on defect was that:

i. The risk of infection with hepatitis C was known to the treating doctors, for whom it was a risk worth running for the sake of the patient in need of a transfusion.
ii. Avoidability or unavoidability is a circumstance for the purpose of Article 6.
iii. The legitimate expectation of people generally was not that blood would be 100 per cent clean but that all legitimately expectable (reasonably available) precautions had been taken.
iv. It would therefore be necessary to investigate whether the producers had taken all legitimately expectable steps to avoid the risk of the product being defective.

[21] See para. 31, where Burton J lists in detail a number of points of common ground.
[22] From 1 March 1988.

c. The claimants' fallback case on defect, in consequence, was:

i. That the defendant's case is contrary to the intention of the Directive as revealed by the *travaux préparatoires*, the Recitals and the observations of the Advocate General and the European Court of Justice in *Commission v UK*, requiring as it did an investigation of fault in all but name.
ii. That nevertheless, the investigation required by the defendant's case in fact reveals that throughout the relevant period the producers *had* failed to take all legitimately expectable steps to avoid the risk of the product being defective: (1) From 1 March 1988 in failing to perform routine surrogate testing of blood donors; (2) From 1 January 1990 in failing to perform anti-hepatitis C Elisa testing of blood donations.

Article 7(e) provides: 'The producer shall not be liable as a result of this Directive if he proves . . . that the state of scientific and technical knowledge at the time when he put the product into circulation was not such as to enable the existence of the defect to be discovered.'

a. The defendant's case on Article 7(e) was that in the then state of scientific and technical knowledge, the defect in the particular product could not be discovered, given the shortcomings of both surrogate testing and anti-hepatitis C Elisa 1st generation tests. In other words, the defect has to be discoverable in the blood in the bag in question.
b. The claimants' case on Article 7(e) was that the defence is not available once the risk of the product being defective was known (which had been the case since the 1970s), whether or not the defect can be discovered in a particular product. In other words, the existence of the defect in the population of products in general has to be undiscoverable for the defence to arise.

Comparative law features of the oral argument

Once the trial began, the European law case was opened by referring to the adoption of the *BGB* in 1896, and the evolving interpretation of Article 823, which is the basis for establishing liability due to fault under German law. German law in the 1950s and 1960s found against plaintiffs who had unquestionably been injured but were unable to demonstrate fault against a diligent manufacturer who could show the existence of all possible precautions. Thereafter the law changed, reflecting what English lawyers would call a decision to shift the burden of proof, concluding with the celebrated case of the child injured by the exploding mineral water bottle. This case concerned a young claimant injured by an exploding mineral water bottle resulting from a very fine hairline crack, not discovered despite what was found to be a technical and supervisory procedure in the defendant's factory in accordance with the very latest technology. Both the Court of Appeal of Hamm and the *BGH* had experienced little difficulty in concluding that the bottle was a defective product under Article 6 of the Directive, categorising the bottle as an *Ausreisser*, as a rogue product or sub-standard product. The battlefield in the German courts was Article 7(e) and the young claimant was the victor in the *BGH*. German law was thus presented as an example of legal evolution in accordance with the principles ultimately espoused by the Product Liability Directive. There was then a very thorough examination of the *travaux préparatoires* over a period of about fifteen years, from which, so argued the claimants, one could observe that many of the arguments advanced by the defendants had been voiced, examined and not accepted by the drafters of the Directive. The claimants of course had to concede that it was the words of the Directive which should prevail, and that the *travaux préparatoires* could not supply principles which were not present in the adopted text. It was interesting to observe that the *travaux préparatoires* contained submissions from chambers of commerce, memoranda from governments, and reports by successive chairmen of the Council Working Group charged with the responsibility of reaching a consensus among the Member States. The books and articles published by those involved in the drafting process, especially Professor Taschner, were particularly relied on.

The claimants also referred to English and Scottish cases such as *Smedleys v Breed* [1974] AC 839 (the factory produced 3,500,000 cans of peas a year successfully but was convicted when four caterpillars, of the same colour, shape and density as the peas, escaped detection in its food preparation processes and were discovered in a can of peas), and *Donoghue v Stevenson* [1932] AC 562[23] (concerning the alleged snail in the bottle of ginger beer) was invoked as authority for the proposition that what manufacturers claimed was ridiculously severe nonetheless could make

[23] It should be recorded that, despite its absence from the lists of authorities in both the Lloyd's Rep Med and the All ER reports of *A v NBA*, the great case of *Donoghue v Stevenson* was referred to in argument on at least ten occasions! Reading the dissenting speeches in *Donoghue v Stevenson* was a salutary reminder that famous cases were not foregone conclusions; Mrs Donoghue was fortunate in having a dogged solicitor who believed he could change the law.

good law. There had been two recent English decisions under the CPA,[24] which the trial judge considered. The conclusion of the *BGH* was echoed[25] (albeit *obiter*) by Ian Kennedy J in *Richardson*:

> This provision [Article 7(e)] is, to my mind, not apt to protect a defendant in the case of a defect of a known character merely because there is no test which is able to reveal its existence in every case. (Para. 285)

A certain amount of time was devoted to the United States, where the commercialisation of the blood industry led to a high incidence of infection and a corresponding number of lawsuits, to which a number of legislatures had reacted by enacting so-called shield laws immunising blood banks from liability in certain circumstances. Indeed, New Jersey and Illinois judgments were duly cited in the judgment.

An Australian case[26] of toxic[27] oysters was considered, but the wording of the Australian statute's equivalent of Article 7(e) was subtly different, alluding to the discoverability of the defect in 'the action goods'. This, it was held, provided a defence since the presence of hepatitis A virus in any given oyster could not be discovered.

The language of Articles 1, 4, 6 and 7 of the Directive as well as its Recitals was reviewed at length. Of the nine European Union languages, the judge was the only person who attempted the modern Greek texts, and the Finnish text was not consulted. Most attention was given to the English, French, German, Italian and Portuguese texts. The Livenote transcribers of the shorthand record of the hearings included linguists[28] who were able to produce accurately typed German, French, Italian or Spanish in the transcript delivered to the judge and counsel at the end of the day. Emphasis was placed on the fact that the explanatory memoranda adopted by other Member States usually made recitals of certain principles relevant to the construction of the Directive. Much time was also devoted to the opinion of Advocate General Tesauro and the judgment in *Commission v UK*.[29]

[24] *Iman Abouzaid v Mothercare (UK) Ltd* (Court of Appeal, 21 December 2000); *Richardson v LRC Products Ltd* [2000] Lloyd's Rep Med 280, a decision at first instance in respect of a failed condom which Ian Kennedy J held not to be defective.

[25] Ian Kennedy J cleaves to the CPA in the course of his judgment and does not mention the Directive at all. While counsel had referred him to *Commission v UK* and the Article 7(e)/Section 4 (1)(e) linguistic discrepancy, he was not apparently referred to the *BGH* decision.

[26] *Graham Barclay Oysters v Ryan* [2000] FCA 1099.

[27] They were contaminated with the hepatitis A virus.

[28] Assisted by one counsel's polyglot son.

[29] Case C-300/95 [1997] All ER (EC) 481.

The judgment

The resolution of these issues as to the true and proper construction of the Directive, having entailed wide-ranging comparative arguments, led to a judgment which refers to authorities from eight[30] jurisdictions and numerous learned books and papers.[31]

The learned judge directed himself that he should approach the *travaux préparatoires* with caution.[32] Bearing in mind that he should be alive to there being an 'autonomous' or Community meaning or construction for harmonising pan-European legislation, the judge welcomed the guidance to be obtained from considering the official different language versions of the Directive and was tentatively prepared to look at how the Directive had been implemented and judicially applied in other Community countries;[33] a little later in his judgment he shows more enthusiasm for judicial decisions elsewhere in Europe for reasons both of comity and harmony, in approaching this piece of common legislation.[34] The judge attached great importance to the Directive's recitals as aids to its construction, listing the significant ones at an early stage.[35]

The judgment makes many citations from the academic literature in respect of both Article 6 and Article 7(e). In part this is because of the dearth of previous judicial decisions, particularly on Article 6, but it also demonstrates a willingness by the judge to adopt a broad and purposive approach to the task of construction that faced him. The judge, in formulating his conclusions on Article 6, underpins them at the outset by reference to European academic literature.[36]

The court decisions that carried most weight with the judge and clearly gave him most assistance were *Commission v UK* and the decision of the *BGH* in the mineral water bottle case, both cases directed at Article 7(e) but both offering some assistance on Article 6. It is interesting to observe that the opinion of Advocate General Tesauro (in *Commission v UK*) needed to be consulted in its original Italian to see that at one point he had used the subjunctive, which had not been carried over into the official English translation.[37] The judge took on the task of analysing the *BGH*'s very dense judgment in the mineral water bottle case and came

[30] England, ECJ, New Jersey, Illinois, Germany, Holland, France and Australia.

[31] The reader should know that the judgment, even by English standards, is long: as handed down it is 170 pages long containing 284 paragraphs (105 pages in Lloyd's Law Reports, Medical containing 283 paragraphs).

[32] Para. 15.i. [33] Para. 15.ii. [34] Para. 44.

[35] Para. 14. [36] Para. 55. [37] Para. 53.i.a.

to the conclusion: 'What the *BGH* was primarily saying is that if the risks are known, unavoidability of the defect in the particular product is no answer.'[38] Burton J's conclusions on Article 6 may be summarised thus:

a. The words *all the circumstances* are not exclusive; neither are they unlimited. They are not to be subjected to a restricted construction *eiusdem generis* to the specific examples given in Article 6. Having regard to other language versions,[39] in particular the French where '*notamment*' (≊ 'notably') is used rather than 'including', the specific examples given in Article 6 are intended to be the most significant circumstances. *All the circumstances* are to be construed as all *relevant* circumstances.
b. *Avoidability* (i.e. the defendant's case on Article 6) is not one of the *circumstances* to be taken into account within Article 6.[40] It is not a relevant circumstance, being outwith the purpose of the Directive,[41] which was to relieve consumers not merely of the need to prove fault or negligence but also of the need to show that the producer had taken all legitimately expectable steps. Furthermore, had *avoidability* been relevant, it would have been a significant circumstance departing from the purpose of the Directive and as such would have been mentioned specifically in Article 6.
c. The first step is to identify the harmful characteristic which caused the injury. The next step is to conclude whether the product is standard or non-standard. If the respect in which it differs from the series includes the harmful characteristic, then for the purpose of Article 6 it is non-standard. The judge preferred this approach to that taken in the United States[42] of categorising product defects as design, manufacturing

[38] Para. 53.ii.

[39] In Para. 34.ii. the judge observes: '[a possibility is] *that they* ["all circumstances"] *are to be construed as the most significant examples of the circumstances. There was some support for this proposition, both by way of some exemplars in European legislation – from which it could be suggested that European draftsmen had considered that the matters actually set out as examples were the ones most worthy of mention – and also by reference to the French language version of Article 6, which used the word, before the list of the circumstances, "notamment", and the German, which used "insbesondere", both of which I take to mean "in particular" or "especially" – although other language versions use phraseology more similar to the English "including"*.'

[40] Para. 63.

[41] Having regard, in particular, to the recitals of the Directive, recitals 2 and 6 being most apposite.

[42] See the American Law Institute's Third Restatement of the Law of Torts 1998, Cap. 1, Section 2 Categories of Product Defect.

or labelling[43] defects, which approach has commonly been adopted by academic writers. The judge saw[44] no reason to take this approach (he was not invited to do so by either party) and observed both that the Directive made no attempt to categorise defects and that the attempt to fit any particular situation into one of these 'boxes' in fact gave no assistance in carrying out the task of deciding under Article 6 whether the product is defective. Materials in the *travaux préparatoires* deflected the judge from taking the 'risk/utility' approach to defect favoured by the US Second Restatement on Torts (1965).[45] He was encouraged in his course of preferring 'standard/non-standard' as part of the test of defectiveness by the fact that both Italy and Spain by express legislation had provided that non-standard products would automatically be defective within Article 6 of the Directive, an example of implementing legislation in other Community countries feeding our debate.[46]

d. In the case of non-standard products it will be relevant to compare them with other products on the market and to consider whether the public at large accepted the non-standard nature of the product, but that is not the end of the matter as the court has to decide the question what is the *legitimate* expectation as to safety of the product, which may be higher or lower than the public expectation.
e. If the unsafe product is standard for the purpose of Article 6, then the judge acknowledged that the process may be more difficult,[47] though questions of *avoidability* would remain irrelevant and social acceptability would only arise through knowledge of the unsafeness.[48]
f. The judge proceeded to hold:
    i. that blood infected with hepatitis C was non-standard[49]
    ii. that the public had not taken it to be socially acceptable for non-standard units of blood to infect patients with hepatitis C,[50] the knowledge of the medical profession being irrelevant to that consideration[51]
    iii. that the public at large were entitled to expect that the blood transfused to them would be free from infection[52]
    iv. that the blood which infected each of the claimants was defective for the purpose of Article 6.
g. Burton J went on to address the defendant's case on defect and having heard a large body of factual and expert evidence, having made a number of findings of fact, having taken into account:

[43] Instructions and warnings. [44] Paras. 39 to 41. [45] Para. 35.i. [46] Para. 36.
[47] Para. 73. [48] Para. 65.ii. [49] Para. 73. [50] Para. 65.ii.
[51] Para. 80. [52] Para. 80.

i. all the *circumstances* on the defendant's construction of Article 6,
ii. the fact that the precautions of the introduction of surrogate testing and earlier introduction of routine screening were not taken

he came to the conclusion[53] that 'such blood so infected on and after 1 March 1988 did not provide the safety which persons generally are entitled to expect'. Burton J's conclusions[54] on Article 7(e) may be summarised thus:

a. Article 7(e) derogates from the purpose of the Directive and should be construed strictly for that reason.[55] The judge had already used the very restrictedness of the Article 7(e) defence as an aid to construction when considering Article 6.[56]
b. The *existence of the defect* means the existence of the generic defect, not the defect in the particular product.[57]
c. Article 7(e) protects the producer in respect of the unknown generic defect; its purpose is to protect the producer against liability for the '*inconnu*', not to provide a defence in the case of damage caused by a known but undetectable generic defect.[58] In his analysis of Article 7(e) the judge acknowledges the guidance of *Commission v UK* and suggests that his conclusions are in line with the decision of the *BGH* and the majority of academic writers. When encapsulating the *travaux préparatoires* for the purpose of Article 7(e),[59] the judge records that originally the intention of the Commission was that the Directive should impose liability even for the '*inconnu*', meaning the inclusion of liability for true development risks; the outcome of the legislative process was the opposite and became Article 7(e). This was a further reason for concluding as the judge did in respect of Article 7(e): 'Hence it protects the producer in respect of the unknown (*inconnu*).'[60]
d. Accordingly non-standard products may qualify under Article 7(e); 'However once the problem is *known* by virtue of accessible information, then the non-standard product can no longer qualify for protection under Article 7(e).'[61]
e. Throughout the relevant period the generic defect of blood sometimes being infected with hepatitis C[62] was well known and

[53] Para. 173. [54] Paras. 74 to 77.
[55] Para. 75. Note that in the Danish Kidney case the ECJ said much the same in relation to Article 7(a), treating it as a given but going through a similar thought process (see paragraph 15 of the judgment).
[56] Para. 64. [57] Para. 74.iii. [58] Para. 76. [59] Para. 52. [60] Para. 76.
[61] Para. 77. [62] Or NANB.

the defendant could not therefore establish a defence under Article 7(e).

Burton J also addressed the consequence had the defendant's construction of Article 7(e) been accepted[63] and resolved several causation issues and a number of damages issues. It is not proposed to discuss those matters here.

Envoi

Participating as advocates in the case was a great honour. No other European country would devote so much care and resources by so many specialised lawyers to settling a question of product liability for personal injuries. The judge can have handled little else for about six months. The courtroom was filled with medical and legal authorities who came and went. The atmosphere was quiet, orderly, courteous, *confraternelle* and intense, qualities that are not necessarily found in every Member State. The Legal Aid authorities in England are to be commended for making enough money available to permit a good job to be done. As advocates we had the privilege of very thoroughly prepared written pleadings, the loose rein but firm grip of very experienced instructing solicitors, a broad and deep survey of the academic literature in at least twelve countries, excellent professional relations with our opponents (throughout the case) and the undistracted attention of an interested and talented member of the judiciary with a gift for languages and an interest in the development of the law.[64] The quality of the judgment, its thoroughness and comprehensiveness, reflect the amount of money and time which the legal system in our country traditionally affords to the resolution of important matters affecting ordinary people. By continental European standards this was luxury justice.

Recently Mr Justice Lightman gave an interesting lecture.[65] Without dissenting from many of his observations (e.g. about the value of good preparation and pre-trial resources), we respectfully but firmly disagree with his suggestion that a continental European approach to civil litigation would deliver a better *quality* of civil justice than is provided by the systems

[63] Paras. 181 to 187.

[64] And, also in accordance with the traditions of the English Bar, all the barristers and the judge had a dinner together, and the menu for the dinner contained such dubious delicacies as *Potage générique, Agneau réformé par Directive, Fromage résolumment anglais sans référence aux normes européennes*, capped with *Café de l'avenir* (the which beverage was named in the (ill-founded) expectation that an appeal was inevitable).

[65] 6th Edward Bramley Memorial Lecture, University of Sheffield.

we enjoy in the UK. We have each of us had the privilege of pleading both in the UK and in its civil law neighbours across the channel. It may be worth concluding by recording some differences. The English tradition used to give greater weight to oral pleading. Written arguments – so-called 'skeletons' – were matchstick-thin, and in the old days were often not used at all. Today, skeletons have become fleshy, and the oral portion has become more focussed. But the oral portion is still a highly demanding exchange of views with a well-prepared judge. Counsel expects to be thoroughly cross-examined. That which is not relevant is rebuffed. The judge advances several theories to test the argument.

The French approach is quite different. Commonly the oral argument is heard in total judicial silence: counsel have no inkling whether they are being relevant, persuasive or tedious. The judgment is usually short, sometimes very short (French *Cour de cassation* judgments may have one sentence of reasoning). The written pleadings (customarily two for and two against) are pieces of advocacy, more carefully polished than an English skeleton, closely responding to the arguments of the adversary.

We would submit, as our personal and no doubt idiosyncratic conclusion, that the relative weights accorded to written and oral submissions are reversed between England and France. The care given to crafting individual judgments is higher in England than in France and consequently, a French judgment is 'only' a decision about the case-in-hand. England takes more care with a single judgment than France, and individual English judgments can be major sources of new legal principle. It is very unlikely that in France 120 infected patients advancing novel legal theories would have received such a thorough examination of their claims. It is very rare that one first instance French or Belgian judgment would shape the flow of future legal developments. We can be proud that the English legal system could deliver high quality justice to people of modest means pursuing a case with a difficult legal theory and complex scientific facts.

Postscript by Nicholas Underhill QC[66]

I am grateful to have been given the opportunity to comment briefly on Michael Brooke and Ian Forrester's lucid and fair-minded account of the *Hepatitis C* litigation. I need not argue the toss on the (very) few points

[66] Fountain Court Chambers. Nicholas Underhill QC was the defendants' leading counsel.

where I disagree with their exposition of the issues and the submissions, still less argue whether the decision was correct. The area of interest for readers of this book is the extensive use made in the course of the trial of comparative law materials. The authors clearly explain how central the use of such materials was to their presentation of the claimants' case. If I had more space I should be inclined to argue that it does not follow that they were central to the determination of the decisive issues. The parties agreed on most of the points of principle: see the section of the judgment headed 'Common ground', which contains a valuable summary of the correct approach to the Act.[67] Although the Judge referred at some points in that summary to comparative law materials, there was nothing that could not have been clearly derived from the terms of the Directive and the Act themselves. The only fundamental difference of principle as regards Article 6 – whether so-called 'avoidability' was a relevant circumstance – was one on which the authorities and academic materials hardly touched.

However, there is no opportunity here to develop this provocative thesis. I will confine myself to drawing attention to three specific points, which may not clearly emerge from the authors' account.

First, the authors write feelingly of the assistance which they received from Dr Taschner, the Commission official who had had primary responsibility for the Directive from its genesis through to its final adoption. As they say, it was their original intention to call Dr Taschner as a witness. His witness statement not only gave a factual account of the prolonged gestation of the Directive but also expressed strong views about the intended meaning and effect of the relevant provisions. The Defendants opposed the admission of this evidence in principle. In relation to English legislation it would of course be wholly improper to adduce the evidence of the promoter or the draftsman of a piece of legislation as to what he intended it to mean. The Defendants argued that the position should be no different in relation to EU legislation. Indeed the objections here were *a fortiori*. The genesis of the Directive was bitterly contested. Different Member States took widely different views as to just how strict the new strict liability regime should be. The result is generally acknowledged to have been a political compromise. It would be extremely dangerous for a court to entertain evidence from one of the protagonists in that debate since his intention as to the effect of the Directive could not be taken to

[67] See para. 31, where Burton J lists in detail a number of points of common ground.

represent the eventual (and largely notional) 'collective intention'. Although the authors may be formally correct to say that it was eventually 'agreed' that they would not seek to rely on Dr Taschner's evidence, that agreement was only reached after the Judge had made it plain that he accepted the validity of the Defendants' objection. The point seems to me important because it is sometimes thought, or assumed, that familiar domestic rules as to the admissibility of evidence can be ignored when 'Euro-issues' are in play. That may be so where the rules are purely local and technical; but where, as here, they reflect legitimate objections of principle they should apply equally whatever the source of law being relied on.

My second point is not dissimilar. The authors explain that they obtained from the archive of the European Commission a mass of minutes and associated materials showing the formal progress of the draft Directive. These went far beyond the drafts which appeared in the Official Journal and the other formal *travaux préparatoires* which are sometimes relied on. The Defendants objected to the admission of these materials – partly because of their sheer untranslated dullness, but also as a matter of principle. The trouble with such materials is that they can give the illusion of completeness but in fact only tell part of the story. In this case, for example, the minutes largely ceased at the crucial moment when the Directive entered the black hole of consideration by the Council of Ministers. It was impossible to find out from them what considerations – if what was no doubt largely a matter of political horse-trading can be so dignified – influenced the final form of the Directive. Again, there was no formal ruling; but the Claimants agreed to a short summary of the legislative history based almost wholly on materials from the Official Journal, and virtually none of the minutes were referred to in Court. Again, the moral is that the introduction of Euro-issues is not *carte blanche* for unrestricted reference to the legislative history.

My third point is somewhat different. Our prolonged discussion during the trial of a variety of comparative law materials often left me with the feeling that we were skating – enjoyably and with a fine display of linguistic talent (my own lagging behind that of the Claimants' counsel) – on very thin ice. At any point we might fall through the surface and discover ourselves seriously out of our depth. Comparative law materials are not easy to use properly. If they are not in English they have to be translated: even when translated, unfamiliar terminology, concepts and procedures have to be explained if basic misunderstandings are to be avoided. There is no expert available to the Court, which is accordingly dependent on counsel. In our case Mr Forrester was as fair as he was learned, and when he offered the Court a translation of an untranslated passage in an article, or in the parallel text of the Directive, it could be accepted without reserve – though the passage of arms about the significance of the use of the subjunctive in one sentence in the Italian version of the Advocate General's Opinion in *Commission v UK* possibly tested the parties' mutual confidence. But it is dangerous in principle to be thus reliant. Without a sure and impartial guide it is very easy to go astray.

Superficiality is a risk in other ways as well. The Claimants' counsel, as they have explained, had done extensive research in the library of the Max Planck Institute. The Defendants' counsel had in turn had great assistance from Professor Stapleton[68] in mining the very thick seam of product liability law in the US (and the narrow but rich seam of the *Oysters* litigation in Australia). But it was not realistic to draw the Court's attention to any but a very small proportion of this material. Hundreds of pages of copied materials – from both sides – were not in the end deployed. I hope we were intelligently selective. The Judge in any event showed himself keenly able to identify points of principle out of a wide variety of disparate materials. But the fact is that English lawyers cannot hope to educate either themselves or the Court to a full understanding of the subtleties of foreign legal systems. Comparative law materials are best used to illustrate or illuminate broad points of principle: even the most learned cannot become good German or US lawyers in the space of a single trial.

This postscript is intended as a counter-balance to the main article and has accordingly focussed on qualifications to the authors' main thesis. But I would not want it to be thought that the comparative law materials deployed in the *Hepatitis C* case were of little value, still less that they were of little interest. Anyone reading Burton J's formidable judgment will see how deeply they penetrated the argument – and also with what vigour counsel and the Court debated them.

Afterword by Mr Justice Burton[69]

A number of reflections occur to me in relation to the *Hepatitis C* litigation, by reference to the need for consideration of comparative law and its relevance to the decision:

[68] See footnote 14 above. [69] The trial judge.

1. Although the decisions of foreign courts are, in the English courts, strictly speaking only a part of the evidence, because evidence of foreign law is at English law to be treated as evidence of fact, nevertheless our modern systems now enable us to dispense with any problems with admissibility: hence the cases and the relevant academic works, whether extracts from textbooks, learned treatises or articles from journals, are collected together and bundled, and, in a long case, delivered to the judge before the trial starts.
2. In this case such 'foreign law' authorities and the academic articles were efficiently copied, indexed and paginated into files which rendered it easy for me to be able to underline and 'sticker up', with colour-coded tabs (essential in a case such as this where in the end there were not far off 100 files, including more than ten containing comparative law authorities and written submissions). This could be done both during the process of speed reading prior to the hearing, before I was fully understanding what all the issues consisted of, and then again during the hearing as they were given more detailed consideration and explanation. I was given some time for pre-reading all the documents prior to the trial starting. With the modern system of 'skeletons' (very often, at any rate in a long case, a misnomer for the lengthy written submissions which are delivered) supplied by way of exposition of each party's case, a judge can obtain a relatively informed grasp in advance by reading the submissions with care, and by speed-reading particularly those documents or, in the case of these comparative law questions, authorities and articles, which are specifically referred, or cross-referred, to in the submissions. Not only did we look at authorities from more than a dozen different jurisdictions (cases which became familiar friends, such as the '*German Bottle case*'[70] and the '*Danish Kidney case*'[71]) but we considered learned contributions from academic writers from the UK, US, Australia, Germany, Italy and France.
3. The decisions of other national courts in Europe are, of course, of great interest, but they are normally at best persuasive. However, where they are decisions seeking to construe or enforce the same European Directive, and we all ought together to be aspiring towards a common or 'autonomous' meaning of that Directive, then such comparative study becomes the more essential. Of course, unless and until there is a definitive conclusion by the European Court binding on all the

[70] *BGH* 9/5/95. [71] See footnote 16 above.

national courts, we may, nevertheless, each be arriving at our own different result.

4. It is in my experience very rare, short of the House of Lords, for a court to have the opportunity to look at so much foreign law and academic authority as we did in the *Hepatitis C* case. This was not just because of the importance of the case and the time which had been set aside for the hearing, but I think largely because of the novelty of the issues and arguments, at any rate in an English court. There has been a considerable jurisprudence developed in the United States which, on analysis, did not appear to be of great assistance in the interpretation of the somewhat differently drafted European Directive, but, that apart, there was little jurisprudence throughout the world, and certainly very little in England and Wales. In attempting to arrive at the correct solutions, an English judge in those circumstances had to look abroad at any rate for his starting point, and the parties gave me that opportunity.
5. The same novelty meant that whereas, on some occasions, in a long case it may be possible, as the proceedings continue, for a judge to be reaching provisional conclusions, or even provisionally drafting parts of his judgment in advance, this was not possible for me. Indeed I had an entirely open mind and was very much swayed first one way and then the other as the argument and evidence continued and developed. This meant that, once the case finished, I was able with a blank sheet of paper to re-read not only my notes but, more importantly and more accurately, the transcripts of the forty-nine days of evidence and argument, and in particular to reconsider the bundles, including the comparative law. I was given some five weeks 'time-off' to write the judgment, and I just about managed it in the deadline, working the sort of hours which I had thought I had left behind at the Bar!
6. The full and detailed oral argument was in my view essential to ensure both proper investigation of the issues and to put me in a position to arrive at an informed and reasoned decision. Bad ideas (whether coming from Counsel or from the Judge) can be tested and discarded. Good ideas can actually emerge in the course of discussion, but in any event can be tested and developed. Misunderstandings can be eliminated. Difficult arguments can be explained and reiterated. The need for oral argument, both in respect of the legal submissions and in due course by reference to the factual disputes, the time necessary for exploration and assimilation of the documents and above all the need for examination and cross-examination of the considerable number of important

witnesses, both factual and expert, meant that it took a great deal of co-operation, hard work and case management to achieve a situation in which everything that any one wished said or read was completed in forty-nine days of hearing.

7. It is certainly right that my judgment ended up very much longer – perhaps at least ten times longer – than any of the cases which we had been considering at any rate in European jurisdictions. Perhaps it is right to suggest that the traditional English legal proceedings are a luxury. But it is certainly the case that it is expected of the judge to give full reasons, analysing all the evidence and law before him or her, and in a case such as *Hepatitis C*, by reference to the British system, after a three-month trial, this inevitably meant a long judgment. One of the authors of this article, Ian Forrester QC, has told me that in conversation with some European judges he has found them astonished that our judgments are of the length they are, and he says (although I am not sure I believe him!) that they wish they were permitted or encouraged to follow suit. The time when this kind of detailed analysis, giving proper credit to the arguments, both of law and fact, put before the judge during the course of the hearing, is of particular importance is, naturally, at the ground-breaking stage. *Hepatitis C* was the first case in England and Wales in which any detailed consideration had been given to all the relevant aspects of the European Directive, and there were very full and thorough arguments by very able counsel to be resolved. It may be that the very setting out in detail of my reasoning, which had to be given in the judgment, contributed to a decision not to appeal.
8. Perhaps the most important matter to emphasise, from the judge's point of view, under our system, is of course the fact that our procedure is adversarial. Absent a case in which a judge happens to be familiar with an authority of which none of the parties in front of him had previous knowledge, in which case he would draw it to their attention and give them an opportunity to make submissions on it, the judge depends upon being 'fed' with information and authorities from the various parties in front of him. We are not expected to do our own research and we do not have any system of researchers or clerks to do any original work for us. It is therefore interesting to me to read in this article how it came about that the various documents were collected and put before me. But I made my decision solely on the basis of those documents and authorities. At one stage prior to trial I asked the parties whether they thought it would be a good idea if I were

accompanied by an expert assessor (as is now occasionally the case in our courts), who would have no part to play in the decision-making, but could assist the judge in relation to reading and assimilating the documentation, particularly on medical matters. The parties were both strenuously opposed to the idea, and I did not pursue it, because in fact I agreed with them. There is clearly a risk in the appointment of an assessor, that the judge will find himself delegating either some part of his understanding or possibly some part of his decision-making to someone else: and at least the parties knew who it was that they were in the process of educating and then persuading during the hearing. But the result of this fact, that it is the judge who is being educated by the parties, and not carrying out his own independent research, is that sometimes outsiders do not understand why points are not dealt with by the judge. Indeed such an experience occurred to me in this case. Professor Stapleton, the leading expert in the field of consumer law, to whom reference has been made above,[72] was kind enough to take me out to lunch some months after the judgment and, from her deep understanding of the law, she belaboured me over points that I did not seem to have taken into account. I was able to indicate that, so far as I could see, such points, even if otherwise available to either of the parties on the particular facts, had not in fact been put before me. This means that perhaps the *Hepatitis C* case, notwithstanding that it was not appealed, will not be the last word on the subject!

[72] See footnote 14 above and the author of Chapter 15 of this work.

3

Spanish product liability today – adapting to the 'new' rules

MIQUEL MARTÍN-CASALS*

Introduction: the application of the Spanish Product Liability Act by the courts[1]

Until 2003 the judgments of the Spanish Supreme Court were referring to the Spanish Product Liability Act (*Ley de responsabilidad civil por los daños causados por productos defectuosos* (hereafter, Product Liability Act

* The author wishes to express his indebtedness to the Spanish Ministry of Science and Technology for the award of the SEC2002–03728 R&D grant for the *Project on the Contribution of Spanish Tort Law to European Tort Law (II)*, within the framework of which this paper has been drafted.

[1] On the Spanish Product Liability Act see Josep Solé Feliu, *El concepto de defecto del producto en la responsabilidad civil del fabricante* (Valencia: Tirant lo Blanch, 1997); Sonia Rodríguez Llamas, *Régimen de responsabilidad civil por productos defectuosos* (2nd edn, Pamplona: Aranzadi, 2002); Domingo Jiménez Liébana, *Responsabilidad civil: daños causados por productos defectuosos* (Madrid: McGraw-Hill, 1998); Fernando L. De La Vega García, *Responsabilidad civil derivada del producto defectuoso* (Madrid: Civitas, 1998) and Patricia Cillero De Cabo, *La responsabilidad civil del suministrador final por daños ocasionados por productos defectuosos* (Madrid: Civitas, 2000). See also, among many others, Miquel Martín-Casals, 'The Likely Impact of the Act of 6 July 1994 Implementing the EC Directive on Product Liability in Spain', *European Business Law Review* 1995: 37 et seq.; Mª Ángeles Parra Lucán, 'Notas a la Ley 22/1994, de 6 de julio, de responsabilidad civil por los daños causados por productos defectuosos', AC 1995, pp. 723–52; Sílvia Díaz Alabart and Mª Carmen Gómez Laplaza, 'La responsabilidad civil por los daños causados por productos defectuosos', AC n° 25, 1995: 534 et seq.; Mª Carmen Gómez Laplaza, 'La responsabilidad por los daños causados por productos defectuosos en la Unión Europea. Presente y futuro', AC n° 15, 2000: 15 et seq. and Miquel Martín-Casals and Josep Solé Feliu, '20 Problemas en la aplicación de la Ley de responsabilidad por productos defectuosos y algunas propuestas de solución (I) and (II)', *Práctica Derecho De Daños: Revista de Responsabilidad Civil y Seguros* 9 (2003): 6–34 and 10 (2003): 5–25. From a comparative point of view see: Miquel Martín-Casals and Josep Solé Feliu, 'Responsabilidad por productos en España y (Des)Armonización Europea', *Revista de Responsabilidad Civil y Seguros* 4 (July-August 2001): 1–17; Miquel Martín-Casals and Josep Solé Feliu, 'La responsabilidad por productos defectuosos: un intento de Armonización a través de Directivas', in Sergio Cámara Lapuente, *Derecho privado europeo* (Madrid: Colex, 2003), pp. 921–48.

or LRPD))[2] only *obiter dicta*, as a sort of reminder of its existence. They dealt with facts that had taken place before the new regulation implementing the Product Liability Directive was applicable and, therefore, they applied the rules of the General Act for the Protection of Consumers and Users (*Ley general para la defensa de consumidores y usuarios* (hereafter, Consumer Protection Act or LGDCU)),[3] an Act which had governed product liability in Spain since 1984.[4]

Errors and omissions excepted, STS 21.2.2003 (RJ 2003\2133) was the first judgment where the Supreme Court applied the Product Liability Act implementing the Directive. In this case, a bottle of white lemonade exploded while the claimant was putting it into his shopping basket in the supermarket. The splinters of glass injured both his face and one eye, and caused him the partial loss of sight in his left eye. The victim filed a claim against the soft-drink and the bottling companies seeking a damages award of 36,520,000 Pta (approx. €220,000). The Court of First Instance decided in favour of the claimant, but awarded the substantially lesser sum of 7,720,000 Pta (approx. €46,000), and this judgment was confirmed by the Court of Appeal and, finally, by the Supreme Court.[5]

Whereas decisions of the Supreme Court have been scarce so far, there has been an ever-growing body of judgments of the Courts of First Instance and Courts of Appeal – increasing dramatically from 2001 to 2003 – that have been applying the Product Liability Act.

In this paper I am going to analyse the application of the Product Liability Act by the Spanish Courts of Appeal. The decisions of these courts show a knowledge of the Act that is still somewhat superficial, and this frequently gives rise to decisions that are often ambiguous or equivocal, sometimes doubtful, and, occasionally, even blatantly wrong. Some misunderstandings of key concepts of the Product Liability Act result from the fact that judges seem to have put the rules of the Product Liability Act 'on top', so to speak, of the knowledge that they already had of the rules dealing with product liability in the 1984 Consumer

[2] Ley 22/1994, de 6 de julio, *de responsabilidad civil por los daños causados por productos defectuosos* (BOE n° 161, 7.7.1994).

[3] Ley 26/1984, de 19 de julio, *general para la defensa de los consumidores y usuarios* (BOE n° 176, 24.7.1984).

[4] So, for instance, among many others, SSTS 28.12.1998 [RJ 1998\10161]; 9.3.1999 [RJ 1999\1368] or Auto TS 20.7.1999 [RJ 1999\5055].

[5] For a comment on this decision see Miquel Martín Casals and Josep Solé Feliu, 'Aplicación de la Ley de responsabilidad por productos defectuosos: la explosión de una botella y el defecto de fabricación', in *Diario La Ley*, 20. junio 2003, p. 1 et seq.

Protection Act. In these cases, the courts have not always been aware of the relationship between the new Act and the old one or, even, of the relationship between the new Act and the general tort and contract law rules. Inconsistencies or misleading interpretations have also arisen from the fact that courts have tried to make a construction of the Product Liability Act which is consistent and coherent with general principles of Spanish law, but which might run counter to a proper interpretation of the product liability provisions implementing the Directive.

Consumer Protection Act or Product Liability Act: which rules apply?

It is well known that the Spanish Product Liability Act implementing the Directive came into force on 8 July 1994 and that one of the first things the implementing Act had to resolve was its compatibility with the 1984 Consumer Protection Act.

The Consumer Protection Act had been poorly drafted in the wake of the *colza* or rape oil case, which caused the intoxication of over 15,000 persons, and whose eventual result was 300 deaths and several thousand severely impaired victims.[6] This Act referred both to defective products and services and provided for two liability regimes: (1) a fault regime, with a rebuttable presumption of fault (Art. 26 LGDCU) and (2) a strict liability regime for products and services that met certain general conditions (of purity, efficiency or security, undergoing technical, professional or systematic control, etc.), or that had been enumerated in the Act (for instance, food products, cleaning products, medicines, healthcare services, gas and electricity services, electrical appliances, means of transport, motor vehicles, toys and other products targeting children) (Art. 28 LGDCU).[7]

When the implementation of the Product Liability Directive was under analysis, some legal scholars and the Ministry of Health and Consumption contended that it was a *minimum* Directive and that Art. 13 Directive permitted the preservation of the Spanish product liability regulation in

[6] The case has been dealt with in the decisions SAN 20.5.1989, STS 23.4.1992 [RJ 1992\6783] and STS 2ª 26.9.1997 [RJ 1997\6366] and has given rise to a damages award of over 500 billion Pta (approx €3 billion).

[7] See Rodrigo Bercovitz Rodriguez Cano, in Rodrigo Bercovitz and Javier Salas, *Comentarios a la Ley general para la defensa de los consumidores y usuarios* (Madrid: Civitas, 1992), Com. Art. 28, p. 715.

force, since it was deemed to be more protective and was 'pre-existent' to the notification of the Directive. However, this position was rejected by the Ministry of Justice, which prepared the draft of the Act finally passed by Parliament. This Act now in force states: (1) 'This Act shall not apply to those products that have been put into circulation before the Act came into effect, which shall be governed by the provisions in force at the time' (Sole Transitional Provision LRPD) and (2) 'Arts. 25 to 28 of the Consumer Protection Act shall not be applicable to civil liability resulting from damage caused by defective products included in Article 2 of this Act' (First Final Provision LRPD).

According to the interpretation which some Spanish scholars thought correct,[8] the Product Liability Directive is not, as a matter of fact, a *minimum* Directive and the provisions of the Consumer Protection Act can apply solely to products put into circulation before 8 July 1994, i.e. the date on which the Product Liability Act came into force, or to damage caused by defective immovables and services, irrespective of the date on which they were made or rendered, i.e. to other situations not coming within the scope of the Product Liability Act.

However, the Court of First Instance no. 5 of Oviedo, dealing with the case of a claimant who had received a blood transfusion in an institution operated by the defendant, *Medicina Asturiana*, in the course of which she was allegedly infected with the hepatitis C virus, entertained some doubts about the relationship between the old Consumer Protection Act and the new Product Liability Act. In this case, the claimant had sought compensation from the defendant for the damage suffered according, *inter alia*, to Arts. 25 to 28 of the Consumer Protection Act, which offered more extensive rights than those which the victims of damage may rely on under the Product Liability Act. *Medicina Asturiana* had challenged the applicability of those articles of the Consumer Protection Act in the light of the already mentioned First Final Provision of the Product Liability Act and, so, the Court of First Instance requested a preliminary ruling on the proper interpretation of Art. 13 of the Product Liability Directive. This article provides that this Directive 'shall not affect any rights which an injured person may have according to the rules of the law of contractual or non-contractual liability or a special liability system existing at the moment when this Directive is notified'.

[8] In this sense see, *inter alia*, Jiménez Liébana, *Responsabilidad civil*, p. 498 and Martín Casals and Solé Feliu, 'Responsabilidad por productos en España', pp. 4–6.

On 25 April 2002, the European Court of Justice, in deciding this case (*María Victoria González Sánchez v Medicina Asturiana*), as well as in two other judgments issued on the very same day, confirmed that the Product Liability Directive is not a *minimum* Directive.[9] In the case at stake, it held:

> [N]or can Article 153 EC . . . be relied on in order to justify interpreting the directive as seeking a minimum harmonisation of the laws of the Member States which could not preclude one of them from retaining or adopting protective measures stricter than the Community measures . . . the margin of discretion available to the Member States in order to make provision for product liability is entirely determined by the Directive itself and must be inferred from its wording, purpose and structure . . . [I]t is important to note that unlike, for example, Council Directive 93/13/EEC of 5 April 1993 on unfair terms in consumer contracts (OJ 1993 L 95, p. 29), the Directive contains no provision expressly authorising the Member States to adopt or to maintain more stringent provisions in matters in respect of which it makes provision, in order to secure a higher level of consumer protection.[10]

Moreover, it added that:

> Although Articles 15(1)(a) and (b) and 16 of the Directive permit the Member States to depart from the rules laid down therein, the possibility of derogation applies only in regard to the matters exhaustively specified and it is narrowly defined. Moreover, it is subject *inter alia* to conditions as to assessment with a view to further harmonisation, to which the penultimate recital in the preamble expressly refers. In those circumstances Article 13 of the Directive cannot be interpreted as giving the Member States the possibility of maintaining a general system of product liability different from that provided for in the Directive.[11]

However, this impossibility of maintaining a general system of product liability different from the one resulting from the implementation of the

[9] On this and other decisions of the ECJ on product liability, see Luis González Vaqué, 'La Directiva, 85/374/CEE relativa a la responsabilidad por productos defectuosos en la jurisprudencia del TJCE: de los riesgos del desarrollo a la franquicia de 500 euros', Enero 2003, Unión Europea Aranzadi: 5–17.

[10] See Judgment of the Court (Fifth Chamber) of 25 April 2002. *María Victoria González Sánchez v Medicina Asturiana SA*. Reference for a preliminary ruling: Juzgado de Primera Instancia e Instrucción n° 5 de Oviedo – Spain. Approximation of laws – Directive 85/374/EEC – Product liability – Relationship with other systems of liability. Case C–183/00. European Court reports 2002, p. 1–03901, paras. 24–7.

[11] Ibid., paragraphs 29–30.

Directive, even after this and other judgments of the European Court of Justice had been issued, was still not clear to some Courts of Appeal. So, for instance:

The Court of Appeal of the Balearic Islands, in a decision issued in July 2002 (SAP Baleares 15.7.2002 [JUR 2002\245264]) (i.e. almost three months after the judgment of the European Court of Justice was issued), holds the supplier of a defective component part of a toilet strictly liable pursuant to the old Consumer Protection Act, arguing that this Act is still applicable to products in accordance with the compatibility with the domestic provision dealing with contract and tort liability provided by Art. 13 Directive.

In a similar way, the Court of Appeal of Cordoba, in a decision issued in June 2002 (SAP Córdoba 19.6.2002) (i.e. also after the judgment of the European Court of Justice), considers that a discussion of which rules apply is 'a trivial matter', holds the defendant liable for the damage caused, and declares that the defendant must be compensated for the property damage caused by a power surge which is assessed at an amount of €105.18 'no matter which rules are applied'. Furthermore, it is worth noting that this amount is well below the threshold established by the LRPD.

Sometimes decisions do not even bother to consider which rules apply. In SAP Segovia 31.7.2002 (AC 2002\1233), dealing with personal injuries suffered by the victim who drank, in a bar, a liquid from a bottle which was labelled 'grape juice', but which in fact contained a caustic liquid, the court held the manufacturer, its insurer and the owner of the bar jointly and severally liable according to Art. 28 LGDCU. Although the decision does not refer to the moment when the bottle was put into circulation, it is very unlikely that this happened before the Product Liability Act came into force, i.e. before 8 July 1994.

Alongside these decisions, the decisions that take into account the First Final provision of the LRPD and correct the wrong allegation of the parties with regard to the applicable rules are becoming more and more frequent (for instance, SAP Sevilla 5.3.2002 [JUR 2002\205647], SAP La Coruña 21.6.2002 [AC 2002\1348] or SAP Vizcaya 9.2.2002 [AC 2002\104]). However, with regard to the applicable norms some fine-tuning is still very necessary: so, for instance, by contrast to what SAP Vizcaya 9.2.2002 [AC 2002\104] states, the moment when a defective airbag is put into circulation is not related 'to the moment when the permit allowing the car to circulate was issued'.

Strict liability *versus* fault liability. Which grounds for liability?

Some decisions are not very clear with regard to whether the Product Liability Act gives rise to strict liability or to fault liability. The distinction between these two liability regimes is, of course, known in Spanish law, although sometimes the difference is a bit blurred in practice by the fact that, with very few exceptions, in fault liability pursuant to Art. 1902 CC, i.e. the general tort liability provision for fault, fault is regularly rebuttably presumed. Nonetheless, this would not explain serious confusions such as in SAP Orense 10.11.1999 [AC 1999\2092], in a case of a car bursting into flames due to a manufacturing defect and thereby harming vehicles which were parked in the vicinity, where the court declared that in spite of the strict character of the liability regime provided by the Product Liability Act 'this does not mean that it can do without a finding of fault . . . fault is presumed or, put another way, the claimant does not carry the burden of proof and it is the defendant who has to establish that he acted with due care'. In a similar way, SAP La Coruña 21.6.2002 [AC 2002\1348], dealing with the damage caused to the teeth of the victim when chewing a biscuit which, due to a manufacturing defect, contained hard pieces of sugar, identifies 'defect' with 'fault' and states, unperturbed, that 'Art. 5 LRPD establishes that the victim has to prove the defect, the damage and the causation link between both. These conditions, in a few words, coincide with the classical conditions for fault liability in tort required by Art. 1902 CC.'

It is possible that legal scholarship has also contributed, to some extent, to fostering confusion when it has seen echoes of fault liability in some of the defences provided by Art. 6 LRPD.[12] Some decisions seem to confirm this idea: so, for instance, SAP Las Palmas 23.4.2002 [JUR 2002\167362], dealing with damage caused by a defective vehicle, states that the Product Liability Act does not modify the fault approach of Art. 1902 CC and 'even establishes for certain cases defences with a clear mark of fault, as results from Art. 6'. Also SAP Ciudad Real 26.11.2002 [JUR 2002\32632], after declaring that the Product Liability Act provides for a strict liability regime, classifies the different defences according to different rationales and identifies the development-risk defence with 'foreseeability of the risk' and considers that this defence shows that the Act does not establish a proper strict liability regime.

[12] So, for instance, Rodriguez Llamas, *Régimen de responsabilidad civil por productos defectuosos*, p. 134.

One can agree with Horton Rogers that the distinction between fault liability and strict liability displays many shades and that there is a sort of 'continuum' between fault liability and strict liability.[13] However, it is difficult to admit that a strict liability regime becomes a fault liability one by the mere fact that it accepts a specific case which can be more or less linked to a finding of fault as a defence. In fact, the European Court of Justice, dealing with the English implementation of the development-risk defence, had already declared in *Commission of the European Communities v United Kingdom*[14] that '[i]n order for a producer to incur liability for defective products under Article 4 of the Directive, the victim must prove the damage, the defect and the causal relationship between defect and damage, but not that the producer was at fault'.[15] In this sense, SAP Tarragona 18.7.1998 [AC 1998\1546] had also rightly set out that the LRPD 'provides for a strict liability regime' and that 'the defendant cannot be exonerated from liability by proving that he acted with due care, since he can only avail himself of the defences laid down in Arts. 6, 8 and 9 LRPD'.

The legal concept of 'product': products or services?

In spite of the fact that a movable joined or incorporated into another immovable is not a movable according to domestic Spanish law (cf. Art. 334.3 CC) and, by contrast, it is a product according to the Product Liability Act (cf. Art. 2 LRPD), the concept of 'product' has not given rise to much hesitation.

Courts of Appeal have not had much trouble identifying products when dealing with bottle caps that go off violently (SAP 18.4.2000 [AC 2000\1214]), tanks that break (SAP Tarragona 18.7.1998 [AC 1998\1546]), medicines that cause harm (SAP Huesca 18.4.2000 [AC 2000\1214]), airbags that are defective (SAP Asturias 17.11.2003 [JUR 2003\

13 W. V. Horton Rogers, 'England', in Bernhard A. Koch and Helmut Koziol (eds.), *Unification of Tort Law: Strict Liability* (The Hague; London; New York: Kluwer Law International, 2002), p. 101.

14 Judgment of the Court (Fifth Chamber) of 29 May 1997. *Commission of the European Communities v United Kingdom of Great Britain and Northern Ireland.* Failure of a Member State to fulfil obligations – Article 7(e) of Directive 85/374/EEC – Incorrect implementation – Defence precluding liability for defective products – State of scientific and technical knowledge. Case C-300/95. European Court reports 1997, page I–02649.

15 Ibid., paragraph 24.

277690]), or even Spanish omelette sandwiches spread with mayonnaise containing salmonella (SAP Córdoba 10.4.2000 [AC 2000\1395]).

Since Art. 2 LRPD considers gas and electricity to be products, Spanish Courts of Appeal have applied the Product Liability Act to damage caused by power surges,[16] breakdown of power transformers,[17] propane gas explosions,[18] and explosions of butane gas cylinders.[19] So, for instance, SAP Albacete 9.3.2000 [AC 2000\1145], in a case of damage caused by the explosion of a butane gas cylinder, declares that 'product' according to the LRPD, includes 'the gas itself and the cylinders [movables] with its accessories'.

Although in the case of damage caused by electricity most decisions draw the distinction between product and service with accuracy, in a few cases courts have had some difficulty when distinguishing whether the damage had been caused by a product, being then governed by LRPD, or by a service, being then governed by the LGDCU. This is the case for instance, in SAP Tarragona 30.4.2002 [JUR 2002\185670] or SAP Barcelona 11.11.2003 [JUR 2004\5832], where the court holds that the damage caused by a power surge is damage caused by a service and that LDGCU applies.

The legal concept of 'defect'. Manufacturing defects or useless products?

With regard to defect, Art. 3.2 LRPD contains a specific provision which, deviating from the Directive, applies to manufacturing defects only and states that '[i]n any case, a product is defective if it does not offer the safety regularly offered by the rest of the issues of the same series'. This provision establishes a presumption of the existence of a defect when the requirements that it includes are met and entails an exception to the general rule provided by Art. 5 LRPD, according to which '[t]he injured person seeking to obtain compensation for the incurred damage must prove the defect, the damage and the causal relationship between the two'.

[16] In this sense, *inter alia*, SAP Huesca 24.11.1998 [AC 1998\8667], SAP Huesca 24.6.1999 [AC 1999\1476], SAP Asturias 20.11.2001 [JUR 2001\35199] and SAP Sevilla 24.9.2003 [AC 2003\1698].

[17] So, for instance, SAP Toledo 16.3.2000 [AC 2000\959].

[18] For instance, SAP Salamanca 15.3.2000 [AC 2000\1367].

[19] Among others, SSAP Badajoz 8.4.1999 [AC 1999\674] and Albacete 9.3.2000 [AC 2000\1145].

Art. 3.2 LRPD has been used often in the cases of bottles that explode and provides a yardstick that Spanish courts had already used within the framework of the old Art. 28 LGDCU.[20] So, for instance, it is applied by SAP Granada 12.2.2000 [AC 2000\851], in a case where a cap of a Coca-cola bottle seriously injured the eye of a little girl while she was opening it. Or by SAP Cádiz 16.3.2002 [JUR 2002\140327], dealing with the explosion of a bottle of tonic water which took place while the victim was taking it from a fridge in a shop, where the court states that the defect of the product 'results from the simple circumstance of the explosion of the bottle without any external grounds that could give rise to this effect, something which, by itself, meets the conditions required for establishing the proof of the defect'. However, by contrast to Italian law, which contains a similar rule (cf. Art. 5.3 Italian Decree),[21] Spanish legal writing considers that this presumption can be rebutted. The defendant can prove that 'other circumstances' (cf. Art. 3.1 LRPD) may indicate that, in spite of the fact that the product offers a level of safety which is lower than the level offered by the other issues of the same series, it still offers the safety which a person may legitimately expect and, therefore, that it is not defective. One of these 'other circumstances' may be 'the presentation of the product' (cf. Art. 3.1 LRPD), since the external aspect of a product can give rise to a certain safety expectation (for instance, the defective bottle had clearly noticeable cracks). The 'improper use of the product' may also be one of these 'other circumstances' and, since Art. 3.1 LRPD does not offer a closed list of these 'other circumstances', other aspects which are relevant in establishing the safety which a person may legitimately expect may also be taken into account.[22] The courts are also very well aware that the notion of the

[20] See, for instance, SSTS 23.6.1993 [RJ 1993\5380]; 4.10.1996 [RJ 1996\7034].

[21] See, for instance, Gustavo Ghidini, in G. Alpa, U. Carnevali, F. di Giovanni, G. Ghidini, U. Ruffolo and C. M. Verardi, *La responsabilità per danno da prodotti difettosi* (Milan: Giuffrè, 1990, p. 48), who understands that once it has been established that a particular issue does not offer the safety regularly offered by the rest of the issues of the same series, the producer can no longer prove that the defect did not exist, not even by invoking any of the 'other circumstances' provided by Art. 5 which are regularly used to establish it. See also Maria Leonarda Loi, in Roberto Pardolesi and Giulio Ponzanelli, 'La Responsabilità per danno da prodotti difettosi', *Le Nuove Leggi Civile Commentate*, n. 3, maggio-giugno, 1989, p. 550.

[22] See in more detail Josep Solé Feliu, *El concepto de defecto del producto en la responsabilidad civil del fabricante* (Valencia: Tirant lo Blanch, 1997), pp. 605–11 and María Ángeles Parra Lucán, 'La responsabilidad civil por productos y servicios defectuosos. Responsabilidad civil del fabricante y de los profesionales', in L. Fernando Reglero Campos (Coord.), *Tratado de responsabilidad civil* (2nd edn, Cizur Menor: Aranzadi /Thomson, 2003), p. 1317.

defect is a key element in the whole system and, therefore, they rightly hold that, pursuant to Art. 5 LRPD, the defect must be regularly proven by the claimant and that this rebuttable presumption of the defect introduced by Art. 3.2 LRPD is exceptional.[23]

The divide between defects for lack of utility and defects for lack of safety has not generally posed great problems so far. It must be admitted that it is not always easy to draw a clear-cut distinction between (a) products that are defective because they are unsafe and, in our case, do not meet the consumers' expectations test, and (b) products that are defective because they do not meet the utility expectations of the particular contracting consumer, according to what had been expressly or tacitly agreed in a contract. However, if the defect, as many decisions hold, is a key element of the whole system, it is worth striving for clarity on this point.

There are some decisions which, if they ever reach the Supreme Court, will require a clear rectifying statement. This is the case of SAP Valencia 16.9.2002 [AC 2002\1657], where the claimant had purchased an irrigation engine from a supplier who, in turn, had obtained it from the manufacturer. The engine did not work properly, and it had to be repaired and some of its parts replaced. No personal injury occurred. No damage to other property arose and not even damage to the engine itself took place. Nevertheless, the Court considered, verbatim, that the case was *a clear case of a manufacturing defect* and *held the manufacturer liable for all expenses in accordance with the provisions of the Product Liability Act* (emphasis added).

Likewise, in SAP Córdoba 30.7.2003 [AC 2003\1142], a taxi driver suffered some malfunction in the taxi which caused the vehicle to be off the road for seventeen days while it was still under the guarantee period. The Court had no hesitation in wrongly interpreting half a dozen provisions of the Product Liability Act, held the seller, *Opel Spain*, liable *pursuant to the Product Liability Act* (emphasis added) and ordered a damages award of €1,359 for the seventeen days during which the taxi-driver could not use the car.

The legal concept of 'manufacturer': back door for the supplier?

Before the Product Liability Act came into force, Art. 26 LGDCU permitted the victim of a defective product to file a claim against the

[23] See, among many others, SSAP Tarragona 18.7.1998 [AC 1998\1546]; Zaragoza 27.9.1999 [AC 1999\1661]; Córdoba 30.10.2000 [AC 2000\2097] and Albacete 9.3.2000 [AC 2000\1145].

manufacturer, the importer and the supplier, together or individually, without establishing any order of priority. The idea that, according to the Product Liability Act, the victim would normally sue the manufacturer, in certain cases only the importer, and exceptionally, i.e. in the cases expressly established by the rules transposing the Directive, the supplier is not always properly understood by victims and courts. So for instance, in SAP Badajoz 8.4.1999 [AC 1999\674], referring to the damage caused by the explosion of a butane gas cylinder due to a leak in the cylinder that was attributable to a manufacturing defect, the Court of Appeal had no problem finding the supplier jointly and severally liable with the manufacturer and its insurance company.

This decision does not accord with the Product Liability Act. However, it must be pointed out that the Spanish Act contains a provision (the Sole Additional Provision of the Act), which can give rise to liability for the supplier well beyond the provisions of the Directive. This provision sets forth that '[t]he supplier of a defective product shall be responsible, as if he were the manufacturer, when he has supplied the product with knowledge of the existence of the defect. In this case, the supplier may bring a claim for recovery against the manufacturer or importer.' Although it is very likely that this provision was meant to hold liable those suppliers who had supplied defective products with intent, courts seem to have turned this liability of the supplier into liability for fault.

So, for instance, in SAP Barcelona 19.4.2002 [JUR 2002\184459], where the victim suffered a personal injury as the result of being knocked by the hydraulic tube of an industrial machine, the court holds the supplier liable, according to the Sole Additional Provision of the LRPD, arguing that, since he was an expert in that sort of product, he should have detected the defect. By contrast, SAP Cáceres 21.6.2002 [JUR 2002\226019], where a toy that had been purchased inside a sealed box was defective, the court stated that the supplier could not have known of the defect when he received the product and, therefore, he could not be held liable according to this Additional Provision.

On this point it might be useful to remind Spanish courts that the European Court of Justice in *Commission of the European Communities v French Republic*,[24] dealing with the French transposition of the Directive which in Art. 1386–7 *Code Civile* equated the supplier with the producer,

[24] Judgment of the Court (Fifth Chamber) of 25 April 2002. *Commission of the European Communities v French Republic*. Failure by a Member State to fulfil its obligations – Directive 85/374/EEC – Product liability – Incorrect transposition. Case C–52/00. European Court reports 2002 page I–03827.

declared that '[s]ince the Community legislature had competence to harmonise the laws of the Member States in the field of product liability, it was also competent to determine the person who was to bear that liability and the conditions under which that person was to be sued'.[25]

Defences, in particular, the full development-risks defence for public bodies

It is very likely that the defence that has been most commonly invoked by the defendants is the one referring to the fact '[t]hat, given the circumstances of the case, it can be presumed that the defect did not exist at the time the product was put into circulation' (Art. 6.1 (b) LRPD). This is likely to be so because, according to its wording ('it can be presumed that the defect did not exist'), the Article does not seem to require full proof of the non-existence of the defect. Nevertheless in SAP Santa Cruz de Tenerife 19.4.2002 [AC 2002\898], dealing with cuts to the tongue of a victim who drank beer from a bottle which contained pieces of broken glass, the court rejects this defence out of lack of proof. The manufacturer had argued that it was impossible for these pieces of glass to have entered the bottle before it was put into circulation. The court held that it had been established that the bottle contained pieces of glass and that the manufacturer had not proven sufficiently that they had entered the bottle afterwards. SAP Cantabria 19.6.2002 [JUR 2002\212110] decided in a similar way with regard to the damage caused by an elevating platform that broke.

With regard to the development risk defence it is worth mentioning that in spite of the fact that Art. 6.1 (e) LRPD provides that '[t]he manufacturer or the importer shall not be liable if they prove: (e) That the scientific and technical knowledge existing at the time the product was put into circulation did not allow for appraisal of the defect', Art. 6.3 LPRD provides that this defence cannot be invoked '[i]n the case of *medicines*, foods or food products for *human consumption* . . .' (emphasis added).[26]

[25] ECJ Decision, para. 39.

[26] Spanish bibliography on this topic is extensive. Among many others see Pablo Salvador Coderch and Josep Solé Feliu, *Brujos y aprendices. Los riesgos de desarrollo en la responsabilidad de producto* (Madrid: Marcial Pons, 1999); María Paz García Rubio, 'Los riesgos de desarrollo en la responsabilidad por daños causados por productos defectuosos. Su impacto en el Derecho español', *Actualidad Civil* 35 (1998): 853–70; José Luís Inglés Buceta, 'Riesgos del desarrollo y accesibilidad: la Sentencia del Tribunal de Justicia de las Comunidades Europeas de 29 de mayo de 1997, con un apóstrofe sobre el nuevo Artículo

According to the Spanish provisions, 'medicines' includes both prescription and over-the-counter medicines. The reference 'for human consumption' applies to medicines, in order to exclude medicines for animals, since according to the Spanish rules 'medicines' are both for human consumption and for animals.[27] Foods and food products also exclude animal food, which is in accord with the Spanish regulations on food and food products.[28]

The liability of public bodies, by contrast, is governed by a different Act (*Legal Regime of Public Administrations and General Administrative Procedure Act* 1992 [hereafter, LRJAP]).[29] In its original wording Art. 141.1 LRJAP provided that recoverable damage was only the damage stemming from harm that the person who has suffered it 'does not have the legal duty to endure'. Although it was considered that the public bodies could exonerate for *force majeure*, a series of decisions issued in the early nineties, dealing with the tort liability of public healthcare centres for the damage caused by blood transfusions infected with HIV, considered that this was not a case of *force majeure* and held the public healthcare centres liable.[30]

In 1999, the 1992 Act was amended by Ley 4/1999, of 23.1.1999.[31] Fearing a second wave of litigation, in this case with regard to HIV, and arguing that the concept of *force majeure* needed 'fine-tuning', the following paragraph was added to Art. 141.1 LRJAP:

141.1 de la LRJAP-PAC', *Derecho de los Negocios*, October (1999: 15–28; Javier Lete Achirica, 'Los riesgos de desarrollo en materia de responsabilidad por los daños causados por los productos defectuosos. Comentario a la sentencia del Tribunal de Justicia de las Comunidades Europeas de 29 de mayo de 1997', *Actualidad Civil* 28 (1998): 685–93 and Elena Vicente Domingo, 'Responsabilidad por producto defectuoso, responsabilidad objetiva, riesgos del desarrollo y valoración de los daños', *La Ley* 5034 (13 April 2000).

[27] See Arts. 6 and 8 Ley 25/1990, 20 December, *del medicamento* (BOE n° 306, 22.12.1990).

[28] See Art. 1.02.01 *Código alimentario español* (Decreto 2484/1967, de 21 de setiembre (BOE n° 248 to 253, of 17 to 23.10.1967, amended by RD 1353/1983, de 27 de abril, BOE n° 126 27.05.1983)).

[29] Ley 30/1992, de 26 de noviembre, *de Régimen Jurídico de las Administraciones Públicas y del Procedimiento Administrativo Común* (BOE num. 285, 27.11.1992 [corrección de errores BOE num. 311, 28.12.1993 and num. 23, 27.1.1993]).

[30] So SSTS 4ª 5.6.1991 [RJ 1991\5131], 4ª 10.6.1996 [RJ 1996\5007], STSJ Cataluña, Social, 9.12.1992 [AS 1992\6357]. However, 1997 marks a turning point in the opinion of the courts, and decisions progressively begin to accept the *force majeure* defence (see, for instance, SSTS 4ª, 22.12.1997 [RJ 1998\737], 4ª 3.12.1999 [RJ 1999\9349], 4ª 5.4.2000 [RJ 2000\3284], 4ª 9.10.2000 [RJ 2000\9420]).

[31] Act Amending the Legal Regime of Public Administrations and Common Administrative Procedure Act (Ley 4/1999, de 13 de enero, *de modificación de la Ley 30/1992, de 26 de noviembre, de Régimen Jurídico de las Administraciones Públicas y del Procedimiento Administrativo Común* [BOE num. 12, 14.1.1999]).

> [T]he damage resulting from the facts or circumstances which could not have been foreseen or avoided according to the state of scientific or technical knowledge existing when the damage occurred shall not be recoverable, without detriment to the social benefits that the law may provide for these cases.

It must be stressed that the development risk defence that public bodies can invoke refers to all sort of products, not just blood transfusions or blood products and, accordingly, public bodies can be exonerated from liability in all cases of development risks.

This difference of treatment between private and public producers has given rise to an intense debate. Some legal writers have declared that this amendment does not give rise to any objections.[32] Others have contended that this provision is unconstitutional, and therefore that it could be challenged before the Constitutional Court by any First Instance or Appellate Court that has to apply it and entertains doubts about its constitutionality (the so-called *cuestión de inconstitucionalidad*).[33] The grounds are as follows: Art. 106.2 of the Spanish Constitution provides: 'Private individuals, under the terms established by the law, shall have the right to be indemnified for any harm they suffer in any of their property and rights, except in the cases of *force majeure*, whenever such harm is the result of the functioning of the public services' [emphasis added].

The Constitution allows exoneration from liability of public bodies only in the case of *force majeure* and, in spite of the reasons given for amending Art. 141.1 LRJAP and introducing a full defence in all cases of development risks, development risks are not, strictly speaking, a case of *force majeure* (they are closer to '*caso fortuito*', a fortuitous event close to a *force majeure* which is internal to the activity of the person causing the harm and which could have been avoided if it could have been foreseen).[34]

Other legal writers argue that this duplicity of rules introduces a duality of legal regimes which will be a disincentive for research by public bodies

[32] See Fernando Pantaleón Prieto, 'Cómo repensar la responsabilidad civil extracontractual (también la de las administraciones públicas)', in Juan Antonio Moreno Martínez (Coord.), *Perfiles de la responsabilidad civil en el nuevo milenio* (Madrid: Dykinson, 2000), pp. 439–65, at p. 462.

[33] See Jesús Jordano Fraga, 'La reforma del artículo 141, Apartado 1, de la Ley 30/1992, de 26 de noviembre, o el inicio de la demolición del sistema de responsabilidad objetiva de las administraciones públicas', *Revista de Administración Pública* 149 (May–August 1999): 321–36, at 333 and 336.

[34] In this sense, see Jordano Fraga, 'La reforma del artículo 141': 333–4.

manufacturing products[35] or that foreign manufacturers supplying their products to Spain will prefer to supply them to public bodies.[36] These arguments point out possible negative effects of the duality of regimes but say nothing about their legality or conformity with other legal rules in force.

Recently, another legal writer has pointed out that this duality of regimes infringes on the rights of the patients of public hospitals (and I would add, of all citizens who use medicines, food and food products which had defects that scientific and technical knowledge could not have detected) and that it also infringes on the equality of the legal position of public bodies and private manufacturers acting in the same market.[37]

However, it must be pointed out that with regard to the interpretation of the principle of equality contained in Art. 14 CE[38] the Spanish Constitutional Court has been quite restrictive. In the decision STC 181/2000, of 29 June, regarding the constitutionality of the legal tariffication scheme for traffic accidents, the Constitutional Court has held that not treating victims equally in different cases of liability does not give rise to an infringement of the equality principle. Moreover, as the legal liability regime established for public bodies applies in exactly the same way to all citizens, following the Constitutional Court, discrimination cannot take place.

On this point I would like to stress two arguments that, I think, can be put forward in order to claim that the provision dealing with the development risks defence of public bodies infringes the Directive.

First, this provision refers to the state of scientific or technical knowledge 'existing when the *damage occurred*'. By contrast, Art. 7(e) Directive sets forth that '[t]he producer shall not be liable as a result of this Directive if he proves: that the state of scientific and technical knowledge *at the time when he put the product into circulation* was not such as to enable the existence of the defect to be discovered' (emphasis added).

In the case *Commission v France*,[39] decided on 25 April 2002, the European Court of Justice has held that '[w]ith regard to the arguments based

[35] Salvador Coderch, 'Prólogo', in Salvador and Solé, *Brujos y aprendices*, p. 15.

[36] Inglés, 'Riesgos del desarrollo y accesibilidad': 15–28, at 24.

[37] In this sense, Seuba Torreblanca, Sangre contaminada, responsabilidad civil y ayudas públicas, cit., p. 312 et seq.

[38] Article 14 [Equality]: 'Spaniards are equal before the law, without any discrimination for reasons of birth, race, sex, religion, opinion, or any other personal or social condition or circumstance.'

[39] Case C-52/00. European Court reports 2002, p. I–03827, point 47.

on Article 15 of the Directive, it should be noted *that whilst that provision enables the Member States to remove the exemption from liability provided for in Article 7(e) thereof, it does not authorise them to alter the conditions under which that exemption is applied*' (emphasis added). A key element of the architecture of the Directive is the moment when the product was put into circulation. The domestic legislation can take the exemption of liability dealing with the development risks defence as it is . . . or leave it. But it cannot start changing its key elements.

Secondly, let us imagine, however, that the State amends Art. 141.1. LRJAP and refers the relevant moment to the moment when the product was put into circulation, thus bringing the wording of this provision in line with the wording of the Directive.

It is likely that in this case the objection that could be raised would go much further, since the Product Liability Directive does not establish any distinction between public law regimes and private law regimes. To give an example: tort liability of private persons is governed in Spain by the provisions of the Civil Code and by specific statutes (for instance, nuclear energy, air traffic, consumer protection Acts, etc.). These Acts do not apply to public bodies, which are governed by the already mentioned *Ley* 30/1992 as amended in 1999.

Liability of public bodies, even when they act as private individuals, will always be governed by this Act (cf. Art. 144 LRJAP), and therefore it will exclude the application of all other rules. Does this mean that the Product Liability Act implementing the Directive can be also excluded? Rather I would say that it cannot be excluded because the norm implementing the Directive binds both private persons and public bodies. In this sense the European Court of Justice has decided cases in which the rules implementing the Directive have been applied to public bodies.[40] Moreover, although it is true that the existence of a Directive cannot alter the internal or domestic distribution of legislative powers, and therefore it is possible for a regional Act (provided that the region involved has legislative power) and a State Act to implement the same Directive, it is at least arguable that the State can implement a Directive twice, i.e. make one implementation for private individuals and another for public bodies.

[40] Although it was not a case related to the development risk defence, in the Judgment of the Court (Fifth Chamber) of 10 May 2001, *Henning Veedfald v Århus Amtskommune*, Reference for a preliminary ruling: Højesteret – Denmark. Approximation of laws – Directive 85/374/EEC – Liability for defective products – Exemption from liability – Conditions. Case C-203/99, the European Court of Justice applied the Danish norms implementing the Directive to a public body.

Recoverable damage: how to compensate non-pecuniary loss and the problem of the 'lower threshold'

With regard to recoverable damage provided by Art. 10 LRPD, two main problems, referring, respectively, to compensation for death and personal injury and to the threshold for property damage, have arisen.

Compensation for death and personal injury

With regard to compensation for death and personal injury Art. 10.1 LRPD provides that '[t]he civil liability regime provided by this Act includes death and personal injury' and Art. 10.2 LRPD adds that '... non-pecuniary losses may be compensated pursuant to the general civil legislation'. As a sector of Spanish legal writing explains, if these provisions are read together they clearly indicate that 'death and personal injury' are included in the liability regime provided by the Product Liability Act and refer solely to all pecuniary losses, such as loss of earnings, as well as all the expenses resulting therefrom (for instance, medical expenses, rehabilitation expenses, medicines, etc.). By contrast, the legal regime provided by the Product Liability Act excludes all the damage that can qualify as 'non-pecuniary' which, however, can be recovered according to the domestic rules.[41] It is true, however, that this was not the only possible implementation of Art. 9 Directive when it provided that '[t]his Article shall be without prejudice to national provisions relating to non-material damage'. As French legal writing interpreting Art. 1386.2 *Code Civile* understands,[42] or as has been recently carried out by the German legislature in the recent amendment of the German Product Liability Act,[43] the legislature implementing the Directive could have included non-pecuniary losses within the framework of the corresponding Liability Act. However, this has clearly not been the case in Spain.

[41] Among others see, for instance, Parra Lucán, 'La responsabilidad civil por productos y servicios defectuosos. Responsabilidad civil del fabricante y de los Profesionales', in Reglero Campos (Coord.), *Tratado de responsabilidad civil*, pp. 1335, and Sonia Rodríguez Llamas, *Régimen de responsabilidad civil por productos defectuosos* (2nd edn, Cizur Menor (Navarra): Aranzadi, 2002), pp. 183 et seq.

[42] See, *inter alia*, Philippe le Tourneau, *Responsabilité des vendeurs et fabricants* (Paris, *Dalloz*, 2001), n. 317, p. 93.

[43] See the new text of §§7 and 8 of the German Product Liability Act (ProdHaftG), as amended by the *Zweites Gesetz zur Änderung schadensersatzrechtlicher Vorschriften*, vom 19.Juli.2002 (Bundesgesetzblatt Jahrgang 2002, Teil I Nr. 50. Bonn, 25.Juli.2002) and Staudinger/Oechsler (2003), §§7– 8 ProdHaftG, pp. 481–3 and Münchener Kommentar / Wagner (2004), §§7–8 ProdHaftG, pp. 2442–5.

In Spanish law if the claimant also wants to recover non-pecuniary losses it seems that, besides the conditions for the application of the Product Liability Act, the claimant should prove the conditions required according to the general domestic legislation that entitles him or her to this recovery. However, Spanish courts usually understand that 'compensation for death and personal injury' encompasses not only compensation for pecuniary loss (medical expenses, loss of earnings, etc.) but also for the so-called *daño corporal*, which, in a similar way to the Italian *danno biologico*, includes the 'impairment in the health or in the bodily or mental integrity of a human being, which is certain and real and independent of the pecuniary and non-pecuniary results that it produces'.[44] So, for instance, in SAP Granada 12.2.2000 [AC 2000\851], a case where a cap of a Coca-Cola bottle seriously injured the eye of a little girl while she was opening it, the Product Liability Act is applied and, according to this Act, awards damages for both pecuniary and non-pecuniary loss, the latter including, among others, *daño corporal*.

Moreover, to assess the award for damages courts have frequently resorted to the legal tariffication scheme included in the Road-Traffic Liability Act (LRCSCVM).[45] So, for instance, in SAP Cantabria 19.6.2002 [JUR 2002\212110], dealing with personal injury caused by an elevating platform that broke down, the court uses this legal tariffication scheme as a reference for the assessment of personal injury, pointing out that the use of the scheme is not mandatory in this case 'but is convenient in order to preserve the principles of legal equality and certainty'.

The Road-Traffic Liability Act expressly admits the autonomy of personal injury in relation to non-pecuniary loss and provides that 'the amount in damages awards for non-pecuniary loss is the same for all victims in the cases of damage for personal injuries and is understood in the sense of respect or restoration of the right to health' (Annex, I 7).[46] According to the legal tariffication scheme, some expenses resulting from

[44] Ricardo de Ángel Yagüez, *Tratado de responsabilidad civil* (Madrid: Universidad de Deusto-Civitas, 1993), p. 698; Elena Vicente Domingo, *Los daños corporales: tipología y valoración* (Barcelona: J. M. Bosch, 1994), p. 323.

[45] *Ley de responsabilidad civil y seguro en la circulación de vehículos a motor*, as established by the Additional Provision 8 (DA 8ª) of the Ley 30/1995, de 8 de noviembre, de ordenación y supervisión de los seguros privados (BOE num. 268, 9.11.1995) (Act for the ordering and supervision of private insurance, which modifies the Act of Use and Circulation of Motor Vehicles).

[46] This is also understood by J. A. Xiol Rios, 'Daño patrimonial y daño moral en el sistema de la Ley 30/1995', [1999] *Revista de responsabilidad civil, circulación y seguro* (RRCCS) 306. See also J. Fernández Entralgo, *Valoración y resarcimiento del daño corporal* (Madrid, 1997), p. 88.

the accident will be compensated in full and separately as long as the victim proves their existence and amount. Actually, point 6 of the first Part of the scheme expressly provides that 'in addition to the awards established according to the Tables, all medical and hospital expenses will be compensated for in any case and also, in the cases of death, burial and funeral expenses'.

However, one of the major shortcomings of this tariffication is that it not only mixes in the tariffication 'biological' damage and other heads of damage – such as pain and suffering, unrelated to health impairment – but also that it extends tariffication to loss of earnings, i.e. pecuniary losses, resulting from death and personal injury. Therefore, if the tariffication scheme is used, it is impossible to leave compensation for non-pecuniary loss out of the award and, in addition, loss of earnings resulting from permanent disability must be compensated for *in abstracto*, i.e. without being able to take the actual pecuniary loss sustained fully into account.[47] Another difference is that, whereas the use of the tariffication scheme in the area of traffic liability is mandatory and a misinterpretation of its provisions can be quashed by the Supreme Court, in the case of product liability courts are not compelled to use the scheme and they do not even apply it by analogy. What the courts do when referring to the tariffication scheme is to use it freely, as 'an orientation' only and, therefore, a misinterpretation of its provisions does not seem to offer the possibility of the decision based thereupon being quashed before the Supreme Court. However, this trend towards the application of the tariffication scheme may be reversed in the future, since the Supreme Court in STS 20.6.2003 [RJ 2003, 4520] has recently rejected its use in cases of personal injuries suffered in types of accidents other than traffic accidents, under the consideration that even if it is applied 'for guidance only' it can be detrimental to the claimant.

In some other cases, and according to a correct interpretation of the Spanish Act implementing the Directive, the courts have excluded compensation for non-pecuniary losses from the framework of the Product Liability Act and they have resorted to the domestic legislation in order to compensate for them. In these cases, however, the courts have not considered it necessary for the conditions required to apply domestic legislation to be proven (as, for instance, the proof of fault) and, by applying this legislation in addition to the Product Liability Act, have awarded a global

[47] For more details see Miquel Martín-Casals, 'An Outline of the Spanish Legal Tariffication Scheme for Personal Injury Resulting from Traffic Accidents', in Helmut Koziol and Jaap Spier, *Liber Amicorum Pierre Widmer* (Vienna; New York: Springer, 2003), pp. 235–51.

damages award without indicating which part of it corresponded to pecuniary and which to non-pecuniary losses. This is the case, for instance, in SAP Santa Cruz de Tenerife 19.4.2002 [AC 2002\898], where the court is very well aware of the fact that the Product Liability Act does not compensate for non-pecuniary losses, but awards a lump sum of €3,000 for all pecuniary and non-pecuniary losses considering that all the requirements for the application of the domestic legislation, albeit not having been proven, have been met.

The 500 ECU threshold

With regard to the 500 ecu threshold, we may think of the well-known Italian saying 'traduttore, traditore' which reminds us how treacherous translations can be. This is the case of the 500 ECU provided by Art. 9(b) of the Directive, i.e., the English 'lower threshold of 500 ECU', which turns into a German 'Selbstbeteiligung von 500 ECU', a French 'déduction d'une franchise de 500 Écus', an Italian 'detrazione di una franchigia di 500 ECU' or a Spanish 'deducción de una franquicia de 500 ECUS'.

In contrast to the Italian transposition norm (which leaves aside the 'deduction' of the Directive and stands for the 'threshold' effect in the implementing norm), Art. 10.1 LRPD follows the same translation of the Directive and provides that in this case 'se deducirá una franquicia de 65,000 PTA', which seems to lead inevitably to the construction that this amount does not only operate as a threshold for filing a claim but also to the idea that such an amount will have to be deducted, i.e. discounted or subtracted, from the final damages award.

Spanish legal writing contended initially that this amount was meant as a threshold only and that, once the claimant could file a suit because the property damage incurred was above that amount, no deduction whatsoever had to be made and the claimant could recover in full.[48] Nowadays, however, the deduction theory prevails and, accordingly, legal writing considers that this amount is always to be deducted from the award for damages.[49]

[48] Rodrigo Bercovitz Rodríguez-Cano, 'La adaptación del derecho español a la Directiva comunitaria sobre responsabilidad por los daños causados por productos defectuosos', EC, n° 12, pp. 83–130, at p. 113; María Ángeles Parra Lucán, *Daños por productos y protección del consumidor* (Barcelona: J. M. Bosch, 1990), p. 584.

[49] *Inter alia*, see Jiménez Liébana, *Responsabilidad civil*, p. 402; Martín Casals and Solé Feliu, 'Responsabilidad por productos en España', p. 12 and, changing her original opinion, Mª Ángeles Parra Lucán, 'La responsabilidad civil por productos y servicios defectuosos.

What is, however, this amount or, in other words, at which rate are these 65,000 PTA to be converted into euros? In the legal provisions implementing the Directive in other European countries the domestic legislator had also converted the amount of 500 ecus into the national currency. So, for instance, the German legislator fixed the amount of 1,125 DM and the Belgian an amount of 22,500 Belgian francs. However, the legislators of these countries have adapted the amounts expressed in their national currency to the euro and have expressly modified their Acts implementing the Product Liability Directive.[50]

Since the Spanish legislator has been silent on this point, two possible interpretations arise. According to the general rules that governed the introduction of the euro in Spain, it can be argued that this amount must be converted into the amount of euros resulting from the conversion rate established between the euro and the peseta (1 euro = 166.386 PTA), which gives a result of €398.658.[51] A second possible interpretation might contend that the amount of 65,000 PTA is just the conversion of the amount of 500 ecus set out in the Directive, and therefore that rule provided by Council Regulation (EC) No 1103/97 of 17 June 1997 *on certain provisions relating to the introduction of the euro*[52] applies. According to Art. 2 of this Regulation '[e]very reference in a legal instrument to the ECU, as referred to in Article 109g of the Treaty and as defined in Regulation (EC) No 3320/94, shall be replaced by a reference to the euro

Responsabilidad civil del fabricante', in Reglero (Coord.), *Tratado de responsabilidad civil*, p. 1337. See also De la Vega García, *Responsabilidad civil derivada del producto defectuoso*, pp. 62–3.

50 For Germany see *Zweites Gesetz zur Änderung schadensersatzrechtlicher Vorschriften*, vom 19.Juli.2002 (Bundesgesetzblatt Jahrgang 2002, Teil I Nr. 50. Bonn, 25.Juli.2002), where §9 adapts the amounts expressed in German Marks to the euro in several Acts, including the 1.125 DM of §11 ProdHftG (German Product Liability Act), which are converted into 500 euros. For Belgium see 20 Juillet 2000. – *Arrête royal portant execution en matière de justice de la loi du 26 juin 2000 relative à l'introduction de l'euro dans la législation concernant les matières visées à l'article 78 de la Constitution.* – [C – 2000/03478], Moniteur Belge 30.08.2000, p. 29492, providing that 'L'article 13 modifiant l'article 11, §2, al. 3, de la loi du 25 février 1991 relative à la responsabilité du fait des produits défectueux adapte au taux d'un euro pour un écu les montants inscrits en francs belges dans cette loi qui applique une directive européenne.'

51 See Council Regulation (EC) No 2866/98 of 31 December 1998 *on the conversion rates between the euro and the currencies of the Member States adopting the euro* (OJEC L 359, 31.12.1998). With regard to conversion rates, especially of those amounts which had not been adopted on 1 January 2002, see Art. 26 of the *Ley 46/1998, de 17 diciembre, de introducción del euro* (BOE 18.12.1998, num. 302, p. 42460).

52 Council Regulation (EC) No 1103/97 of 17 June 1997 *on certain provisions relating to the introduction of the euro* (OJEC L 162/1, 19.6.97).

at a rate of one euro to one ECU', a rule which gives rise to the amount of €500, and a result which I consider preferable, since it is more in line with the original uniformity.

Recently arguments in favour of abolishing the threshold have been put forward. It has been argued, along with other reasons, that a dramatic increase in the cases of product liability – a risk that the threshold was intended to prevent – has not occurred. Further, it has been argued that in certain economies, full compensation for property damage caused by a defective product is, from the social point of view, the most desirable option. It has also been said that the revival of consumer arbitration as an adequate device to solve the problems posed by small claims for damage caused by defective products is not coherent with the existence of a threshold which specifically excludes compensation for petty or unimportant damage. The exclusion on the grounds of preventing an increase in court costs from taking place loses its strength if the claims are channelled through the much less expensive and quicker proceeding of consumer arbitration. Finally, because in other areas of liability of professionals with regard to consumers (package travel, consumer credit, etc.) there are no deductions which partially exonerate the professional counterpart that is held liable.[53]

It is difficult to assess how sound these arguments are but I think that some of them are at least doubtful. I will refer to one of them only: that an increase of claims is not going to take place because of the Product Liability Act.

Although it is still very early to reach a firm conclusion, the decisions issued over recent years show a tendency for an increase in a certain type of claim which in one way or another disregards the existence of a threshold and which could be described in this way: a consumer, normally covered by a first-party multi-risk home insurance, sustains property damage (frequently, in an electrical appliance) and collects payment from the insurer. Then the insurer subrogates and files a claim against the producer. Since the current trend of the Courts of Appeal seems to be either to disregard the existence of the threshold or to consider that the conditions required by the general civil legislation (especially negligence or fault of the producer) have also been met, suing for petty sums can be worth the trouble for the insurer: if he wins the case he will not only collect the small amount but also the costs and lawyer's fees. However, the incentive

[53] In this sense, Juan José Marín López, *Daños por productos: estado de la cuestión* (Madrid: Tecnos, 2001), pp. 121–2.

is not very great, since lawyer's fees for the winning party can never exceed a third of the total amount of the claim in the proceedings (Art. 394.3 LEC). This is, for instance, the case in the judgment of the Court of Appeal of Cordoba (SAP Córdoba 19.6.2002 [JUR 2002\212207]), where a power surge caused property damage of €105. The insurance company filed a claim pursuant to the Product Liability Act against the electricity company. The decision, which not even once refers to the Product Liability Act threshold or deduction, compensates the insurance company in full.

The possibility of deduction is not even mentioned in a judgment of the Court of Appeal of Valencia (SAP Valencia de 17.9.2002 [AC 2002\1658]), referring to the property damage caused by a leak in a boiler due to a manufacturing defect. The decision awards €11,800.65 as compensation for the property damage suffered by the claimant without even referring to the deduction established by the Act (Art. 10.1 LPRD).

When the court is aware of the existence of this provision and mentions it, it simply declares that the proven facts show that both the conditions required by the Product Liability Act and the general provisions governing fault liability in tort (Art. 1902 CC) have been satisfied. Fault of the producer is not only rebuttably presumed but simply derived from the mere fact of the existence of a defect in the product. In this sense, see the Court of Appeal of Ciudad Real (SAP Ciudad Real 26.11.2002 [JUR 2002\326332]), in a case in which a defective drive belt of a car harmed the vehicle in which it was incorporated and where the defendant wanted the threshold amount to be deducted, arguing that fault of the defendant had not been shown; the court stated that 'taking into account the defect that has been detected, it can be inferred that the control and check procedures used by the manufacturer either have not been sufficient or have not functioned properly, thereby giving rise to the placement of a product with a serious defect on the market, according to which all conditions of liability required by Art. 1902 CC are met'.

Conclusion

A non-Spanish reader could have the impression that the intention of this paper is to point out the mistakes made by the Spanish Courts of Appeal and to hint that they have not been able to cope with the Product Liability Act implementing the Directive. This, however, has not been the author's aim, but rather it has been to show the state of the actual application of the Act at the end of 2003. Some of the misinterpretations of the Act can be attributed to the 'novelty' of an Act which, although almost ten years old, has only recently begun to be applied. These problems can be and, hopefully, will be easily corrected when these cases start reaching the Supreme Court. A few papers in those journals read by judges with alluring titles such as 'All the Possible Mistakes in the Application of the Product Liability Act and How to Avoid Making Them' could also contribute to overcoming this problem. Nevertheless, the first decision of the Supreme Court has not been very promising. Besides other minor mistakes, and in spite of the fact that it was issued almost one year after *Medicina Asturiana* and the other decisions of the European Court of Justice, it once more referred to the possible application of the old General Act for the Protection of Consumers and Users (LGDCU), pointing out that Art. 27.1 (c) LGDCU becomes 'decisive' when, both according to the First Final Provision of the Spanish Product Liability Act and to *Medicina Asturiana*, the old Act is no longer applicable to defective products put into circulation after the Product Liability Act came into force.[54]

Other difficulties that Spanish courts will have to overcome are even more worrying. They are related not to a simple misinterpretation of the Act but to the existence of domestic legal principles and traditions which are different from those that underpin the implementing Act and the Directive. So, for instance, compensation for non-pecuniary loss is far more widely accepted in Spain than in some other European countries and, in contrast to, for instance, Germany before the 2002 reform,[55] it has never been excluded from statutes providing for strict liability regimes. Therefore, it is not self-evident why the judge must resort to the general tort liability rules to compensate for these losses or to decide on aspects excluded from the Directive such as, for instance, the recoverability of the amount of damages under the threshold. Although a much more detailed examination would be required, these aspects show that harmonisation through Directives is a difficult road to travel along and that the further development of common European Principles is necessary if the process of rapprochement of the European legal systems is to be pursued.

[54] For more details about these decisions of the Spanish Supreme Court see Martín Casals and Solé Feliu, *Aplicación de la Ley de responsabilidad por productos defectuosos*, pp. 1–2.

[55] See Jörg Fedtke and Ulrich Magnus, 'Germany', in Bernard A. Koch and Helmut Koziol (eds.), *Unification of Tort Law: Strict Liability* (The Hague; London; Boston: Kluwer Law International, 2002), p. 166.

4

Interaction between the European Directive on Product Liability and the former liability regime in Italy

ELEONORA RAJNERI

Introduction

Fifteen years after the implementation of the European Directive on product liability no more than ten cases have been decided by Italian courts. Trying to explain the EC Directive's impact on the Italian legal system, I will first describe the former liability regime engineered by the courts and by the scholars on the matter: usually, when a new social problem arises requiring a legal solution in a civil law system, the courts intervene before the legislator. Therefore, since the EC Directive has been enforced, it has started to interact with the solution previously adopted by the courts. I will then examine the application of the new law, pointing out in particular how the open-ended definition of 'defect' is interpreted and applied. The applications are not exempt from incoherence due to the ambiguous nature of product liability law, constantly shifting between tort law and contract liability. After comparing the former and the latter regime, we find that the EC Directive does not give any further advantage to consumers; on the contrary it provides several limitations to their right of claim. This makes other regimes more attractive. In particular, the EC Directive missed the opportunity to face the procedural problems arising from a mass tort case in order to improve access to justice. Consequently, whenever the consumer chooses to sue someone other than the manufacturer under a concurrent regime, or chooses not to sue any one, the product liability law fails to achieve its functions.

Italian background to the European Directive

The social problem of injuries caused to consumers by defective products had already been worked out in Italy (as in the other European Member States), when the EC Directive on product liability came into force. The solution adopted was substantially the same everywhere and consisted in channelling the liability for these injuries towards the manufacturer. But the instruments used in order to achieve this solution were different in the different Member States.

In Italy the solution was engineered by the courts using instruments already existing in the legal system. The instruments available were: the liability related to the sale contract law, the general provision of Art. 2043 c.c. on fault liability and one of the strict liability hypotheses described by the legislator.

Instead of enlarging contractual liability beyond parties linked by privity, the Italian courts chose general tort law with some adjustments.[1] This choice led to a 1964 case ruled on by the *Corte di Cassazione*:[2] Mr and Ms Schettini ate some biscuits produced by Saiwa which had allegedly gone off. Because of the defect Mr and Ms Schettini suffered food poisoning and, as a result, an economic loss due to the medical fees. Mr Schettini, who, by chance, was a lawyer, sued the manufacturer, claiming compensation. He argued that the manufacturer was liable under art. 2043 codice civile (hereafter c.c.) that states: '(Q)ualunque fatto doloso o colposo che cagiona ad altri un danno ingiusto, obbliga colui che ha commesso il fatto a risarcire il danno.'[3] Hence, the prerequisites of the liability are: the damage, the causality and the agent's fault.

The claimant proved the damage by medical expertise. The causality was considered proven by the fact that the producer offered to change the defective product with another one when Mr and Mrs Schettini wrote him a letter complaining about the injury. But, as the defendant objected, the claimant was unable to prove the manufacturer's fault.

The problem was that theoretically Italian courts are not allowed to increase the strict liability hypothesis detailed by the legislator because these are exceptions to the general principle of fault liability and, as exceptions, they are in *numerus clausus*. Of course, none of the legislative provisions concerned the manufacturer's liability for defective products.

[1] Since 1960 Italian doctrine started to rethink the role of the civil liability as an instrument for distributing the profit between entrepreneurs and consumers; in particular attention was paid to the strict liability rule as an instrument for making the firm liable. See P. Trimarchi, *Rischio e responsabilità oggettiva* (Milano, 1961); S. Rodotà, *Il problema della responsabilità civile* (Milano, 1964).

[2] Cass. civ. 25-5-1964 n. 1270, *Foro it.*, 1965, I, 2098.

[3] 'If an act committed through fault or intention causes an unjust damage to somebody else, then the person who has committed the act must compensate the damage.'

The Court resolved the problem affirming that this is not a strict liability case, because the manufacturer's fault is still relevant, but the fault does not have to be proven by the claimant as it is *in re ipsa*, i.e. by the fact that the product had a defect and that this defect caused an injury to the claimant.[4]

In practice, the court created a sort of liability which is half way between strict liability and fault liability: fault is still necessary, but the burden of proof has been reversed in order to protect the claimant's position.

In some pharmaceutical product cases, courts have increased the manufacturer's liability by applying the strict liability provision of art. 2050 c.c. Under this rule the person who causes damage to somebody else while he is carrying out a dangerous activity is held strictly liable unless he is able to prove not only that he was not at fault, but also that he used all the appropriate (i.e. existing) measures in order to avoid the risk of injuries.[5] In *Fiorasi v Soc. Crinos* the claimant argued that she got hepatitis because of an infected blood product used for the manufacture of Trilergan, a medicine she was taking for her cephalalgia treatment. In that case the court held that putting into circulation a potentially injurious product is a dangerous activity under art. 2050 c.c.[6] Therefore the manufacturer was held strictly liable considering that he did not succeed in proving that he had taken all the appropriate measures in order to avoid the risk of damage, as we will see in more detail below.

The implementation of the European Directive

Italy implemented the EC Directive in 1988 with the d.p.r. n. 224, which follows quite literally the European provisions, including the rule of the development risk defence and the threshold of compensation for injuries caused to products other than the defective one.

The European solution for product liability has been implemented over and above a system of legal rules already engineered by courts and by scholars. Nevertheless the Italian courts did not seem to feel any gap or any interruption between the old and the new discipline. Indeed, in a case which began before the enforcement of the EC Directive, but decided

[4] It is known that an improper use of the presumption is a typical judicial device to introduce a legal change avoiding the trauma of a breakdown in the system. See M. Franzoni, *Colpa presunta e responsabilità del debitore* (Padova, 1988), p. 2.

[5] Cass. civ. 15-7-1987 n. 6241, *Foro it.*, 1988, I, 144; Cass. civ. 27-7-1991, *Nuova giur. civ.*, 1992, I, 569; Cass. civ. 20-7-1993 n. 8069, in *Giur. it.*, 1993, I, 1, 1118.

[6] Cass. civ. 15-7-1987 n. 6241.

afterwards, the *Corte di Cassazione* held that the new discipline could be useful in order to enlighten the correct application of the old one.[7]

The claimant claimed compensation for physical injury which had occurred when he was a twelve-year-old child and his hand was crushed by the chain joint of a swing. Because this joint was built like a pair of scissors, his thumb was severed from his hand. The crucial point of the case was to decide whether or not the conduct of the victim was reasonably foreseeable by the manufacturer. Surprisingly the court stated that the swing's manufacturer was not liable because the child's conduct (he was standing on the machine instead of sitting properly) was not one that could be considered reasonably foreseeable. Therefore the product was not defective following the definition of 'defect' given by the European Directive.

The concept of defect was indeed the question most often discussed in the first applications of the product liability law.

Definition of a product's defect

The definition of defect is based on the concept of expectations: on one side the consumer's expectations about the safety of the product, on the other side the manufacturer's expectations about the use of the product. Hence an objective concept of defectiveness (i.e. a general standard of safety fixed by the law) does not exist. This means that the consumer is free to buy a less expensive product as long as he lowers, at the same time, his expectations on safety. This is exactly what happens whenever a consumer chooses, for example, to save money by buying a cheap car instead of a more expensive one: he knows that the cheaper car has (among other disadvantages) fewer safety features. As a consequence of his conscious choice he has to be more careful using this product than if he had bought the more expensive one.

Concerning the manufacturer's expectation, the product is defective under the law only if the damage occurred when the consumer used it in the normal way, i.e. foreseeable from the manufacturer's point of view. If the consumer used the product in a way that is not considered normal by the court, then he is held responsible for his own conduct.

In other words, the European law takes into consideration the interaction between the user's and the manufacturer's conduct in order to

[7] Cass. civ. 29-9-1995 n. 10274, *Foro it.*, 1996, 954.

distribute the liability between them in such a way that the damage is the responsibility of the one in the best position to foresee it and, consequently, to prevent it.[8]

The role of warnings and advertising

Because the product's defectiveness is based on expectations, warnings and instructions accompanying the product assume a great importance in the court's decision as instruments which make explicit the parties' expectations. For example, in *Tentori Umberto v Ditta Rossin s.n.c.* the consumer suffered physical injuries because the front fork of his mountain bike broke while he was cycling up a mountain.[9] The Tribunal asserted that the use of this kind of bicycle on an inaccessible mountain road is normal, considering that the product was advertised by the manufacturer as an off-road bicycle. Consequently the manufacturer was held liable because he had not made the bicycle with appropriate materials. A housekeeper who was injured by a needle hidden in the earth of her flowering plant, was considered negligent under the EC Directive because she had not worn gloves, as was recommended by the manufacturer's instructions written on the wrapping. Thus, the manufacturer escaped liability because he had written on the wrapping: 'for use with proper instruments for gardening, like spades, rakes, hoes, gloves and so on' and, by consequence, he transferred the duty of care to the user.[10]

In other words a proper instruction or a proper information about the product can neutralise the danger related to certain uses of it. On the other hand, the missing information can be the reason for the detection of its defectiveness, as is the case decided by the Tribunal of Vercelli, 7 April 2003. Here the tribunal held the manufacturer liable for the damages caused by the explosion of a coffee machine, because he failed to advise the user that the valve of the machine had to be changed every two years. However, this kind of decision can be criticised whenever they charge the

[8] P. Trimarchi, 'La responsabilità del fabbricante della direttiva comunitaria', in *Riv. soc.*, (1986) 595.

[9] Trib. Monza, 20-7-1993, in *Giur. it.*, 1995, 323.

[10] Tribunale di Roma, 22-11-2001, in *Giur. Romana*, 2002, p. 137. Actually it has to be noted that the housekeeper did not suffer serious physical injury: she was only claiming for her psychological stress (she had undertaken tests in order to check whether she had caught some infection or not). So, probably, the tribunal would have better exempted the manufacturer from his liability by explicitly asserting the injury's irrelevance instead of assessing the product's defectiveness.

manufacturer with a duty to inform the consumer even about facts of common knowledge.

The expectation test and the distribution of liability between the parties

Taking advantage of this flexible definition of defectiveness, the manufacturer defends himself most of the time by putting the blame on the consumer's conduct. This happens when he alleges either that the victim was negligent having being warned about the danger and having nevertheless ignored the warning (as in the gardener case), or that the product was used by the victim in a way that could not be reasonably expected (as in the swing case).

In the case of a ladder that collapsed causing injuries to the gardener who was working on it, the Tribunal held the manufacturer liable after having verified through witnesses that the ladder had been used in a normal, foreseeable way when the accident occurred.[11]

Lissoni v De Bernardi and Tessitura Lissoni s.r.l. is the classic design case:[12] an industrial machine with exposed parts injured an inattentive worker. The victim argued that the machine should have been designed with safety features to prevent such accidents. The defendant argued that the risks could have best been avoided by the user exercising care because he should have known that such a machine was dangerous. To solve such a dispute the court had to decide if the machine provided the safety that a person should reasonably be entitled to expect. The law does not specify if the relevant expectations are those of the user or those of the buyer. The first problem arose from the fact that here the victim was not the person who bought the machine, i.e. the person who made a cost–benefit analysis deciding how much to spend on the machine. Hence the court could not deduce the user's expectations by taking into account some objective elements like the price paid for the product. Probably it would have been better to make the victim sue the employer under labour law;[13] then the employer, as the product's buyer, could have sued the manufacturer under product liability law: it would have been clear, in this case, that the relevant expectations were those of the buyer. Probably the ambiguity of the product liability law (which is constantly shifting between

[11] Trib. Milano 31-1-2003, in *Danno e resp.*, 2003, 634.

[12] Trib. Monza 11-9-1995, in *Resp. civ. e previdenza*, 1996, 371.

[13] In fact, the victim sued both the manufacturer and the employer under the product liability law and general tort law, as I will explain below about joint and several liability.

contract liability and tort law)[14] arises precisely from the fact that it has to take care not only of buyers, but also of bystanders. However, because of the vagueness of the expectation test and because of this ambiguity, the court must proceed intuitively. Here the court affirmed that the worker could not have known that the machine was dangerous because there was no evidence in the case that he had started to work a long time before the accident occurred. Therefore it rejected the manufacturer's defence, asserting also that the machine was especially unsafe for a short worker like the claimant.[15]

Manufacturer liability

When courts assess the parties' conduct using words like foreseeability, expectations, possibilities of avoiding risk and so on, they somehow evoke the concept of fault, emphasising the fact that the EC Directive does not bind the manufacturer with an absolute strict liability. The line of reasoning is more or less the following: the manufacturer is liable unless the victim used the product in a way not reasonably expectable (i.e. not foreseeable by the manufacturer). Thus, if the product has been used in an expected way, then the manufacturer is liable unless he warned the consumer of the danger. In any case, if the consumer's use was reasonably expectable and if the manufacturer did not warn him about the danger, he is not nevertheless liable if he could not avoid the injury because 'the state of scientific and technological knowledge at the time when he put the product into circulation was not such as to enable the existence of the defect to be discovered' (art. 7(e)). This means that the manufacturer is not liable if it was impossible for him to avoid the risk of damage. When there is a little space where the manufacturer can be kept safe from liability or, in other words, when there are precautions which cannot be required of the manufacturer, then this is not an absolute strict liability regime. Obviously the regime will be closer to fault liability or to strict liability, according to the way of interpreting this impossibility. Whenever the court takes into account subjective elements like the possibility of a particular manufacturer avoiding the risk, then the court is closer to liability for fault. In other words, there is an uninterrupted line connecting fault liability

14 About the nature of the liability for defective product see G. Alpa and M. Bessone, *La responsabilità del produttore* (Milano, 1999), pp. 266–7.

15 In other words the physical characteristics of the victim, instead of requiring him to be especially careful, increased the manufacturer's liability.

and absolute strict liability.[16] This line passes through the objectivisation of the fault as standard of care,[17] goes towards the fault *in re ipsa* and comes to strict liability with the exemption provision.

In conclusion the absolute strict liability of the manufacturer exists only in the manufacturing defect case, as is made explicit by Art. 5 of the Italian law ('a product is defective if it does not provide the safety level normally provided by other products of the same series'); it does not properly exist in the design or in the warning case.

Court's pro-claimant attitude: joint and several liability

Even if the enforcement of the new law has not been perceived by judges as a real change in the system, it, nevertheless, seems to have increased their concern for consumer protection. In fact, in the few other applications of European product liability law, the Italian courts took a clearly pro-claimant attitude; this is demonstrated by the fact that they are more than ready to take for proven the causality in cases where the burden of proof on the claimant was hard to discharge ('presunzione legale' in Italian law).[18]

In a 1995 case the Tribunal of Milan held liable the manufacturer and the seller of a bunk bed which collapsed the first night after its installation, seriously injuring the person who was sleeping below.[19] Considering the

[16] The theory that there is a *continuum* between the tort of negligence and strict liability is put forward by P. G. Monateri, 'La responsabilità civile', in dir. Rodolfo Sacco, *Trattato di diritto civile* (Torino, 1998) 1013.

[17] Some authors remark that fault detection increasingly means to measure somebody's conduct with a general standard of diligence rather than examining his psychological attitude. See F. Busnelli, 'Nuove frontiere della responsabilità civile', in *Jus*, 1976, 49; M. Bussani, *La colpa soggettiva* (Padova, 1991). About the objective and subjective concept of fault see also, G. Alpa and P. Bessone, *Atipicità dell'illecito* (Milano, 1980), p. 109.

[18] The change of emphasis is made clear by the various cases where the courts rejected claimant claims under the former regime. For example in *Stubing Solvi v AEG Telefunken* the manufacturer of a television that exploded was not held liable for damages because the consumer had kept the machine turned on in the stand-by mode (Trib. Roma 17-9-1987, in *Resp. civ. e previdenza*, 1988, 225). In *Tamburella v Artsana* the thermometer manufacturer was exempt from liability for physical injuries caused by the breakage of the product because of the consumer's contributory negligence (Trib. Roma 27-4-1988, *ivi*, 1989 684). In a 1964 case the manufacturer was exempt from liability for a toy gun that injured a child because the Court assumed that the child had not used it properly (App. Genova 5-6-1964, in *Foro padano*, 1964, I, 725). In 1972 the tribunal exempted the manufacturer from liability for damages caused by a household appliance because the user's conduct was considered contributory negligence (Trib. Pavia, 22-12-1972, *Il monitore dei trib.*, 1973, 129).

[19] Trib. Milano 23-3-1996, *I contratti*, 1996, 374.

difficulty of assessing whether the responsibility was more that of the manufacturer who designed the bunk bed or of the seller who installed it without remarking on the defective installation instructions, the tribunal assumed that there was a joint and several liability for the injury that occurred. In other words the tribunal used Art. 9 of the Italian law, which explicitly allows the manufacturer to share his liability with any other person who has been found liable for the same injury. In this sense it is clear that the legal provision represents a benefit not only for the claimant (who can claim compensation from more than one liable person) but also for the manufacturer (who can share his liability with another person). It does not matter if, as in this case, the manufacturer is held liable under product liability law and the other person under contractual law, because the Italian legal system allows the non-concurrence of contractual liability and civil liability for the same injury.[20] And it does not matter if the EC Directive allows joint and several liability only among persons who have been held liable for the same injury 'under the Directive's provision', because the Italian law does not require this last limitation.[21]

In the aforementioned case of the short worker and the textile machine, the tribunal held jointly and severally liable both the machine's manufacturer and the employer who bought the machine, without specifying too precisely under which legal provision the latter was held liable. Instead of applying the employer's liability, or the seller's liability, the tribunal evoked vaguely general tort law.

Recovery for emotional distress

What is also interesting to observe in these two cases is the tribunal's opinion on recovery for emotional distress. Under the usual interpretation of Art. 2059 c.c. it is recoverable only if the fact which caused the

[20] P. G. Monateri, *Il cumulo di responsabilità contrattuale e extracontrattuale* (Padova, 1989).

[21] The commentator on the Italian law who noticed this imprecision has suggested that the expression 'other persons' should be better interpreted as 'other producers' in order not to betray the Directive's *ratio* (D. Poletti, 'Commento a art. 9, pluralità di responsabili', in Pardolesi and Ponazanelli (a cura di), *La responsabilità per danno da prodotti*, in *Nuove leggi civ. commentate*, 1989, 600). But Italian courts do not seem to have taken note of this suggestion. Concerning the ECJ's decision on French law which refused the possibility for Member States to increase the liable persons under the Directive provision, it should be noted that Italian courts have increased the liable persons but not under the same law (Case C-52/00, *Commission v France* [2002] ECR I-3827). However the Directive's *ratio* is betrayed, as I will point out below.

injury is also relevant under criminal law. In order to qualify this as a crime, the manufacturer's fault has to be proven. As under product liability law fault does not matter (assuming that it is a strict liability case), the courts have affirmed explicitly that this damage is not recoverable.[22] Nevertheless, because in these cases another person has been held liable under general tort law (which in contrast requires fault), the court assumed that the Art. 2059 c.c. requirements were fulfilled and, consequently, ordered both to compensate also the emotional distress.

Nevertheless it is also to be remarked that recently the courts have extended the possibility of compensation for non-material damages, overruling the doctrine which excludes this compensation in strict liability cases. In 2003, in the case about the explosion of a coffee machine, the Tribunal of Vercelli held that the fact that the manufacturer is strictly liable under the European Directive does not preclude a finding of liability also for non-material damages when fault is proven. Therefore, considering that the lack of information proves the manufacturer's fault, the tribunal condemned him to pay also for non-material damages. Going further the Corte di Cassazzione held that non-material damage has to be compensated also in strict liability cases because there the fault, even if not investigated by the court, is presumed as existing by the law.[23] Under this new doctrine, it is relevant to establish if the Directive charges the manufacturer with an absolute strict liability, or with a strict liability which presumes the existence of the fault.

The use of presumptions

In *Facanabia v F.lli Saclà s.p.a.* the judge agreed with the claimant's claim for compensation for physical injuries which occurred when he bit a small piece of metal hidden in rice seasoned with 'Condiriso', a product supplied by F.lli Saclà s.p.a.[24] The victim sued F.lli Saclà assuming that the small piece of metal was in the 'Condiriso' and not in the rice. The judge did not even question the claimant's assumption and did not allow the defendant to give evidence of the fact that he had taken all reasonable care to avoid this kind of damage: the judge stated that this evidence was already contradicted by the fact that the damage had occurred. So, by

[22] Trib. Roma 17-3-1998, in *Foro it.* (1998) I, 3660; Trib. Milano 31-1-2003, cit;

[23] C. Cass. 12 May 2003 n° 7282, in Resp.civ.e prev., 2003, 682 – the case concerns the damages caused by a car accident.

[24] Giudice di pace di Monza 20-3-1997 n. 1386, in *Arch. civ.*, 1997, 876.

just verifying the damage, the judge presumed defect and existence of causality!

Drawing a consumer model

Case by case, distributing the loss for defective products between manufacturers and consumers and assessing their respective conducts, the courts draw a model of the consumer balancing two different needs. On the one hand the consumer needs legal protection because the asymmetric information between him and the manufacturer makes him weaker. On the other hand, the actions of the consumer should not always be justified by the law (unless the legislator decides to assume a paternalistic attitude), because the consumer has to be diligent and aware, i.e. responsible for his own acts. Unfortunately the Italian consumer model does not always look quite coherent; when he is twelve years old the consumer has to sit up straight on a swing and, being a housekeeper, a woman has a duty to wear professional gloves when she takes care of her flowering plant; but a short worker can be less diligent when using a dangerous machine, and, in any event, being a lawyer, a person can eat a bad and (probably) smelly biscuit with the certainty of getting compensation for food poisoning!

The (dis)advantages of the European Directive in competition with other liability regimes

These cases (as well as the classic case of the sparkling water bottle that exploded in the hands of the innocent consumer[25] and a couple of others)[26] are at this moment all the Italian applications of the EC Directive on product liability.

Several explanations have already been given as to the low impact of product liability law in Europe (especially compared with the over litigation of American product liability law). In particular the difficult access to justice for the European consumer, who cannot take advantage of the American contingency fees system, has been mentioned. As a matter of fact the cost-shifting rule makes litigation too risky for many consumers. This means that only a few of them claim for damages and, among these, the great majority accept the settlement offered by the

[25] Trib. Roma 17-3-1998, in *Foro it.*, 1998, I, 3660.

[26] Trib. Napoli 28-2-2002, in *Giur. napoletana*, 2002, 247; Trib. Viterbo 17-10-2001, in *Rass. giur. umbra*, 2001, 206.

manufacturer who is trying, on his side, to avoid the bad publicity of public proceedings.

Furthermore, European consumers have little interest in claiming for damages because the social security system already provides for compensation.[27]

Besides the fact that product liability law has not often been litigated on in Europe, the question arising now is why the enforcement of the EC Directive on the matter has not sensibly increased this litigation. The comparison between the EC Directive's provisions and the former regime emphasises the fact that the EC Directive does not provide Italian consumers with greater protection. Indeed, from the defendant's point of view, the reversion of proof used by Italian courts can give the same result as the provisions of the EC Directive. In reality to prove that the manufacturer was not at fault can be as difficult as giving evidence for the development risk defence. Concerning the manufacturer's exemption from liability in case of unforeseeability of consumer conduct or in case of consumer fault, the same results are achieved in tort law using contributory negligence or the lack of causality.

In cases of defective pharmaceutical products the consumer's protection seems to be even greater in the previous regime. As I said above, in this situation Italian courts were used to apply Art. 2050 c.c.[28] Under this law anybody who, carrying out a dangerous activity, causes an injury to somebody else is held strictly liable unless he is able to prove that he has used all appropriate measures in order to avoid the risk of injury. Commentators on these cases observe that the liability regime is harder for the manufacturer under Art. 2050 c.c. than under product liability law. There is the view that the requirements for the fulfilment of the exemption are higher than those for the development risk defence because the former does not allow any allusion to subjective considerations.[29] Therefore the Italian legal system, under pressure from the thalidomide and infected blood products cases, adopted a more severe approach against

[27] A. Cavaliere, 'The Economic Impact of Product Liability and Product Safety Regulations in the European Union', in *Quaderni del dipartimento di economia pubblica e territoriale*, Pavia, n. 4, 2001.

[28] See n. 5.

[29] D. Caruso, 'Quando il rimedio è peggiore del male: emoderivati infetti e responsabilità civile', in *Foro it.* (1988) I, 150; A. Busato, 'I danni da emoderivati: le diverse forme di tutela', *Resp. civ. e previdenza* (1994): 70; A. Barenghi, 'Brevi note in tema di responsabilità per danni da emoderivati difettosi tra obiter dicta e regole giurisprudenziali' in *Giustizia civ.*, 1994, 1044.

pharmaceutical manufacturers, i.e. exactly in the field where the USA doctrine has softened the product liability law.[30] Nevertheless, as long as this liability does not noticeably increase insurance costs as happened in the USA, it is quite unlikely that in a competitive market pharmaceutical producers will stop research for innovations, simply because of the fear of compensation claims.

Limitations to the consumer's right of claim

In addition to the fact that the EC Directive does not charge the manufacturer with a heavier liability than the former regime, it also fixes many limitations to the consumer's right of claim. First, under Art. 10 the proceeding has a limitation period of three years, instead of the five-year prescription period for the tort of negligence law suits. Then, under Art. 11 the victim's right expires within ten years from the date on which the producer put into circulation the product that caused the damage. A similar provision does not exist in general Italian tort law.

Furthermore there are limitations on the recoverable damages. Damage to the same defective product is not recoverable. Damage to products other than the defective one can be recovered only over the threshold of L. 750,000 and, in any case, only if they are products for private use or consumption. This last provision, in particular, excludes the recoverability of the economic loss under product liability law. In contrast, Italian tort law does not exclude their recoverability. Concerning emotional distress, as I have said, the courts assert that they are not recoverable because Art. 2059 c.c. requires evidence of fault, and the evidence of fault is lacking in an absolute strict liability case.

Hence, all these limitations (which are not always justified under a coherent legal theory as has been noticed)[31] quite often make alternative legal regimes more attractive to consumers than product liability law. The person who has been injured by a defective product can choose between suing the manufacturer under product liability law or suing the seller or the retailer under the contract of sale law or under the tort of negligence, whenever claiming for economic loss or for emotional distress or whenever the product liability lawsuit has already expired and the other has not. Or, as happened in the industrial machine case and in the bunk-bed case, the claimant can combine all the possible lawsuits for the same damage.

30 See for example the discussion in S. C. California 31-3-1988 *Brown v Abbot Laboratories.*

31 J. Stapleton, *Product Liability* (London: Sweet and Maxwell, 1994), pp. 303–40.

Product liability function betrayed

Whenever the consumer sues someone other than the manufacturer for damage caused by a defective product, he betrays the theory underlying product liability law. The first aim of this law is to channel the liability for defective products to the manufacturer because he is considered the cheapest cost avoider, i.e. because he is the subject in the best position to take all the appropriate steps in order to avoid the risk of damage.[32] This interpretation of the law arises from the definition of defect, that, as we have seen above, distributes the cost of the accident between the parties according to which one of them was in the best position to avoid it. Secondly, this interpretation is also made clear by the development risk defence provision, which exempts the manufacturer from liability related to damage which he could not absolutely prevent with the knowledge he had on the date in which he put the product into circulation. In other words, the balance between the function of compensation and the function of deterrence is theoretically in favour of that of deterrence.[33] But, in practice, whenever the injured person sues somebody other than the manufacturer or whenever he gives up his claim for compensation, then product liability law fails to fulfil the deterrence function which was one of the reasons for its implementation. These considerations seem to be confirmed by the fact that some years after the implementation of the EC Directive, the European Council passed Directive n. 92/59 which, in order to improve precaution measures, introduces *ex ante* regulatory controls on product safety and states that putting a defective product into circulation is a crime.[34]

[32] Calabresi, as is very well known, elaborated the theory of the cheapest cost avoider, as the person who is in the best position to make the cost–benefit analysis between accident costs and accident avoidance costs: G. Calabresi, *The Costs of Accidents, a Legal and Economic Analysis* (New Haven: Yale University Press, 1970); G. Calabresi and J. Hirschoff, 'Towards a Test for Strict Liability in Torts' (1972) 81 Yale LJ: 1054, 1060.

[33] The balance between the deterrence function and the compensation function is totally in favour of the latter in the solution adopted in New Zealand in 1972. This solution consists in insuring compensation of all personal injuries through administrative tools instead of tort law.

[34] The Directive has been introduced in the Italian legal system with d.lg. 17-3-1995 n. 115. For an examination of the interaction between this law and product liability law see F. Cafaggi, 'La responsabilità dell'impresa per prodotti difettosi', in N. Lipari (a cure di), *Diritto privato europeo*, II, Padova, pp. 996–1031; D. Siniscalco, 'Regole economiche e principi giuridici a confronto: il caso della responsabilità del produttore e della tutela dei consumatori', in U. Mattei and F. Pulitini (eds.), *Consumatore, ambiente, concorrenza: analisi economica del diritto* (Milano, 1994), pp. 39–45.

Access to justice in mass tort cases

In order to improve the application of the EC Directive the legislator should have included provisions that give consumers some further instruments of protection that did not exist in the former regime. In particular, considering the problem of access to justice, the Directive could have taken care of the mass tort question. In fact the concern about product liability arose precisely from cases like thalidomide or asbestos, i.e. cases where the same product defect injured a plurality of people. Lacking a mechanism like the American class action, every injured person has to initiate his own lawsuit against the manufacturer under product liability law. This mechanism has several disadvantages. First of all, the plurality of lawsuits creates the risk of diverging judgments among courts on the same matter. This is exactly what happened in Italy with the Trilergan case. Because of the use of infected blood products, Trilergan caused hepatitis infection to many patients between 1974 and 1975. Trilergan's manufacturer (sued by a number of injured parties with different lawsuits) argued that at the date on which it put the product into circulation the test for the detection of hepatitis infection in blood products was only experimental, and for this reason it did not have to be used at that time. In one case the court applied Art. 2050 c.c., but considered that the defendant had fulfilled the exemption evidence of having used all the appropriate measures in order to avoid the risk of damage.[35] In another case, the same exemption provision was not applied, it being considered that the manufacturer should have used the RIA test, even if it was only experimental.[36] Another tribunal applied Art. 2043 c.c., instead of Art. 2050, and stated that the manufacturer was not liable because the claimant did not give evidence of his fault.[37] In contrast, elsewhere, the evidence of fault was considered as given.[38]

Secondly, the lack of the class action does not help to solve the problem of access to justice due to the high costs. It is true that all the people injured in the same circumstances can use the *litis consortium* procedure, asking for the unification of their lawsuits in front of the same judge. Nevertheless, because this procedure does not have something like the 'opt out' mechanism, the opportunistic behaviour of those that prefer to wait for the result of other people's lawsuits, instead of bearing on their own shoulders the risk of the uncertainty related to new case law,

[35] App. Roma 17-10-1990, in *Giur.it.*, 1991, 816.

[36] Cass. civ. 15-7-1987 n. 6241, in *Foro it.*, 1988, I, 144.

[37] Trib. Napoli 9-10-1986, in *Resp. civ. e prev.*, 1988, I, 475.

[38] App. Trieste 16-6-1987, in *ivi*, 1989, 334.

cannot be avoided. This means that, especially in controversial cases, the mechanism of *litis consortium* is not able to combine a significant number of claimants.

Furthermore, with the *litis consortium*, the judge is not allowed to settle the amount of compensation once for everybody, but he has to assess every single claim or send back the lawsuits to other judges for individual compensation.[39] In other words this solution raises procedural costs in such a way that it makes it completely inefficient.

The *Associazione Altroconsumo v Fiat auto s.p.a.* case is telling from this perspective.[40] It was proved that some 'Dedra' cars caused physical injuries because their exhaust pipes allowed a small quantity of gas into the car when driven. The claimant sued Fiat under Art. 3 of L 30-7-1998 n. 281 which allows consumer associations to claim for precautionary measures in order to avoid the risk of damage to consumers. The judge ordered Fiat to make a public announcement of the defect which had occurred, inviting the owners of the defective cars to take them back for repairs. The point is that consumer associations are not legally entitled to claim for damages on behalf of injured parties. So injury compensation depends on the individual's initiative and it is obvious that when the damage is not considerable, the consumer does not want to take the risk of losing his lawsuit for a small amount of money. This means that if on the one hand the deterrence function is achieved through the manufacturer's fear of loss of his reputation (as a consequence of the application of legal provisions other than product liability law), on the other the compensation function is missed most of the time.

Conclusion

The access to justice problem, the several limitations to the consumer's right of claim for a defective product, the lack of more useful instruments of protection than those already provided by the former system, all make the product liability law neglected by consumers. Its minimal litigation, of course, harms the achievement of its functions.

The deterrence function is achieved through the instruments of other legal provisions (passed by the legislator in consideration of the low impact of product liability law), such as the *ex ante* regulatory

[39] For example, Trib. Roma 27-11-1998, in *Foro it.*, 1999, 314.

[40] Trib. Torino 17-5-2002, in *Danno e resp.*, 2003, 75. See also C. Poncibo, 'Le azioni di interesse collettivo per la tutela dei consumatori', *Riv. crit. del dir. priv.*, 2002, 659–69.

control and the consumer associations' right to claim for precaution measures.

The compensation function is also missed most of the time, especially for small claims, because product liability law does not provide any special instruments to solve the procedural problems of mass tort cases.

The harmonisation function announced by the Directive in its preamble has not been achieved either. This is firstly because it has never been proved that manufacturers' decisions within the EC were significantly influenced by the contrasting regimes on product liability in the Member States and secondly because it has never been proved that surviving local differences (due also to the various options left open by the Directive) are insignificant under this concern.

At present, the only function that seems to have been achieved by the EC Directive (with the co-operation of the ECJ's interventions)[41] consists in putting a ceiling on manufacturer liability rather than a floor for consumer protection.

Moreover it is clear that the aims of the European Union are to create incentives which promote commercial trading between Member States and technological innovation. Consumer protection is an incentive in this sense, as long as it does not turn into a paternalistic attitude. That is probably what the European Council aimed to avoid by putting a ceiling on national manufacturer liability. More precisely the limit is put above the national legislators' intervention, but it provides a certain amount of flexibility to the courts, which can use the various open-ended definitions of the EC Directive to adapt their decision to the individual case.

[41] Case C-183/00 *González Sánchez v Medicina Asturiana SA*; Case C-52/00 *Commission v France.*

5

L'exception française? The French law of product liability

DUNCAN FAIRGRIEVE*

Introduction

The preamble to the 1985 European Directive on Product Liability declares that harmonisation of national rules is necessary in view of the fact that disparities are liable to distort competition, to affect the free movement of goods and lead to differences in the level of protection offered to consumers against physical injury and damage to goods caused by a defective product.[1]

The interaction between Community law and the national laws of the Member States has been a complex process. The purpose of this paper is to analyse the reception of this aspect of European law in one system, that of France.

The French law on product liability has traditionally adopted a pro-consumer approach, engineered mainly by the intervention of the courts. Professor John Bell has noted that the French law of product liability is essentially a creature of judicial and doctrinal interpretation of the Napoleonic Code.[2] Professor Malinvaud has also described how the judiciary have been active in shaping the law:

> Guided by the desire to compensate as fully as possible the victim, that is to say the consumer of the product, the case law has created a new positive law whilst respecting the texts, at least in appearance.[3]

* I am very grateful to Stefan Lenze for his comments on a previous draft.

[1] Preamble, para. 1. Council Directive of 25 July 1985 on the approximation of the laws, regulations and administrative provisions of the Member States concerning liability for defective products (85/374/EEC), OJL 210.

[2] J. Bell, *French Legal Cultures* (London: Butterworths, 2001), p. 79.

[3] P. Malinvaud, 'La Responsabilité civile du fabricant en droit français', *Gazette du Palais* 1973.2.463 (translated by Professor John Bell, *French Legal Cultures* (London: Butterworths, 2001), p. 79). De la Rochère and Mihac argue that 'French Courts have applied the general provisions laid down in the Civil Code. However, as we will see, these rules and principles

It will be shown in this chapter that following the chronic delay on the part of the French legislator to implement the European Directive, the French courts themselves acted, and moulded the case law in a way inspired by the themes underpinning the European provisions.

The subsequent legislative intervention and the implementation of the Directive was by no means the end of the story. The manner in which the Directive was transposed and the subsequent litigation raise some key questions about the harmonisation effort in this area.

Damages liability under French law

Damages liability in France is divided into two parallel regimes deriving from public law and private law, both with dual sets of principles governing liability. The law applicable depends essentially on the identity of the defendant, whether a public law or private law entity. For a long time, the sets of principles applied by the administrative law and private law courts were very different. The recent trend has, however, been for a growing parallelism, as the courts are increasingly aware of the difficulty of justifying two different standards of liability. Nonetheless, there are still important differences in the rules applied by the courts, in areas such as causation and quantum of damages.

Public law liability before the public law courts is essentially a case law development, based upon an extensive notion of administrative fault (*faute de service*), and a number of heads of no-fault liability. Private law liability stems from the Napoleonic Civil Code. The substantive law of product liability is heterogeneous, and essentially made up of the court's interpretation of contract and tort law principles laid down in the Civil Code. The implementation of the European Product Liability Directive has also added a new route for claimants.

Product liability cases may arise before both sets of courts, but the great majority of products claims evidently concern private sector manufacturers, and proceed before the private law courts. This chapter will thus focus on private law.

In private law products cases, a variety of avenues may be pursued by a claimant. The traditional approach to product liability derives from an interpretation by the courts of the principles of both contract and

have been profoundly modified when applied in the product liability field in order to comply with the sense of justice and for better protection of the victim' ('France', in D. Campbell, *International Product Liability* (London, 1993), p. 231).

tort law laid down in the Napoleonic Civil Code, promulgated in 1804. With the implementation of the European Directive, claimants in civil law actions now have an alternative, and, to some extent, supplementary, cause of action under Articles 1386–1 to 1386–18 of the French Civil Code.

In summary then, a claimant bringing an action in France in respect of an allegedly defective product has several civil law causes of action available to him: contractual and tortuius claims under the Civil Code; the Product Liability Directive as implemented in French law. These will be examined in turn.

Law of contract[4]

Liability in contract is the cornerstone of the general product liability system in France. Article 1147 of the Civil Code lays down that a party to a contract in French law is liable for damages caused by the non-performance of his contractual obligations 'whenever he fails to prove that such non-performance results from an external cause which cannot be imputed to him, even though there is no bad faith on his part'.

In respect to sales contracts, *contrats de ventes*, the Civil Code imposes two principal obligations on the seller: an obligation to deliver the goods and an obligation to guarantee the goods he sells.[5] The latter obligation is the most important in the context of product liability. It should also be noted that under French law, a party to a contract is not only bound by the provisions stipulated in the said contract, but is also bound by duties developed by the courts. There are a series of such obligations, of which the most important is the *obligation de sécurité*. We will examine in greater depth the *obligation to guarantee against defects* and the *obligation de sécurité*.

Obligation to guarantee against defects

The case of defective goods which cause either personal injury or property damage to the buyer is governed by several provisions set forth in the Civil

[4] Note should be made of the principle of *non-cumul des responsabilités* (principle of the non-concurrence of actions) according to which a party to contract may not sue the other party for damages in delict, as long as the facts from which the delictual liability would otherwise arise are governed by one of the contract's obligations.

[5] Article 1603 CC.

Code referred to as the 'latent defect warranty' ('*garantie contre les vices cachés*').[6] The origins of this obligation can be traced back to Roman law.[7]

With respect to latent defects, Article 1641 CC provides that the seller of products guarantees the goods sold against hidden defects rendering the goods improper for the use for which they are intended.[8]

Four conditions must be met for the warranty to apply:[9] (1) the product is defective; (2) the defect was hidden; (3) the defect was present prior to the transfer of property of the goods; (4) the defect is material enough to render the product unfit for use or to materially reduce its value.

In principle, contractual product liability requires the existence of a sale contract between the defendant and claimant. Importantly, however, the 'latent defect warranty' has been extended by the courts to all buyers and sub-buyers in the distribution chain. A consumer can thus sue the manufacturer directly for latent defects in products sold to him by a retailer.[10]

A variety of remedies are available for the breach of this warranty, including recovery of the purchase price, rescission of sale, and a damages claim. For damages to be awarded, the Civil Code lays down the condition that the seller knew of the defect at the time of sale.[11] However the French courts have softened the burden of having to prove knowledge by first applying an evidential presumption that professional sellers should, due to their special professional expertise, be aware of, at the time of sale, latent defects in the products which they sell.[12] As Taylor has explained, this has subsequently been transformed into a substantive rule: professional sellers are strictly liable to the buyer for damage caused by hidden defects in the goods.[13] The broad notion of 'professional seller' ensures that this rule extends to both manufacturers of a product and also professional resellers such as distributors or retailers.

[6] See Articles 1625, 1641–8 CC.

[7] See discussion in Bell, *French Legal Cultures*, p. 79.

[8] 'The seller is held to warrant against latent defects in the thing sold which make it improper for the use for which it is intended or which so impair such use that the buyer would not have acquired it, or would only have paid a lower price, if he had known of them.'

[9] See Articles 1641–8 CC.

[10] Cass com 24 November 1987, Bull Civ IV N°. 250.

[11] Article 1645 CC: 'Where the seller knew of the defects of the thing, he is liable, in addition to restitution of the price which he received from him, for all damages towards the buyer.'

[12] Cass civ 1 24 November 1954 JCP 955.II.8565.

[13] S. Taylor, 'The Harmonisation of European Product Liability Rules: French and English Law' 48 (1999) *International and Comparative Law Quarterly*: 419, 425.

Despite this judicial liberalism, there are several weaknesses in bringing an action based on the 'latent defect warranty'. The primary problem has been the short limitation period. Article 1648 CC originally provides that these actions 'must be brought by the buyer within a short time, depending on the nature of the material defects and the custom of the place where the sale was made'. This was interpreted to mean that the buyer must file a claim within a 'short period' of the date of discovery of the latent defect, or the date when the defect could reasonably have been discovered.[14]

Pursuant to a legislative amendment in 2005, the action must henceforth be brought within two years of the discovery of the defect (Article 1648 CC as amended).

Obligation de sécurité

Over and above the 'latent defect warranty', the French *Cour de Cassation* has reinforced the protection afforded in product liability cases by developing the notion that *vendeurs professionels* undertake an obligation to deliver a safe product.

In a number of cases during the 1990s, the French *Cour de Cassation* reinforced the protection afforded in product liability cases by developing the notion that '*vendeurs professionels*' undertake an obligation to deliver a safe product over and above the 'latent defect warranty' or *garantie des vices caches*. The extent of the obligation, known as an *obligation de sécurité*, is impressive. The *Cour de Cassation* has stated that 'the seller acting in his professional capacity must deliver products that are free from any defects likely to cause harm to people or goods'.[15] Sellers and manufacturers are thus subject to an '*obligation de résultat*' (strict liability): the products must guarantee 'the necessary level of security which a consumer expects'.

This *obligation de sécurité* also applies equally to sellers and manufacturers.[16] The French case law has developed to provide that the contractual action for failure to deliver safe products passes to the downstream

[14] Cass com 18 February 1992, Bull civ IV N°. 82; Com 3 May 1974 JCP 1974.II.17798.

[15] The 'vendeur professionel' 'est tenu de livrer un produit exempt de tout défaut de nature à créer un danger pour les personnes ou les biens' (Cass civ 1, 20 March 1989, *Dalloz* 1989.581, note Malaurie). Cf Cass civ 1, 11 June 1991 JCP 1992.I.3572 obs Viney.

[16] It was developed on the basis of Article 1135 CC, which allows the court to imply contractual terms (see Cass civ 1, 20 March 1989, *Dalloz* 1989.581, note Malaurie).

buyer or user, thereby avoiding problems arising from the lack of direct contractual relationship, in common law parlance the problem of the privity of contract.[17]

This case law was heavily influenced by the European Directive.[18] Indeed, in a decision handed down in 1998, only a few months before the implementation of the Product Liability Directive in France, the *Cour de Cassation* delivered a judgment explicitly following the wording of the Directive and held that the producer is under a 'safety duty' when selling a product, such safety being that 'which a person is legitimately entitled to expect'.[19] Consequently, even before the transposition of the European Directive, its effects were being felt in the case law. The *Cour de Cassation* had to some extent remedied the inaction of the legislator.

Tort law

The cornerstone of French tort law is Article 1382 of the French Civil Code which provides: 'Any act whatever of man, which causes damage to another, obliges the one by whose fault it occurred, to compensate it.'[20]

Under Article 1382 CC, proof of fault on the part of the defendant is a prerequisite of liability. However, the notion of fault has a rather different meaning in French law than in the common law.[21] This is illustrated in the sphere of product liability.[22] An extensive notion of fault has been

[17] See Cass civ 1, 9 March 1983, Bull civ I N°. 92; JCP 1984.II.20295. See also De la Rochère and Mihac, 'France', p. 234.

[18] F. Leduc, *La Responsabilité du fait des choses: Réflexions autour d'un centenaire* (Paris: Economica, 1997) pp. 97 and 100; Bell, *French Legal Cultures*, p. 87.

[19] Cass civ 1, 3 March 1998, *Dalloz* 1999 Jurisprudence 36; RTDC 1998.683. The text of this judgment and analysis of the decision may be found on the BIICL Product Liability Database, which may be accessed at www.biicl.org. Cf Cass civ 1, 28 April 1998, *Dalloz* 1998 IR 142; RTDC 1998.684; JCP 1998.II.10088 (reference to 'les articles 1147 et 1384, alinéa premier, du Code Civil, interprétés à la lumière de la directive CEE n°. 85–374 du 24 juillet 1985').

[20] '*Tout fait quelconque de l'homme, qui cause à autrui un dommage, oblige celui par la faute duquel il est arrivé, à le réparer.*'

[21] J. Bell, S. Boyron and S. Whittaker, *Principles of French Law* (Oxford: Oxford University Press, 1998) pp. 357–8. For the differences in conception of fault in governmental liability cases, see D. Fairgrieve, *State Liability in Tort: a Comparative Law Study* (Oxford: Oxford University Press, 2003).

[22] For an excellent in-depth analysis of this point, see S. Taylor, *L'Harmonisation de la responsabilité du fait des produits défectueux: une étude comparative du Droit anglais et du Droit français* (Paris: LGDJ, 1999).

developed. After initially requiring proof of specific wrongful behaviour on the part of the defendant, the French courts have now shifted the focus of analysis from the producer's behaviour to the product itself, merely requiring the proof of delivery of a defective product: 'delivery of a defective product is sufficient to establish fault on the part of the manufacturer or the distributor'.[23]

The claimant has thus practically been exempted from having to prove fault so long as he can demonstrate that the products were defective and that such defective products were the cause of his damage or injury. So, the mere marketing of defective products constitutes proof of the manufacturer's fault. This is an important development of the law in favour of the victims of product defects. A strict liability '*obligation de sécurité*' thus applies under both the law of contract and tort. Manufacturers and suppliers are subject to this duty in respect of either a buyer under contract or a third-party victim. In some cases, the result has thus been an eliding of the contractual and delictual duties in order to focus upon the notion of 'defect'.[24]

Article 1384 (1) of the French Civil Code

Article 1384 (1) of the French Civil Code provides that: '[o]n est responsable non seulement du dommage que l'on cause par son propre fait, mais encore de celui qui est causé par le fait des personnes dont on doit répondre, ou des choses que l'on a sous sa garde.'[25]

The French courts have broadly interpreted the provisions of Article 1384 (1) CC so as to impose strict liability for the 'deeds of things within one's keeping'.[26] An employer is thus strictly liable as a *gardien* of factory machinery for the personal injuries which it caused. In these cases, the only defences are if a *gardien* can show *force majeure* or contributory fault of the victim.

[23] Cass civ 1 18 July 1972, Bull civ 1 N°189.

[24] Cass civ 1, 28 April 1998, *Dalloz* 1998 IR 142; RTDC 1998.684; JCP 1998.II.10088. The influence of European law again should be recognised. Taylor summarises this development of the law as follows: 'French judges have therefore anticipated the incorporation of the Directive by centring liability on the notion of "defect", but do not allow a development risks defence' (Taylor, 'Harmonisation of European Product Liability Rules', 419, 427).

[25] 'A person is liable not only for the damages he causes by his own act, but also for that which is caused by the acts of persons for whom he is responsible, or by things which are in his custody.'

[26] Bell, Boyron and Whittaker, *Principles of French Law*, pp. 371–83.

The notion of liability for things in one's keeping might seem *prima facie* to exclude product liability, given that the essence of the subject matter is a transfer of the product from the producer or supplier to the consumer. However, the French courts have asserted that *la garde* may be split and have drawn a distinction between the *garde du comportement* and *garde de la structure*. The former is the person who is responsible for harm caused by the thing's behaviour, the latter is the person responsible for harm caused by its defects. In this way, the manufacturer of the product may be considered to have retained control over the structure of a product, even if it lost the *garde du comportement* in favour of the owner. Liability may stem from the responsibility for the structure of the product.

The application of Article 1384 CC in product liability cases is, however, limited, as, in order to apply the distinction between *garde du comportement* and *garde de la structure*, the courts have required in proof that the object in question has 'its own internal dynamism' ('un dynamisme propre').[27] There are some cases in which Article 1384 CC has been applied in the product liability field, but these have generally been limited to situations involving products which have exploded, where no other basis for liability was readily apparent.[28] The recent French jurisprudence thus suggests that the courts are taking a restrictive view of Article 1384 CC in products cases.[29]

Implementation of the Directive

The traditional approach to product liability has been modified by the European Directive. The implementation of the European Product Liability Directive 85/374/EEC into French law has been a complex and painful process. Only under the threat of heavy financial penalties did France finally implement the European Directive, a full ten years after the deadline, on 19 May 1998.[30] The implementation was effected by modifying

[27] But see the application of Article 1384 CC in a vaccination case: TGI 5 June 1998 *Dalloz* 1998 *Sommaires Commentés* 336.

[28] Taylor, 'Harmonisation of European Product Liability Rules', 428; de la Rochère and Mihac, 'France', p. 251.

[29] See e.g. the recent tobacco case: *Cour de Cassation*, 2 civ., 20 Nov. 2003; Consorts Gourlain contre SA SEITA, JCP 2004.II.10004; *Dalloz* 2003.2902, conclusions Kessous, note Grynbaum. The text of this judgment and analysis of the decision may be found on the BIICL Product Liability Database, which may be accessed at www.biicl.org.

[30] The delay in implementation was attributable to a number of causes. There was a good deal of hesitation about the appropriate vehicle for the introduction of the new rules. Initially, the idea was to benefit from the need to implement the Directive in order to

the French Civil Code, and the new provisions are contained in Article 1386–1 to 1386–18.[31]

However, the long story of the French grappling with the 1985 Directive did not end here. The European Commission considered that the Directive had been incorrectly implemented into French law, and infringement proceedings under Article 226 were brought. The European Court of Justice's important decision in this case was delivered in April 2002. In the same year, another important case was brought, this time involving a preliminary reference from a Spanish court. These cases will be examined in reverse order.

González Sánchez v Medicina Asturiana SA

A Spanish judge made a preliminary reference to the European Court of Justice (ECJ) under Article 234 EC in order to gain a ruling on a question concerning the interpretation of Article 13 of the Product Liability Directive.

The question was raised in proceedings between Ms González Sánchez and Medicina Asturiana SA concerning compensation for damage allegedly caused by Medicina Asturiana during the course of a blood transfusion.

A Spanish Statute of 19 July 1984 provided for a system of strict liability enabling consumers and users to obtain compensation for damage caused by the use of a thing, product or service. A subsequent Statute was adopted on 6 July 1994 in order to transpose the Product Liability Directive into Spanish law. Ms González Sánchez sought to rely on the former more favourable law.

The Spanish court sought to ascertain whether Article 13 of the Directive entailed that the rights conferred under the earlier Statute were

effect a total reform of the provisions of French law governing products, and a working party chaired by the distinguished academic Professor Jacques Ghestin was formed. The proposals duly submitted by the Ghestin group were, however, subject to a good deal of criticism, and were not acted upon by the Government. A more limited reform was then set slowly in motion, limited mainly to introducing the provisions of the Directive and ensuring conformity with the pre-existing domestic provisions. A number of further problems however arose delaying the adoption of this project. The second chamber of the French Parliament, the Senate, was consistently hostile towards the introduction of the development risk defence, considered to be contrary to the traditional approach of French law. (See *Lamy Droit Economique* (Paris: Lamy, 2002), para. 6523.)

31 See C. Larroumet, 'La Responsabilité du fait des produits défectueux après la loi du 14 mai 1998' 1998 *Dalloz* Chr 311; G. Viney, 'L'Introduction en droit français de la Directive européenne du 25 juillet 1985 rélative à la responsabilité du fait des produits défectueux' *Dalloz* 1998 Chr 291.

limited or restricted as a result of the Directive's transposition into domestic law.

The arguments before the court revealed two very different conceptions of harmonisation in this area. The Spanish Government and the Commission maintained that Article 13 of the Product Liability Directive could not be interpreted as enabling the victim of damage to rely, in regard to the products coming within the Directive's scope, on a more favourable system of liability.

On the other hand, the claimant in the Spanish case, as well as a number of other Member States,[32] advocated a radically different interpretation of Article 13. In their view the harmonisation brought about by the Directive was incomplete. Article 13 should not be interpreted as precluding the application of the pre-existing systems of liability, which may be more favourable to the victim of damage. It would plainly be contrary to the Directive's objective for its transposition to result in less protection for the victim.

The Court indicated that the Directive did not simply effect a minimal harmonisation; it, in fact, was a 'complete' harmonisation.[33] Relying primarily on a textual analysis of the legal basis of the Directive,[34] the Court held that 'Article 13 of the Directive cannot be interpreted as giving the Member States the possibility of maintaining a general system of product liability different from that provided for in the Directive.' The Member States may only maintain other systems of contractual or non-contractual liability where they are 'based on other grounds, such as fault or a warranty in respect of latent defects'. Therefore, the Spanish legislative scheme had been superseded: any scheme 'founded on the same basis as that put in place by the Directive and not limited to a given sector of production does not come within any of the systems of liability referred to in Article 13 of the Directive'. The claimant was not entitled to the benefit of a Spanish statute that conferred wider rights on consumers than the Directive.

The ECJ's view seems to be thus that, while the Directive is not intended to interfere with pre-existing general liability rules under tort or

[32] The Greek, French and Austrian Governments.

[33] Case C-183/00 *González Sánchez v Medicina Asturiana SA* [2002] ECR I–3901. It also held, in the joined case, that 'the Directive seeks to achieve, in the matters regulated by it, complete harmonisation of the laws, regulations and administrative provisions of the Member States' (Case C-52/00 *Commission v France* [2002] ECR I-3827, para. 24).

[34] The Court observed that the Directive was based on Article 100 of the EEC Treaty (amended to Article 100 of the EC Treaty, now Article 94 EC), and that that legal basis provides no possibility for the Member States to maintain or establish provisions departing from Community harmonising measures.

contract, where they are 'based on other grounds, such as fault or a warranty in respect of latent defects', or with special liability systems relating to specific types of products, it does preclude the coexistence of a *general* system of product liability based on the same foundation as that in the Directive.

The decision thus squarely addresses the question of harmonisation in the sphere of product liability.[35] However, the response that it gives is not entirely uncontroversial. On the contrary, this decision has provoked much controversy within the academic community in France. Before we analyse this further, we must turn to the companion case on the interpretation of Article 13, *Commission v France.*

Commission v France

In this case, the European Court of Justice addressed the action brought by the Commission against France for incorrectly implementing Directive 85/374/EC.[36] In its decision, the ECJ tackled as a preliminary matter the question whether the Directive was a 'complete, or merely a minimum, harmonisation of the laws, regulations and administrative provisions of the Member States'. It made it clear that it preferred the former option, rehearsing the arguments deployed in the aforementioned reference from the Spanish Court, and stating in a particularly striking passage of its judgment that:

> the Directive seeks to achieve, in the matters regulated by it, complete harmonisation of the laws, regulations and administrative provisions of the Member States.[37]

In respect of the substance of the infringement proceedings, the ECJ indeed found that France had incorrectly implemented the Directive. Three specific aspects of the French implementation incurred judicial displeasure: damage; liability of suppliers; and defences.

(1) Damage

Under Article 9 of the Directive, reparation for damage to goods of a type intended for private use is subject to a lower threshold of 500 Euros.

[35] For discussion of this point, see G. Howells, 'Product Liability – a Maximal Harmonization Directive?' December (2001) *European Product Liability Review*: 10.

[36] Case C-52/00 *Commission v France* [2002] ECR I-3827.

[37] Para. 24.

However, the new provisions of the French Civil Code covered, unlike Article 9(b) of the Directive, *all property* damage. The lower threshold was thus omitted.[38] The European Court held that on this point the implementation was faulty.[39] The Directive's strict liability regime was designed to be applicable only to significant injury in order to avoid an excessive number of disputes.

(2) Liability of suppliers

Under Article 3(3) of the Directive, the liability of the supplier is conceived as only subsidiary liability, applicable where the producer is unknown. Suppliers may avoid liability by identifying the producer or the person who supplied them with the product.

However, French law takes a different approach. Under the provisions of the Civil Code, a professional supplier '*est responsable du défaut de sécurité du produit dans les mêmes conditions que le producteur*'.[40] A supplier cannot avoid liability simply by identifying the producer or upstream supplier. The Civil Code equates the position of the supplier with that of the producer.

The French provisions offer more protection for the victim, who will often prefer to pursue in the courts his or her local supplier. Nonetheless, the ECJ upheld the Commission's complaint. The choice had been deliberately made to put the burden of the litigation on the producer. The supplier is liable only on an ancillary basis. This reduces the likelihood of multiplying proceedings. French law was not in line with this approach.[41]

(3) Defences

Article 7 of the Directive provides that the producer shall not be liable as a result of the Directive if he proves:

38 Article 1386–2 of the Civil Code.

39 A similar decision was reached in Case C-154/00 *Commission v Greece* [2002] ECR I-3879.

40 Article 1386–7: 'A seller, a hirer, with the exception of a finance lessor or of a hirer similar to a finance lessor, or any other professional supplier is liable for the lack of safety of a product in the same conditions as a producer.'

41 This may also have an impact in Denmark where a similar principle of *action directe* applies. Note that the Danish presidency proposed an amendment of the Directive to make the (equal) liability of suppliers optional for Member States. However, this proposal was watered down by the Council in its resolution of December 2002, in which the Council decided that 'there is a need to assess' this point. I am grateful to Stefan Lenz for this point.

- that the defect is due to compliance of the product with mandatory regulations issued by the public authorities; or
- that the state of scientific and technical knowledge at the time when he put the product into circulation was not such as to enable the existence of the defect to be discovered.

These two defences have been introduced into French law but made explicitly subject to the condition of observance by the producer of an obligation to monitor the product. A producer is unable to invoke such a defence where the defect in the product was discovered within ten years of putting the product into circulation, and during that period the producer did not take the appropriate measures to avoid the damaging consequences. This provision thus imposes a post-marketing obligation to warn consumers of the dangers of products, and to take appropriate evasive action once the defect is revealed. The ECJ decided that this supplementary burden on the producer was contrary to the provisions of the Directive.[42]

Parallel regimes and extent of harmonisation

The most controversial aspect of the recent decisions is their effect, or rather *perceived* effect, on the traditional French case law concerning product liability, due to the interpretation of Article 13. It is worth laying out the wording of this Article in full:

> This Directive shall not affect any rights which an injured person may have according to the rules of the law of contractual or non-contractual liability or a special liability system existing at the moment when this Directive is notified.

Traditionally viewed as permitting the co-existence of parallel contractual and extra-contractual actions,[43] the Directive's promoters assumed that as the Directive would ensure a more favourable position for the victim than existing rules, it would finish in practice by replacing alternative actions.[44] However, as we have seen in French law, the transposed version of the EC Directive actually in some ways represents a less favourable

[42] A number of key provisions of the French Civil Code are thus in breach of EU law. In a new 'Simplification of Law' Act passed on 9 December 2004, the three offending aspects of the French Civil Code have been modified to bring it in line with the Product Liability Directive.

[43] Taylor, 'Harmonisation of European Product Liability Rules', 419, 420.

[44] EC Bulletin No. 11/ 76, No. 30 page 20.

approach than the pre-existing rules of the Civil Code as interpreted by the courts.

In its decisions, the European Court of Justice has taken a trenchant view of Article 13. It has held that Article 13 *does not mean* that a Member State can maintain a *general* system of product liability different from that provided for in the Directive. Rather Article 13 posited the co-existence of product liability systems *of a different type*, 'based on other grounds, such as fault or a warranty in respect of latent defects' or with special liability systems relating to specific types of products. Any scheme 'founded on the same basis as that put in place by the Directive and not limited to a given sector of production' was seemingly not encompassed within Article 13.

This decision has created much disquiet in France. It has been interpreted by commentators as undermining the traditional approach to product liability. It is seen as having a particular impact on the French case law creation of an *obligation de sécurité*. This case law is not a special liability system, as defined by the ECJ: it certainly does not have a sectoral application. Nor does the French case law creation of an *obligation de sécurité* have a different legal basis to the European Directive. Indeed, as we have already seen, the Directive was the explicit source of inspiration for the *Cour de Cassation*.

As Professor Calais-Auloy states in a case-note on the recent decisions, entitled 'Ménace européenne sur la jurisprudence française concernant l'obligation de sécurité':[45]

> Le régime instauré par la jurisprudence française s'applique à tous les secteurs de production: il est un 'régime général de responsabilité' au sens que donne la Cour de Justice à cette expression. Il ne pourrait donc être maintenu que s'il reposait sur un fondement différent de celui de la directive. Or la jurisprudence française se fonde, comme la directive, sur une obligation de sécurité concernant les produits. C'est la raison pour laquelle le système jurisprudentiel des responsabilités ne peut, aux yeux des juges européens, se maintenir en concurrence avec celui transposé de la directive.[46]

Under the ECJ's interpretation of Article 13, the co-existence of the *obligation de sécurité* regime with that under the Directive would seem to

[45] Viney adopts a more nuanced interpretation: JCP 2002.I.177.

[46] J. Calais-Auloy, 'Menace européenne sur la jurisprudence française concernant l'obligation de sécurité du vendeur professionel' Dalloz, 2002. 2458.

infringe Community law. It is thus incumbent upon the French courts to reinterpret the current rules in order to effect the goal of 'complete harmonisation'.

This outcome has been criticised by many French observers. It undermines the traditional robust protection of consumers in French jurisprudence, and deprives them of the benefits of the pre-existing case law, for instance in terms of the generous limitation period for actions based on an *obligation de sécurité*.[47] Maximal harmonisation was not necessary or advisable in an area where consumer protection is now paramount. Professeur Viney pulls no punches in her analysis of the case law. She commences a recent case-note with the observation:

> La CJCE a rendu, le 25 avril 2002, à propos de l'interprétation de la directive du 25 juillet 1985 relative à la responsabilité du fait des produits défectueux, trois arrêts qui ne sont assurément pas de nature à séduire les consommateurs européens![48]

As for the concrete effects in the short term, some commentators are resigned to the faithful application of the ECJ's interpretation of Article 13 and the ousting of the *obligation de sécurité* in this sphere. Others have pointed out that the *obligation de sécurité* may enjoy a continued vitality by means of the application of Article 1382, a regime explicitly allowed to co-exist and one in respect of which it is increasingly accepted that liability is satisfied by a breach of the *obligation de sécurité*.[49]

Conclusion

The recent decisions of the ECJ raise important questions about harmonisation within the sphere of product liability. The ECJ has made it clear that it prefers the option of maximal harmonisation, with the Directive seeking to achieve a 'complete harmonisation'. The ECJ's reasoning was

[47] Under the Civil Code, the limitation period for actions based on contract is generally thirty years: Article 2270–1. Under the Directive, the limitation period is three years after the Victim has knowledge of the defect and the identity of the manufacturer (Art. 10), and ten years after the placing of the product on the market. Such short limits do not apply in the French system. The discovery of an obligation of security has allowed the French courts to circumvent the short delay for *garantie de vices cachés* laid down in Art. 1684 CC.

[48] JCP 2002.I.177.

[49] The *Cour de Cassation* has held in respect of *obligation de sécurité* that '*les tiers à un contrat sont fondés à invoquer tout manquement du débiteur contractuel lorsque ce manquement leur a causé un dommage, sans avoir à rapporter d'autre preuve*' (Cass Civ 1, 18 July 2000, N°. 99–12135).

predominantly textual.[50] Taking a step back from the exact wording of the Directive and its legal basis, one might question the need for such an approach. Professor Howells has questioned the need for maximal harmonisation in the sphere of product liability:

> Mere disparities in national laws may not be sufficient justification if they create only abstract risks of barriers to trade or non-appreciable distortions in competition. Thus, in keeping with the subsidiarity principle, it could be argued that what is needed is a harmonisation of product liability law to the extent that injured persons get a fair deal in all states and there are sufficient sanctions to ensure that civil product liability encourages proper research and development. However, this need not require complete harmonisation. After all, the United States seems to manage an internal market with some significant differences remaining between state product liability laws.[51]

Limits on space preclude an evaluation of the extent to which 'complete harmonisation' is achievable in respect of product liability laws. Certainly at present other aspects of both substantive and procedural law have undermined the goal of harmonisation in this sphere. The Community law on product liability does not extend to crucial areas affecting consumer protection such as causation, recourse actions, calculation of damages and access to justice.[52]

[50] The following arguments were raised. The Directive was based on Article 100 of the EEC Treaty (amended to Article 100 of the EC Treaty, now Article 94 EC), and that legal basis provides no possibility for the Member States to maintain or establish provisions departing from Community harmonising measures. The Product Liability Directive, unlike other Directives, contains no provision allowing the Member States to adopt or to maintain more stringent provisions in order to secure a higher level of consumer protection.

[51] G. Howells, 'Product Liability – a Maximal Harmonization Directive?', December (2001) *European Product Liability Review*: pp. 10, 13.

[52] Concerning English and French law, see Taylor, *L'Harmonisation de la responsabilité du fait des produits défectueux*.

6

German product liability law: between European Directives, American Restatements and common sense

STEFAN LENZE

Introduction

Product liability has today in Germany established itself as a separate niche of tort law that is of particular relevance for consumers and business. In both doctrine and practice it is a field that is inextricably linked to global developments. The fundamental change in case law in 1968[1] which practically focussed the issue of negligence liability on the question of defect was no doubt influenced by the developments in the United States surrounding *Henningsen v Bloomfield Motors Inc.*,[2] *Greenman v Yuba Powers*[3] and the adoption of §402A of the Restatement of Torts Second (1965). With the implementation of the European Directive on Product Liability[4] in 1990, a second pillar of liability was added to the existing system. The question since then is whether and to what extent the Directive has made an impact. The current product liability debate in the Unites States is particularly helpful in this context, for the Third Restatement of Torts: Products Liability (1998) describes the situation under negligence law quite accurately, while the Directive at first sight shows more similarity to Section 402A of the Restatement Second of Torts. This is not to say that product liability is an American or European import. That a producer is liable if it fails to adopt a reasonable alternative design was decided by the Stuttgart Court of Appeal in 1907,[5] and the Reichsgericht found in the Brunnensalz case of 1915[6] that proof of a manufacturing defect was sufficient to establish a *prima facie* case of negligence. The subsequent developments have been refinement.[7]

[1] BGHZ 91, 53 (Chicken Pest). [2] 161 A.2d 69 (N.J. 1960). [3] 377 P.2d 897 (Cal. 1963).
[4] Directive 85/374/EEC on liability for defective products, OJ 1985 L 210/29.
[5] OLG Stuttgart OLGE 18, 69 ff. (Electric Wood Saw).
[6] RGZ 87, 1, 3 (Piece of Glass in Bottle).
[7] See G. Brüggemeier, *Common Principles of Tort Law* (London: BIICL 2004), p. 128.

The practical implications of the globalisation of product liability can be seen in the case of Bayer, whose shares dropped by 26 per cent in March 2003 when the German drug manufacturer faced a class action in the United States, alleging a defect in the anti-cholesterol product Lipobay. Another example is the recent blow to the brand name of Mitsubishi in Japan on account of product defects in cars,[8] the effect of which can be felt at board level and on the assembly lines of DaimlerChrysler in Stuttgart.

Product liability based on pre-market defects

The German law of product liability is today based on three sources: the law of contract, the traditional (fault-based) law of torts and strict liability. These regimes form, according to a general principle of German law, concurrent legal bases and Article 13 of Directive 85/374/EEC on liability for defective products ('Product Liability Directive')[9] preserves this juxtaposition.

Contract

Contract law does not play a major role in the German law of product liability. Contractual liability only arises where the claimant and the defendant are in a contractual relationship, i.e. in an ordinary sale of goods situation. This means a buyer usually can not sue the manufacturer of a defective product, as there is no contractual relationship between them. Although the idea of a contract conferring rights on third parties exists in German law (§311 (3) BGB), it generally does not provide a remedy in product liability claims.[10]

A claim in contract requires breach of a contractual duty (§280 BGB). The most relevant breach of a contractual duty with respect to product liability is delivery of a defective product (§§434, 437 BGB). A product is defective according to §434 BGB if it does not conform with the contract.[11] The concept of defect is therefore primarily based upon a mutual

[8] See the chapter by L. Nottage, in this collection. [9] OJ 1985 L 210/29

[10] Note, however, that the doctrine of third party contracts has developed since it was rejected by the Bundesgerichtshof in the Chicken-pest case (BGHZ 53, 91 ff) with respect to product liability cases. One situation for a third party claim would be, for example, an employee of a manufacturer suing another manufacturer who sold his employer a defective machine as a result of which he was injured.

[11] See also Article 2 of the Directive on consumer goods and associated guarantees (1999/44/EC).

(subjective) idea of the product's features. The expressly agreed quality can be higher or lower than the average quality of those products. Where the parties did not (expressly or impliedly) agree on a certain quality, goods will be defective (1) if they are not fit for the purpose communicated to, and recognised by, the seller, or (2) if they are unsuitable for the ordinary use to which products of such kind are normally put.

As a consequence of Directive 1999/44/EC on certain aspects of the sale of consumer goods and associated guarantees, the seller is also liable for statements on specific characteristics of the product made by the manufacturer (or his representative), particularly in advertising or labelling (§434 (1) 3 BGB). The seller is, however, not liable for statements if he did not know nor should have known of those statements, or if he corrects those statements before contracting, or if those statements could not have influenced the decision of the buyer.

Contractual liability for defective products, in principle, requires that the seller was at fault as to the delivery of a defective product. §280 (1) 1 BGB, however, in effect sets up a rebuttable presumption that the seller knew, or should have known, of the defective condition of the product. Yet in practice the seller will often be able to rebut the presumption of fault, for it is under no general obligation to verify the quality of each product. The seller only has a duty to check that a product is free of defects where such an examination is reasonable in view of the circumstances.

Tort

Product liability in Germany is primarily based in tort law. It comprises liability for breach of a general duty of care (*Verkehrspflicht*) under §823 (1) BGB and breach of statutory duty (*Schutzgesetz*) under §823 (2) BGB.

1. Breach of a duty of care

Most product liability claims have, so far, been brought on the basis of a breach of a duty of care. In the area of product liability, manufacturers have the duty to undertake every safety precaution that is technically possible, practical and economically reasonable.[12] The intensity of the duty of care depends on the magnitude and the probability of the foreseeable risks of harm.[13] In economic terms, the manufacturer is negligent if the increased

[12] BGH NJW 1990, 906, 907 (Horse Box); BGHZ 104, 323, 325 (Lemonade Bottle).

[13] BGH VersR 1960, 609, 611; MünchKomm/Wagner §823/249; Larenz/Canaris, Schuldrecht II/2, §76 III 4 b.

(marginal) costs of the untaken safety precaution would have been less than the expected damages.[14]

The duties of the manufacturer span from designing the product to its manufacture and marketing. In each of these stages, certain 'defects' can happen. The courts and legal writing have therefore identified three known types of defects: manufacturing defects, design defects and instruction defects. However, in the context of negligence, the term 'defect' probably craves more confusion than clarification, and it is helpful to bear in mind that liability depends on a breach of duty, not on a 'defect'.[15] The idea behind using the term 'defect' in negligence goes back to the case law of the *Bundesgerichtshof*, according to which the claimant only has to prove that the product was 'defective' at the time when it left the manufacturer, while it is for the manufacturer to show that – despite the defect – it did not breach a duty of care, i.e. that he could not reasonably have known of or avoided the defect.[16] This rule is most effective in the case of manufacturing defects where proof of a factual product flaw is sufficient. In classic design defect and warning cases, the concept of 'defect' as the trigger element for the reversal of proving fault has a very limited meaning. The decisive point here is how one allocates the burden of proving the elements of a negligence claim.

(a) **Manufacturing duties** A manufacturer has the duty to organise the production process in such a way that the risks of manufacturing defects are minimised. A product has a manufacturing defect if the product departs from its intended design.[17] The claimant can prove the existence of a defect by direct or circumstantial evidence. Thus, the claimant only needs to show that the product malfunctioned in a way that is ordinarily the result of a defect.[18] Contrary to the situation under the Product Liability Directive,[19] the claimant also needs to prove that the product was already defective at the time of marketing. In effect this requires the

14 *United States v Caroll Towing Co.* 159 F.2d 169 (2nd Circ. 1947); S. Shavell, *Foundations of the Economic Analysis of the Law* (Cambridge, MA: 2004), pp. 190 ff; MünchKomm/Wagner §823/42.

15 MünchKomm/Wagner, §823/572.

16 BGH 51, 91 ff. (Chicken Pest) manufacturing defect; BGHZ 67, 359 (Floating Switch) design defect; BGHZ 116, 60 (Toddler Tea) instruction defect; but see also BGHZ 80, 186 (Derosal) instruction defect.

17 MünchKomm/Wagner §823/584; *Restatement Third of Torts: Products Liability* §2 (a).

18 S. Lenze, 'Beweis des Produktfehlers', thesis, forthcoming; *Restatement Third of Torts: Products Liability* §3.

19 See Article 7(b).

claimant to show with greater precision than under the Directive the specific nature of the defect.[20] Where the claimant can prove a manufacturing defect, it can make out a *prima facie* case of negligence. The defendant can free itself from liability if it can prove that there were no reasonable safety precautions available to detect and/or avoid such a defect.[21]

(b) Design duties In order to establish that a product is negligently designed, it is helpful to focus on the 'untaken precaution' of the manufacturer.[22] The first step in a negligence claim is to identify what the manufacturer *could have done* to reduce the foreseeable risks of harm but failed to do. Once the untaken precaution is identified, the question is whether this precaution *should have* been taken. In product liability terms, a product is negligently designed if the overall safety of the product could have been increased by altering the design, and if the additional safety benefits of that alteration outweigh the additional costs.[23] This parallels the situation under Section 2 (b) of the Restatement Third (Products Liability). In order to make out a *prima facie* case of defective design, and thus negligence, the claimant only needs to show the existence of a safer and practical design alternative.[24] The manufacturer is not liable, however, if it can prove that the 'costs' (including any disadvantages to the consumer and the public) of altering the product would outweigh the benefits of the increased level of safety.[25] The manufacturer can also free itself from liability if it can prove that, taking into account the state of technical and scientific knowledge at the time of marketing, it could not have known

[20] This may be different where the manufacturer, due to intrinsic, particular risks in the manufacturing process, is bound to ensure the safe state of the product before it leaves the premises (BGHZ 104, 323 (Lemonade Bottle); BGH NJW 1993, 528 (Sparkling Water Bottle I); BGH NJW 1998, 2611). But see also OLG Koblenz NJW-RR 1999, 1624, 1625 (Water Bottle).

[21] BGHZ 51, 91, 105 ff. (Chicken Pest); BGHZ 104, 323, 325 ff. (Lemonade Bottle); BGHZ 129, 353, 361 ff. (Mineral Water Bottle II); OLG Koblenz NJW-RR 1999, 1624, 1625 (Water Bottle).

[22] M. Grady, 'Untaken Precautions' 18 (1989) *J. Leg. Stud.* 139, 143; §3 Comment i of the *Restatement Third of Torts (General Principles)* Tentative Draft No. 1; similarly C. v Bar, *Verkehrspflichten* (Berlin 1980) 157; Larenz and Canaris, Schuldrecht II/2 (Munich: Köln 1994) §76 III 1 d.

[23] Lenze, *Beweis des Produktfehlers*; similar Münch/KommWagner §823/581 f. For an explanation of the cost/benefit test see D. Owen, 'Towards a Proper Test for Defective Design Defectiveness', 75 (1997) *Tex. L. Rev.* 1661, 1687 ff.

[24] Lenze, *Beweis des Produktfehlers*. See also LG Köln NJW 2005, 1195 (1200).

[25] That is in effect what the Bundesgerichtshof says in BGH NJW 1990. 906, 907 (Horse Box); note that this allocation of the burden of proof departs from the Third Restatement (see §2 Reporters Note Nr. 4 to comment f).

of the defect.[26] However, this defence is not available where the manufacturer, because of the nature of its activities, is under an obligation to carry out its own research and product testing independently of the existing state of technical and scientific knowledge.[27] In effect, negligence can therefore require a higher degree of care than the 'strict liability' rule under the Product Liability Directive.

(c) **Warning duties** Where it is not possible to design a product without risks, manufacturers are under a duty to provide adequate instructions and warnings to reduce unavoidable product risks (risk-reduction warnings) and to enable consumers to make an informed choice as to whether they want to take that risk (informed-choice warnings).[28] The producer thereby not only needs to warn of dangers present in the ordinary use of the product but also of dangers related to any foreseeable misuse.[29] The extent of the duty to warn generally depends on the level and nature of the risk, and the probability of its manifestation.[30] The information duties, however, are limited by general consumer knowledge. That means there is no need to warn of risks which are generally known to its possible users.[31] The courts have thus denied a duty to warn of the dangers of tobacco,[32] alcohol,[33] chocolate bars[34] or liquorice.[35]

In order to establish a *prima facie* case of negligence, the claimant only needs to show that the warnings were reasonable in hindsight, that is, considering the knowledge of the risks at the time of trial.[36] It is then for the defendant to prove that it could not have known of the product's unsafe condition at the time of marketing. What is more, in many circumstances there will be a (rebuttable) presumption that the claimant would have adhered to reasonable instructions and warnings.[37]

[26] BGH VersR 1960, 1095, 1096 (Cooling Device); MünchKomm/Wagner 823/579.

[27] BGHZ 116, 60, 70 (Toddler Tea I).

[28] Kullmann/Pfister, *Produzentenhaftung*, Kz. 1520/38.

[29] BGH VersR 1987, 102, 103 (Zinc Spray); BGH NJW 1989, 1542 (Asthma Spray); BGHZ 116, 60, 65 (Toddler Tea I); BGH ZIP 1995, 747 (Toddler Tea III); BGH VersR 1999, 892 (Paper Shredder); OLG Hamm NJW-RR 2001, 1248 (Log Flume); OLG Düsseldorf, 20/12/2002, 14 U 99/02 (Chocolate Bar).

[30] BGHZ 80, 186, 192 (Derosal).

[31] BGH NJW 1986, 1863, 1864; BGH NJW 1996, 2224 (Lubricating Gel); OLG Hamm NJW-RR 2001, 1248 (Log Flume); OLG Düsseldorf, 20/12/2002, 14 U 99/02 (Chocolate Bar).

[32] OLG Frankfurt NJW-RR 2001, 1471 OLG Hamm NJW 2005, 295.

[33] OLG Hamm NJW 2001, 1654.

[34] OLG Düsseldorf, Decision of 20 December 2002, 14 U 99/02.

[35] LG Bonn, 19.4.2004 – 9 = 603/03 (Haribo).

[36] BGHZ 116, 60, 70 (Toddler Tea I).

[37] BGHZ 116, 60, 73 (Toddler Tea I).

(d) *Prima facie* case of negligence without proof of the type of defect In order to establish a *prima facie* case of negligence, the claimant is not in all circumstances required to prove the specific type of defect. The claimant only needs to show that the damage was caused by an objective safety deficit of the product existing at the time when it was put into circulation.[38] An objective safety deficit can be inferred from the malfunctioning of the product where a defect is the most likely explanation for the damage.[39] However, this kind of circumstantial evidence requires that the harm is ordinarily the result of a product defect, and that causes other than a product defect are extremely unlikely.[40] The situation under German negligence liability is thus comparable to Section 3 of the Restatement Third (Products Liability).

2. Breach of statutory duty

Manufacturers are also liable for intentional or negligent *breach of a statutory or regulatory provision* meant to protect other persons. It makes no difference whether the provisions are based on federal, state or EC law. Important examples of such provisions can be found in the Appliances and Product Safety Act, the Food Act, the Drug Act, the Medical Devices Act and the Criminal Code.[41] While the claimant here needs to prove the breach of a statutory/regulatory duty, the defendant can free himself from liability if he establishes a defence.[42] Breach of non-binding product safety standards is indicative of negligence but not conclusive. Compliance with product safety statutes or non-binding product safety standards is properly considered in determining whether the manufacturer was negligent, but it is also not conclusive.

Subject of the duty A duty of care in tort can attach to all persons who are involved in the production and marketing of a product, although the characteristics of the duty may vary depending on the role of the individual person. In contrast to the situation under the Product Liability

[38] BGH NJW 1996, 2506, 2507 (Furniture Polish); BGHZ 51, 91, 105 (Chicken Pest).

[39] That is the effect of BGHZ 67, 359, 362 (Floating Switch); BGH NJW 1996, 2506, 2507 (Furniture Polish).

[40] Lenze, *Beweis des Produktfehlers.*

[41] Geräte und Produktsicherheitsgesetz, Lebensmittel- und Bedarfsgegenständegesetz, Arzneimittelgesetz, Medizinproduktegesetz and Strafgesetzbuch.

[42] BGHZ 51, 91 ff. (Chicken Pest). The situation is thus identical to Section 14 of the *Restatement Third of Torts (General Principles)* Tentative Draft No. 1. Under 4 (1) of the *Third Restatement (Products Liability)* the manufacturer is liable independently of any excuse.

Act (see below), the supplier can be liable in tort, regardless of whether the 'producer' can be identified.[43] A duty of care can also attach to members of management, who thus may be personally liable for product defects and post-marketing failures.[44]

Product Liability Act

The PLA implements the Product Liability Directive to introduce liability for *defective* products. Compared to tort law, the PLA sets stricter limits on recoverable damages as well as on the group of liable persons; it also does not apply to post-marketing defects. Given the existence of an effective system under tort law, the PLA has rarely been applied. However, as it is now possible to recover non-material damages under strict liability regimes (as of 1 August 2002),[45] this could change. The PLA applies only to products that have been put on the market after 1 January 1990. §1 I PLA sets up the basic rule by which producers are liable for personal injury or property damage caused by defective products.

1. Defect

As under the Directive, a product is defective under §3 PLA 'if it does not provide the safety a person is entitled to expect, taking all circumstances into account, including:

(a) the presentation of the product;
(b) the use to which it could reasonably be expected that the product would be put;
(c) the time when the product was put into circulation'.

(a) Tripartite concept of defect Although neither the PLA nor the Product Liability Directive distinguish between different types of defects, German courts, through case law, have (re-)established the three known categories of defects: manufacturing defects, design defects and instruction (warning) defects.[46] This has far-reaching consequences for the

[43] BGHZ 139, 43 (Fireball I) and BGHZ 139, 79 (Fireball II).
[44] BGH VersR 2001, 381 (Toddler Tea IV); BGH NJW 1975, 1827; BGH NJW 1987, 372.
[45] Second Act to change the rules relating to damages (Zweites Gesetz zur Änderung schadensersatzrechtlicher Vorschriften BGBl. 2002 I, 2634 ff.)
[46] BGH NJW 1995. 2162 (Sparkling Water Bottle II); OLG Düsseldorf, 20.12.2002, 14 U 99/02 (Chocolate Bar); OLG Hamm NJW-RR 2001, 1248 (Log Flume).

application of the concept of defect. In this tripartite concept, certain provisions only apply to certain categories of defects.[47] The most important effect of this partition of defect is that strict liability in fact only remains for manufacturing defects.[48] The issues underlying the question whether a product is defectively designed, or whether the manufacturer has failed to warn consumers of product dangers, largely echo the questions arising in negligence.[49]

As with all other courts in the EU, German courts – bound by the definition of defect in the statute – refer to 'consumer expectations' to determine the existence of a design defect. In fact, reference to what consumers are or are not entitled to expect in many cases simply couches the underlying questions in the terms of the statute. Consumer expectations obviously matter most with respect to instructions and warnings.[50] As far as manufacturing and design defects are concerned, consumers' expectations only have an ancillary function to adjust the departure-from-design test (manufacturing defects) and the cost-benefit test (design defects) and to help establish a *prima facie* case of defect.[51]

(b) Manufacturing defects As far as manufacturing defects are concerned, reference to consumer expectations is in most cases redundant. It does not make things clearer to say that consumers are 'entitled to expect that a product does not depart from [its intended design]'.[52] This is different, however, in the case of atypical manufacturing defects – 'non-standard' products – such as blood. The fact that a batch of blood is infected with HIV or hepatitis-C does not automatically render the product defective,[53] for there is – unlike in the case of exploding bottles – simply

47 For example, Art. 6 I(c), 6 II only to design and warning defects, Art. 7(b) only to manufacturing defects, Art. 7(d) only to design defects, Art. 7(e) and Art. 7(f) only to design and warning defects.

48 BGH NJW 1995. 2162 (Sparkling Water Bottle II); compare §2 (a) *Restatement Third of Torts: Products Liability.*

49 OLG Düsseldorf, 20.12.2002, 14 U 99/02 (Chocolate Bar); OLG Hamm NJW-RR 2001, 1248 (Log Flume); OLG Cologne, 27.8.2002, 3 U 116/00 (Mountain Bike).

50 Owen, 'Towards a Proper Test for Defective Design Defectiveness', 1661, 1666.

51 Lenze, *Beweis des Produktfehlers.*

52 Compare the circular reasoning in BGH NJW 1995, 2162 (Water Bottle II).

53 *A v National Blood Authority* [2001] 3 All ER 289 at para. 66: 'But it seems to me that the primary issue in relation to a non-standard product may be whether the public at large accepted the non-standard nature of the product – i.e., they accept that a proportion of the products is defective (as I have concluded they do not in this case). That, as discussed, is not of course the end of it, because the question is of legitimate expectation, and the Court may conclude that the expectation of the public is too high or too low.'

no such common consensus on the product 'blood'. However, the fact that a batch of blood is infected is indicative of a product defect, without ultimately deciding the question of whether there is a defect in law.[54]

(c) **Design defects** Whether the Product Liability Directive sets up a strict liability regime for design defects[55] or whether liability for design defects is in effect liability for misconduct[56] is controversial. The preamble to the Directive speaks of 'liability without fault', which does in point of fact only say that 'personal blameworthiness' is not the issue. It does not say whether the objective conduct of the manufacturer is to be disregarded. It makes no difference whether one says 'a product is defective in design' or 'a product is defectively designed'. What matters is what factors a court may consider within Article 6 of the Directive/ Section 3 PLA.

The German courts (like most of their European counterparts)[57] have so far not defined the notion of design defect within the PLA. However, they have (intuitively) noticed that consumer expectations are not of much guidance in a courtroom where there simply are no consumer expectations or the existing expectations are unrealistically high or lag behind the level of safety achieved by the latest technology. Where the safety of product design is in question, courts therefore particularly take into account any existing statutes, regulations or (non-binding) standards.[58] Breach of statute or regulation will inevitably render the product defective, while breach of a non-binding product standard is indicative of a defect.[59] Compliance with binding product safety laws or product standards does not by itself prove that the product is free of defect but is indicative of it being safe.[60]

[54] That is consistent with Mr Justice Burton's interpretation of defect in *A v National Blood Authority*, ibid.

[55] Unclear in the Preamble to Directive 85/374 ('liability without fault' – but what is fault?); different in Taschner/Frietsch, *Produkthaftungsgesetz und Produkthaftungsrichtlinie* (Munich 1990) Art. 1/1; H. Taschner, 'Die künftige Produzentenhaftung in Deutschland', *NJW* 1986, 611 f.

[56] MünchKomm/Wagner, *Einleitung ProdHaftG* 16; W. Lorenz, 'Rechtsangleichung auf dem Gebiet der Produkthaftung', *ZHR* 151 (1987) 1, 13 ff; H. Kötz, 'Ist die Produkthaftung eine vom Verschulden unabhängige Haftung?', F. S. Lorenz (1991), 'Rechtsangleichung', 109, 113.

[57] With the exception of the Austrian Supreme Court, which often uses the definition of the German courts in negligence.

[58] OLG Düsseldorf, 20.12.2002, 14 U 99/02 (Chocolate Bar); OLG Hamm NJW-RR 2001, 1248 (Log Flume); OLG Frankfurt, 1.2.2001, 1 W 11/00 (Tobacco Claim).

[59] Lenze, *Beweis des Produktfehlers.*

[60] Ibid.

To decide the question of defective design in the absence of any legal standard or clear consumer expectations, German writers[61] and the Austrian courts[62] often say that one is *entitled* to expect that a product is 'state of the art'. However, the understanding of this concept varies considerably, ranging from 'the cutting edge technology available at the time' to nothing more than 'good industry practice'. Not least because of the vagueness of this term and the confusion surrounding it, the reference to 'state of the art' should be dropped altogether.

The existence of a safer design alternative is a much clearer test, and it has a basis in Article 6(2) of the Product Liability Directive. Article 6(2) stresses that 'A product shall not be considered defective for the sole reason that a better product is *subsequently* put into circulation.' It follows that the existence of safer products at the time of circulation is a relevant factor. Even if no safer products were available when the contended product was put on to the market, a subsequent improvement of its design can show that the safer design could have been adopted earlier.[63] It goes without saying that in order to be a safer design alternative the proposed design must increase the overall safety of the product.[64] There is a substantial body of case law supporting the position that the existence of an alternative safer design is at the heart of a typical design defect case under the Directive.[65] However, while proving the existence of a safer design is a first step in proving a design defect, it is clearly not sufficient. A reasonable consumer does not and cannot legitimately expect a safer design if that entails a disproportionate loss of utility.[66] This is the second element of any risk–benefit test.

[61] Kullmann/Pfister, *Produzentenhaftung*, Kz. 3604/18a; Taschner/Frietsch, note 55, Art. 6/20; Palandt/Sprau, ProdHaftG §3/9.

[62] Austrian Supreme Court, Decision of 16 July 1998 (Electric Fire) – 6Ob157/98a; 23 September 1999 (Bulldozer) – 2Ob112/98d; 16 April 1997 – 7Ob2414/96t (Power Cable).

[63] Austrian Supreme Court, Decision of 11 May 2000 – 8Ob192/99i (Garden Shredder); cf. *A v National Blood Authority* para 72.

[64] OLG Saarbrücken NJW-RR 1993, 990, 991 (Police Revolver).

[65] OLG Cologne, Decision of 22 August 2002 – 3 U 116/00 = 13 (2003) *European Product Liability Rev.* 40 ff.; *Abouzaid v Mothercare* [2000] All ER (D) 2436, para. 27 ('It is clear that more could have been done, for example a non-elasticated method of attachment . . .); *Boogle v McDonald's* [2002] EWHC 490 QB; Austrian Supreme Court, Decision of 5 December 2002 – 8 Ob 192/99i (Extension Ladder) = 13 (2003) *European Product Liability Rev.*; Austrian Supreme Court, Decision of 16 July 1998 – 6 Ob 157/98a (Electric Fire); Decision of 19 September 2002 – 3 Ob 71/02 s (Industrial Machine). Beschl. v. 19.09.2002 – 3 Ob 71/02 s.

[66] *Boogle v McDonald's* [2002] EWHC 490 QB at para. 80. ('They expect precautions to be taken to guard against this risk but not to the point that they are denied the basic utility of being able to buy hot drinks to be consumed on the premises from a cup with the lid off.')

A further question is whether the production costs of a safer design alternative are a relevant factor within Article 6.[67] The argument that production costs cannot be said to be in the expectations of a reasonable consumer is not exactly strong. Most writers[68] and courts[69] accept that the price of a product is a relevant factor, arguing that the price, unlike costs of production,[70] determines the safety expectations of a consumer. However, if anything, the price may tell the buyer something about the product, but the price is also said to be relevant if a mere user, or even a bystander, is injured who has no idea how much the buyer paid for the product.[71] The price of a product is also objectively not a good indicator of how safe a product is. It depends on an array of factors that have all but nothing to do with safety, like competition or trends.[72]

What consumers are *entitled* to expect is that a design is as safe as it can be considering its true social costs (disadvantages of pecuniary or non-pecuniary form).[73] Here, as in negligence, one starts by identifying the specific precaution which the manufacturer could have taken to make the product safer, or *façon de parler* the specific design feature that would have increased the overall safety of the product.[74] So far, the situation under Article 6 Directive is similar to that under §2 (b) of the *Restatement Third of Torts: Products Liability*. Contrary to the position taken there,[75]

67 In favour of considering the production costs: MünchKomm/Wagner *ProdHaftG* §3/24; Staudinger/Oechsler *ProdHaftG* §3/87 ff.; against consideration of production costs: Taschner/Frietsch, Art. 6/22 ff.; Kullmann/Pfister *Produzentenhaftung*, Kz. 3604/18c.

68 Kullmann/Pfister, *Produzentenhaftung*, Kz. 3604/18a; Palandt/Sprau, ProdHaftG §3/9.

69 Austrian Supreme Court, Decision of 5 December 2002 – 8 Ob 192/99i (Extension Ladder) = 13 (2003) *European Product Liability Rev.* 40; *A v National Blood Authority*, para. 71, 'Price is obviously a significant factor in legitimate expectation, and may well be material in the comparative process.'

70 Kullmann/Pfister Kz. 3604/18c.

71 Staudinger/Oechsler, *ProdhaftG* §3/89.

72 The only set of circumstances in which the price of a product is a real indicator of the product's safety is in a real strict liability system, in which the manufacturer pays for all damages caused by its product. But then the cheaper product would be the safer product, for the manufacturer would internalise the costs of accidents (see Shavell, *Foundations of the Economic Analysis of the Law*, 214 ff.).

73 Are consumers (buyers, users, bystanders) not entitled to expect that the benefits of a product outweigh its costs because the person who bought the product, due to imperfect information, made a wrong assessment of the true social costs of a product (price and costs of accidents)?

74 Similarly Owen, 'Towards a Proper Test', 1661.

75 According to §2 comment f, 'To establish a prima facie case of defect, the plaintiff must prove the availability of a technologically feasible and practical alternative design that would have prevented the plaintiff's harm.' 'Technically, though, the burdens of production and persuasion [as far as the risk-utility aspects are concerned] are on the plaintiff' (§2, Reporter's Note Nr. 4).

however, the claimant should only carry the burden of proving that the overall safety of the product could have been increased by altering the design in a practical manner and without an unbalanced loss of utility.[76] The procedural means of pre-trial discovery in Europe (at least on the continent) are not such as to enable the claimant to gather the relevant information he requires to demonstrate what it would cost the manufacturer to alter the design in the proposed manner. The manufacturer must be allowed, however, to rebut the claimant's *prima facie* case of defect if it proves that the costs of altering the design would outweigh the benefits of the extra safety gained through altering the design.[77] It should be noted that the extra level of safety is not usually expressed in financial terms if it primarily includes a reduced risk of personal injury.[78]

(d) Inherently dangerous products Some products cannot be designed in a safer way but still contain a considerable risk of harm. For example, a new vaccine against HIV could currently not be replaced with a substitute product (as an alternative design). However, if this vaccine causes another severe form of autoimmune disease in 10 per cent of applications, its risks will probably outweigh its utility. This case differs from the classic design defect case, for the issue here is not whether there is 'something wrong' in the design. The design of the vaccine is, by current standards, as good as it can be. The issue is whether the risks are so high that the product 'should not be sold at all'.

Generally speaking, consumers are *entitled* to expect that a product that cannot be made any safer be 'not sold at all' if its overall risks outweigh its overall utility.[79] The shift from focussing on the relative safety characteristics of a product (micro balancing)[80] to focussing on its overall risk–utility relation (macro balancing)[81] is significant. It represents a shift from judging the standard of care *within the activity* of designing a product to the dangerousness *of engaging in the activity* of selling this product.[82] This overall risk–utility analysis creates specific

[76] Lenze, *Beweis des Produktfehlers.* [77] Ibid.

[78] See §3 comment h of the *Restatement Third of Torts (General Principles) Tentative Draft No. 3.*

[79] MünchKomm/Wagner §3/32; see also the reasoning in *Potter v Chicago Pneumatic Tool*, 694 A.2d 1327, 1333.

[80] Owen, 'Towards a Proper Test', 1661, 1673 ff. [81] Ibid.

[82] There is a remarkable similarity between the liability rule for 'excessively dangerous products' and the liability rule for manufacturing defects. In both instances, the liability rule

problems. It is questionable whether courts always possess the required information to judge the overall risks and utilities of a product.[83] What is more, in judging the overall social benefits and social costs of a product, the courts may in certain situations take on the role of a legislator or regulator.[84]

Two situations should be distinguished. The overall risk–utility test is not normally problematic when applied to a certain product *within a class* of products, especially when the product is intended to have an objective utility, as is the case with drugs. A court is perfectly able to decide, if necessary with the help of experts, whether or not the risks of a drug outweigh its utility.[85] The overall risk–utility test can be more problematic if the product in question in effect represents a *class of products*, especially when the product is intended to give subjective pleasure. Can a court, for example, say whether the total social costs of alcohol, cigarettes, chocolate bars and liquorice outweigh their total social utilities? Even if one accepts that courts engage in 'social ordering', they may not duly hold their view, or that of an expert, over the general consensus of the public and the preferences of consumers. It is probably in these cases where consumer expectations matter most in the context of 'design' defect. Thus the German courts do refer to consumers' expectations when it comes to products of this nature.[86]

does not focus on the conduct (due care) of the manufacturer within its activity but on the dangerousness of engaging in that activity. The difference is that selling water bottles is on a risk–utility balance not negligent, for the risk of harm, though well known, is extremely small and the utility of reusable glass bottles quite high (environmentally friendly), so that a special rule is needed to make manufacturers liable for product flaws (and thus internalise the risks). But selling water bottles would certainly be negligent if the probability of a product flaw was 10 per cent.

[83] J. Henderson/A. Twerski, 'Achieving Consensus on Defective Products' 83 (1998) *Cornell L. Rev.*: 867, 885 with further references.

[84] D. Owen, 'Moral Foundations of Products Liability Law' 68 (1993) *Notre Dame L. Rev.*: 427, 468 ff.; it should be noted that the relevant authority in Europe can ban a particular product, even if it essentially represents a product category, if it is on a risk–utility balance 'unsafe' in terms of the General Product Safety Directive 2001/95/EC.

[85] Given that a drug manufacturer will not usually produce only one drug, a verdict that this product fails risk–utility standards only affects the way in which the enterprise runs its business. Where a manufacturer produces only one product, as is the case with some tobacco companies, the verdict bars manufacturers from that activity, which is a much more intensive restriction of their constitutional rights.

[86] OLG Frankfurt NJW-RR 2001, 1471 (Beer); OLG Hamm NJW 2001, 1654 (Tobacco); OLG Düsseldorf 20/12/2002, 14 U 99/02 (Chocolate Bar); LG Bonn, 19.4.2004 – 9 = 603/03 (Liquorice/Haribo). What the courts fail to address, however, is whether there is a safer and practical design alternative for these products.

(e) Warning defects Warning defects are determined by the same factors as in negligence.[87]

2. Proof of defect without proving the specific defect

The claimant does not in all circumstances have to prove the specific nature of the defect. To establish a *prima facie* case of defect, the claimant only has to establish that the product 'did not provide the safety that one is entitled to expect' (Article 6 of the Directive, §3 PLA).[88] There may not always be an exact technical explanation ready at hand as to why a product did not do what it was expected to do. If a product fails in circumstances where one is entitled to expect that it does not fail this makes out a *prima facie* case of defect.[89] Generally speaking, the higher the expectations of safety to which the typical consumer is entitled, the lower the extent to which the claimant has to investigate the exact nature of events leading to the product's failure – and vice versa.[90] This rule of evidence is based on Community law – not on national law.

However, this sort of 'malfunction evidence' will in practice only apply where the proper functioning of the product can be said to be within the expectations of a typical consumer.[91] In many situations, particularly involving complex design matters, the consumer will not know whether the product could be made just 'that tick safer'. In these cases particularly, proof of defect will require proof of a safer and practical design alternative by means of expert evidence.

Where the claimant, by proving the malfunctioning of the product, makes out a *prima facie* case of defect, it is for the defendant to establish the specific cause of the product's failure. In order to do that, the defendant will at first need to establish whether the alleged unsafe condition is due to the design features of the product or to a departure from that design. If the malfunction is caused by the design, and the manufacturer can identify the design feature that caused the harm, the burden of production and

[87] OLG Frankfurt NJW-RR 2001, 1471 (Beer); OLG Hamm NJW 2001, 1654 (Tobacco); OLG Düsseldorf 20/12/2002, 14 U 99/02 (Chocolate Bar); LG Bonn, 19.4.2004 – 9 = 603/03; AG Nuremberg NJW 2004, 3123; Austrian Supreme Court, Decision of 15 February 2004-606 7/036. (Haribo); MünchKomm/Wagner §3/33; Staudinger/Oechsler §3/48.

[88] Lenze, *Beweis des Produktfehlers.*

[89] Ibid. See also Austrian Supreme Court, Decision of 25 May 2004-406 94/04. Wrong therefore is *Foster v Biosil*, London County Court, Judgment of 18 April 2000.

[90] S. Lenze, 'Proof of Defect' 9 (2002) *European Product Liability Review* 40 ff.; S. Lenze, 'Zum Beweis des Produktfehlers' 6 (2003) *Produkthaftpflicht International*: 242; S. Lenze, 'Strict Liability for Manufacturing Defects – What Proof is Needed?' 11 (2003) *European Product Liability Review*: 44.

[91] *Soule v General Motors Co.*, 882 P.2d 298, 308 ff.

persuasion reverts to the claimant who needs to demonstrate the existence of a safer design alternative – and the game starts again.[92] If the damage is caused by a manufacturing defect, the defendant is strictly liable (unless he has a defence under Article 7). The same applies if the defendant cannot establish the specific nature of the defect.

3. Defences

§1 (2)–(4) PLA stipulate a number of defences. The most important defences are the 'defective – but not at time of circulation' defence and the 'development risks' defence.

The producer is not liable if 'it is to be assumed' that the product was free from defect at the time of circulation but only became defective post-marketing, for example because of product tampering or misuse. This defence only makes sense in case of product flaws, for a design or warning defect cannot occur post-marketing. What this defence really means is that it is for the manufacturer to tell a post-marketing product flaw from a manufacturing defect. Although the German rules on standard of proof generally require establishing a very high probability of the relevant facts, an autonomous interpretation of the Product Liability Directive suggests that the manufacturer is not liable if, on a balance of probabilities, it is more likely than not that the defect came into being post-circulation.[93]

The producer is also not liable if 'the state of scientific and technical knowledge at the time when he put the product into circulation was not such as to enable the existence of the defect to be discovered'. According to the European Court of Justice, this requires proof that it was objectively impossible to discover the harmful characteristics of the product, taking into account the most advanced state of scientific and technical knowledge at the time the product was put into circulation (i.e. not just the knowledge of a certain industry).[94] However, such knowledge must be accessible.[95] The *Bundesgerichtshof* maintains that this defence does not apply to manufacturing defects.[96]

[92] Lenze, *Beweis des Produktfehlers*. Note that the situation is different from *Soule v General Motors*, according to which the 'manufacturer may not defend a claim that a product's design failed to perform as safely as its ordinary consumer would expect by presenting expert evidence of the design's relative risks and benefits' (882 P.2d 298, 308).

[93] See S. Lenze, 'Defective but not at Time of Circulation' 11 (2003) *European Product Liability Review*: 35, 36.

[94] Case C-300/95, *Commission v UK*, at para. 26; see also H.-J. Kullmann, *Produkthaftungsgesetz* (3rd edn 2002), §1/5 b.

[95] *Commission v UK*, note 29, 29.

[96] BGH NJW 1995, 2162.

4. Causation

The German courts, just like the courts of the other Member States, apply the national rules on causation to the PLA although it is based on a European Directive that clearly includes causation as an element (Articles 1 and 4). In theory, courts should therefore apply common rules on causation.[97] As a practical matter, it will in most instances not make a great difference if the courts of the Member States apply their national rules on causation, for the rules differ not much in standard cases. However, in certain instances, courts should be encouraged to look across the national borders to see whether 'there is law elsewhere'.[98] The House of Lords in *Fairchild*[99] has set a good example in this direction.

Special problems arise, for example, where it cannot be ascertained which of several generic products did in fact cause the damage. According to §830 I 2 BGB, participants in a tort[100] are jointly and severally liable 'where it cannot be ascertained which of several participants caused the damage through its conduct'. It is controversial whether several individual producers can be seen as 'participants'. On the reading of the House of Lords, §830 I 2 BGB should be interpreted as to mean that several people are participants if they all 'contributed to the risk of injury'. The *Bundesgerichtshof* would add: provided that other causes for the injury can be excluded. The rule may therefore apply in cases where the claimant cannot prove which of the products *he had actually used* in fact caused the damage.[101] However, it does not apply where he cannot even say *which* products he had used – which is the typical situation where some courts in the US in certain circumstances have applied the concept of *market share liability.*

Damage The PLA only covers damage flowing from personal injury or damage to property other than the defective good. It does not cover damage to property not ordinarily intended for private use, damage to the product itself, (other) pure economic loss or property damage of less than €500. As of 1 August 2002, compensation for pain and suffering is included within the range of recoverable damages (§8 sentence 2 PLA).

[97] Compare Article 288 (2) EC. [98] *International and Comparative Law Quarterly.*

[99] *Fairchild v Glenhaven Funeral Services* [2002] UKHL 22; [2003] 1 AC 32.

[100] Albeit seeded in tort law, this provision also applies to the law of contract as well as to strict liability (BGH NJW 1999, 3633).

[101] BGH NJW 1994, 932 (Toddler Tea II).

In the case of personal injury caused by one product, or by generic products with the same defect, the maximum liability is €85 million (§10 PLA). This provision was originally included in the Product Liability Directive in order to guarantee insurability for development risks. The implementation of both the development risks defence and damage caps is incoherent, as liability for design and instruction defects – this is where development risks can occur – essentially parallels the issues underlying a negligence standard. It is nevertheless applicable law in Germany.

Liability based on breach of post-marketing duties

Post-marketing duties of producers exist as general duties of care (negligence) and statutory duties.

Duty of care

The manufacturer's duties of care do not end with the marketing of the product. Courts have stated that for a considerable time manufacturers are obliged to monitor their products and take appropriate measures, including the issue of warnings.[102] Failure to comply with post-marketing duties is a ground for liability. Unlike under the defect-focussed case law in negligence, the *Bundesgerichtshof* maintains that there is no general shift in the burden of proof regarding breach of such a post-marketing duty, i.e. the claimant usually needs to show that the manufacturer should have discovered the risk in question through product monitoring and testing.[103]

Whether and to what extent there is a duty to recall products is highly controversial.[104] What seems clear is that there is no duty to recall a product that was not objectively defective at the time of marketing. A Porsche from 1950 without head rests may be unsafe under today's standards, but it was not (and never will become) defective in the legal sense.[105] The

[102] It is controversial whether there is a duty to recall a product that is defective at the time of marketing but whose risks were not known at that time; see MünchKomm/Wagner §823/604 ff.

[103] BGHZ 80, 199 (Derosal).

[104] Against a duty to recall products: G. Brüggemeier, 'Produktsicherheit und Produkthaftung' 151 (1988) *ZHR* 511, 525–6; MünchKomm/Wagner §823/603 ff.; in favour of such a duty: OLG Karlsruhe, Decision of 2 April 1993 – 15 U 293/91; OLG Munich VersR 1992, 1135 Kullmann/Pfister, *Produzentenhaftung*, Kz 1520 Bl. 62 f.

[105] The situation is the same as under Article 6 (2) of the Product Liability Directive.

question is more difficult, however, when the product was – in hindsight – defective but the dangerous characteristics were not known at the time of marketing. This would be the case if a manufacturer had used asbestos in the construction of the brakes although a safer material with similar safety characteristics existed. Even if one were to accept that a duty to recall products may exist under certain circumstances, considering the high costs of a product recall, this would require that there is a considerable risk for the health of consumers and that a recall is the only reasonable possibility to protect consumers against that risk.[106]

Product safety laws

While post-marketing duties in the past were mainly the domain of negligence, the transposition of the revised General Product Safety Directive (2001/95/EC) will shift the focus further towards breach of statutory duty, under the transposition legislation, the Appliances and Product Safety Act (*Geräte- und Produktsicherheitsgesetz*, GPSG).[107]

Manufacturers are also obliged to conduct proper market surveillance, including the taking of test-samples, and to implement appropriate measures if product risks emerge post marketing. This includes warning suppliers and the public of product risks, using appropriate means. What type of warning is appropriate depends on the nature of the product and the relationship to suppliers and customers. For example, where suppliers and customers are known, personal letters, email and telephone may be appropriate means of contact. In anonymous customer relationships, manufacturers may have to use the media and the internet to issue warnings effectively. Manufacturers are further under a duty to withdraw a product from suppliers, or recall a product from customers, where the nature and seriousness of the risk requires such action (§5 I no. 1 c GPSG).[108] A new duty for manufacturers and suppliers is the duty to instantly notify the competent authority if they notice that their products pose any risks to life or health of persons, or if there is reason to believe that such risks exist (§5 II GPSG).[109]

[106] OLG Karlsruhe, Decision of 2 April 1993 – 15 U 293/91; OLG Munich VersR 1992, 1135; Kullmann/Pfister, *Produzentenhaftung*, Kz. 1520/62 f.

[107] *Geräte- und Produktsicherheitsgesetz* of 6 January 2004 (BGBl. 2004 I 2).

[108] See also C. Schieble, *Produktsicherheitsgesetz und europäisches Gemeinschaftsrecht* (Baden Baden: Nomos, 2003) 64, 177 and 228 ff.; for recalls under the general duty of care see Foerste in Westphalen (ed.), *Produkthaftungshandbuch* §24/233 ff.

[109] See also C. Schieble, note 14, 65.

Failure to take the 'appropriate action' will normally lead to liability. Whether and what action is appropriate is not to be judged with hindsight but in consideration of the circumstances at the time when such action was due. However, this is an objective standard focussing on the danger of the product, not on the capabilities of the individual manufacturer. However, it is currently unclear whether failure to recall a product under the requirements of the GPSG is a cause for liability. Clearly, if the relevant authority has ordered a recall, failure to comply with that order will render the producer liable. If there has been no recall order, however, liability will presumably not arise in circumstances where, considering the costs and benefits of such action, it was reasonable not to recall the product, i.e. there is no liability where there would be no liability in negligence.

Liability for drugs

Background

Liability for drugs under the German law of product liability to some extent differs from the Product Liability Directive. The Drug Act 1976 is the only special product liability regime in Europe that existed prior to and is thus exempted from the Directive (Article 13). It includes liability for development risks and renders insurance compulsory. It also incorporates new rules on causation and special rules governing disclosure of information, both of which were introduced in 2002.[110] The Drug Act of 1976 was enacted against the background of the thalidomide crisis of the late 1950s, which had struck Germany particularly badly. This incident highlighted the necessity of reviewing the quality, efficacy and safety of medicinal products prior to their marketing, authorisation and sale.

Scope of the Drug Act

The Drug Act only applies to drugs and other medicinal products which hold (or are bound to hold) a marketing authorisation. It does not, for example, apply to veterinary medicines, homeopathic preparations and medicinal products used in clinical trials. The potentially liable 'pharmaceutical enterprise' is the entity named on the packaging that has placed

[110] See also I. Brock, 'German Parliament Passes the Second Act to Change the Rules Relating to Damages' in Lovells, *European Product Liability Review*, June 2002 at 16 f.; http://www.lovells.com (Publications – Newsletters).

the product on the German market. Injuries suffered from these medicinal products may be covered by the Product Liability Act and liability based on tort.

Defective drug

According to §84 (2) no. 1 of the Drug Act, the 'pharmaceutical enterprise' is liable if 'a drug, used correctly, has harmful effects which, taking into account the state of medical knowledge, exceed a tolerable level'. That is the case if the overall risks of the product outweigh the overall benefits (macro balance) or if the risks could have been reduced by the adoption of a reasonable safer design (micro balance).[111]

Alternatively, the distributor is liable 'if the injury is caused by an instruction which does not adequately represent the state of medical knowledge' (§84 (2) No. 2). The labelling requirements for the summary of product characteristics and the package insert leaflet are laid down in Articles 11 and 59 of Directive 83 (2001) EC. Product information must, in a clear and appropriate way, point to any product risks and side effects known at the time of circulation, and point out any serious possibility of such risks and side effects. The product information must also include instructions relating to the correct use of the drug and it must in certain circumstances also highlight the possible consequences of foreseeable misuse.[112] There is no formal 'learned intermediary defence', whereby the warning of doctors is sufficient. However, it is difficult for the patient to prove that he would not have taken the drug in the presence of warnings if the prescribing doctor had been made aware of the risks.

Causation

The claimant, in principle, needs to prove a causal link between the defective drug and the damage. Yet there are exceptions to this rule.

In 2002 the German legislator, in an unprecedented fashion, changed the rules on causation.[113] According to the new rules, actual causation between the application of the drug and the damage is presumed if the drug in question is, in the actual circumstances, capable of causing such

[111] For an economic analysis of the German Drug Act, see Blantzenberg, 'Ökonomische Analyse des deutschen Arzneimittelhaftungsrechtes', PharmR 2000, 39.

[112] BGHZ 106, 273, 284 (Asthma Spray).

[113] For an overview, see Bollweg, 'Die Arzneimittelhaftung der AmG', MedR 2004, 486; Pflüger, 'Kamsalitätsvermutung', PharmR 2003, 363. Wagner, 'Reform der Arzneimittelhaftung', VersR 2001, 1334.

damage (§84 II 1 Drug Act).[114] This rule does not, however, apply 'if, in the actual circumstances, a different instance is capable of causing the damage' (§84 II 3 Drug Act). However, another drug which also may have caused the injury is *not* regarded as a 'different instance'. This is different if this drug is not considered defective (e.g. because its harmful effects are acceptable in the light of the benefit–risk assessment).

Whether the new causation rules are in compliance with EC law remains to be seen. There are sound reasons why the new rules may contravene Article 13 of the Product Liability Directive. Article 13 allows special product liability systems to remain applicable if they existed at the time when the Directive was adopted by the Council, i.e. on 25 July 1985. The German Drug Act dates back to 1976, yet the amendments relating to causation were enacted in 2002. The question thus is whether Article 13 allows changes to existing systems. The European Court of Justice recently made clear that the Product Liability Directive seeks to achieve maximum harmonisation within its scope.[115] That suggests a narrow reading of Article 13, one that does not allow the German legislator to go it alone in the EU and change the only (national) co-existing product liability regime in a way that would, after eighteen years of practical symmetry with the Directive, make a real difference.

Compulsory insurance

A party placing a medicinal product on the German market must be insured against all liability under §84 of the Drug Act, either through a German insurance company or by obtaining a confirmation of cover from a credit institution in Germany or within the EU. The German insurance industry has created a 'pharma pool' through which all major insurance companies pool the statutory strict liability risk, thus facilitating affordable insurance premiums.

Liability for genetically modified products

The Genetic Engineering Act came into force on 1 July 1990 and aims at protecting human beings and the environment against dangers which may

[114] See OLG Koblenz NJOZ 2004, 2983.

[115] Case C-52/00, *Commission v France* [2002] ECR I-2553; Case C-154/00, *Commission v Greece* [2002] ECR I-3879; Case C-183/00, *González Sánchez v Medicina Asturiana* [2002] ECR I-3901.

arise from genetic engineering. It also establishes a legal framework for relevant research and development and the exploitation and promotion of this technology. Activities conducted in genetic laboratories are classified into four containment levels according to the degree of risk they involve. §§32 ff. of the Genetic Engineering Act provide for the operator's absolute liability if damage is caused to third parties as a result of properties of a genetically modified organism. Liability is limited to a maximum amount of €85 million. The Act also includes liability for development risks (i.e. there is *no* development risks defence).[116] Liability based on the Genetic Engineering Act covers material as well as immaterial damages (the latter as of August 2002). In so far as the Genetic Engineering Act derogates from the Product Liability Directive,[117] one could query its compliance with Article 13 of the Directive (see above).

State compensation schemes

State compensation schemes play some role in German product liability law. Thalidomide victims have a right to benefits provided by a public foundation established in 1971.[118] Another public foundation has been set up to help patients who were infected with HIV through contaminated blood products before 1 January 1988.[119] In both cases, the endowments are shared by the state and the relevant pharmaceutical companies. There is also financial aid available for a specific group of people who have been infected with the hepatitis-C virus through particular batches of vaccine.[120]

Most notably, however, there is a special compensation scheme for accidents at the work place and occupational diseases.[121] A large part of asbestos litigation, for example, is for this reason redirected to the social security system.

[116] §37 II GentechnikG.

[117] That is, particularly with regard to products without marketing approval (compare §37 II GentechnikG).

[118] Gesetz über die Errichtung einer Stiftung 'Hilfswerk für behinderte Kinder', BGBl. I 1971, 2018 ff.

[119] Gesetz über die humanitäre Hilfe für durch Blutprodukte HIV-infizierte Personen, BGBl. I 1995, 972 ff.

[120] See I. Brock, 'State Compensation for HCV Infections in the Federal Republic of Germany' December (2002) *European Product Liability Review*: at 16–17.

[121] The competent institutions are the Bundesberufsgenossenschaften.

Practice and procedure

Pre-trial discovery

German law has traditionally been fairly restrictive regarding pre-trial discovery and document disclosure in particular. There is no pre-trial discovery procedure and no general claim for disclosure that would help the claimant establish liability. Recent reforms of the Code of Civil Procedure (CCP)[122] and the Drug Act, however, have introduced tighter rules for the disclosure of documents.

Under §84a of the Drug Act, the injured person can now request that the manufacturer (and the relevant authority) provide information on known effects, side effects and interactions of a drug. Procedural law now gives the court power to order the disclosure of documents in the possession of a party (or a third person) if a party makes substantiated reference to the content and implications of those documents (142 CCP). However, this does not mean a change of heart from the generally restrictive approach to the disclosure of documents in German law.[123]

Experts

Many product liability cases deal with issues which are highly technical in nature. These cases always require the opinion of experts. According to German procedural law, it is the duty of the judge to instruct experts for the purpose of giving expert evidence in court. Counsel for the claimant and the defendant file their briefs prior to the trial, presenting the facts and legal issues relevant to the case. The judge then – usually after a preparatory hearing – formally orders the hearing of evidence and instructs the experts. The claimant and the defendant will not use their own appointed experts at first. However, the parties have a right to obtain their own expert opinions on a consultancy basis (in addition to the reports delivered by court-appointed experts) on the questions at issue.

Trial on preliminary issues

There is no trial on preliminary issues in the German law of civil procedure. For example, at no time does the court decide on the *admissibility*

[122] Gesetz zur Reform des Zivilprozesses vom 27.7.2001, BGBl I, 1887 ff.

[123] See further I. Brock, 'Does Discovery Find its Way into the German Rules on Civil Procedure?' (2002) Lovells, *European Product Liability Review*, at 28 f.

of scientific evidence, for it appoints the experts itself. Furthermore, the court cannot split the trial to decide on certain *preliminary issues* (e.g. causation) first. What the court can do, however, is focus on certain issues (e.g. causation) first, take evidence on them – and then 'discuss' the outcome with the parties. Courts may also initially take a decision on the merits, while reserving the assessment of damages until later (§304 CCP).

Each party may in certain circumstances *prior to the trial* request that the court appoint an expert to give an opinion on the cause of injury or defect[124] (§485 II CCP). This may, depending on the opinion, prompt the claimant to withdraw the claim or it may lead to a settlement. The claim for disclosure under the Drug Act can be litigated separately, prior to the damage action.

Fee arrangements and legal costs

Lawyers in Germany are not allowed to work on a 'no win – no fee' basis or to agree on contingency fees.

The losing party must generally reimburse the winner's legal fees and court costs. Fees and costs are calculated on the basis of the amount of damages claimed. To cover the costs of litigation, legal insurance is available. An uninsured claimant sues at his own risk, which increases proportionally to the amount claimed. This may prevent some claimants from claiming unrealistically high compensation amounts simply to improve their position in settlement negotiations. However, with legal insurance becoming increasingly common in Germany, this effect loses significance.

More recently companies which offer financing of claims have been emerging in Germany. This effectively operates similarly to contingency fee arrangements. The company guarantees coverage of the costs of litigation in return for a 20 to 30 per cent share of the amount of compensation realised. These companies will consider the amount of money in dispute and the claimant's prospects of success.

Class or representative actions

Class actions or similar means of bundling mass tort actions are not available under German law. In cases of serial damages, however, it is possible for one particular lawyer or firm to coordinate litigation. Mass

[124] Defect here, in the strict sense, refers to contract law, but there seems to be no reason why it should not apply to 'product liability defects' as well.

tort actions are therefore often settled out of court. Companies financing litigation have recently tried to set up a fund for group or mass tort cases to pursue the claims assigned to it.

Representative actions are not available in the areas of product liability and product safety. Although the Injunction Act 2002 *(Unterlassungsklagegesetz)* gives certain bodies the right of representative action where 'consumer protection laws' are being infringed, this Act does not apply to provisions related to product risks such as, for example, the Product Safety Act. 'Consumer protection' in this context refers to business-to-consumer practices only.[125]

[125] See the legislative intention to the Act, BT-Drucks. 14/2658 at 52–3 and Directive 98/27/EC on injunctions for the protection of consumers' interests.

7

Dutch case law on the EU Product Liability Directive

CEES C. VAN DAM

Introduction

The Dutch Act to implement the European Directive on Product Liability (PL) entered into force on 1 November 1990.[1] Since 1 January 1992 the relevant provisions can be found in art. 6:185–193 BW. According to these provisions the producer may invoke the development risk defence (art. 6:185 s. 1 sub e) but the liability of the producer is not limited (art. 16 Directive).[2]

Since the Directive had to be implemented on 30 July 1988 (art. 17 Directive), the Netherlands exceeded this term by more than two years. There are two published cases as regards damage caused by products which were put into circulation between 30 July 1988 and 1 November 1990. In one case the court (Hof Leeuwarden) explicitly interpreted Dutch law in accordance with the PL Directive.[3] In another case the Hoge Raad did not make clear whether or not it did so.[4]

In the implementation Act, the Netherlands did not provide a limitation of the liability of the producer, which would have been possible according to art. 16 of the Directive.[5] Neither did the Act derogate from Article 7(e);

[1] For an overview of Dutch Product Liability law, see I. Giesen and M. Loos, 'Liability for Defective Products and Services', in Ewoud Hondius and Carla Joustra (eds.), *Netherlands Reports to the Sixteenth International Congress of Comparative Law* (Antwerp, Oxford; New York: Intersentia 2002), pp. 75–113, also published at http://www.ejcl.org/64/art64-6.html (Electronic Journal of Comparative Law).

[2] L. Dommering-van Rongen, *Product-aansprakelijkheid. Een rechtsvergelijkend overzicht* (Deventer: Kluwer, 2000), pp. 7 ff.

[3] Hof Leeuwarden 18 March 1998, NJ 1998, 867 (Tetra Werke/Kuiper), with reference to ECJ 8 October 1987, Case 80/86, Rep. 1987, 3969 (Kolpinghuis). See about this case also para. 7 and Dommering-van Rongen, *Product-aansprakelijkheid*, p. 88.

[4] HR 24 December 1993, NJ 1994, 214 (*Leebeek v Vrumona*); see para. 4 and Dommering-van Rongen, *Product-aansprakelijkheid*, p. 14.

[5] Under the general law of damages (art. 6:109 BW), the courts have a discretionary power to mitigate the amount of damages, but only if full compensation in the given circumstances would have evident unacceptable consequences. See also HR 28 May 1999, NJ 1999, 510 (G./H.).

this provision implies that the producer can invoke the development risk defence (see also para. 2).

The previous Dutch case law with regard to product liability did not differ much from the PL Directive. In the Halcion decision the Hoge Raad held that it is unlawful (*onrechtmatig*) to put a defective product into circulation, using the same definition of defect as in art. 6 of the PL Directive.[6] However, next to the unlawfulness requirement, it had to be established that the producer knew or ought to have known of the defect and that he was able or should have been able to prevent the defect (*toerekening*). Sometimes the courts laid the burden of proof of the opposite on the producer.[7]

In cases of pure economic loss and of damage to commercial goods caused by a product (thus cases to which the Directive does not apply, see art. 9), the Hoge Raad follows a comparable path. The rule is that it is unlawful (*onrechtmatig*) to put a product into circulation that causes damage when it is used in a normal way and in accordance with its purpose.[8] In principle this implies that the producer is not liable if the damage is caused by a wrongful use of the product. This would differ from the defectiveness requirement of the Directive, which requires the producer to take into account wrongful conduct of the user of the product, at least to a certain extent. The criterion of the Hoge Raad has been criticised because it would easily establish the unlawfulness of putting cigarettes into circulation.[9] The general approach of the Hoge Raad is that it applies a kind of expectation test in order to establish unlawfulness and not a kind of risk–utility test.[10]

This implies that the main difference between the regime of the directive and that of general tort law is that the latter regime additionally requires

[6] HR 30 June 1989, NJ 1990, 652, note CJHB (Halcion); see also HR 2 February 1973, NJ 1983, 315, note HB (Leaking Hot Water Bottle) and HR 15 March 1996, NJ 1996, 435 (*Ateliers Belges Réunis v Kuijt*).

[7] Hof Amsterdam 27 June 1957, NJ 1958, 104 (*Ford v Den Ouden*); Hof Den Bosch 18 January 1995, TvC 1995, 207 (*W. v Hero*); Hof Amsterdam 27 August 1998, VR 1999, 67 (*Steifensand v Vos*). See however also Rb. Breda 11 November 1969, NJ 1971, 427 (*Hendriks v Weco*).

[8] HR 6 December 1996, NJ 1997, 219 (*Du Pont v Hermans*); HR 22 October 1999, NJ 2000, 159, note ARB (*Koolhaas v Rockwool*); HR 22 September 2000, NJ 2000, 644 (*Vladeko v VSCI*); HR 29 November 2002, NJ 2003, 50 (*Helm v Aerts*). This rule is connected with the issue of the burden of proof: see HR 24 December 1993, NJ 1994, 214 (*Leebeek v Vrumona*), about which para. 4.

[9] A. R. Bloembergen, note under HR 22 October 1999, NJ 2000, 159 (*Koolhaas v Rockwool*).

[10] Giesen and Loos, 'Liability for Defective Products and Services', para. 2.2; Dommering-van Rongen, *Product-aansprakelijkheid*, p. 32.

that the unlawful act can be attributed to the producer (*toerekening*). This is the case if the producer knew or ought to have known about the defect and if he had been able or ought to have been able to prevent it. The courts have interpreted this requirement in a restricted way. Generally, the establishment of unlawfulness leads to the factual presumption of *toerekening* and it is up to the producer to prove that he could not have known or prevented the defect.[11]

In cases in which the damage occurs many years after the product has been put on the market, the claim of the victim can be extinguished according to art. 11 of the Directive. This provision holds that the rights of the injured person shall be extinguished upon the expiry of a period of ten years from the date on which the producer put into circulation the actual product which caused the damage. In these kinds of cases the victim has to take refuge in general tort law, which provides longer limitation periods. According to art. 3:310 al. 1 BW a claim for damages expires five years after the victim became aware of both the damage and the person responsible. In any case the claim expires twenty years after the event that gave rise to liability. If the damage is caused by a dangerous substance (for instance a poisonous fluid leaking from a defective tank) this term is extended to thirty years (art. 3:310 al. 2).

By the end of 2002 not more than six cases which were directly or indirectly related to the Directive were published. In the following paragraphs these decisions will be briefly analysed.

Defect and development risk defence

This case, which has been quoted in the English NBA case,[12] was about a claimant who, during heart surgery, received HIV-infected blood.[13] It was assumed that the blood had been given by a donor who had only just contracted HIV, such that his infection could not be detected by a test during what has been called 'the window period'. The first question to be

[11] See the case law mentioned in note 8 and furthermore I. Giesen, *Bewijs en aansprakelijkheid* (2001), pp. 232–3, who points out that it is not clear whether the courts in these cases decide that there is a reversal of the burden of proof, a factual presumption of *toerekening* or an obligation for the producer to provide the victim with information in order to enable him to prove his claim.

[12] *A v National Blood Authority* [2001] 3 All ER 289.

[13] Rb. Amsterdam 3 February 1999, NJ 1999, 621 (HIV-Contaminated Blood). See also the critical comments of Dommering-van Rongen, *Product-aansprakelijkheid*, p. 40 and pp. 114–15.

answered was what the claimant was entitled to expect with regard to the safety of the donor blood as provided in art. 6. The District Court agreed with the claimant that, '. . . taking into account the vital importance of blood products and that in principle there is no alternative, the general public expects and is entitled to expect that blood products in the Netherlands have been 100 per cent HIV-free for some time. The fact that there is a small chance that HIV could be transmitted via a blood transfusion, which the Foundation (defendant) estimates at one in a million, is in the opinion of the Court not general knowledge. It cannot therefore be said that the public does not or cannot be expected to have this expectation.'[14]

This decision in which the Court considered the blood product to be defective is in accordance with the English decision in the NBA case[15] and the decision of the German Bundesgerichtshof in the Exploding Mineral Water Bottle case. The expectation of the public is not to be related to the statistical expectations (which would imply that safety expectation lies under 100 per cent) but to the legitimate individual expectation (which implies that safety expectation is 100 per cent).

As has been stated by Rogers: 'the public had been generally aware of the risk of untraced infected samples of blood, the individual user was entitled to expect that his bag of blood was infection-free and was not to be taken to be participating in a form of Russian roulette'.[16] This implies that an announcement to the general public about the small risk caused by blood products would not alter the fact that the individual user is entitled to expect 100 per cent safety. Therefore, it might be concluded that the courts, when establishing the defect of a product, are only allowed to take into consideration safety information which is communicated to the individual user.

The second decision of the court concerned the interpretation of art. 7(e) of the Directive (regarding the development risk defence). The court decided that this defence does not apply only to the knowledge of the risk but also to the avoidability of it. Since in this case it was scientifically impossible to detect the HIV contamination during the so-called window period, the court rejected the claim of the patient. In the English NBA case[17] and the German Mineral Water Bottle case it was held that

[14] Translation derived from *A v National Blood Authority* [2001] 3 All ER 289, nr. 44 iii.

[15] *A v National Blood Authority* [2001] 3 All ER 289.

[16] *Winfield and Jolowicz on Tort* (London: Sweet and Maxwell, 2002) 358, with reference to *Richardson v LRC* [2000] PIQR P164 (at [65]).

[17] *A v National Blood Authority* [2001] 3 All ER 289.

the development risks defence only applies to the fact whether the risk could be known, not whether it could be avoided. The latter view can be considered to be the right one. This means that the Amsterdam District Court wrongly dismissed the claim of the patient.

Presentation of the product and expected use

Art. 6 holds that a product is defective when it does not provide the safety which a person is entitled to expect, taking all circumstances into account, including the presentation of the product and the use to which it could reasonably be expected that the product would be put.

This provision had to be applied in a case concerning a sixteen-year-old girl, who inserted a mini tampon in a wrong way: she inserted it in the urethra and not in the vagina. She only succeeded in doing so after, following advice from her mother, she had put vaseline on the tampon. After the insertion she could not get the tampon out and surgery was necessary. The girl suffered damage and held the producer of the mini tampon liable.

The court dismissed her claim. Firstly, it decided that the instructions for use were clear enough, even for those using the product for the first time. Secondly, it deemed the design of the tampon not to be defective, because it was only possible to insert it incorrectly with a lot of effort and pain (and vaseline).[18]

Proof of the defect

The peculiar feature in the Dutch product liability case about a lemonade bottle was not that it exploded but that the top of the bottle broke off.[19] This happened when the barman in the canteen of a football club tried to

[18] Rb. Zwolle 24 April 2002, Praktijkgids 2002, 5921 (*X v Johnson and Johnson*).

[19] HR 24 December 1993, NJ 1994, 214 (*Leebeek v Vrumona*), about which also Dommering-van Rongen, *Product-aansprakelijkheid*, p. 14. See also Hof Leeuwarden 21 December 1994, TvC 1995, p. 122: a cyclist suffered damage when the fork of his bike broke. After investigation of the fork, the producer destroyed or mislaid it. The court considered that this fact had to be taken into account to the detriment of the producer as regards the burden of proof of the defect. The court accepted the statement of the cyclist with regard to the place of the crack and with that the cause of the defect. An opposite decision can be found in Hof Amsterdam 27 August 1998, VR 1999, 67 (deskchair): soon after a deskchair broke it was welded by the employer of the victim; for that reason the court put the burden of proof of the defect on the victim.

open it. The barman was injured and held the producer of the lemonade bottle liable.

The accident took place in the autumn of 1988, a few months after the EC Directive had to be implemented in Dutch law. As has been mentioned, the implementation Act entered into force more than two years later. This implied that the Dutch court was obliged to interpret Dutch law in accordance with the Directive. If the Dutch Hoge Raad did so, then it did so by implication only.

The key issue in this case was the burden of proof of the defect, because the producer denied that the bottle was defective and argued that it was likely that the bottle had broken owing to another cause, probably that of using too much force.

Article 4 of the Directive holds that the injured person has to prove the defect. It is clear that he could not prove the defect by simply showing the broken bottle, since the bottle could also have been broken because of wrongful conduct of the barman. On the other hand it would be too burdensome to oblige the barman to prove the defect of the bottle itself, since this is in practice hardly possible. The Dutch Hoge Raad took an intermediate view and decided that if the barman could prove that he had opened the bottle in a normal fashion, this would lead to the factual presumption that the damage had been caused by a defect of the bottle. It was then up to the producer to rebut this presumption and to prove that the bottle was nevertheless not defective.[20] This decision can be seen as an application of the *res ipsa loquitur* rule, a rule which is also applied in other European legal systems.

Proof of causal relationship between defect and damage

The injured person has to prove the causal relationship between the defect and the damage (art. 4). This can be illustrated by the following decision.[21] Ms Boerman bought an ice-cream at Alberto's Snackcounter. It was a Jive ice-cream, produced and pre-packed by Motta. After eating the ice-cream Ms Boerman was thought to have contracted paratyphus. She suffered damage for which she held Alberto liable. Alberto was not the producer

[20] In accordance with the regime of the PL Directive, the Hoge Raad furthermore decided that the producer had to prove that the defect did not exist when it was put into circulation (cp. art. 7 sub b), that the defect could not have been discovered at an earlier date (cp. art. 7 sub e) and that the product was not used in accordance with its intended use (art. 6 al. 1 sub b).

[21] Ktg. Zwolle 4 July and 5 December 2000, Praktijkgids 2001, 5699 (*Boerman v Alberto*).

of the ice-cream, so this is not a genuine product liability case but, as I will point out, the causation issue that was raised could also have arisen in a claim against the producer.

Experts had concluded that a number of ice-creams which were sold by Alberto were contaminated with salmonella. The court deemed it beyond reasonable doubt that Ms Boerman had bought one of these contaminated ice-creams. This was sufficient to conclude that there was a breach of contract by Alberto. But was there also a causal connection between this breach of contract and the damage to Ms Boerman? Paratyphus can be caused by the salmonella microbe, more specifically by the salmonella paratyphi. In this case there is an incubation period of seven to twenty days and Ms Boerman got ill only two days after eating the ice-cream. The salmonella enteritidis has a shorter incubation period and can cause the same symptoms. This microbe was also found in the contaminated ice-creams. However, the hospital had diagnosed that Ms Boerman was infected by a salmonella microbe but it had not made a more specific diagnosis. So, although it was likely that Ms Boerman had got ill as a consequence of eating the ice-cream from Alberto, this was not beyond doubt. Who had to bear the risk of this uncertainty? In accordance with the case law of the Dutch Hoge Raad, the Court decided that it was up to Alberto to prove that Ms Boerman would have suffered the same damage if she had not eaten the ice-cream.

The judge referred to the so-called 'reversal rule' of the Hoge Raad. This rule determines under which circumstances the burden of proof regarding causation can be reversed.[22] The plaintiff has to prove which risk has been created by the defendant and that specifically that risk has materialised.[23] If these requirements are met, the burden of proof with regard to causation will be reversed. This means that the defendant has to prove that there is no causal connection between the breach of duty and the damage. This reversal rule does not apply if the facts of the case are unclear or if it is not plausible or likely that the claimed damage has been caused by the breach of duty.[24] With these decisions the Hoge Raad has narrowed the scope of the reversal rule substantially.

[22] See about this so-called 'omkeringsregel': HR 26 January 1996, NJ 1996, 607, note WMK (Dicky Trading II); HR 16 June 2000, NJ 2000, 584, note CJHB (Sint Willibrord); C.C. van Dam, Aansprakelijkheidsrecht (DenHaag: Boom, 2000), nr. 810; I. Giesen, *Bewijs en aansprakelijkheid* (2001), p. 116 ff.

[23] HR 19 January 2001, NJ 2001, 524, note JBMV (*Ter Hofte v Oude Monnik Motors*).

[24] HR 29 November 2002, RvdW 2002, 190 (TFS/NS); HR 29 November 2002, RvdW 2002, 191 (*Kastelijn v Achtkarspelen*).

Up till now, the rule has not been applied in (genuine) product liability cases.

This reversal of the burden of proof resembles the so-called *McGhee*-test of Lord Wilberforce. He said: 'It is a sound principle that where a person has, by breach of duty of care, created a risk, and injury occurs within the area of that risk, the loss should be borne by him unless he shows that it had some other cause.'[25] As a general rule this statement has been rejected as demonstrated in *Wilsher*,[26] although in the *Fairchild* case the rule was applied with regard to liability for indivisible diseases.[27]

A comparable rule applies in German law with regard to the so-called *Verkehrspflichten* (duties of care). The rule holds that if the damage falls within the scope of protection of the duty of care, there is a rebuttable presumption that there is causation between the breach of duty and the damage (*Anscheinsbeweis*).

So, although the concept of rebuttable presumption is well known, the question is whether (and if so, how) this concept will be applied in cases of product liability to which the Directive is applicable. In most legal systems the courts are also entitled to shift the burden of proof from the plaintiff to the defendant. This is not a rule but an option open to the courts to use in the established circumstances of the case. In Dutch law this follows from art. 150 Civil Procedure Act (Wetboek van Burgerlijke Rechtsvordering).

Information about the identity of producer or importer

Mohammed Al Kholali bought an electric cooker in an 'It's' shop. When he used this cooker at home a fire broke out. It was assumed that this fire had been caused by a defect in the electric parts of the cooker. The plaintiff, who did not have fire insurance, held 'It's' liable for the damage. Initially 'It's' acknowledged liability but three weeks later denied it and referred the plaintiff to the importer of the cooker.

The decision of the President of the District Court of Breda[28] focused on the application of art. 3(3) of the Directive (art. 6:187 al. 4). This provision holds: 'Where the producer of the product cannot be identified, each supplier of the product shall be treated as its producer unless he

[25] Lord Wilberforce in *McGhee v National Coal Board* [1973] 1 WLR 1 (HL).

[26] *Wilsher v Essex Area Health Authority* [1988] AC 1074 (HL).

[27] *Fairchild v Glenhaven Funeral Services Ltd* [2002] 3 All ER 305.

[28] Pres. Rb. Breda 8 December 2000, KG 2001, 28 (*Al Kholali v It's Electronic*).

informs the injured person, within a reasonable time, of the identity of the producer or of the person who supplied him with the product.'

The President of the Court decided that the withdrawal of the acknowledgment could be considered as a justified use of the reasonable time mentioned in this provision and dismissed the claim against the supplier. As a consequence of this the plaintiff had to hold the importer liable for the damage but he was bankrupt. The plaintiff argued that application of art. 3(3) of the Directive in this case was not reasonable on three grounds: the importer was bankrupt, 'It's' was a big nationwide chain of shops and the plaintiff did not have fire insurance. The President of the Court rejected these arguments because they were irrelevant in the context of the Directive.

Putting a product into circulation

Kuiper bought a (refill) CO_2 capsule from the Dutch importer of a German producer (Tetra Werke). The capsule was intended to be used in a CO_2-system which was also brought onto the market by Tetra Werke. Kuiper suffered damage and held Tetra Werke liable. The question was raised whether the producer had put the capsule into circulation. The court held that this was the case since Tetra Werke had passed the capsule on in the chain of distribution.[29]

The position of the supplier

Closely related to the issue of product liability is the position of the supplier. Someone who suffers damage from a defective product that he has bought himself can also hold the supplier liable, in particular if the latter did not waive his liability (successfully).[30]

In a landmark case, the Dutch Hoge Raad gave a clear answer to this question. The case was about a nursery that had bought a fertiliser which appeared to be contaminated. It was established that the purchased fertiliser did not have the qualities the purchaser was entitled to expect on

[29] Hof Leeuwarden 18 March 1998, NJ 1998, 867 (*Tetra Werke v Kuiper*); see about this case also para. 1 and Dommering-van Rongen, *Product-aansprakelijkheid*, p. 88.

[30] The supplier can avoid liability under the Directive by providing information about the identity of the producer (art. 3 al. 3) but this does not affect his contractual liability as a supplier. In the present case the District Court and the Court of Appeal had decided that the supplier did not provide the purchaser with a copy of his general contract terms. For that reason they were not applicable to this case (art. 6:233 BW).

the basis of the contract (art. 7:17 BW). The issue to be decided by the Hoge Raad was whether it was required that the supplier knew or ought to have known about the contamination, and, more generally, about the defect of the sold product. The Hoge Raad decided that it was irrelevant whether the supplier had known or ought to have known about the defect. The court added that, in very special circumstances, the decision could be different but it did not point out what kind of special circumstances it aimed at.[31]

This case was about a kind of damage to which the Directive does not apply: the defective product intended for private use or consumption did not cause damage to a person or to property (art. 9). If this had been the case, the position of the supplier would have been different. Art. 7:24 al. 2 BW holds that if a good is sold by a professional to a consumer and the defect falls under the scope of art. 185 ff. BW, the producer is solely liable. This means that in these cases the liability for defective products in the sense of the Directive is channelled exclusively to the producer. However, the supplier is liable if he knew or ought to have known of the defect, if he guaranteed the absence of the defect, or if the claim concerned material damage under the amount of €500. This statutory provision implies and the above-mentioned case shows that a professional-buyer is better protected than a consumer-buyer.[32]

The DES-case: proof of causation

The DES case of the Dutch Hoge Raad has gained international attention.[33] The case was referred to in the *Fairchild* decision of the House of Lords, mainly because it is aptly described in Walter van Gerven's casebook on tort law.[34]

The case concerned the liability of a large number of producers that could have caused injury to a large number of plaintiffs, by putting a defective product on the market. The defective product was DES, a medicine destined to protect against premature birth, which was taken by pregnant

[31] HR 27 April 2001, NJ 2002, 213, note JH (*Oerlemans v Driessen*).

[32] For this reason art. 7:24 al. 2 has been criticised: see Asser-Hijma, *Koop en ruil*, 6th edn, Deventer: Tjeenk Willink, 2001, nr. 445; Dommering-van Rongen, *Productaansprakelijkheid*, pp. 93–4.

[33] Hoge Raad 9 October 1992, NJ 1994, 535, note CJHB (*DES v Daughters*).

[34] *Fairchild v Glenhaven Funeral Services Ltd* [2002] 3 All ER 305; Walter van Gerven, Jeremy Lever and Pierre Larouche, *Cases, Materials and Texts on National, Supranational and International Tort Law* (Oxford: Hart, 2000), pp. 447–52.

women during pregnancy, mainly in the forties, fifties and the beginning of the sixties of the last century. Children of these mothers appeared to suffer from fertility problems and daughters had a high risk of cervical cancer.

Since pharmacists were also allowed to produce DES, there were numerous producers and the so-called DES-daughters could not prove from which producer they had obtained DES.

The Directive of course did not apply to this case. Before the Hoge Raad the question of unlawfulness was left aside and the decision focussed on the causation issue. The Hoge Raad applied art. 6:99 BW, which holds: 'Where the damage may have resulted from two or more events for each of which a different person is liable, and where it has been determined that the damage has arisen from at least one of these events, the obligation to repair the damage rests upon each of these persons, unless he proves that the damage is not the result of the event for which he himself is liable.'

The court decided that this provision does not require that the plaintiff identifies and summons all possible liable persons. The provision would apply if the plaintiff proves that (a) the summoned producers had put DES into circulation in the relevant period and that they were liable for doing so; (b) that other producers also had put DES into circulation in the relevant period and that they were also liable for doing so; (c) that the plaintiff has suffered damage as a consequence of using DES but that it can not be established from which producer the used DES was obtained.

If these requirements are met, the summoned parties are jointly liable, unless this would be unacceptable from a reasonableness point of view given the circumstances. A relevant factor is the probability of the chance that the damage of the victim is caused by an event for which no liable person can be determined.[35]

The decision has caused mixed reactions. There was understanding for the attempt to help the victims out of the evidentiary quagmire. Some commentators had less understanding for the consequence of the decision that the producer can possibly be liable for a larger amount of damage than that which he could have caused. This downside of the decision could have been prevented by choosing a way of market-share liability.[36] However, the

[35] HR 9 October 1992, NJ 1994, 535, note CJHB (Des). See for an overview of Dutch articles on this decision: Van Gerven, Lever and Larouche, *Cases*, p. 227. See also Giesen and Loos, 'Liability for Defective Products', para. 4.2.

[36] Advocate-General Hartkamp argued in favour of this solution in his Conclusion (advice) before the decision, nr. 12–15, following the decision of the Supreme Court of California in *Sindell v Abbott Laboratories* 607 P.2d 924 (1980), which was also a case about the liability of the producers of DES.

Hoge Raad considered that this would have another downside: market-share liability would wrongly put the risk of insolvency of the producer on the victims.[37]

Conclusion

The small number of decisions suggests that producers, importers, national agents and their liability insurers are inclined to settle product liability claims out of court, in order to prevent the development of case law by the courts.[38] They might fear that case law will tend to be favourable to consumers and that as a consequence of this the floodgates of claims will be opened. A closer look at the cases also shows, however, that four out of five genuine cases under the Directive date from 1998 or later. Perhaps this is an illustration of the trend that the number of claims against producers is increasing.

[37] However, if the causal connections had been known, the victim could also have been confronted with an insolvent defendant; see W. E. J. Akkermans, *Proportionele aansprakelijkheid bij onzeker causaal verband* (Tilburg: Tjeenk Willink, 1997), pp. 362 ff.

[38] J. Spier, *De uitdijende reikwijdte van de aansprakelijkheid uit onrechtmatige daad* (1996) 237; see also Report from the Commission on the Application of Directive 85/374 on Liability for Defective Products, COM (2000) 893 final, p. 10: according to German and Dutch insurers 90 per cent of the claims are settled out of court. See, further, Giesen and Loos, 'Liability for Defective Products', para. 6.1.

8

Defect in English law – lessons for the harmonisation of European product liability

GERAINT HOWELLS

Comparative law in the courtroom

Comparative law has figured prominently in recent high profile English tort cases;[1] none more so than in the judgment of Mr Justice Burton in *A v National Blood Authority*.[2] This was particularly striking for it was a first instance decision and might signify that comparative law in the future will not be the sole preserve of the appellate courts. Admittedly it was an important case and a decision of a High Court judge.[3] Comparative law will probably not be cited too frequently in fast track cases in the county court. Nevertheless it is something practitioners may have to grapple with more often than they might have anticipated a decade ago. Burton J's analysis was also unique because of its extensive analysis of academic literature, both from England and other jurisdictions. The striking feature of the judge's use of comparative law was the impression one gained that he really did use comparative law. It was not merely added on to the reasoning, or used to support a conclusion. The judge seemed genuinely to be looking for guidance from the comparative sources.

A combination of factors might explain the use of comparative law in this way. The case concerned the application of Part I, Consumer Protection Act 1987, which implemented the European Product Liability Directive. Thus the way the European Court of Justice (ECJ) and courts in other Member States had interpreted the Directive might have special

[1] See Lord Goff's cameo discussion of German law in *White v Jones* [1995] 1 All ER 691 and the extensive use of comparative law to embolden the judges in *Fairchild v Glenhaven Funeral Services* [2003] 1 AC 32 to impose liability on tortfeasors, where it was impossible to determine which one had caused the harm.

[2] [2001] 3 All ER 289. For an analysis of this case by the present author see G. Howells and M. Mildred, 'Infected Blood: Defect and Discoverability: a First Exposition of the EC Product Liability Directive' 65 (2002) *Modern Law Review*: 95.

[3] For further discussion of the use of comparative law in this case, see chapter 2.

relevance. There was also a paucity of national case law to guide the judge. Few cases had been decided under the new law and the judge was keen to differentiate the new strict liability rules from negligence. Thus, of necessity, the judge was forced to seek inspiration from elsewhere.

However, the use of European and comparative law in this way should also be applauded for assisting in the harmonious application of EC law across Europe. National judges respecting the supremacy of European law should help ensure consistent application within the Member States. Indeed, Burton J took guidance from the ECJ's decision on the development risks defence in *Commission v United Kingdom*;[4] although he is not uncritical of the decision and indeed perhaps interpreted it with an overly pro-claimant gloss.

With regard to the supremacy of European legislation, Burton J is, if anything, arguably too willing to acknowledge the supremacy of the Directive for he simply disregarded the Act and applied the Directive. The problem therein perhaps lies more with the EU's approach to directives than with the judge. Directives had originally been intended to give Member States a certain latitude in implementation, but subsequent developments have limited that discretion markedly. This perhaps leads into broader debates about the degree of harmonisation that is necessary. We cannot tackle that large agenda here, but it is relevant for, as we shall see, there are differences not only in the substantive law, but also the way it is practically applied and the EU needs to consider whether or not such differences are matters for concern.

However, Burton J's judgment perhaps demonstrates another form of judicial co-operation that is needed to ensure the smooth implementation of directives. That is the need for national judges to be open to bilateral influences from other jurisdictions. Burton J was very willing to study other jurisdictions' case law, even when he disagreed with it. Indeed the fact that he sometimes disagreed with judgments in other jurisdictions has important lessons for the development of European law. This must mean that the application of the law is uneven across Europe. Cases do not always reach the ECJ; either because the litigation does not advance that far – the National Blood case was not appealed – or as in the German mineral water bottle case[5] the German Supreme Court took the rather dubious view that the answer was so obvious that no reference was necessary. Europe needs to consider whether these differences at the level of application are

[4] C-300/95 [1997] ECR I–2649. [5] [1995] NJW 2162.

problematic. If they are considered problematic, ways should be found to address them.

At the British Institute of International and Comparative Law conference the present author floated the idea that there should be a database of European product liability case law.[6] He had in mind a mechanism for assisting lawyers seeking guidance on interpretation where there was no ECJ jurisprudence and little national case law. Such a database might also highlight instances of application and the Commission would be able to consider whether legislative intervention was desirable.

The inspiration for the database proposal came from the CLAB database the Commission has established for unfair terms.[7] A product liability database might be of even greater practical application, for where there is national case law – as there is in abundance in relation to unfair terms – lawyers may well be content to seek guidance from it rather than look further afield. However, the CLAB database might nevertheless be invaluable in drawing attention to divergent approaches.

Strict liability is different from negligence

There has only been limited case law in the United Kingdom on the strict liability provisions. We will concentrate on the case law dealing with the central concept of defectiveness and the related development risks defence.[8] One of the important features to emerge from the recent case law is the judicial willingness to accept that strict liability is – in practice as well as theory – a different standard from negligence.

In *Abouzaid v Mothercare*[9] the Court of Appeal imposed strict liability for a defective 'Cosytoes' fleece liner whose metal buckle had injured a child attempting to affix it to his sibling's pram. The Court stressed that there was no liability in negligence.

Much of what follows will be based on the judgment of Burton J in the *National Blood* case. The National Blood Authority were found liable for

[6] *Product Liability in Comparative Perspective*, held at the Institute on Thursday 30 January 2003.

[7] http://europa.eu.int/clab/: see H. Micklitz and M. Radeideh, 'CLAB Europa – Die Europäische Datenbank missbräuchlicher Klauseln in Verbraucherverträgen' [2003] *ZEuP*: 85.

[8] Other cases have dealt with who is a producer (*Relph v Yamaha*, 5 July 1996); limitations (*Smithkline Beecham v Horne-Roberts* [2002] 1 WLR); and causation (*XYZ and others v Schering Health Care Ltd* [2002] All ER 437).

[9] [2000] All ER (D) 2436.

supplying blood infected with hepatitis C, despite there being no means of detecting such contamination at the time of supply. An understanding of that judgment requires an appreciation of the judge's concern to differentiate strict liability from negligence. This was in the face of much academic criticism that strict liability was at best a form of super-negligence and was really little different from negligence when the challenge was related to the product's design. Jane Stapleton was at the forefront of academic analysis downplaying strict liability.[10] Indeed such pessimism seemed justified given the wording of the law and the extra-judicial comments of a Law Lord that some kind of risk–utility balancing would have to be undertaken.[11] It seemed that the expectations of consumers on which the defectiveness standard was based would be no more than that a producer would do what was reasonable. Mr Justice Burton was keen to counter such pessimism.

In truth the defectiveness standard was so open-textured and the rationale behind the Directive so opaque that almost any gloss could be given to them. It is to Mr Justice Burton's credit that he did not simply adopt the pessimistic approach, which was being reinforced by developments in the US where the *Third Restatement of Torts: Product Liability* was effectively restricting strict liability to manufacturing defects. However, the lack of material from which to build a theory of strict liability both afforded the judge the opportunity to be creative and also exposed him to criticism. This is inevitable, for he was attempting to create policy by way of explanation of concepts whose creators had not explained their function adequately or even adopted a structure that was internally coherent.

Traditionally it has been argued that negligence was concerned with producer conduct and strict liability with the condition of the product. It will be argued that this approach may be wrong, if the reference to condition requires a finding of a physical defect. Liability certainly extends to defects arising from expectations, which might have been inflated by marketing and labelling. It will be argued that the enduring legacy of Burton J's judgment should be the ability to take account of general perceptions of safety that are reasonably held. Breach of this legitimate expectation is not proof of a defect, rather it is the actual defect itself. This abstract approach may not endear itself to practitioners. Where there is no physical defect it may be harder to convince people of the justice of imposing

[10] Her major work in this field is *Product Liability* (1994).

[11] Lord Griffith, P. Val and R. Dorner, 'Developments in English Product Liability Law: a Comparison with the American System' (1988) 62 *Tul LR*: 353.

liability. Indeed even Burton J was keen to analyse the facts in such a way as to suggest a physical defect. Yet it will be argued that the abstract approach is the better way to interpret the judge's decision and provides an opportunity for reconciling divergent approaches to the application of the defectiveness standard across Europe.

General standard

> Art. 6(1) provides that:
>
> 'A product is defective when it does not provide the safety which a person is entitled to expect, taking all circumstances into account, including:
>
> a. the presentation of the product;
> b. the use to which it could reasonably be expected that the product would be put;
> c. the time when the product was put into circulation.'

Central to any discussion of how English law deals with defectiveness is the approach of Burton J in the *National Blood* case. He accepted that this was a consumer expectation rather than risk–utility standard, although the term 'legitimate expectations' was preferred to 'entitled expectations'. Burton J adopted the reasoning of Bartl, a German author, that the judge was 'an informed representative of the public at large'.[12] The legitimate expectations could be higher or lower than the actual expectations of the public and indeed had to be determined even where the public had no expectations, for example, in the case of a new product. The judge acts as a reflector of community standards and performs the role of a jury in the US. Later it will be commented that English judges when performing this function of applying the law feel the need to give more detailed reasons than some of their continental counterparts. This may help explain some continuing differences in the practice of product liability between the Member States.

Products may fail to satisfy legitimate expectations for a number of reasons. Some of these may relate to the condition of the product: it may be a 'lemon' because of a manufacturing error, use of poor quality materials or due to contamination. Alternatively poor instructions or lack of warnings could defeat safety expectations. Equally the public might have expected an alternative design, which contained fewer risks. However, so long as the expectations of safety are legitimate (query to what extent

[12] See H. Bartl, *Produkthaftung nach neuem EG-Recht* (Landsberg: Lech, 1989).

reasonableness is relevant?) then a product which fails to meet that standard of safety should result in liability. There should be no need to prove why it did not meet those safety expectations. This should be the feature that distinguishes strict liability from negligence. The defect is the failure to meet legitimate expectations. Failure to meet these expectations is not merely evidence of a defect: it is the defect.

Of course it also has to be borne in mind that the defectiveness standard is only intended to set minimum standards. Liability will not attach merely because harm could have been avoided by taking additional safety precautions. The question is whether the product affords appropriate levels of safety. However, to prevent a finding of defectiveness any risks must be socially acceptable. The object of the law is not to force all products to have the highest safety standards, merely to make them acceptably safe.

Relevant factors

Burton J believed the strict liability standard was intended to be different from negligence. One way he underlined this was by deciding that 'all the circumstances' meant all relevant circumstances and that the directive had singled out the most significant. Others might be relevant, but avoidability of risk was not one and if it had been intended to be one then it would have been mentioned. This was certainly a brave decision given that the directive referred to *all* circumstances.[13] It can be supported on the basis that to introduce such considerations might in the wrong judicial hands reintroduce the fault concept too easily. However, the exclusion of such factors could be seen as going against the role of judge as juror outlined above. In some cases the avoidability of harm might weigh heavily in the calculus; in others, such as probably *National Blood*, the fact the public had not been informed of that unavoidability might mean it should be discounted.

Non-standard products

Burton J was keen to distance himself from the American terminology of manufacturing, design and instruction defects. This seems correct for,

[13] For criticism see C. Hodges, 'Compensating Patients' 117 (2001) *LQR*: 528 and R. Goldberg, 'Paying for Bad Blood: Strict Product Liability after the Hepatitis C Litigation' 10 (2002) *Med L Rev*: 165.

whilst these concepts can be useful heuristic tools, they have been corrupted in the Third Restatement in order only to apply strict liability to manufacturing defects. Indeed the distinctions between the categories are in reality by no means clear. However, Burton J then went on to create his own distinction between *standard* and *non-standard* products. *Standard* products perform as the producer intended, *non-standard* products are deficient or inferior in safety terms because of a harmful characteristic or characteristics.

It is perhaps understandable why the judge adopted this approach. He was going out on a limb and being able to label the infected bags of blood as non-standard made his task easier. However, what is the non-standard product? The judge described as 'too philosophical' the argument that all the bags of blood were equally defective because they contained a risk of infection. It was more comfortable for him to decide on the basis that the infected bags of blood were the non-standard product. Once the harmful characteristic was identified then, as the judge himself said, 'a decision that it is defective is likely to be straightforward'.

However, this approach seems to be assisted too much by the benefit of hindsight. Moreover, it does not fit in with the judge's own reasons for imposing liability. The mere fact of infection did not seem to be enough; it was the fact that the public had not been warned of that danger that seemed decisive. Even if the judge was careful to leave open the issue of whether the blood would have been defective even with adequate warnings, it is hard to conceive that a judge would hold blood to be defective when it was as safe as it could be and the public had been fully warned of inherent risks. Thus the way public expectations of safety had been defeated must have been in reality because they had not been informed of the risk. Damage (the prerequisite for any legal action) would only be suffered by those unfortunate enough to be given infected blood, but all the bags of blood did not offer the safety it was legitimate to expect and hence were defective. People could not expect blood free of infection, as that was impossible to obtain. What they could expect was to be told of the risk so that they could decide whether to face such a risk. The same outcome could have been achieved without drawing the standard/non-standard distinction. One suspects it was a useful psychological crutch for the judge to be able to point to some physical contamination as the defect. However, it does not sit easily with his analysis of why the legitimate expectations had been defeated. Also, as discussed below, the need to identify a physical defect does have serious implications for cases where products may have a potential to cause harm, but the risk has not yet materialised.

Warnings

Although the judgment of Burton J was rightly seen as an important victory for claimants and a signal that strict liability was indeed stricter than negligence, nevertheless doubts must remain about the extent to which it will help claimants in the future. The key factor determining liability seemed to be that the National Blood Authority had not taken steps to inform the public of the risks. His very first conclusion was that the risk had not become socially acceptable. Although the judge was careful not to decide how the case would have been decided had the public been informed, it seems inconceivable that liability would have been imposed in such circumstances.

An important message from the case is that it is not sufficient that the medical profession be informed,[14] the public also has to be made aware of the knowledge. This leads to difficult questions about what steps producers should take to bring risks to the public's attention, especially in cases where the product is not supplied directly to them. Despite one's best efforts it will be hard not to talk about this issue in any terms other than reasonableness of conduct. The fact there had been little effort to engage with the public made the judge's task easier in the instant case. In many cases it might turn upon how many news reports of the risk can be salvaged from archives. Some injured parties might then be denied liability because they were not sufficiently aware of current affairs. Much will turn upon how deep knowledge has to penetrate into society before it is considered to be acceptable. Everyone knows that knives can cut the user, but do sufficient people know of the risk of internal bleeding from aspirin for the producers not to have to specifically warn of the risk?

However, in most cases products are supplied to consumers and warnings can be provided through appropriate labelling. The question of defectiveness will then turn on whether the warning was adequate.[15] *Worsley v Tambrands Ltd*[16] was a case where the manufacturers were able to avoid liability by pointing to warnings that tampons can cause toxic shock syndrome and giving appropriate instructions for use. That case is also important for underlining the fact that defectiveness is concerned with

[14] See Hodges, 'Compensating Patients'.

[15] There may be issues related to warning overload, if too many warnings are given so as to obscure the crucial messages, but one suspects courts will be slow to impose liability on that basis.

[16] Decision of Ebsworth J in High Court, 3 December 1999.

minimum safety standards. It was not relevant that better warnings and instructions could have been given so long as the ones used met the minimum safety standards.

Burton J also noted that warnings could not exclude liability as art. 12 of the directive prohibited limitations or exclusions of liability. There is clearly a tension between warnings which manage expectations and ones which seek to exclude liability. The former are permitted, unless it is submitted they are with respect to risks which it is wholly unreasonable for the producer to expose users to. The latter are not allowed and might extend to warnings which were so general that their purpose is seen to be to avoid liability rather than give the user a genuine estimation of the risks involved.

Implications

The reasoning behind Burton J's judgment supports the abstract approach to defectiveness in so far as the key issue seemed to be not so much the condition of the product, but rather the lack of information provided about the risk of contamination. However, the judge still seemed to need to analyse the problem so that the bags with actual infected blood could be viewed as deviant from the other bags of 'pure' blood. Finding a defect in the mere risk of contamination was not sufficient. Indeed he described such an approach as 'very philosophical'. However, the fact the judge found it comforting to impose liability by relating to bags that actually were contaminated should not undermine the value of adopting an abstract approach to defectiveness.

The value of the abstract approach can be seen from how it might be applied to two earlier cases. *Richardson v LRC Products*[17] involved a condom that ruptured during intercourse and *Foster v Biosil*[18] a breast implant that leaked. Neither claimant succeeded. The result in the former case seems entirely defendable. As Kennedy J noted:

> There are no claims made by the defendants that one will never fail and no-one has ever supposed that any method of contraception intended to defeat nature will be one hundred per cent effective. This must particularly be so in the case of a condom where the product is required to a degree at least to be, in the jargon, 'user friendly'.

[17] Decision of Kennedy J in High Court, 2 February 2000.
[18] Decision of 19 April 2000, 59 BMLR 178.

Such a conclusion seems entirely in accordance with common expectations. The result in the breast implant case, however, seems far more debatable. The decision went against the claimant because the judge in that case, Cherie Booth QC, found that it was not sufficient that the product 'failed in a way which is unsafe and contrary to what persons generally might expect'. She required proof that there was a defect. Under the abstract approach, however, the product would be defective because of the mere fact the product failed in a way that defeated legitimate expectations. If the public do not reasonably expect such a safety risk then liability should ensue. Defect relates to a product which does not offer the safety legitimately expected by the public. This covers inherent risks unless they have become socially acceptable. The blood in *National Blood* could not have been made safer, but liability was still imposed. There is no need to prove how it came about that those safety expectations were defeated. To do so would impose an inordinate technical burden of proof on claimants, the overcoming of which was, as Burton J pointed out, one of the reasons for imposing strict liability.

The abstract approach would also justify the denial of liability in *Bogle v McDonald's*.[19] That involved claims alleging that McDonald's coffee was too hot. The fact that people expect coffee to be hot would, absent other circumstances, be sufficient reason for denying liability with respect to such a socially acceptable risk.

The abstract analysis also assists in resolving two other complicated issues. First, is the problem of products that have a risk of failure. This is most dramatically demonstrated in the case of heart valves whose poor manufacture means they have a higher than acceptable rate of failure. If one fails inside a patient then liability would normally ensue. More complex is the position of a patient faced with the quandary of deciding what to do with such a product, which may or may not fail on him. Under the abstract approach it should be possible to argue that the product did not offer him the safety he was entitled to expect. If he decides to keep the valve, but suffers mental anxiety amounting to a recognised psychological illness as a result, this should be compensated. Alternatively if he chooses to have the valve replaced he can be compensated for having to undergo the operation. Even if after the operation it is discovered that his valve was not faulty, compensation would still be payable as the need for the operation arose from a defect in the product, i.e. the unacceptable high risk of failure.

[19] Decision of Field J 25 March 2002 [2002] EWHC 490.

The above example might highlight some potential differences between the abstract approach to defectiveness favoured by this paper based on the logic of Burton J's approach and the possible way Burton J might in practice be predicted as likely to deal with such problems. His desire to categorise the products in which the risk materialised as non-standard products might cause him only to impose liability where an actual valve can be shown to have had a physical defect. Thus all those who chose not to have the operation, possibly because they were advised against it on health grounds, and those who suffered a second operation to discover there had been no need for it might struggle to obtain compensation. Burton J might not in those cases be willing to find a non-standard product. Liability for standard products can be imposed, but the outcome is more uncertain. Yet, the suffering of such users, in terms of anxiety or having to undergo an operation, resulted from the lack of safety in the class of products just as much as those unfortunate enough to actually have a valve that failed or would have failed. The abstract approach seems to produce a more just solution.

The abstract approach also assists with overcoming some of the evidential difficulties in this area. Under the abstract approach if a product causes harm in a way that is unexpected, then that is not evidence of defectiveness, but rather is proof of defectiveness. Products that fail to provide the level of safety that could legitimately be expected are defective *per se.* This is not a reversal of the burden of proof. It is more than that. Even if the producer could demonstrate that the product was of the best quality possible, there should still be liability if there was not common knowledge or a specific warning of a socially acceptable risk.

Application of defectiveness standard across Europe

Adopting this approach to defectiveness would also help bring English law into line with the approach that seems prevalent in Europe. Continental courts have been prepared to accept that the mere fact that a product causes harm in an unexpected way can be the basis of liability. The French national report in a recent EC Commission sponsored study of the implementation of the Directive gives two classic examples of this approach. The Court of Appeal of Toulouse had to deal with a car accident allegedly caused by defective tyres.[20] The Court relied on the tyre exploding to presume it was defective without being concerned to

[20] Decision of 7 November 2000.

identify the precise cause. A case before the Tribunal de Grande Instance in Aix-en-Provence[21] involved a glass window in a fireplace exploding in circumstances where the precise cause was unknown. In line with the abstract approach favoured in this chapter, the Court held that 'a product is defective when it does not provide the safety which a person is entitled to expect' and it was of no importance that the claimant had not proved the precise cause of the accident.

Continental judges may be freer to decide cases in what might, to common law eyes, appear to be a rather cavalier manner. Their function is seen as merely applying the written law to the facts of the case. British judges feel more responsibility for explaining their reasoning. The abstract approach to defectiveness enables a bridge to be constructed connecting British theory to continental practice. This should help ensure the harmonious development of European law.

Development risks

Although this chapter concentrates on the interpretation of the concept of defect, some words will be said about the related issue of development risks. Indeed Burton J in the *National Blood* case commented that the existence of a restrictive development risks defence meant that it should be the only means of escape available to the producer who had done everything that could reasonably have been expected of him. Thus the existence of the defence supported excluding such considerations from the decision on defectiveness. This makes some sense if one believes there is a logic to the inclusion of the development risks defence. Elsewhere the writer has suggested the defence would be better removed and such issues dealt with in the assessment of defectiveness.[22] Burton J clearly disagrees and equally we have already seen that he would exclude all considerations of avoidability, whereas this chapter proposes considering them, but as only one of a range of factors.

It is also useful to consider how the English courts have received the ECJ decision in *Commission v United Kingdom*. The English courts have certainly not given the development risks defence the overly generous interpretation in favour of the producer that the wording of the defence

[21] Decision of 2 October 2001.

[22] G. Howells and M. Mildred, 'Is European Product Liability More Protective than the Restatement (Third) of Torts: Product Liability?' 65 (1998) *Tennessee Law Review*: 985–1030.

in section 4(1)(e) of the Consumer Protection Act 1987 might suggest. Although no factual situation has yet tested it to the full, Burton J in *National Blood* endorsed the reasoning of the ECJ, although some might find it surprising that he was able to give such a pro-claimant gloss to a decision which was in essence a victory for producer interests.

The ECJ decision left the ambiguously worded UK version in place and introduced a requirement that the state of scientific and technical knowledge must have been accessible to the producer before it would defeat his defence. The example quoted by the Advocate-General was of an article published in a Manchurian journal, which European companies might not be expected to have knowledge of. Burton J was more sophisticated in his analysis, pointing out that Manchuria might be a bad example if the product was particularly associated with that country. Nevertheless he accepted the (possibly questionable) principle that accessibility was a requirement for knowledge to defeat the defence.[23] He simply saw it as more likely to apply in more restrictive circumstances, such as to an unpublished document or research not available to the public.

The actual issue concerning the development risks defence at stake in *National Blood* was whether the defence could apply where the general risk was known, but it was not possible to identify it in any particular product. Liability had been avoided on this ground in an Australian case,[24] but Burton J did not follow that decision as it was based on a slightly differently worded provision. In imposing liability his approach was similar to that of the German Supreme Court, which had held that the development risks defence did not apply to manufacturing or 'non-standard' defects. Burton J differed from the German Supreme Court to the extent that he thought the defence could apply to such defects, but only on one occasion. Once the risk was known of, then it was outside the defence and he was clearly impressed by the Advocate-General's argument that the producer then had to take steps to protect himself by either stepping up experimentation and research investment or taking out insurance.

Thus, once a risk is known about, the development risks defence does not apply even if it is not possible to discover the defect in individual products. The defendants might view this as a harsh decision. Arguably the wording of the defence could have assisted them since it talked about knowledge enabling the *existence* of the defect to be discovered. Also the

[23] See G. Howells and M. Mildred, 'Comment on "Development Risks: Unanswered Questions"' 59 (1996) *Modern Law Review*: 570–3.

[24] *Graham Barclay Oysters Pty v Ryan*, 102 FCR 307.

producers might feel aggrieved that for the purposes of determining defectiveness the judge treated the contaminated blood as a separate category of non-standard products, but for the development risks defence not to apply it was sufficient that the presence of the risk in the generic product was known. These stances are not, however, logically inconsistent even if the defendant might be left feeling hard done by. They reinforce the view that the development risks defence will rarely succeed[25] and might hasten the day when the defence can be removed. That might assist in the development of a more coherent policy.

Currently it is hard to discern what policy lies behind the defect concept and the presence of the development risks defence merely muddies the waters. Whether the strict liability regime should impose liability where the producer has done all that can reasonably be expected of him lies at the heart of the debate and one's view on that will colour any assessment of Mr Justice Burton's decision. The directive gave little guidance. The English courts have given an indication that strict liability should be truly different from negligence, but the impact of this may be diminished by the possibility of circumventing this strict standard by the use of warnings. The judge was aware of the risk that warnings could undermine the rules against exclusion of liability, but it is hard to imagine a producer being held liable for a risk that was reasonable in the context of the product's benefits, and which had been warned of. Of course it is not possible to warn of risks which are not known about and if the development risks defence were removed such cases might be a test for how committed the legal system was to a shift from negligence to strict liability. In most cases, however, the use of warnings will undermine the strictness of the regime. Indeed one might wonder whether the courts would be as quick to impose liability for the unavoidable on a private enterprise rather than a state blood authority.

Development of European private law

Beyond the substantive law, the English product liability cases and the *National Blood* case in particular make a nice case study for the development of European private law. They illustrate the interrelationship between European and national law as well as the links between national

[25] Equally, in *Abouzaid* the defence was considered irrelevant, because the dangers from using elasticated straps were well known and it was simply that no one had applied them to that context (*Iman Abouzaid v Mothercare (UK) Ltd* (CA, 21 December 2000)).

legal systems. It shows that it is possible for a dialogue to be undertaken, but that there are also impediments to harmonisation of laws due to the practice of the courts.

The key question in practice is how easy it will be to convince courts that a product was defective. Some Member States' courts seem relaxed and willing to find so based on the mere fact that the product behaved differently from what might be expected. The English courts have seemed to require more proof of some aspect of the condition of the product that can be viewed as a defect. This chapter has argued that the concept of defect should be read as a more abstract one taking into account factors other than the product's condition. The fact a product does not provide the standard of safety legitimately expected should not merely be evidence of possible defectiveness, but should be considered as being a defect in its own right. The decision of Burton J would be in line with this approach, apart from his desire to describe the infected bags of blood as non-standard. Nevertheless this abstract approach would provide a way of reconciling the emerging case law across Europe.

PART II

European influences

9

Product liability: basic problems in a comparative law perspective

HANS CLAUDIUS TASCHNER

Product liability is the attempt to answer the question of to whom the risk of damage resulting from modern machine-guided mass production should be allocated. Should it be allocated to:

- the victim, as the price for his participation in the advantages of the industrial development, but to be borne as an inevitable Act of God,
- to the state, this means to all taxpayers in solidarity, or
- provisionally to the producer having provided the cause of damage by manufacturing a product which did not meet the safety requirements that the public at large expects – provisionally to the producer, because he alone can distribute his expenses to the rather limited group of product users by incorporating them into his sales price?

The answer to this question seems to be one of perspective: the traditionalist prefers the first choice, a citizen believing in state-organised solidarity the second, and the person devoted to state-free liberal convictions the last one. There are no other solutions than these three. One has to decide.

Good arguments exist for each of these solutions. The Product Liability Directive, issued by the Council of Ministers in 1985,[1] has opted for the third one. This has now been implemented by the fifteen EU-Member States, the ten applicant states, and seven other European states outside of the EU and followed by many non-European states in Asia, South America and by Australia, altogether by nearly forty states.

This chapter concentrates on three main problems: the kind of liability, i.e. negligence or strict liability, which includes discussion of the notion of defect, the question of whether or not a strict liability system needs limits

[1] Council Directive of 25 July 1985 on the approximation of the laws, regulations and administrative provisions of the Member States concerning liability for defective products (85/374/EEC), OJL 210 of 7 August 1985, p. 29.

as to amount, or a ceiling, and liability for the so-called 'development risks'. It follows the comparative law method.

Negligence or strict liability?

Can the problems caused by detrimental qualities of products be solved by applying negligence, or is it necessary to provide for a kind of liability which is not based on personal behaviour? Negligence is defined as the 'interference with the duty to take care', a general definition accepted by all legislations. The respect of this duty necessarily presupposes the opportunity that a person has to choose between a behaviour considered to be such an interference or abstaining from doing so. Abstaining from interfering would free the person of liability even if his activity was the cause of damage or injury to another person: a manufacturer is doing his best to avoid his product acquiring qualities which are detrimental to its users. Beyond this requirement he can not be held liable. When §2(b) chap. 1 of the Third Restatement 'Products Liability', elaborated by the American Law Institute (ALI), which compiles American law and formulates phrases like rules and paragraphs of continental law codifications, uses terms such as 'foreseeable risk of harm' to be avoided by 'adoption of a reasonable alternative design the omission of which renders the product not reasonably safe', here one finds the classical elements of negligence liability.

But this is not the problem of product liability in its proper sense. If a person foresees the 'risk of harm', if he can 'adopt a reasonable alternative design' and if he abstains from doing so, then he shall certainly be held liable. There is no question about this. No other rule is needed. One may call this a liability for products; product liability it is not. The problem lies beyond this line.

What should the law be if a manufacturer has used all available tests to control his products from first design through to the final checks, always applying the greatest of care, but unfortunately a detrimental quality has 'slipped in'? In 1956, the German Bundesgerichtshof[2] decided on the case of a person who had an accident with a new bicycle. This accident was caused by a handlebar breaking due to metal fatigue in the steel used. This metal fatigue had remained undiscovered and was practically undiscoverable. The Court denied liability, not finding any interference

[2] BGH VIZR 36/55, 'Der Betrieb' 1956, at p. 592.

with the duty to take care, and dismissed the claim: the circumstances described here should be considered as inherent in the way modern mass products are manufactured. They are rare and have to be borne by the user.

Was this decision correct?

Not all product deficiencies are of the same nature. Specific differences have led academic writers, firstly in Germany, to distinguish three categories. In the first category, those products manufactured in series, where one of these fails to correspond to what makes a product non-detrimental, are grouped. One speaks of 'manufacturing defect', as in the case just described where one bicycle was defective among thousands of others which had no steel parts with metal fatigue.

The second category consists of products in which the entire series has been designed in such a way that all products have the same deficiency. This was the case of the 1973 aircrash near Paris, where 325 passengers, mostly British, died when a DC-10 operated by Turkish Airlines came down. The rear baggage door on the plane opened outwards instead of inwards. According to the rules of physical science, this way of opening the door was a less appropriate one for the different levels of air pressure when the aeroplane was in flight. Locking the door had to be done by hand, naturally from the outside. The poorly locked door opened after take-off, the sleeves connecting the cockpit and the rudders bent due to the drop in air pressure, and the plane went out of control and crashed. One speaks of a 'design defect' because all DC-10 aeroplanes were designed in the same way.

The third and final category contains products of perfect manufacture and design, but with potentially dangerous properties in the hands of inadvertent users. Therefore, instructions need to be given to warn them of these properties. If the warning is insufficient, we speak of a 'lack of warning'.

The three categories are clearly distinguishable and are not just academic theory. They are accepted in product liability discussions in Europe and were taken over by the American Law Institute (ALI) in its Restatement.

The question arose of whether the same rule should apply in all three categories. The ALI pleads for distinguishing between them. Whereas it recognises in cases of manufacturing defects the necessity to follow the 'strict liability in tort' rule, developed in 1963 by Justice Traynor in

Greenman v Yŭba[3] in California and which spread afterwards to other state legislations in the United States, the ALI proposes to abolish this rule for design defects, returning to negligence-based liability. The definition in §2 (b) chap. 1 just quoted refers only to this category. Therefore, the actual dispute 'strict liability or negligence' centres only around this question.

Before entering this dispute, we will take a brief look at the evolution of decisions about product liability during the late nineteenth and the first half of the twentieth century. It is worthwhile noting that all cases decided in this period by European and American courts belong to the 'manufacturing defect' category: the explosion of some engines of a railroad company, 1884 French *Cour de Cassation*;[4] glass splinter in salt extracted from mineral water, 1915 German *Reichsgericht*;[5] the broken wheel of a motor vehicle, 1916 *MacPherson v Buick Motor Company* New York High Court;[6] breaking of a motor car suspension, 1925 French *Cour de Cassation*;[7] a rotten snail in a lemonade bottle, 1932 *Donoghue v Stevenson* House of Lords;[8] underwear incorrectly treated with a certain chemical product, 1936 *Grant v Australian Knitting Mills* Appellate Court London;[9] the broken handlebar of a bicycle, 1956 German *Bundesgerichtshof*;[10] contaminated serum in vaccination ampoules, 1968 'Fowlpest' German *Bundesgerichtshof*;[11] to mention only a few. The term 'design defect' was not yet invented.

In these cases, liability was denied or recognised. When it was denied, the courts could not find negligence, as in the German bicycle case. But in the cases where courts felt compelled to compensate the victim, it is interesting to read the grounds of liability. Courts come either to an extensive interpretation of negligence or, mainly in Great Britain and Germany, a reversal of the *onus probandi*, the burden of proof of fault, from claimant to defendant. Such a change in procedural rules led, in practice, to a change in material law because the person having the burden of proof would normally be unable to show proof and would lose the case. This procedural remedy, invented by the courts, shows the uneasiness of judges over traditional negligence which results in a claim being dismissed because negligence cannot be found. In Great Britain, the Appellate Court did so in the 1936 *Grant* case[12] applying the Parömia *res ipsa loquitur*, circumstances speak for themselves. In 1968, the German *Bundesgerichtshof*

[3] *Greenman v Yuba Power Products, Inc.* 59 Calif.2nd 57, 377 P 2nd 897.
[4] S.1886.1.149; D.P. 1885.1.357. [5] RGZ 87,1. [6] 217 N.Y. 282; 111 N.E. 1050.
[7] D.P. 1926.1.9. [8] [1932] AC 562. [9] [1936] AC 85.
[10] See footnote 2 above. [11] BGHZ 51, 91. [12] See footnote 9 above.

followed in the *Fowlpest* case[13] with the same pattern: if the cause of the damaging factor can only be located within the premises of the producer, his negligence is presumed. It would be unjust for the victim, said the court, to be forced to prove circumstances within the enterprise which would only allow the conclusion that the producer was negligent. The factory of the manufacturer is not accessible to him. It is therefore the defendant who must show that he did not act negligently. These half-way solutions showed the need to change the law, but they were not definite ways to reach a satisfactory result.

If the design defect is defined, as the ALI does, as 'a foreseeable risk of harm to be avoided by adoption of a reasonable alternative design the omission of which renders the product not reasonably safe', one pleads for negligence. This result will be strengthened if there is the application of the risk–utility test, developed also in the United States, to know whether a product is defective or not: the utility of the product for users, the probability of damage, economic capacity of the producer to avoid damaging qualities of his product without too heavy costs, the producer's ability to transfer his insurance costs via sales prices to the consumer and so on.

The notion of defect, which European judges are now bound by and which is based on the concept of lack of 'safety which a person', i.e. the public at large, 'is entitled to expect' (Article 6 of the Product Liability Directive), does not go into such detail. It should not be denied that one or the other of the characteristics mentioned of the risk–utility test may be of interest in evaluating the safety which the public at large legitimately expects. Certainly, clear-cut objective elements as the basis of a definition would be welcomed, but they do not exist. Whether a product is serviceable or not does not apply here. Serviceability is a term which is appropriate to be used for the law of sales. But the question here is not whether the product worked or not. The French traditional law since the end of the nineteenth century has been based on the law of sales (art. 1645 code civil), which irrebuttably presumed fault of the *vendeur professionel*, the professional vendor. This was dogmatically wrong, even if the result of this French case law is to be welcomed. The goal is to protect life and limb, and to a certain extent the property, of the product user. The corresponding notion to this requirement is safety, not utility. The term 'risk' corresponds to safety. The only question left is the degree of safety. This is a problem of social acceptance. From social acceptance,

[13] See footnote 11 above.

logically, follows expectation. This term refers to the product quality as such, not to whether or not the producer has carried out all necessary tests and taken all available precautions. Such an interpretation has to be rejected as the High Court in *A v National Blood Authority* did.[14] It would mean reintroducing negligence liability by the backdoor, as Justice Burton said.

To know whether the quality of the product in question – even a detrimental one – is socially accepted is best answered by adding the determining adverb 'legitimately': it is the *nobile officium* of judges to qualify a product as defective or not. The rear baggage door of an aeroplane with an unsafe locking system is an unacceptable quality of this plane, whereas high-percentage alcoholic beverages or tobacco are harmful qualities of the respective products, but socially accepted and therefore not defects.

The majority of the suggested characteristics of the risk–utility test are undoubtedly in favour of the producer. It is hard to accept that a producer's financial ability to bear the costs of an alternative design should be a determining factor of whether his product was defective or not. If a producer is unable to manufacture a safer product in design, then he must abstain from production.

The specific situation in cases of design defects resides in the fact that the producer developing his product creates its qualities. In design, by necessity, he has to look ahead to see what defects he must avoid, unlike manufacturing defects which he may be unable to avoid. 'Risk of harm', 'to avoid this risk by adopting an alternative design the omission of which renders his product unsafe', is an element which would allow cases falling in this category of design defects to be solved by applying negligence – under the condition that very high standards of ability and care are required from responsible engineers.

When the people of ALI have been asked how they would decide the DC-10 case applying their principles – in favour of the victims or the producer – the answer was a certain astonishment: 'Of course in favour of the victims.' This means they would not hesitate to apply very widely the negligence rule of §2 (b) of the Restatement. This shows that in practice the American legal system in force, the envisaged law reform in that country and the European Directive based legislations have all come to the same result, and thus are much closer than academic disputes would have us believe.

[14] *A v National Blood Authority* [2001] 3 All ER 289 (Burton J).

When the Product Liability Directive was drafted, there was discussion as to whether or not to differentiate between manufacturing and design defects over liability. The overwhelming opinion in the Council was not to do so. So the strict liability rule of Article 1 of the Product Liability Directive covers design defects as well. The convincing argument for doing so was that in the case of design defects as well as in manufacturing defects 'liability turns on the existence of a defect alone . . . no question of foresight of the danger arising for consideration'.[15] The other argument was to ensure legal security: a clear-cut definition of both categories is not easy. Would it not be a paradise for defence lawyers to try to bring each case under the second category in order to win the case, if negligence were allowed in design defect cases? There would no longer be manufacturing defects. Only the uniformity of applicable liability leads to the legal security needed mainly for the insurability of a producer's risk.

To sum up: there are only three conditions for a product liability claim, enumerated in Article 4 of the Product Liability Directive: damage, defect and causation. The producer's conduct is entirely unimportant. His liability is 'defect based', not 'fault based'. Foreseeability or avoidability is irrelevant. 'Defect' is an objective notion. It refers to safety, and to nothing else. The identification and qualification of the properties of a product depend on what the public at large, not the consumers, believes. It is up to the courts to decide what the public at large believes.

Is the limitation of the amount of damages an essential feature of strict liability?

The next problem to be discussed is connected with the principle of strict liability even if it has arisen only in one country. In Britain, it might be said: 'So what? No problem with us.' When basic product liability problems are considered in a comparative law way and in the context of European approximation of laws, one can not simply set aside this aspect: is limitation of the amount of damages, a ceiling, an essential feature of strict liability as such? German law believes it is. The German delegation in the Council fought to see it introduced in the entire Community and, when this appeared impossible, it fought for the option to provide it if a Member State wishes to do so. This is the reason why Article 16 is found

[15] See C. Newdick, 'The Development Risk Defence of the Consumer Protection Act 1987' (1988) 47 *CLJ* 455.

in the Product Liability Directive, and this option was later exercised by that country as well as Spain and Portugal.

The arguments in favour of providing for a ceiling whenever liability is strict are based on the presumption that liability without a ceiling would be boundless and therefore not bearable for the person liable. Furthermore, it has been alleged that unlimited liability would not be insurable. In German law strict liability is found in traffic law (motor vehicles, the railway, air traffic), in the transport of energy (lines for electricity, gas pipes), atomic energy, pharmaceutical products and recently products originating from genetically modified organisms. In all cases, there are two kinds of ceilings, an overall ceiling covering the entire damage and an individual ceiling case by case.

These arguments in favour of a ceiling are weak, if not wrong. If liability is not bearable, then the natural consequence is the debtor becoming bankrupt. This is the correct solution in liberal economies. A ceiling leads to sharing the burden of damage between the victim and the person liable. Is there a justification for such a sharing? In some countries' legislation, the possibility exists for the judge to reduce the amount of damages in unusual cases. But again, is such a reduction justified in normal cases of product liability? The only justification in one case or the other would be to keep the enterprise alive. This is not a sufficient reason for a general rule. Victims are not a means for guaranteeing the survival of companies.

The argument about unlimited strict liability being uninsurable is wrong. Insurers do not care about limitations. They underwrite contracts whenever these are profitable. Insurers fix their covers according to the risk insured, whether the customer's liability is limited or not. Above the ceiling there is apparently less of a need to insure. But one should be careful. Courts may easily find negligence when they wish to protect victims.

Limitation of liability is not an essential feature of strict liability. It is unknown in other legislation. It should not be taken into consideration. In the European Union, Member States should not follow the German example; on the contrary, they should help German law to get rid of this mistake. They have the chance to do so. Article 16(2) of the Product Liability Directive provides for abolishing the 'ceiling' option on a proposal made by the Commission, and decided subsequently by the Council. The requirement of a unanimous decision, Article ex-100, now Article 94, as mentioned in Article 16(2) of the Product Liability Directive, is overruled by the new Article 100 (a), now Article 95, which permits a majority vote. Germany, Spain and Portugal together have only twenty-three votes with no blocking minority (twenty-six votes). Reference to subsection 4 of article 95 allowing national provisions to be upheld if specific national reasons justify it is not available. What is needed only is the Commission's proposal, but the Commission seems to be too shy to offer one.

Development risk liability

The final topic to be approached seems to be a burning one according to learned articles, books or debates. It is not. The question is rather theoretical: 'Should the so-called "development risk liability" be included in the strict liability system or not?'

Again, this ambivalent notion should, first of all, be narrowed down. Contrary to what may be understood, this notion does not cover the case of whether the producer of an out-moded product not possessing today's improved safety devices should be liable if the damage would not have occurred with a new product. The lack of a smoke warning system in a mobile home – the case has been decided in the United States – which was produced and marketed years before the fume poisoning case happened does not render this old product defective just because new series of new mobile homes are now equipped with this modern safety device. The degree of safety has to be determined retrospectively at the moment the product was first put into circulation. If the product was, according to the conviction of that time as decided by the court, not defective, it did not become defective if the expectancies of the public at large became higher. There is no room for producer's liability. Any other solution is unacceptable for industry. The user of outmoded products is acting at his own risk. Article 6(2) of the Product Liability Directive says this clearly, even if this rule is superfluous. Article 6(1)(c) fixes the time of marketing as the decisive moment to qualify the properties of the product, not the time of causing the damage.

'Development risk liability' means only and very precisely the case where the product has harmful properties at the moment of marketing, but these were unknown because the scientific or technical means of discovering them were lacking. Only a very few cases can be quoted. One of those is the following: in the 1980s, the 'Immuno' case came under consideration in Germany. A company, which had been producing for years a well-known and successful drug to protect haemophiliacs for a certain period, imported blood from the United States. This blood was used as raw material for the drug. All known and available tests, such as hepatitis for example, were carried out. All were negative. Unfortunately, the imported blood was contaminated with an unknown virus, the HIV virus causing AIDS. The virus was only discovered years later. Half of the 4,500 well-organised haemophiliacs in Germany got sick and died. Because the 1976 German Pharmaceutical Act[16] provides for strict liability of the producer including this kind of case, the victims were compensated except for their pain and suffering. At that time, German law still excluded compensation for this kind of damage when strict liability was applied. This has been recently modified. By an out-of-court settlement, the victims received 9.4 million Deutschmarks for this non-material damage.

This case shows the characteristics of 'development risks liability' as it should be understood: an objectively harmful product, which would have been considered as defective at the time of manufacturing, if only the damaging properties had been known, but where there are no means available in science and technology for discovering them. Article 7(e) of the Product Liability Directive formulates the 'state of scientific and technical knowledge' as a criterion. This again is an objective notion. Reference is made neither to 'the producer of products of the same description as the product in question', as section 4 (1)(e) Consumer Protection Act[17] says, nor to the best-qualified specialist, not even in a faraway country. Reference is made only to the general state of science and technology. 'State of scientific and technical knowledge' means the overall sum of what scientists and technicians in their respective areas have achieved as common performance in their ongoing research and skill. Again, a producer's conduct and his personal knowledge, but also his lack of general accessibility to scientific knowledge, are without relevance. The provision should only 'protect the producer in respect of the unknown (*inconnu*)'.[18] That is all that Article 7(e) is doing, nothing more, or, as the German Bundesgerichtshof said: 'Liability should only be excluded when the potential danger of the product could not be detected because the possibility to detect it did not (yet) exist at the time of marketing.'[19]

According to the Product Liability Directive system and its underlying philosophy, this case should be covered. Dogmatically there are no reasonable and genuine elements for excluding it. It was only for political

[16] 'Gesetz zur Neuordnung des Arzneimittelrechts' (Act to reorganise the law concerning pharmaceutical products), Bundesgesetzblatt I, 2445.

[17] Consumer Protection Act, 1987 Chapter 43, 15 May 1987, part 1 'Product Liability'.

[18] See footnote 14 above. [19] BGHZ 129, 353.

reasons that the Council did not take this case on board. But this exclusion was, at the time, considered as only provisional: Member States were granted an option to include this kind of liability under Article 15(1) of the Product Liability Directive, and the Council agreed to modify the Directive after ten years, i.e. in 1995, abolishing this exclusion, subsection 3 of the same article. It is well known that only Luxemburg, faithful to its alliance with France and Belgium, preserved its traditional liability in this field, whereas the other two countries having the same legal system denied it, leaving Luxemburg alone. From the newcomers, only Finland has introduced this liability. To abolish this exclusion is hopeless. Even if the Commission were to dare to submit a proposal in this respect, the necessary Council majority would not be obtainable.

It is interesting to note that France and Spain could not avoid including 'development risk liability' for products derived from human blood (France) and food-stuff (Spain). It is obvious that both countries drew on the consequences of national catastrophes in those areas: France with blood contaminated by HIV, and Spain with rape seed oil *colza*. The 1976 German Pharmaceutical Act,[20] reaping the consequences of the thalidomide catastrophe in the sixties, also provides, as mentioned, producer's liability in development risk cases. Considering these legislations, a remark should be allowed here: why do states lock the stable door only after the horse has bolted?

To be quite clear about this: if something happens outside those areas and legislations mentioned which has to be qualified as a 'development risk liability' case, there would be no protection of the victim under actual European legislation: no producer's liability, no state compensation or help. It is questionable whether this is an acceptable situation.

A final observation: the debates around product liability during the past few decades have had an unexpected, but highly welcome result: in the discussions on the different aspects and best solutions to its problems in seminars or learned circles, a new topic suddenly appeared on the agenda: 'risk management'. Speakers, mostly industrial consultants, explained to producers how they could avoid the damaging consequences of their products by safer designs, safer manufacturing conditions and better final control to avoid liability. This new understanding of production, which is now very common, is perhaps the best result that the Product Liability Directive could have had. The 1992/2001 Council Product Safety

[20] See footnote 16 above.

Directive[21] follows the same lines. It has had good success. This has to be said in answering all critical remarks claiming that the Product Liability Directive was unnecessary because there were no cases at the benches. There is still plenty left to be decided, so there should not be worries about there being enough work to keep the lawyers busy.

[21] Directive 2001/95/EC of the European Parliament and of the Council of 3 December 2001 on general product safety, OJL 11 of 15 January 2002 p. 4 modifying the Council Directive 92/59/EEC of 29 June 1992, OJL 228 of 11 August 1992 p. 24.

10

The development risks defence

MARK MILDRED

Introduction

The question how the regime of liability without fault which the Product Liability Directive 85/374/EEC ('the Directive') sought to deal with unforeseeable defects has evoked considerable political debate amongst Member States and controversy among commentators. This chapter seeks to describe the issues arising in determining the meaning and scope of the defence, the light shone upon them by reported decisions and the questions which are yet to be resolved whether by the jurisprudence of Community courts or by legislative reform.

History

The protracted and inadequately transparent negotiations over the terms of the Directive have been covered before.[1] It is, however, of relevance to recall the fact that the presence of the development risks defence inspired such disagreement among Member States as to result in the derogation permitting them to omit it from their implementing legislation.[2]

After the publication of the first draft of the Directive in 1976 the Council of Europe produced the Strasbourg Convention on Product Liability in 1977.[3] In the same year the English and Scottish Law Commissions produced Reports on Product Liability.[4] All four recommended the omission of the defence. The first two were eclipsed by publication in 1979 of the

[1] For a full analysis, see J. Stapleton, *Product Liability* (London: Butterworths, 1994) chapter 3.

[2] Article 15 (1) of the Directive.

[3] European Convention on Product Liability in Regard to Personal Injury and Death, Strasbourg, 27 January 1977. This achieved no support and was never brought into effect. It is tempting to speculate on the role played by the absence of the development risk defence in the fate of this proposal.

[4] Law Commission Report No. 82 and Scottish Law Commission Report No. 45 (Cmnd 6831) (1977).

second draft, leading to the final form of the Directive and the latter two by the Pearson Royal Commission on Civil Liability and Compensation for Personal Injury which rejected comprehensive reform in favour of sectoral change limited to personal injury cases and excluding damage to property.[5] Any impetus for domestic change was bound to be constrained by the Community reform process.

The negotiations over the second draft took six years and it is likely that the inclusion or exclusion of the defence provided a major battleground in the eventual completion of the Directive. The Commission's desire to exclude the defence was effectively over-ruled by the Member States' representatives. The defence as finally incorporated in the Directive reads:

> 7. It shall be a defence for the producer to prove: . . . . .
> (e) that the state of scientific and technical knowledge at the time when he put the product into circulation was not such as to enable the existence of the defect to be discovered.

The presence of the defence in the Directive has led to uncertainty amongst commentators over the rationale for its inclusion in a regime intended to dispose of the fault criterion and the extent to which its presence must import the criterion of the reasonableness of the producer's conduct.[6]

Implementation

Only Finland and Luxembourg have chosen to omit the defence from their implementing legislation in full. The second of these, at least, has a small manufacturing, as opposed to service, sector so that the defence may be seen as of little consequence. In Germany the defence does not apply in respect of medicinal products liability, which is governed by the Pharmaceutical Products Law of 1976.[7] Spain has generally implemented the defence but excluded it in relation to medical products, food-stuffs and food products for human consumption, which are governed by the Consumer Protection Act 1984.[8] The explanation is widely believed to be a reaction to the widespread epidemic of poisoning caused by the sale of defective cooking oil.[9] In France the defence is excluded in relation to

[5] Cmnd 7054 (1978).
[6] See Stapleton, *Product Liability*, pp. 225–9. [7] *Arzneimittelgesetz.*
[8] The exemption of the defence in relation to these products is contained in Article 6.3 of the *Ley de responsabilidad civil por los daños causados por productos defectuosos.*
[9] In the early 1980s a widespread supply of Colza cooking oil was held responsible for 600 deaths and approximately 25,000 cases of non-fatal poisoning.

human body parts and products derived from them.[10] Again, this is partly the consequence of a notorious case relating to infection of patients suffering blood clotting disorders with HIV from blood concentrate products.

In the United Kingdom the implementation process itself caused controversy.[11] The Government was determined and able to secure inclusion of the defence but sought to express it in terms wider than those of Article 7(e) of the Directive. In the Parliamentary process the House of Lords favoured literal implementation of the words of the Directive.[12] In the event the Bill was passed on the last Parliamentary business day before the General Election and the price of its passage was the incorporation of a defence framed in words apparently wider than those of the Directive: 'the state of scientific and technical knowledge at the relevant time was not such that a producer of products of the same description as the product in question might be expected to have discovered the defect if it had existed in his products while they were under his control'.[13]

The meaning of the defence

This alteration by expansion of the wording provided by the Directive (to which almost all other implementing Member States had strictly adhered)[14] brought out into the open a debate about the meaning of the defence which others had glossed over in the implementation process. Whilst there is little official record of the discussions during the legislative process, in anecdotal evidence from Professor Hans Claudius Taschner, the civil servant leading the legislative passage of the draft Directive, the requirement for unanimity and the potential deadlock led to the passage of a form of words which left unresolved which of the competing interpretations was to be preferred.[15] Unanimity of Member States was required

[10] Law 98–389 of 19 May 1998, Article 13 which incorporates a new Article 1386–12 into the *Code Civil.*

[11] The Directive was implemented by Part 1 of the Consumer Protection Act 1987 (hereinafter 'the Act').

[12] See House of Lords Debates, 9 March 1987, cols. 849–51 and 14 May 1987, cols. 786–7.

[13] Section 4 (1)(e) of the Act.

[14] Save for Italy which provided for a 'defence when the state of . . . knowledge . . . was not such that the product could have been considered defective': Article 6(1)(e) of the Decree of the President of the Italian Republic of 24 May 1988, No. 25.

[15] For example in a seminar for aspirant members of the EU organised by the TAIEX office of the European Commission in Brussels in June 1996. It is clear from his writings that he is inclined to the narrow interpretation of the defence. See for example C. Miller, *European Initiatives: the European Communities in Comparative Product Liability* (London:

to complete the Directive on the legal basis on which it was introduced.[16] Such official evidence as exists suggests opposition to exclusion of the defence for fear of suppressing innovation.[17]

In essence the competition of interpretation is between absolute undiscoverability[18] and undiscoverability by reasonable means.[19] Proponents of the first maintain that the second would reduce the regime of the Directive to one of negligence. Proponents of the second refer to Recital 7 to the Directive which establishes a fair apportionment of risk between producer and consumer as the basis for the defences available to exonerate the producer and argue that the narrow interpretation, entailing a requirement to prove a worldwide negative, would deprive the defence of any practical effect. Variations upon this theme run through the limited jurisprudence on the proper interpretation of the defence, to which we may now turn.

Decided cases

There is surprisingly little authority on the legal meaning of the defence. The existing cases fall into three categories: the early cases, the judgment of the European Court of Justice in *EC v UK* and cases (in particular the English Hepatitis C case) interpreting the judgment of the ECJ.

Early cases

The earliest invocation of the defence in England was by a manufacturer of yoghurt which had incorporated in its product hazelnut puree contaminated with a toxin clostridium botulinum B manufactured by another company.[20] Driven to particularise its defence that the toxin was

BIICL, 1986) at p. 11: '. . . due to the *absolute* lack of scientific and technical knowledge, the existing defect could not be discovered' (emphasis added). See also 'Harmonisation of Products Liability Laws in the European Community' 34 (1999) *Texas International Law Journal*: 21. It may, however, be the case that, as the senior Commission official responsible for the draft, the validity of his perception may have been undermined by the failure of the Member States to toe the Commission line on the general scheme of the Directive including the proposed exclusion of the defence. See also the comments of Nicholas Underhill QC appended to chapter 2.

[16] Article 100 of the Treaty of Rome.

[17] European Parl Working Documents 1978–9, DOC 246/78, pp. 26–7 and European Parl Working Documents 1979–80, DOC 71/79, pp. 16–17.

[18] 'The narrow interpretation'. [19] 'The wider interpretation'.

[20] *Stephenson v Healds of Fleetwood* (unreported), Queen's Bench Division, Manchester District Registry.

not discoverable in the existing state of scientific and technical knowledge by a yoghurt manufacturer, the company admitted the existence of tests for the toxin which could be carried out in some, but not all, microbiological laboratories but denied that any such tests were available to it or customarily undertaken by yoghurt manufacturers. This approach would, if accepted, have evidently allowed defendants an even wider exemption from liability than would have been conferred by the 'reasonable means' interpretation of Article 4(e) of the Directive.[21] In the event the case was settled before judgment so that no judicial assessment of this line of argument is available.[22]

The first major judgment in relation to Article 7(e) was that of the Bundesgerichtshof in a case arising out of an injury to the eye of a nine-year-old child by the explosion of a re-used mineral water bottle.[23] The bottles were subject to an intensive system of inspection and quality control. There was a conflict on whether the explosion had resulted from a hairline crack or a chipped area. If the latter (which appears to have been treated as the more likely), the court decided that the chipped area could have been detected and thus was discoverable, so that the defence would not apply. If, however, the explosion resulted from a hairline crack, the defence would still not apply because it would be a rare and inevitable production defect not covered by Article 7(e) even though it was inevitable despite reasonable precautions.

The court decided that the defence covered only undetectable dangers resulting from the construction (in the context a near synonym of 'design'), as opposed to the production, of the product. Since the danger of explosion of bottles which were somehow flawed (rogue products or 'lemons', in German *ausreisser*, literally 'runaways') had been known for a long time the defence would not apply. In this and an Austrian case also relating to a mineral water bottle there was also reliance on the defence under Article 7(b) that it was probable that the defect did not exist at the

[21] Since the test would have become, in effect, custom and practice of the industry rather than the conventional test of negligence. This would, of course, have provided compelling evidence that the English interpretation of the defence exceeded the test set by the Directive.

[22] For a fuller account, see M. Mildred, 'The Impact of the Directive in the United Kingdom' in M. Goyens (ed.), *Directive 85/374 on Product Liability: Ten Years After* (Louvain-la-Neuve: Centre de Droit de la Consommation, 1996), pp. 52–4.

[23] Case VI XR 158/94, judgment dated 5 September 1995, hereinafter 'the German Water Bottle case'. The judgment of the Bundesgerichtshof overruled the Court of Appeal (Berufungsgericht) which held that the development risks defence was available to the manufacturer because the latest state of science and technology could not have detected the defect in the bottle.

time it was put into circulation by the defendant.[24] This was also unsuccessful and a detailed discussion of the latter defence is outside the scope of this chapter.

The assertion that the defence had no application to manufacturing defects reflects the stance taken in a Unilateral Declaration by the United Kingdom upon adoption of the Directive.[25] In the *English Hepatitis C* case the judge rejected the traditional classification of defects as production (or manufacturing), design and information defects in favour of distinguishing between standard and non-standard products.[26] He thus chose to equiparate '*ausreisser*' with non-standard products so as to avoid the disqualification of manufacturing defects from the protection of Article 7(e) and interpreted the decision as saying 'that, if the risk is known, unavoidability of the defect in a particular product is no answer'.[27]

The court refused to refer the question to the European Court of Justice on the grounds that the interpretation of the provision was not disputed in the national jurisprudence or the academic literature and the court did not seek to depart from the jurisprudence of the Court of Justice. This is in itself surprising since the Directive is silent on the question whether any exemption from the ambit of the defence is conferred upon manufacturing errors: rather the defence appears on its face to be available to cover all types of error without discrimination. Stapleton points out that the impetus to exclude manufacturing errors from the scope of the defence reflects a fear that its inclusion would result in a more manufacturer-friendly environment for claims under the Directive than for the 'covert strict liability for manufacturing errors' regime in negligence.[28] Further, as Howells points out, the question itself is not straightforward.[29] Is the existence of rare failures a cost of strict liability to be spread across the market or is the disproportionate cost of an infallible quality control system a reason for exempting the producer from liability for the consequences of that very fallibility? In this context, Newdick floats a distinction between the capacity of scientific knowledge to understand the existence of a defect and the inability of technology to permit discovery of that defect (or *quaere*

[24] 4 Ob 87/97s 8 April 1997.

[25] Department of Trade and Industry 1987 and also the Explanatory Memorandum for Draft Product Liability Act, BT-Dr. 11/2447 of 9.6.1988, p. 15.

[26] *A v The National Blood Authority* [2001] 3 All ER 289 (hereinafter 'the Hepatitis C case').

[27] Ibid., at para. 53 (iii).

[28] J. Stapleton, 'Restatement (Third) of Torts: Products Liability: an Anglo-Australian Perspective' (2000) *Washburn Law Journal* 363. See also C. Newdick, 'The Future of Negligence in Product Liability' 103 (1987) *LQR*: 288–310, at 291.

[29] *The Law of Product Liability* (London: Butterworths, 2000) para. 4.249.

to detect it at reasonable cost).[30] If that distinction were employed, the defence would protect products where a theoretical risk was accepted but the actual defect in the particular product escaped detection. The point of this would be to avoid the social inutility occasioned by an obligation to test the individual product to destruction in order to discover whether it was one of those in which the theoretical risk had crystallised. This question of interpretation will recur in the consideration of three later cases.[31]

In the Western High Court of Denmark a manufacturer of glue was unsuccessful in its reliance on the defence when the glue dissolved in the presence of condensed water in the pipes in which it was employed.[32] The reasons given were that the court-appointed expert was able to discover the reason for the failure of the glue and that the defendant had previously received a similar claim in respect of the same product.

The infringement proceedings

After more than six years of unproductive negotiation and the formal preliminaries, infringement proceedings against the UK were commenced by the Commission in September 1995 under Article 169 of the Treaty of Rome.[33] The Commission sought a declaration that, by failing to take all the measures necessary to implement the Directive, and in particular Article 7(e) thereof, the United Kingdom had failed to fulfil its obligations under the Directive and under the Treaty. In Article 169 proceedings, the burden of proving the infringement rests upon the Commission. In this case, in the absence of any decisions by the Court of Justice or any court in any of the Member States on the meaning of Article 7(e), the Commission had to demonstrate that section 4(1)(e) of the Act was incapable of bearing the same legal meaning as that of Article 7(e).

1. The legal meaning of the provisions

The elucidation of the legal meaning of Article 7(e) involves a number of considerations. The legal basis for the Directive was Article 100 which allows directives to be made to approximate laws which directly affect the

30 C. Newdick, 'The Development Risk Defence of the Consumer Protection Act 1987' (1988) *CLJ*: 455–76, at 472.

31 The *Hepatitis C* case; *Scholten v OLVG Hospital Amsterdam*, 3 February 1999, *Nederlandse Jurisprudentie* 199, 621; and *Graham Barclay Oysters Pty Ltd v Ryan* (2000) 177 ALR 18.

32 UfR 1997.203 V. Judgment of 14 November 1996.

33 Case CC-300/95. The Opinion of the Advocate General and the Judgment of the Court of Justice are reported together at 1997 ECR I-2649; [1997] All ER (EC) 481.

establishment or functioning of the common market. The first Recital calls for approximation of the laws of the Member States to eliminate distortion of competition and the fettering of free movement of goods within the market and to avoid different degrees of consumer protection arising in different Member States. From this it is clear that economic interests have a part to play in the process. The second Recital asserts the proposition that liability without fault is the only adequate means of achieving a fair apportionment of the risks inherent in modern technological production. Some commentators treat this as establishing the over-riding principle to govern the construction of the Directive[34] that fair apportionment is the basis for the availability (in the seventh Recital) of a number of exceptions to the rule of liability without fault. There is nothing here to be found to suggest any other constraint on liability or any reference to the personal or generic characteristics of the producer as a determinant of the liability standard. It is noteworthy that none of the other defences available to the producer refers to or involves personal responsibility or fault: they rather protect those who could be categorised as outwith the regime created by the Directive, for example those who made no supply, or no supply in the course of a business, or whose product was not defective. This may touch upon (but does not determine) the competition between the wide and narrow interpretations of the defence.

2. The arguments of the parties

The Commission argued that the test in Article 7(e) is objective in the sense that it refers to a state of knowledge and not to the knowledge or the ability or capacity to acquire knowledge of a particular person or class of persons. The Act, on the other hand, implies an assessment referable to what may be expected of a reasonable producer, if not the actual producer, of the type of products in question. The Directive requires the producer to show the impossibility of discovering the defect rather than the fact, or likelihood, that a person in the same or a similar situation as or to his own would not have discovered it. Under the Act, on the other hand, proof that the producer took standard or reasonable steps to discover the defect will exonerate him. The incorporation into the defence of a reasonableness test is, in effect, reintroducing fault-based liability by the backdoor, albeit with the burden of proof reversed. There is already ample safeguard for the producer in the concept of 'defect'. A product is only

[34] See Howells, *Law of Product Liability*, para. 4.11.

defective if it is not as safe as persons generally are entitled to expect. The burden of showing that is on the claimant. The only stage at which reasonable standards could possibly be relevant is when the claimant must prove that the product is defective, not when the producer must prove that the defect was undiscoverable. The Commission submitted that, since the defence created an exception to the fundamental principle of strict liability, it should be narrowly construed in accordance with the normal approach of the Court. The Commission gave as an example the case of a chemical manufacturer who, in common with the rest of the industry, and, excusably, did not read an article in a certain basic science journal published in German which clearly established the risk of cell damage in humans exposed to a chemical manufactured by the company. It was argued that there would in these circumstances be a viable defence under the Act (because a producer of products of the type in question could not be expected to have discovered the defect) but not under the Directive (because the defect was clearly discoverable).

The United Kingdom replied that the tests administered by the two provisions were the same, both being objective. The examination of the state of scientific and technical knowledge was not directed to what the producer in question actually knows, but to the knowledge which producers of the 'class of producer in question, understood in a generic sense' might objectively be expected to have. The answer could only be that the ambiguity in the Directive should be given the wide interpretation and the wording of the Act accordingly reflected it. The more substantive point made by the United Kingdom (and referred to only in the Advocate General's Opinion) was that, if the relevant state of knowledge did not correspond in some way to the ability of the producer in question to discover the defect, the defence could never succeed unless the producer could show that no one in the world could have discovered it.[35] A defence which is unattainable in practice cannot provide the required fair apportionment of risk and thus could not have the meaning contended for by the Commission. A more appropriate approach was to provide an objectively verifiable standard – that of the capacity of persons in the same generic position as the actual producer to discover the defect. One could object, however, that a defence which was only to be available in the rarest circumstances was what many commentators imagined was intended.[36]

[35] *EC v UK*, paragraphs 10 and 11.

[36] H. C. Taschner, *ProdukhaftungsR und EG-Produkthaftungsrichtlinie* (2nd edn 1990).

3. The Opinion of Advocate General Tesauro

The Advocate General's Opinion confirmed that the true question for the Court was whether the national provision was capable of only one interpretation which was manifestly different from the Community provision and hence incompatible with it.[37] He reflected that one of the reasons for the introduction of the draft Directive was that injured consumers frequently went uncompensated as a result of the difficulty in proving negligence on the part of the manufacturer whereas the latter could pass its liability costs on to consumers generally in the overall price of the product. He began his elucidation of Article 7(e) itself by saying that the test was not the custom and practice of the industry in question, but rather whether available knowledge would have permitted eradication of the defect. Neither expense nor practicability nor failure to keep abreast of changes in the state of knowledge will absolve the producer from failure to discover the defect. The Advocate General went on to reflect on the meaning of 'state of knowledge' which does not develop in a linear manner and to which theories once thought erroneous or speculative may in time be admitted.[38] He advised that the word 'state' does not connote simply a majority or establishment view but rather the most advanced opinion. After setting an exceedingly demanding standard in relation to what it is discoverability of which would deprive the producer of the defence, the Advocate General changed tack by stating that this reinforced the obligation to deal with all *foreseeable* (emphasis added) risks either by increasing research and experimentation or by instead insuring against liability for any damage caused.[39] Use of the word 'foreseeable' makes it plain (although not explicitly acknowledged) that the wider interpretation of the defence was being addressed. One isolated opinion as to the potentially defective or hazardous nature of the product is sufficient to take the defect out of the realm of unforeseeability although the speed and scale of dissemination of a discovery would affect its discoverability for the purpose of Article 7(e).[40]

The Advocate General then concluded that 'state of knowledge' must be construed to include all data in the information circuit of the scientific community as a whole, bearing in mind, however, on the basis of a reasonableness test, the actual opportunities for the information to circulate.[41] As a result of this gloss on the words of both the Directive and

[37] *EC v UK* paragraph 14. [38] Para. 21.
[39] Para. 22. [40] Para. 23. [41] Para. 24.

the Act in favour of the wide interpretation, the Advocate General had no difficulty in rejecting an irremediable conflict between the two provisions. This was despite finding an undeniable ambiguity in the Act which, he said, 'insofar as it refers to what might be expected of the producer, could be interpreted more broadly than it should'.[42]

The rationalisation of the conflict rested on three arguments. First, consideration of the producer was central to both the Directive as a whole and to Article 7(e) which 'although it does not mention him, is aimed at the producer himself as the person having to discharge the burden of proof in order to avoid incurring liability'.[43] This argument seems to imply that, because the producer is the defendant, the standard by which he should be judged is that of producers, notwithstanding the language of the provision itself. The second asserted the objectively verifiable knowledge of producers as a whole as the key criterion, but again limited this to such most advanced knowledge as was 'objectively and reasonably obtainable and available'.[44] Thirdly the contention that the Act in effect introduces a quasi-negligence test was rejected on the basis that the burden of establishing the defence rests on the defendant.[45] The confusion between the substantive standard and the burden of proof is puzzling.

4. The judgment of the Court of Justice

The Court approached the task of interpretation of the legal meaning of the defence by separating the question into two parts: discoverability and state of scientific and technical knowledge. It confirmed that Article 7(e) is not specifically directed at the practices and safety standards in use in the industrial sector in question but concerned, 'unreservedly, . . . the state of scientific and technical knowledge, including the most advanced level of such knowledge'.[46] The state of knowledge is, the Court said, not that of which the actual producer 'actually or subjectively was or could have been apprised, but the objective state of scientific and technical knowledge of which the producer is presumed to have been informed'.[47] That is all the Court of Justice had to say on the subject: a discussion of the key phrase 'state of . . . knowledge' and of the definition of 'knowledge' as opposed to hypothesis and the like is absent. The Court did not expressly approve but equally did not dissent from the Opinion of the Advocate General which included as part of the state of scientific and technical knowledge 'one

[42] Para. 25. [43] Para. 26. [44] Ibid. [45] Para. 27. [46] Para. 26. [47] Para. 27.

isolated opinion (which, as the history of science shows, might become, with the passage of time, *opinio communis*)' as to the potentially defective and/or hazardous nature of the product. This would deprive the manufacturer of the defence.[48] Under the first limb, therefore, the Court set a high standard for producers to satisfy in relation to the means of discoverability.

That standard was, however, limited by the second limb of the Court's analysis. The only basis it offered for the making of the presumption of the producer's knowledge of the defect was that the relevant knowledge must have been 'accessible' at the time at which the product was put into circulation but no explanation of what is meant by the word accessible was offered.[49]

The Court ended by giving five reasons for rejecting the Commission's view that there was a clear conflict between the two provisions and, therefore, for dismissing the application. The first uncontroversially pointed out that, under both provisions, the burden of establishing the defence rests on the producer.[50] The second referred to the fact that the definition of state and degree of knowledge in the Act is not tied to that of the producer.[51] Even so, however, that knowledge is related by the language of the Act to the expectation (a concept to be found in the Directive only in the context of the definition of 'defect') that a producer of the type of goods in question would or might have discovered the defect. The third reason was that the wording of the Act does not suggest that the test will be whether the producer has taken reasonable care by the standards of the industrial sector in question.[52] Finally the Court referred to the failure of the Commission to refer to any decision of the domestic courts inconsistent with the Directive[53] and stated that there was nothing to suggest that English courts would not interpret section 4(1)(e) in the light of the wording and purpose of the Directive.[54]

5. Discussion

The decision of the Court is unhelpful in a number of respects: the basis for the presumption of what information the producer had, the meaning of the words 'accessible', 'knowledge' and 'state of knowledge', the ambiguous meaning of Article 7(e) recognised but not articulated, let alone resolved and the question whether the lack of case law does or does

[48] Para. 22. [49] Para. 28. [50] Para. 34. [51] Para. 35.
[52] Para. 36. [53] Para. 37. [54] Para. 38.

not matter.[55] The separation of the concepts of state of knowledge and discoverability may appear to give substance to both the narrow and the wide interpretations of the defence. In fact the reliance of the Court on the criterion of accessibility moves the fulcrum of the debate well towards the wide interpretation.

There are ironies in the judgment: acknowledgment of the ambiguity of the language of Article 7(e) lays the ground for a future reference to the Court from a judgment of a court in a Member State – the clarity assumed by the Bundesgerichtshof in the German Water Bottle case has proved illusory. The lack of case law which precluded a definitive judgment on the meaning of s. 4(1)(e) of the Act interacted with the failure of the Court of Justice to resolve the ambiguity in Article 7(e) so that the Infringement Proceedings were doomed to failure. A third and more journalistic irony was the view of the Advocate General that the proceedings were premature in the absence of any decisions of domestic courts.[56] The consumer movement had, on the contrary, castigated the Commission for taking almost ten years to bring the matter to the Court.

Cases after the Infringement Proceedings

In *Scholten v OLVG Hospital Amsterdam*, the Amsterdam District Court at first instance decided that blood which contained the HIV virus after the introduction of screening tests for that virus had been introduced was defective.[57] The chance of viral contamination was about one in a million but the public was entitled to expect 100 per cent safety, particularly since that small risk was not general knowledge and thus could not affect the entitled expectation of consumers. The defendants raised a defence under Article 7(e) on the basis that it was impossible to detect the virus, given the practical inability of the defendants to employ the emerging PCR test. The court held that the defence applied to the avoidability as well as the knowledge of the defect and therefore succeeded because '[detection of the virus by the PCR test] could not have been expected of the Foundation'.

[55] For commentaries on the decision, see C. Hodges, 'Development Risks: Unanswered Questions' 61 (1998) *MLR*: 560–70; M. Mildred and G. Howells, 'Comment on "Development Risks: Unanswered Questions"' 61 (1998) *MLR*: 570 and 'Is European Products Liability More Protective than the Restatement (Third) of Torts: Products Liability?' 65 (1998) *Tennessee Law Review*: 985–1030; J. Stapleton, 'Products Liability in the United Kingdom: the Myths of Reform' 34 (1998) *Texas International Law Journal*: 45 and 'The Conceptual Imprecision of Strict Liability' 6 (1998) *Torts Law Journal*: 260.

[56] Para. 29.

[57] 3 February 1999, *Nederlandse Jurisprudentie* 199, 621.

As was pointed out by Burton J in the Hepatitis C case (a) the criterion of 'expectation' is relevant only to Article 6 considerations and not to discoverability under Article 7(e), and (b) it is not clear whether the applicability of the development risk defence to production defects was argued.[58] Taking these factors with the fact that the decision was at first instance, it is submitted that this successful invocation of the defence is of little authority.

In *Richardson v LRC Products Ltd* the claimant sued a condom manufacturer whose product ruptured during intercourse so that she became pregnant.[59] The judge found that the condom was not defective since failure of the product did not of itself prove a defect in circumstances in which the producer and consumer alike acknowledge that inexplicable failures occur on a regular basis. The judge went on to deal *obiter* with the development risk defence raised by the defendants. He found that the defence would not have availed the defendants: 'The test provided by the statute is not what the defendants knew but what they could have known, if they had consulted those who might be expected to know the state of the research and all available literature sources. This provision is . . . not apt to protect a defendant in the case of a defect of a known character merely because there is no test which is apt to reveal its existence in every case.'[60]

In *Abouzaid v Mothercare (UK) Ltd* a twelve-year-old child was helping his mother attach a fleece-lined sleeping bag to a pushchair in 1990.[61] While he was attempting to secure the bag by buckling two elastic straps one strap slipped from his grasp and injured his left eye. The producer appealed against a confused finding of liability. The Court of Appeal decided that the product was defective in respect of its design and the information supplied with it. The development risk defence was rejected by the Court. Pill LJ found that an absence of record of previous similar accidents (said to be evidence of the state of technical knowledge, but doubted by Pill LJ) went to the question of foreseeability in negligence and not to discoverability.[62] Since the risk giving rise to the defect identified by expert evidence was identifiable at the time the product was put into circulation in 1990, the defect was discoverable. Chadwick LJ considered that the defence was not engaged since a simple practical test revealing the design defect could have been carried out before 1990. That it had not

[58] At paragraph 53 (iv). But see the text following note 51 above. The enthusiasm of Burton J for *EC v UK* is hard to square with his decision to ignore the text of the Act.

[59] [2000] Lloyd's Law Reports (Medical) 280.

[60] Transcript pp. 14–15.

[61] [2000] All ER (D) 2436.

[62] At para. 29.

been carried out resulted from the manufacturer's failure to consider it, rather than anything connected with the state of scientific and technical knowledge. It is hard to know whether Chadwick LJ was expressing a preference for the wide construction of the defence when he said that it enabled a producer to escape strict liability 'if he can show that, having regard to the state of scientific and technical knowledge at the time, he was not at fault in failing to discover the defect'.[63] If not, he was falling into the language of negligence and replicating the confusion of the judge at first instance.

In a French case the Toulouse Court of Appeal disallowed the development risk defence pleaded by a butcher whose horsemeat had infected the claimant with trichinellosis.[64] The Court uncontroversially (in the light of the result of the Infringement Proceedings) decided that the defence referred not to the state of knowledge of which the producer could reasonably have been informed but the existing and accessible state of knowledge at the time the product was placed on the market.

The judgment of Burton J in the *Hepatitis C* case litigation contains an unusually broad comparative review of the Directive, is widely viewed as the most comprehensive analysis of the concepts of defectiveness and development risks and has attracted considerable critical comment.[65] The judgment in general goes straight to the Directive and largely ignores the parallel words of the Act for interpretative purposes. In his interpretation of the development risks defence Burton J resorted to the objects of consumer protection and facilitation of compensation and the opportunity in Recital 16 for Member States to exclude the defence or to confine the ambit of the defence within a narrow compass.[66] The object of the defence was to see whether the defect could be discovered or eliminated.

Perhaps surprisingly Burton J relied heavily upon the judgment of the Court of Justice. As we have seen in that case the Advocate General not only imported the language of negligence in his use of the words 'producer's obligation to deal with all *foreseeable* risks',[67] but went on to limit the

63 At para. 44.

64 Judgment of 22 February 2000. *Gazette du Palais*, 30 August 2001, para. 11.

65 Apart from the extensive discussion in this volume at chapter 2, see C. Hodges, 'Compensating Patients' 117 (2001) *LQR*: 528; G. Howells and M. Mildred, 'Infected Blood: Defect and Discoverability: a First Exposition of the EC Product Liability Directive' 65 (2002) *MLR*: 95.

66 Para. 75.

67 Advocate General's Opinion para. 22. The statutory test goes to the discoverability of defects rather than the foreseeability of risks.

state of knowledge by reference to 'the basis of a reasonableness test'.[68] This seems difficult to square with his general attitude of promotion of consumer protection.[69]

Burton J took up from the Court of Justice the 'Manchuria question'. This was an example adopted in the submissions of the Commission designed to show that the defence was wider under the CPA than under the Directive. It should be borne in mind that the Court of Justice in *EC v UK* was dealing with Infringement Proceedings rather than a reference in an actual private law claim and this altered the focus to some extent from interpretation to compliance. The Commission had argued that a Chinese language local publication in Manchuria might have rendered information discoverable under the Directive but not under section 4(1)(e) CPA. The purpose of the example was the comparison of the outcomes under the two wordings rather than an attempt to fix the criteria for 'discoverability' or persuade the Court of Justice to confine the defence to the narrow interpretation – the purpose to which it was adapted in the Hepatitis C case. In the event Burton J appears to have followed the ECJ in limiting discoverability by the concept of accessibility and thus to have adopted the reasoning of the Advocate General.

The categorisation of products into standard and non-standard referred to above affected the court's approach to the defence under Article 7(e).[70] A standard product is one which is and performs as the producer intends. A non-standard product is different from the products as they are intended or desired by the producer to be.[71] Once the unwanted effect of the non-standard product has occurred and is known, the defect is discoverable and the defence lost forever.

Since infection of blood and blood products with viruses including hepatitis C virus was known by the producers, a crucial issue was whether the defence applied when there was knowledge of the existence of the defect, but not of how to detect it in particular products. This again reflects the fact that the case was concerned with non-standard products since the defect (infection with virus) was unintentionally present in some but not all blood bags. The court decided to treat as a 'defect' the existence of a problem of safety in the class of products as a whole.[72] Once that problem

[68] Ibid at para. 24.

[69] Judgment of Burton J at para. 75: the defence, as a derogation from the purposes of the Directive, should be construed narrowly.

[70] See text accompanying note 23. [71] Judgment para. 36.

[72] Para. 74 (iii): 'The existence of the *defect* . . . is clearly generic. Once the existence of the *defect* is known, then there is then the *risk* of that defect materialising in any particular product.'

was or should have been known to the producer, the producer could not rely on the difficulty or impracticability of discovering the defect in any particular item. The specificity required for the defence under Article 7(b) which refers to the presence of a defect in a particular product is absent from Article 7(e).[73] If it were otherwise, as the defendants submitted the defence should be construed, the producer would be protected against a known risk occurring after the development period had ended with the discovery of that very risk. 'Known' includes capable of being known from accessible knowledge.[74]

Burton J would allow the defence in relation to a non-standard product on one and only one occasion. The attraction of this approach is that the consumer is not defeated by a risk known in general to exist in a limited fraction of the production run but undiscoverable in the particular product without destroying it. Thus the intended confinement of exceptions to the strict liability rule is maintained.

This approach may be more apt in relation to non-standard than to standard products. It is easier in the former case to use the concept of 'defect' to address the general problem and that of 'risk' to address its materialisation in the particular product. But what of a standard product where the occurrence is not an all or nothing event depending on whether the particular product has the characteristics which differentiate it from the norm?

In the case of a defective standard product much may depend on the way in which the defect is characterised. If the defect in a product is the capacity to cause a certain outcome, the defence will be lost as soon as that capacity is known. Whilst the detail of the difficulties of definition of defect is outside the scope of this chapter, it is worth noting that the capacity to cause harm may as likely trigger a risk–utility balancing exercise as lead to a finding of defectiveness.[75] By definition, however, the defence can only be engaged before the capacity to cause harm has been identified so that the relevance of a warning will only impact on the defence when the product has the capacity to cause more than one kind of damage

[73] In the Australian case *Graham Barclay Oysters Pty Ltd v Ryan* (2000) 177 ALR 18 the Full Federal Court decided that the defendants were entitled to rely on the defence in s 75AK(1)(c) of the Trade Practices Act since the only method of detecting the defect in an oyster would involve its destruction. This contrary approach is justified by the terms of the defence which refer to the defect in the *action* goods (emphasis added).

[74] Para. 77.

[75] This assumes that the approach of Burton J in the *Hepatitis C* case of ignoring this balance in investigating the existence of a defect does not prevail into the future. See his judgment paragraphs 68–9.

and one is alleged to be undiscoverable even though the other has been discovered.[76]

Since the *English Hepatitis C* decision, the Austrian Supreme Court has held that a coffee machine which caught fire for no clear reason was defective, even though the claimant could not explain the mechanism which led to the outbreak of the fire.[77] The defendant ran the development risks defence on the basis that, since 60,000 similar machines had been supplied without any similar incidents, the defect must have been undiscoverable. The Court rejected this argument since the defendant had not proved that it was unknowable at the relevant time that coffee machines could catch fire by reason of 'unavoidable and perhaps undiscoverable defects'. This is a firm application of the defence in keeping with the goals of consumer protection and liability without fault.

Unresolved issues

State of knowledge

The Court of Justice did not resolve the classic difficulty of defining the 'state of scientific and technical knowledge'. As discussed above, the notion that the most advanced idea, however abstruse, counter-intuitive or unsupported by evidence, may set the standard is puzzling.[78] It is unclear how such an approach fits with the concept of a 'state' of knowledge, a phrase which seems to imply some consensus or settled basis.

Accessibility

As a fetter on the effect of such an approach (and, as we have seen, introducing a two-stage test of uncertain textual provenance) the Court of

[76] Suppose a drug can cause damage to joints and to the liver. If the capacity to cause liver damage is discoverable in 2000 but that to cause damage to joints in 2003, it is uncertain when the defence is lost in relation to the latter. Claimants will attempt to define the defect as the capacity to cause injury *per se*. Defendants will wish to define the injury with more specificity. This question goes to the definition of defect but clearly affects the availability of the defence. There is no authority on the question.

[77] 10 Ob 98/02p (22 October 2002) discussed in 11 (2003) *European Product Liability Review*: 37–8.

[78] Contrast the approach of the US Supreme Court in *Daubert v Merrell Dow Pharmaceuticals* Inc 509 US 579 (1993) which sought to refine the concept of the state of scientific knowledge, in particular by insisting that the materials relied upon by expert witnesses in their evaluation of scientific controversies should have undergone peer review.

Justice qualified its view that Article 7(e) is directed 'unreservedly, at the state of scientific and technical knowledge, including the most advanced level of such knowledge' by the requirement that such knowledge must have been accessible.[79] Burton J was content to follow the qualification although he added no elucidation of the meaning of 'accessible' to the gloss imposed on the literal wording of the Directive by the Court of Justice. It is implicit in his judgment that the following would not be considered accessible: (i) an unpublished document and (ii) unpublished research not available to the general public retained within the laboratory or research department of another enterprise. It is not clear whether these are intended to be exhaustive. By inference publication is generally a prerequisite for accessibility.

Does it follow that anything recorded on a searchable database is presumed to be within the producer's knowledge? Or only that in the same language as that spoken by the producer? Or only that contained in the databases which a producer of products of the type in question is in the habit of searching? It is easy to see that the constraint itself raises satellite questions of degree and interpretation.

Knowledge

A further uncertainty concerns the definition of 'knowledge' itself. Traditionally scientific advances are put forward as hypotheses rather than assertions. What is the standard of proof (or level of comfort) required before an idea can fairly be described as knowledge capable of being part of 'the state of . . . knowledge'? Is the idea itself a sufficient element of knowledge or must the controversy be resolved in its favour? This is clearly important: the controversial suggestion that the measles mumps rubella (MMR) vaccine may have a causal role in the development of autistic symptoms was first made in the *Lancet* of 28 February 1998 in these terms 'We have identified a chronic enterocolitis in children that may be related to neuropsychiatric dysfunction.'[80] This suggestion was and is still hotly disputed. It is uncertain whether such a statement is sufficiently robust to qualify as (the most advanced) knowledge.

A related dilemma is the question whether an idea must be complete before it is capable of comprising knowledge. If not, the elements which, if connected together, would have constituted the knowledge will

[79] *EC v UK* at para. 26. [80] A. J. Wakefield, *The Lancet* 151 (1998) 637–41.

themselves, very likely at a far earlier date, defeat the availability of the defence. The Court of Justice did not engage with these problems save to the extent that it decided that the knowledge concerned must be the most advanced. Again, the reason for this was likely to have been the basis for the case – Infringement Proceedings – so that the Court was not inclined to make a judgment on what would and would not have been in issue on a fact-based reference for the interpretation of any of these concepts.

When does a researcher's idea become knowledge? To what extent can the claimant argue that the conjunction of different strands of thought adds up to discoverability? How does this dilemma interact with the provisions of Article 6.2?[81] As Stapleton argued (before the Court of Justice had given prominence to the concept of accessibility): once the criterion for discoverability involves leaps of curiosity or creativity, a succession of value questions are introduced, the inevitable consequence of which is that liability should exist only in respect of defects discoverable by reasonable means, for there is no logical halfway house between absolute undiscoverability (rendering the defence nugatory) and undiscoverability by reasonable means (aping the negligence standard).[82]

Wide or narrow interpretation

Whilst there is as yet no formal determination of the question whether the wide or narrow interpretation of the defence is correct, the introduction of the criterion of reasonableness into the accessibility of knowledge by the Advocate General has gone a long way to suggest that the defence should be given the wider interpretation.[83] Indeed the dictum of the Court of Justice that the accessibility criterion was implicit in the wording of Article 7(e) strengthens this view.[84]

Conduct of the producer

A further concern relates to the conduct of the producer. The general approach of the court is likely to exclude consideration of the conduct of the producer at the instance of either party. It is to be disregarded for the purposes of ascertainment of defect.[85] But it may be taken into account for

[81] An old car is not defective because a later model incorporates air cushions. But how far do the familiar notions of the softness of a balloon, rapid deceleration on impact and the capacity of hard surfaces to cause wounding combine to make the absence of preventive measures a discoverable defect?

[82] See Stapleton, *Product Liability*, pp. 239–42.

[83] Para. 24. [84] Para. 28. [85] Hepatitis C case para. 72.

the purpose of Article 7(e).[86] In the circumstances the remark of Burton J: 'Negligence, fault and the conduct of the producer or designer can be left to the (limited) ambit of Article 7(e)' raised but did not solve the problem.[87] That is not surprising since the context in which the remark was made was whether the defect had to be discoverable in the individual product. It may be that he intended to convey no more than that the defence is the escape route for the producer 'who has done all he could reasonably be expected to do (and more)'.[88]

Exclusion of the producer's conduct from the question of discoverability would, however, allow the producer to fail to take steps to ascertain the true incidence of the unwanted effects of its products with impunity.[89] In the Hepatitis C case the defendants unsuccessfully submitted that they must be given the opportunity to do all they could to avoid injury.[90] Defendants would presumably argue that they are liable to perform the requirements of the regulator and any criticism that they had not gone far enough should be made in negligence. What is not resolved is whether a court should decide whether a defect *would have been* discoverable, for example by the producer taking certain steps.

In the English oral contraceptive litigation, the Committee on Safety of Medicines issued a safety warning relating to the third-generation product in October 1995 after three research reports suggested a significant increase in the incidence of venous thrombo-embolism (VTE) in women using them compared to the incidence in those using second-generation products. Since many of those affected had been exposed to the alleged defect before suspension of the licences, the claimants sought to argue that the defendants could and should have set up post-marketing surveillance studies forthwith upon placing the products on the market. If they had done so, the argument ran, the existence of the defect would have been discoverable far earlier. The defendants relied on the argument that the defence asked only whether (that is, when) the defect had been discoverable and they had been under no obligation relevant to the questions posed by the Directive to take steps to collect, analyse and publish the data. They accepted their obligations under the regulatory regime but no more.

[86] Ibid., para. 73.

[87] Ibid.; the remark at paragraph 49 (ii) 'Article [7(e)] is not concerned with the conduct or knowledge of individual producers' should presumably be read subject to para. 73.

[88] Para. 64.

[89] For the contrary view, see C. Hodges in M. Mildred (ed.), *Product Liability: Law and Insurance* (London: LLP Ltd, 2001), paragraph 2.92.

[90] Para. 75.

The claims were discontinued before the question of interpretation was decided. The difficulty in the oral contraceptive case was that the producers were the only ones able completely to assemble the data from which the 'true' incidence of the adverse effect could be calculated. Anyone else would have no basis on which as quickly to make the suggestion of a raised incidence and the fact that all oral contraceptives cause some incidence of circulatory problems was known and fully warned about.

Thus the defect of which discoverability was in issue was precise and most easily and quickly calculable by the producers themselves. The result of the producer's lack of research might of course affect the question of legitimate expectation. If this led to a finding of defectiveness, it would be undesirable that the same lack of practicable research founded a defence under Article 7(e). The superimposition in the French implementing legislation of a requirement that, in order to take advantage of the defence where the defect was discovered within ten years of the product entering circulation, the manufacturer must have taken steps to avoid the damage and warn of the dangers of the product was struck down by the Court of Justice on the basis that the Directive was a maximum Directive.[91]

Manufacturing defects

There is potentially conflicting authority in the Water Bottle case and the Hepatitis C case. Burton J would square the circle by interpreting the former decision as being based in the language of the rogue product rather than the 'boxing' of defects into production, design, etc. It will be interesting to see how far subsequent judgments in the courts in Member States take up the standard/non-standard approach to defects. Unless that becomes the orthodox approach, far from certain in the absence of any textual basis in the Directive for it, a question fit for decision by the Court of Justice will remain: does the development risks defence apply to manufacturing defects?

Discoverability in the individual product

This issue has been decided different ways in Scholten and Hepatitis C. It is submitted that the reasoning in the latter is more coherent for the reasons set out in the discussion above. The absence of an appeal in the latter case removed the opportunity for a further exposition of the conflicting

[91] Case C-52/00 *Commission v France* [2002] ECR I-3827.

approaches and a further opportunity for that and the possibility of a conclusive reference to the Court of Justice is awaited. The Australian case is a decision correct on the wording of the applicable statutory provision and does not add to the debate over the correct interpretation of the Directive.

Definition of defect

The more precisely the defect is defined, the easier it will be for the manufacturer to succeed in the defence. Claimants will seek to rely upon wide allegations of unsafeness and defendants will urge the court to decide that the defect of which discoverability is in issue must, to give the defence substance, be narrowly particularised. The claimants will in this regard no doubt derive some comfort from the judgment of Burton J in the Hepatitis C case. This definitional problem will principally arise in cases of variable adverse outcomes. There is no authority on the point in such circumstances. Claimants will no doubt urge upon the courts an approach analogous to that taken in common law cases such as *Hughes v Lord Advocate.*[92]

Reform

Every five years the Commission must present a report to the Council of Ministers on the application of the Directive with any appropriate proposals.[93] In addition the Commission was obliged to report to the Council of Ministers in 1995 on the effect of any rulings on the application of the development risks defence and on the effect of the derogation permitted by Article 15(1)(b).[94] In the light of this report the Council would decide whether to *repeal* the defence.[95]

The first report of the Commission in 1995 was extremely short and based on very few cases, given the late implementation of the Directive in many Member States.[96] The 1999 Green Paper was designed as a consultation process in order to inform the report due at the end of 2000.[97] The Green Paper sought information on the application of the defence in practice, whether industry had incurred additional expense in jurisdictions where the defence was unavailable, whether the defence should

[92] [1963] AC 837. [93] Under Article 21.
[94] Article 15(3). [95] Article 15(3) does not refer to amendment of Article 7(e).
[96] COM(95)617 of 13.12.95 based on an impact study carried out in 1994.
[97] *Green Paper: Liability for Defective Products* COM(1999)396 final, 28.07.1999.

continue and, if not, whether damages payable as a result of development risks should be borne by society as a whole or the manufacturing sector concerned.[98]

The responses to the Green Paper did not disclose any major problems with the application of the Directive.[99] The Commission was of the view that there was insufficient evidence for firm conclusions or of the need for change.[100] On the question of the development risks defence replies followed 'party lines': manufacturers cautioned against the suppression of innovations, insurers against the difficulty of setting premia for development risks and consumers against allowing producers to take the benefits of trade without the burdens.[101] The response of the European Commission was to establish an expert group to gather information on the legal application of the Directive and to commission research.[102] The purpose of the research was twofold – to assess the economic impact of strengthening the Directive by removing the development risks defence and the financial limit and to analyse and compare the practical effects of the different legal systems in place in the Member States for the prosecution of product liability claims.[103]

The first is still in progress. The second reported to the Commission in 2003.[104] It acknowledged the development risks defence as a potential source of disharmony but concluded that it was read so narrowly as to avail producers little.[105] The report did not thereby intend to convey that the defence should be given the narrow meaning referred to above but rather that, on whatever interpretation of the wording of Article 7(e) applied, there appeared to have been only one successful compared to six unsuccessful invocations of the defence.[106] In the light of this there

[98] Ibid., 22–5. Whether the constitutional basis for increasing consumer protection (for example by removing the defence) still exists under Article 95 of the Treaty (the replacement of Article 100 under which the Directive was promulgated) is a matter for debate – see S. Weatherill, 'The Commission's Options for Developing UK Consumer Protection and Contract Law: Assessing the Constitutional Basis' [2002] EBLR 497.

[99] *Report from the Commission on the Application of Directive 85/374 on Liability for Defective Products* COM (2000) 893 final, 31.1.2001.

[100] Ibid., 28. [101] Ibid., 17.

[102] Ibid., 28–9. [103] Ibid., 29 and 30–1 respectively.

[104] *Product Liability in the European Union* MARKT/2001/11/D.

[105] Ibid., 49–50. The report did not intend to convey that the defence should be given the narrow meaning referred to above but rather that, on whatever interpretation of the wording of Article 7(e) applied, there appeared to have been only one successful plea of the defence.

[106] *Scholten v OLVG Hospital Amsterdam*, 3 February 1999, *Nederlandse Jurisprudentie* 199, 621. There are now seven unsuccessful attempts to rely upon the defence: personal

seemed to be no reason to consider the defence, particularly as it was seen as an important part of the balancing of interests required by Recital 7.

Conclusion

The controversy surrounding the introduction of the defence has not been followed by its frequent invocation. Further there seem to have been very rare successful pleadings of the defence. This may be less to do with clear definition of the meaning of the defence by the courts of the Union than the low volume of product liability litigation and the heavy pressure towards settlement of disputes engendered by the very high cost of litigation. Indeed, as we have seen, unresolved questions of interpretation of the components of the defence predominate over settled jurisprudence.

It is tempting to speculate that there will, when an appropriate opportunity arises, be a sustained attack by industry on the authority of the Hepatitis C judgment which is widely perceived as having a pro-claimant effect. Whilst such an attack may focus mostly upon the definition of defect, the opportunity to re-visit questions of interpretation of the defence are unlikely to be ignored.

Whatever the outcome of this, the balancing exercise provided by the existence of the defence is likely to remain key to the acceptance of the Directive by industry as a politically acceptable compromise on questions of the appropriate standard for liability without fault and thus the opportunity for reform of the Directive by removal of the defence is highly unlikely to be taken.

communication from Rod Freeman of Lovells, the major author of the report: the German Water Bottle case (Case VI XR 158/94, judgment dated 5 September 1995), *Abouzaid v Mothercare (UK) Ltd* [2000] All ER (D) 2436; Hepatitis C, the Austrian water bottle (4 Ob 87/97s 8 April 1997) and coffee machine cases (10 Ob 98/02p 22 October 2002), the Danish glue case (UfR 1997.203 V. Judgment of 14 November 1996), the French horsemeat case (Judgment of 22 February 2000. *Gazette du Palais*, 30 August 2001, para. 11) and an Irish case in which disclosure of research, safety and quality control documents was refused apparently on the basis that the defence was unlikely to be established given the state of knowledge: *Pierce v Aghadoe Developments and Ballygowan Ltd* (Decision of the Master of the High Court, 29 January 2002). The Tribunal de Grande Instance de Montpellier disallowed the defence pleaded by Institut Pasteur in proceedings arising out of the infection of a young woman with Creutzfeld-Jakob Disease from growth hormone treatment on the basis that the action was not brought under the Directive which had not been implemented in France at the time of commencement: 2ème ch. B, 9 July 2002, JCP 2002 II.10158.

11

Approaches to product liability in the EU and Member States

CHRISTOPHER HODGES

The essential components of product liability

In considering the state and nature of product liability, one needs to remind oneself that several different areas need to be examined:

- substantive law on liability
- mechanisms for funding lawyers and court costs, and the extent and proportionality of the financial risk to claimant and defendant
- rules of procedure
- law on damages
- sometimes, conflict/jurisdictional issues such as proper law, jurisdiction and enforcement of judgments.

This is fertile ground for comparative lawyers, which is made more interesting since all of these areas are potentially subject to reform. But one's ardour is somewhat dampened by the consistent evidence that product liability is not a major phenomenon in any EU state. This is also my personal experience over the past ten or so years in handling claims for a number of manufacturers, covering a range of consumer and industrial product sectors, and their insurers, that may arise in any European jurisdiction. One of the jurisdictions that has consistently been most active for individual claims is Russia, where there are unregulated contingency fees, few controls on the accuracy of media statements, and questionable standards in the judicial system.

Substantive law

The rules on strict liability for defective products are relatively stable (Directive 85/374) and firmly implemented into national provisions of member states and applicant states. There has been a small number of instances of incorrect implementation but the Commission and ECJ are well advanced in sorting these out.[1] In 2002 the Danish Presidency called for amendment of Directive 85/374 to provide for liability of intermediaries after a ruling by the Court of Justice which has implications for Denmark and France, but this issue has not made headway.

There have been some interesting divergences in interpretation of the strict liability provisions by national courts. This paper will not examine these but note a number of decisions that may be considered controversial:

France: Aix-en-Provence decision that the claimant does not have to prove that a defect is the cause of the injury.[2]

UK: The decision in the important Hepatitis C case that adopted a strict interpretation of defect based on the view that consumer protection policy requires compensation to be awarded, and the unavoidability of defect is irrelevant; also that the development risk defence is unavailable where the nature and possibility of the defect is known but it is unknown and unknowable whether it existed in the given product.[3]

UK: A defendant can be substituted outside the ten-year cut-off, when proceedings were instituted before the cut-off but against the wrong defendant.[4]

Netherlands: The 1999 decision that blood products infected with HIV were defective, since patients were entitled to expect 100 per cent safety of blood products for sometime before the mid-1990s, but the development risk defence succeeded on the facts.

Germany: The Supreme Court decision (not referred to the ECJ) that the development risk defence does not apply to manufacturing defects.[5]

Austria: The Supreme Court decision on the notification mechanism under which suppliers may escape liability, which highlights the lack of clarity in Art. 3.1 of 85/374 and also the existence of variations in the national provisions implementing this article.[6]

1 Case C-52/00 *Commission v France*; Case C-154/00 *Commission v Greece*; Case C-183/00 *María Gonzáles Sánchez v Medicina Asturiana SA*.

2 D.2001.IR.3092 (2001, exploding glass in fireplace).

3 Note discussion by C. Hodges, 'Compensating Patients' 117 (2001) *LQR*: 528; G. Howells and M. Mildred, 'Infected Blood: Defect and Discoverability: A First Exposition of the EC Product Liability Directive' 65 (2002) *MLR*: 95.

4 *SmithKline Beecham plc v Horne–Roberts* [2001] EWCA CIV 2006 (CA).

5 BGH, 1995, exploding mineral water bottle; OLG Frankfurt, 1995, food infected with hepatitis A by a cook.

6 [2000] ecolex 12; [2000] Rdw 54; see C. Hodges, 'Product Liability of Suppliers: the Notification Trap' [2002] *ELRev*: 758.

Denmark: A folding ladder which broke was not defective when put into circulation given expert evidence that it was the overloading of the ladder that caused it to break (1999).

National courts can make some surprising decisions. For example, courts in Madrid and Seville held that causation was established simply because the manufacturer subsequently recalled the product.[7] Such a conclusion based on such a sole piece of evidence is quite illogical: products can be recalled for commercial rather than safety reasons.

In order to form a complete picture of European compensation mechanisms, one should note the provisions that apply in the four Scandinavian States for compensation of pharmaceutical injuries. Attractive as these are in their national contexts, the national schemes differ in detail and would not be replicable in other States in view of the economic implications. The reason why the schemes work in their national contexts is their complementarity with other national provisions for compensation, not least the high levels of social security/solidarity mechanisms, which cover certain types of damage/loss and which therefore limit the scope and cost of the pharmaceutical schemes, and the existence of sister schemes for medical injuries.

A further quirk is that Germany has a particular regime for compensation of injuries caused by pharmaceuticals, which is exempt from harmonisation in line with the provisions of the Directive.[8] This German regime was reformed in 2002[9] so as to:

(a) reverse the burden of proof, in that the manufacturer has to prove that the harmful effects of the drug did not originate in its development or manufacture;
(b) introduce a presumption of causation, which the manufacturer would have to rebut, if the damage is of a type for which the drug is qualified;
(c) introduce pain and suffering damages for these claims;
(d) increase the maximum compensation payable.

It is curious, therefore, that the picture across Europe in relation to the substantive law on liability contains a number of variations and that at least some important court decisions raise issues that are controversial and

[7] Decisions in 1996, 1998, 1999 for which the author has brief written reports but not citations.

[8] Directive 85/374/EEC, article 13.

[9] Second Law amending the pre-existing Law of Damages: but there is some uncertainty over whether some of the amendments fall within Article 13.

may fragment the appearance of harmonisation if similar decisions are not reached in other Member States. In this connection, it is interesting that several national Supreme Courts have not referred points to the Court of Justice of the European Communities but have made unilateral decisions.

The area of product liability has been something of an ideological battleground between what might be briefly described as supporters of consumer protection and of commercial continuity. The political colours of these two opposed positions, if taken to extremes, are obvious. None of the arguments for and against the basic provisions or contentious issues in relation to strict liability and the Directive have changed much since 1985 or even 1977. The most significant development that impacts on the balancing of the arguments has, in my view, been in relation to the very considerable expansion of EU legislation regulating product safety. Measures have been introduced that encompass the horizontal provisions of Directive 92/59, now amended by 2001/95, on general consumer product safety, as well as the many vertical provisions, such as the New Approach Directives. This development in regulatory law that specifically impacts upon the safety of products significantly undermines the theoretical argument that product liability can be justified as filling a gap in the regulation of industrial conduct, or an argument for punitive damages. On the contrary, this development tends to support an argument for the introduction of a pre-emption defence on the basis that standards of product safety (testing, design, information, pre-marketing approval, post-marketing vigilance, etc.) are set by regulatory measures and that confusion, double standards/jeopardy through isolated decisions by civil courts should be avoided. In any event, future product liability cases will increasingly be significantly influenced by regulatory standards, as has already been seen, particularly in relation to pharmaceuticals.

National law does, of course, continue to govern liability for fault and breach of contract. It has hitherto generally been said that despite differences of wording and detail, national provisions on contract and negligence are roughly similar in their results. The major difference between national provisions in the product liability context is that most of the Civil Law jurisdictions reverse the burden of proof in fault liability claims, whereas common law jurisdictions do not. Given their general similarity in effect, the level of justification for harmonising national provisions in relation to product liability alone has been recognised as being low. Some areas of consumer protection have been harmonised on a piecemeal basis, which now amounts to significant protection for consumers, notably Directive 93/13 on unfair terms in consumer contracts, and Directive 99/44 on certain aspects of the sale of goods and associated guarantees: the latter is yet to have an impact in practice, but it will be considerable, since it introduces considerable extensions in consumer rights such as in relation to repair, replacement, and refund. However, on the wider front, there are important proposals for the codification of European contract law[10] and non-contractual obligations.[11]

Funding and financial risk

This is in many ways the most important area in the practice of product liability. The issue of whether a claimant, or a claimant's lawyer, can afford to litigate a particular claim is of fundamental practical importance. National law and practice governs here, as yet unharmonised by Community measures, and there are many differences in the national rules. The approaches range from the tariff on legal fees in Germany and Austria to an absence of effective regulation in some other States. Some form of legal aid is available in every jurisdiction but it can range from (fullish) state funding of lawyers, administered by a state entity (UK), to allocation by the Bar or a court of a lawyer (perhaps with little experience) to be paid by public funds (Germany) or to act *pro bono* (and therefore little used). The area is highly complex and political. The Commission's Directive on legal aid[12] is preliminary in scope but potentially far-reaching in effect: it requires Member States to provide effective access to justice and representation, whether by funding of lawyers (how much and on what basis is unspecified) or through some form of contingency mechanism. Scotland has long had a contingency system but it is little used. England and Wales largely replaced a legal aid regime with a privatised conditional fee scheme in 1999:[13] significantly, the uplift on standard fees is regulated and capped: this has lowered the incidence of product liability multi-party claims, and there has been debate over whether this denies access to justice or acts as a filter for unjustified cases that waste costs. Member States have noted

[10] Green Paper on *European Contract Law*, COM (2001) 398, 11.07.2001; Communication from the Commission to the European Parliament and the Council: A More Coherent European Contract Law: An Action Plan, COM(2003) 68, 12.2.2003.

[11] Preparatory work of C. von Bar, *The Common European Law of Torts* (Oxford: Oxford University Press, vol. I 1998, vol. II 2000); note also the series of publications by the European Centre of Tort and Insurance Law, Vienna.

[12] Directive 2003/8, OJ L 26/41, 31.1.2003.

[13] The Access to Justice Act 1999 and the Conditional Fee Regulations 2000, SI 2000/692.

the conflict of interest issues that can arise with contingency systems: the UK protests that this is not an issue in practice.

Procedure

Again, national provisions apply and there are considerable variations of detail within the two broad traditional approaches of Roman/civil law and of common law. This is currently an important and fertile area. Key issues are: is the basic approach essentially adversarial or inquisitorial; is there pre-action and during-action disclosure of evidence, or is the system that each of the parties produce only the documents that each has; are experts controlled by the parties or by the court; is the main submission of evidence and of legal argument within an oral or a written tradition; is there a single trial or does the court hold a succession of hearings in order to assemble evidence piece-meal? My personal experience is that the procedure in some Member States is so complex and drawn out that the system of justice has virtually broken down (Greece, Italy). In contrast, some Member States have introduced significant modernising reforms of their civil procedure rules designed to make litigation simpler, quicker, cheaper and more cost-proportionate, notably the United Kingdom in 1999, followed by the Netherlands in 2001, and Germany in 2002.

The Commission's Directorate-General on Justice and Home Affairs is considering possible moves towards harmonisation of civil procedure across Europe, with the possible end of a Code of Civil Procedure: this is a logical endpoint given the goals of creation of a single market but will not happen quickly! The most significant issue in relation to product liability matters is currently whether a class action mechanism, or its equivalent, exists. This continues to be a contentious issue. Some Member States have introduced new procedures, such as the UK (Group Litigation Orders, 1999), Spain (2001) and Sweden (Class Actions, 2002). Legislators can easily misunderstand and underestimate the effects of reforms in this area, and encourage a litigious environment in which unmeritorious claims can prosper. The English Rule on coordination of multi-party cases[14] can be recommended, as providing for a flexible approach through judicial control in case management and avoiding litigation becoming uncontrollable, such as can occur with opt-out mechanisms. The only EU jurisdiction which has so far experienced a sequence of multi-party claims has been England and Wales (followed by Ireland,

[14] CPR Part 19.III.

with important isolated cases in Spain and Austria), where the very high failure rate of cases is remarkable.[15] Advertising by lawyers can also be an issue.[16]

Damages

This area is subject to national laws, where the approaches can differ, as to the rules on both recoverability (heads, remoteness) and levels of compensation. There are some moves towards harmonisation, for example through compensation levels for motor vehicle accident injuries. The contentious 'hot spot' issue for the product liability arena is whether punitive damages could be justified, although they are not currently generally available (the House of Lords has recently re-ignited the issue in the UK).[17] Any thought for future harmonisation in this area is limited by significant complexities: rules on recoverability and quantum present a major challenge in their own right but the position is enormously complicated by inter-relations with other national approaches to social security or solidarity, where there are again major differences.

Jurisdictional issues

This area is subject to some reform but any substantive changes will probably not have major effect on product liability issues.

- Convention 80/934/EEC on the law applicable to contractual obligations (Rome I) and its reform[18]
- Forthcoming Proposal on law of non-contractual obligations (Rome II)[19]
- Regulation on jurisdiction and enforcement of judgments (formerly Brussels Convention).[20]

[15] C. Hodges, *Multi-Party Actions* (Oxford: Oxford University Press, 2002).

[16] See Lord Steyn, 'Perspectives of Corrective and Distributive Justice in Tort Law', Eighth John Maurice Kelly Memorial Lecture, University College, Dublin, 1 November 2001.

[17] *Kuddus v Chief Constable of Leicestershire* [2001] 2 WLR 1789.

[18] Green Paper on the conversion of the Rome Convention of 1980 on the law applicable to contractual obligations into a Community instrument and its modernisation COM (2002) 654, 14.1.2003.

[19] See Consultation on a preliminary draft proposal, 3 May 2002.

[20] Council Regulation (EC) No 44/2001 of 22 December 2000 on jurisdiction and the recognition and enforcement of judgments in civil and commercial matters.

Does the Community have jurisdictional competence to propose a new Directive on product liability?

Debate in the product liability area during the past few years has tended to concentrate on the socio-legal arguments for and against change to the Product Liability Directive. It is, however, important to consider the circumstances under which the European Community would have jurisdiction to amend that or any other Directive. Directive 85/374 was based on Article 100 EC as it stood in 1985, which provided:

> The Council shall, acting unanimously on a proposal from the Commission, issue directives for the approximation of such provisions laid down by law, regulation or administrative action in Member States as directly affect the establishment or functioning of the common market . . .

The current successor to this measure is Article 95 EC, which provides:

> By way of derogation from Article 94 and save where otherwise provided in this Treaty, the following provisions shall apply for the achievement of the objectives set out on Article 14. The Council shall, acting in accordance with the procedure referred to in Article 251 and after consulting the Economic and Social Committee, adopt measures for the approximation of the provisions laid down by law, regulation or administrative action in Member States which have as their object the establishment and functioning of the internal market.

Article 14 EC provides that the Community shall adopt measures with the aim of progressively establishing the internal market, which shall comprise an area without internal frontiers in which the free movement of goods, persons, services and capital is ensured in accordance with the provisions of the Treaty.

The ECJ has made clear in many judgments that measures must be properly constitutionally based, and not depend simply on the conviction of one or more of the institutions as to the objective being pursued but must be based on objective factors that are amenable to judicial review.[21] It was held in Case C-376/98[22] that measures based on Article 95 EC must actually contribute to eliminating obstacles to the free movement of goods

[21] E.g. Case C-155/91 *Commission v Council* [1993] ECR I-939; Case C-209/97 *Commission v Council* [1999] ECR I-8067.

[22] *Germany v Parliament and Council* [2000] ECR I-8419 (re Tobacco Advertising Directive 98/43).

and to the free movement to provide services or to removing appreciable distortions of competition. A measure must be market-making harmonisation, informed if appropriate under Article 95.3 by public health protection under Article 152 or consumer protection under Article 153, neither of the last two being competent to found jurisdiction for measures themselves. Thus, it is not constitutionally acceptable when considering this type of Community legislation to engage in public health policy – or consumer protection policy – dressed up as market-making.[23]

So the issue is: what is the evidence that there now remain distortions to the free movement of goods or appreciable distortions of competition in relation to product liability within the internal market? There was scant evidence of this in either the First Study,[24] the First 1995 Report[25] or the Second 2000 Report.[26] These showed the very low level of product liability litigation within the Member States, and certainly in relation to trade between them. The 2003 Study similarly reaches the conclusion that there is little evidence that disparities between Member States in the practical functioning of product liability regimes create significant barriers to trade or distortions in competition in the EU.[27] It seems, therefore, that jurisdiction to amend the Directive is lacking. Furthermore, there seems little political will to embark on amendments at present. If amendments were proposed, it is not difficult to envisage a jurisdictional challenge to any proposals to which objection were to be taken.

Conclusion

Product liability is a subject that has significant complexities in that it encompasses areas of access to justice, litigation procedure and levels of compensation as well as substantive liability rules. The market-driven imperative of European harmonisation has produced the introduction of reform of the historic liability rules on contract and fault not by reform or harmonisation of those rules but by the introduction of the new rule

[23] See S. Weatherill, 'The Commission's Options for Developing EC Consumer Protection and Contract Law: Assessing the Constitutional Basis' [2002] *EBLR*: 497.

[24] C. Hodges, *Report for the Commission of the European Communities on the Application of Directive 85/374/EEC on Liability for Defective Products* (London: McKenna & Co, 1994).

[25] COM(95) 617.

[26] Report from the Commission on the Application of Directive 85/374 on Liability for Defective Products COM (2000) 893.

[27] *Product Liability in the European Union: A Report for the European Commission* (London: Lovells, 2003).

of strict liability. Harmonisation of the national rules on contract and fault is likely to emerge, albeit slowly. The other areas (access to justice, etc.) continue to divide European Member States and the process of their harmonisation is beginning, but will take a significant amount of time. Whether these longer-term harmonisation processes bring about significant reforms remains to be seen.

The level of product liability claims in Europe has consistently remained far lower than that which has been produced in the USA by their procedural rules and constitutional climate, given in particular their different situation in relation to availability of healthcare and insurance. It is widely recognised that the overheated liability system in the USA produces economic results that encourage lawyer-led litigation and in which lawyers can reap very substantial and disproportionate rewards. The impact of reforms to European rules on access to justice, class actions, funding mechanisms and damages should be carefully considered so as to avoid these American problems. Existing variations in national rules on litigation procedure and funding constitute significant barriers to consumers in bringing claims and confusion to all litigants and non-national lawyers in understanding some national systems.

The function of a product liability mechanism is primarily to pay adequate compensation to those to whom claimable harm is caused. The system seems to operate effectively in Europe but with significant differences brought about by differing national rules in healthcare and social security provisions, and with important areas of law and procedure that are not yet harmonised. A further function is to impose a deterrent on producers to take care that their products are designed, manufactured and labelled so as to minimise the safety risks of use. Deterrence is of limited value as a mechanism of behavioural control since it acts *post facto* whereas the considerable corpus of regulatory controls may be expected to be of greater impact in acting preventatively. Although there is little data on these points, there seems to be little evidence that there are significant variations in the level of product safety or accidents produced by defective products.

12

Product liability – a history of harmonisation

GERAINT HOWELLS*

Introduction

Rather than discussing whether harmonisation of product liability is desirable or practical or debating how best it can be achieved, this chapter deals with a topic (product liability), which has in fact, since 1985, been the subject of a harmonising directive. This chapter seeks to focus on three issues. First, what has the product liability experience taught us about the need for harmonisation and particularly about the degree of harmonisation required for internal market reasons? Second, how has the Community monitored its legislation and determined whether it needs to be amended? Finally, we will use the central concepts of defect and development risks to consider whether the courts (both national and European) have been able to develop a harmonised approach to interpretation and what can be done to enhance a common development of European principles.

How much harmonisation is necessary?

The Product Liability Directive was introduced as an internal market measure under art. 100 of the Treaty. The drafter of the Directive, Professor Taschner, has on many occasions subsequently spoken of his firm belief that the measure is an internal market and not a consumer protection measure. Thus the first recital to the directive states that 'the existing divergences may distort competition', although it does go on to note that this may entail a differing degree of consumer protection.

One unfortunate side effect of this has been that product liability has not been within the sweep of directives for which the consumer protection Directorate General (DG-SANCO) is responsible. This is regrettable given that it has clear overlaps with other directives under the umbrella of

* This is a version of a paper written for the third edition of *Towards a European Civil Code*, editors A. Hartkamp, M. Hesselink, E. Hendius, C. Jonstra, E. Du Perron and M. Veldman (Ars Aequi Libri, Nijmegen Law International, 2004).

DG-SANCO – most obviously it complements the General Product Safety Directive[1] and in the private law field sits alongside directives on sale of goods[2] and unfair terms.[3] This split of competences might have important consequences for any future development of European private law. At the very least the Commission needs to improve the way it coordinates work between the different directorates.

Germany v European Parliament and Council[4] confirmed that the internal market Treaty provision could only be invoked where either this was necessary to eliminate barriers (or potential barriers) to trade or to prevent distortions in competition. Product liability does not directly impose barriers to trade as it makes no specific requirement of products other than they are not defective. Thus the justification must rest upon the distortion of competition ground. Such distortions must be 'appreciable'.[5] One might be sceptical about the necessity (as opposed to the desirability) for product liability harmonisation given that the US manages to work with a single market containing differing product liability regimes. Indeed certain product liability rules were already common throughout Europe. For instance, most systems had a regime of contractual liability for defects and a tort regime based around fault liability. Possibly instances like the development of a *de facto* strict liability regime in countries like France and the reversal of the burden of proof in Germany provided sufficient excuse for harmonisation.

The US experience should, however, teach us that the single market does not require complete uniformity of product liability law; indeed it needs to be appreciated that the impact of product liability goes beyond substantive rules and depends on issues such as damages, procedural rules and access to justice. We shall see that the Directive was nevertheless intended to be a maximal harmonisation directive not allowing states to increase protection other than in areas where this was provided for expressly by the Directive. It will be argued that this is unjustified. All that the internal market requires is that the rules in the Member States be

[1] Directive 2001/95: OJ 2002 L11/4 amending Directive 92/59.

[2] Directive 1999/44: OJ 1999 L 171/12.

[3] Directive 1993/13: OJ 1993 L95/29.

[4] C-376/98, [2000] ECR I-8419, [2000] All ER (EC) 769. For a fuller discussion of this decision by the present author see 'Federalism in USA and EC – The Scope for Harmonised Legislative Activity Compared' 6 (2002) *European Review of Private Law*: 601. At the same time the Court decided the case of *R v Secretary of State for Health, ex parte Imperial Tobacco and others*, C-74/99, [2000] ECR I-8599 in which the English High Court had referred the question of the same Directive's validity.

[5] Judgment at para. 168.

within a sufficiently narrow band so that they do not create appreciable distortions in competition. Given this premise, it does indeed seem bizarre that the directive did not find it necessary to harmonise whether pain and suffering damages could be recovered, but thought it essential that consumers could not use the Directive to recover the first 500 Euros of property damage in any state!

The lack of discretion of Member States to increase protection has been confirmed in three recent decisions of the European Court of Justice. In *Commission v France*,[6] the French implementing law was condemned for allowing recovery of the first 500 Euros; for making suppliers liable on the same basis as producers; and for imposing the extra condition that the producer must prove that he took appropriate steps to avert the consequences of a defective product in order to invoke the compliance with mandatory requirements and the development risks defence. Similarly Greece was condemned for not introducing the 500 Euro threshold.[7] In *González Sánchez v Medicina Asturiana SA*[8] a victim of infected blood was not allowed to continue to rely on an earlier Spanish law which had been repealed when the Directive was implemented.

The discussion in the above cases centred on an interpretation of Article 13 of the Directive, which provides:

> This Directive shall not affect any rights which an injured person may have according to the rules of the law of contractual or non-contractual liability or a special liability system existing at the moment when this Directive is notified.

The Court in *Commission v France* states that Article 13 of the Directive does not allow Member States to maintain a general system of product liability different from that provided for in the Directive. It goes on to state that contractual and non-contractual liability can, however, exist on grounds such as fault or a warranty for latent defects. It also states that the special liability scheme exception is limited to specific schemes limited to a given sector of production. Given that France extended liability in an Act implementing the Directive, the Court's decision could be easily justified on the basis that the law increases the protection beyond the permitted maximum levels by rules introduced after the notification of the Directive.

It is more problematic, however, to justify the Court's other statement that art. 13 does not give Member States the possibility of maintaining

[6] Case C-52/00, [2002] ECR I-3827. [7] *Commission v Greece*, C-154/00 [2002] ECR I-3879.
[8] Case C-183/00, [2002] ECR I-3901.

a general system of product liability different from that provided for in the Directive. It is well known that the French system of contractual and tortious liability had developed to an extent where its protection probably surpassed that of the Directive.[9] Some French commentators now interpret this decision as meaning that the existing liability system must be reinterpreted so as not to exceed the protection of the Directive.[10] This would be remarkable. The French system might be labelled by jurists as a special liability system, but it is really only the accumulation of a set of contractual and non-contractual rules, whose continued validity had seemingly been expressly preserved by Article 13. Art. 13 might, admittedly, put a brake on the future interpretation of those rules by the courts, but surely should not affect existing jurisprudence. Indeed, it might even be argued that it would be going too far to limit the national courts' interpretation of laws which only incidentally provide liability for defective products. For example, should the development of warranty law be impeded because it happens to have knock-on effects in product liability which exceed the protection offered by the Directive? In the United Kingdom, for instance, one might argue that for parties to a contract a claim in satisfactory quality is an easier route than establishing a defect under the Consumer Protection Act 1987. Does the European Court seriously intend that English sale of goods law needs to be reformed or its development modified because of its product liability consequences? What the Court seems to have failed to appreciate is that product liability is not a simple topic that can be boxed off and delimited within the scope of a directive; rather product liability claims can typically be based on a wide range of contractual and tortious claims.

Similarly the result in *Sánchez* can be justified, but the reasoning might be questioned. Sánchez was in effect complaining that Spain had implemented the Directive by repealing the more protective rules in its 1984 law. It seems perfectly permissible to argue that whilst Article 13 permits Member States to maintain existing systems of liability in place it does not *require* them to do so. They would clearly seem to be free to decide that existing laws should be repealed in favour of the Directive's standard. However, the Court seems to have gone further and indicated that the Spanish Government would not have been able to maintain its 1984 rules in place if it had wanted to do so. It states that the special liability system is limited to specific sectors and continues:

[9] Further, see chapter 5. [10] See Note C. Larroument, *Dalloz* 2002 no. 31, p. 2464 at 2465.

> [the] system of producer liability founded on the same basis as that put in place by the Directive and not limited to a given sector of production does not come within any of the systems of liability referred to in Article 13 of the Directive. That provision cannot therefore be relied on in such a case in order to justify the maintenance in force of national provisions affording greater protection than those of the Directive.[11]

Whilst the special liability system was clearly intended to cover cases like the pharmaceutical regime, it is baffling how the existing Spanish system could fail to be anything other than a species of non-contractual liability whose continued existence was specifically provided for by Article 13. It would be an elementary mistake only to define as non-contractual liability liability based on civil codes or the common law. Thus whilst the decision can be justified as defending the right of Spain to choose not to maintain its existing laws, it should have held that Spain would have had the right to have done so if it had so desired.

From an internal market perspective there would seem to be no reason why product liability has to be absolutely uniform, so long as the range of liability is sufficiently narrow so as not to distort competition. Insisting on complete uniformity might even be viewed as a disproportionate response. The only crucial issue of substantive law which might appreciably affect competition is the development risks defence and this is specifically addressed in the Directive. Other important issues such as the heads of damages available, particularly non-material damage, have been the subject of consultation recently and their approximation could be valuably reviewed.

One of the foci of a recent study carried out by the Commission[12] was the relationship between the strict liability regimes and contractual and non-contractual claims. It would be surprising if the issue of whether the Directive should be the sole source of redress in product liability cases were not on the Commission's agenda, especially given the tone of the recent European Court judgments and the general move towards total harmonisation directives in order to promote the internal market. However, in product liability such a move is both unnecessary and would generate much complexity. Total or maximal harmonisation is only really necessary where rules affect the form of the goods or services so that modification or adaptation to design, labelling or packaging may be required

[11] Judgment para. 33.

[12] The scope of the study was envisaged in COM (2000) 893 at 29–31. This study was carried out by the law firm Lovells and the present author acted as a consultant.

to permit market access. Otherwise rough equivalence of laws will usually suffice. The idea that traders should be able to trade into any Member States without having to have knowledge of national laws on the basis that they can assume them to be the same across Europe is unrealistic. It is illusory in theory and unrealistic in practice.

Indeed boxing off product liability laws and trying to create a uniform European regime is impracticable. The contours of product liability overlap with other areas to such an extent that saying an issue falls within product liability and not other areas like service or environmental liability will be problematic and equally it will be hard to prevent areas like sale of goods law and negligence from having an impact.

Modernisation

The fact that Europe was able to enact a directive on product liability in 1985 was indeed a major achievement, given the fear of a US style liability crisis in the minds of many governments and industries. The fact that its content was ambiguous was understandable given that it was responding to a thalidomide problem and yet had to include a development risks defence option to make sure there was sufficient support to ensure adoption. This was also to be expected given its inspiration had in part at least come from the US. The US had settled on strict product liability in the Second Restatement of Torts in 1964. However, the jurisprudence from the US was confused; unsurprisingly given the variety of state and federal courts which addressed the issue. In particular there was no agreement on the respective roles of consumer expectations and risk–utility in judging product defects. More fundamentally from a historical perspective it is clear that the drafters of the Second Restatement had been seeking a rather modest reform, limited to tidying up the existing sales law and overcoming the evidential problems consumers faced with regard to proving how product defects arose.[13] Subsequently the US addressed this issue in the Restatement of Torts (Third) (Product Liability) and somewhat contentiously sought to bring order to its product liability system by distinguishing between types of defects – manufacturing, design and failure to warn – and in effect restricting strict liability to manufacturing defects. There has been and continues to be much debate as to whether this is the correct restatement of the court's jurisprudence and whether it will be

[13] G. Priest, 'Strict Product Liability: The Original Intent' (1989) 10 Carduso Law Rev 2301.

accepted by the courts. Even if the drafters of the Second Restatement had not foreseen their reform would lead to challenges to product designs and warnings with the attendant broader social impact, this was certainly how the new rules were utilised by many courts. It would seem hard to turn the clock back and view strict liability as having only a marginal impact.

For our purposes, it suffices to note that the EC Product Liability Directive was therefore introduced at a time when product liability jurisprudence was in an embryonic state and at least with some reliance on fledgling US theories, which the US has since revisited and revised. The Directive also had more than the usual scars from the political compromises that 'distinguish' EC legislation. There were overt options on the development risks defence, the exclusion of primary agricultural produce and game and a ceiling on personal injury damages. Other important matters left to national law included the practically important topic of recovery of non-material damages. The Directive also included some significant restrictions, such as the ten-year long-stop on liability, and some other minor irritable aspects such as the exclusion of the first 500 Euros of property damage. The central concept of defect was itself subject to the accusation of opaqueness for, in defining defectiveness in terms of when a product does not provide the safety which a person is entitled to expect, it could easily be accused of being circuitous by including in the definition the very question the definition should be providing the answer to. Moreover, the development risks defence, introduced against the Commission's better judgment, threatened to undermine the strict liability regime which underpinned the reforms.

Fortunately, the Directive had made plenty of provision for its review. The Directive was to be reviewed every five years[14] and the options on the development risk and cap on personal injury after ten years.[15] However, the sole reform to date has been the removal of the exclusion of primary agricultural produce and game.[16] This was intended to be a response to the 'mad cow' BSE crisis, although how any victim of CJD could be expected to invoke the Directive is baffling. They would have to identify which beef, consumed many years before, was infected and responsible for their disease. It smacks more of knee-jerk political reaction than any serious attempt to reform product liability law. The Commission's first report on the Directive had been a very scant document[17] relying on an impact

[14] Art. 21. [15] Art. 15(3) and 16(2).

[16] Directive 99/34 OJ 1999 L 141/20. [17] COM (1995) 617.

study[18] to suggest that given the limited experience to date it was not appropriate to propose reforms. The European Parliament had called for a substantial revision of the Directive when debating the limited reform for primary agricultural produce and game. Although the Commission did not share this view it promised to open up discussion in the form of a Green Paper.[19] This Green Paper canvassed an amazing array of possible reforms, from the modest to the potentially dramatic, but its very breadth seemed to indicate a lack of focus and drive to bring about reforms. This seems to support the view that the Commission wanted to air the issues, but had no urgent desire to see reform. The European Parliament's Committee on Legal Affairs and the Internal Market nevertheless still seems keen on reform.[20] The Commission subsequently issued a Report outlining the responses to the Green Paper and setting out some future steps.[21] One of these was to commission a study on the workings of the directive and future reforms will no doubt have to await the response to that study. Another study on the economic impact of the development risks defence has also been undertaken.

The author was a consultant to the latest Commission study.[22] Without going into the details of that report, it can be noted from general observations that there is no great clamour for major reform. The guiding spirit behind the original directive (Professor Taschner) is no longer at the Commission, though active in academic circles, and seems fairly pleased with the law he introduced. As we have seen, the Commission was dragged into a more extensive review of the law. Industry has not experienced any major disasters. Injured parties tend on the whole to fail on causation issues rather than because there is no potential ground for liability. There have been no major scandals, where an aspect of the Directive, like the ten-year limitation period, for instance, has caused obvious injustice.

The courts have, of course, faced problems with some product claims. The most tricky product related claims to date have concerned blood products, where the risk has resulted from public health scares concerning blood and blood products infected with diseases such as hepatitis C, HIV or new variant CJD. As this is a by-product of a public health problem, the blood industry has been fortunate to escape widespread calls for reform to the law to make it liable in a stricter way. This is in stark contrast to the way

18 Available at www.europa.eu.int/comm/internal˙market/en/goods/liability/index.htm.

19 COM (1999) 396.

20 See its report on the Green Paper of 1 March 2000, A5-0061/2000.

21 COM (2000) 893.

22 See www.Lovells.com.

the pharmaceutical industry was treated in the wake of the thalidomide disaster, where the industry was seen as the cause of the problem. Of course this does not mean that the blood industry should not be responsible for those infected by its products. Indeed this has happened in a significant English case.[23] Simply the blood issue has been seen as a specific social problem not requiring general reform of the law of product liability.

Some important reform issues are on the agenda. France[24] and Denmark[25] in particular seem concerned that the strict liability regime should be capable of being extended to all suppliers. Another major issue is the repeal of the development risks defence, into which the Commission has undertaken a specific study.[26] The ten-year limitation period could also be seen as a potential source of injustice. It would also be useful to ensure non-material damages were recoverable in all countries; although there is a trend in this direction anyway given the reforms to civil liability in Germany.[27]

There could also be a number of minor reforms that would clarify the law. Most obvious is the exclusion of the first 500 Euros from a property damage claim. There is even confusion as to whether this is in fact a threshold, which when breached allows recovery in full (as applies in the United Kingdom), or whether it should be a deduction like an insurance excess as it is treated in the other states. The simplest solution would be to abolish it, especially given that the rationale for the exclusion as a way to reduce claims for small amounts is not very convincing. One can see minor clarifications like this taking place. One would be sceptical about more fundamental reforms to the legislation given the lack of enthusiasm from the Commission combined with a lack of clamour for reform from any interest groups. The lack of a strong reform call from the consumer side might appear strange given some of the shortcomings in the directive as a consumer protection measure. Apart from the lack of any obvious instances of injustices, this quietness from the consumer side may be explained by the fact that the consumer groups that lobbied for the earlier

[23] *A v National Blood Authority* [2001] 3 All ER 289.

[24] Following the recent ECJ decision, discussed above.

[25] During their Presidency of the Council they proposed an amendment, making it clear that Member States could impose liability on intermediaries, to Council: see www.health.fgov.be/WHI3/krant/krantarch2002/kranttekstoct2/021023m05eu.htm.

[26] Fondazione Rosselli, Analysis of the Economic Impact of the Development Risks Clause as a provided by Directive 85/374/EEC on Liability for Defective Products (2004).

[27] The Zweites Schadenersatz-ÄnderungsGesetz would amend s. 8 of the Product Liability Law so as to allow compensation for non-material damage under the conditions set out in the new s. 253(2) of the Civil Code.

reforms have now moved on to newer and higher-profile topics and have not been involved in the application of the law, which has been carried out by private practitioners. This leaves the question of whether the courts can by themselves bring order to this area of law. This will be tested by their approach to the central jurisprudential topics of defect and development risks.

Defect and development risk

The concept of defect and the development risks defence can be criticised for vagueness, but their very imprecision could provide the opportunity for the courts to develop a meaningful approach. The European Court of Justice in particular could be an important source of guidance for the development of product liability law given its ability to bind the Member States' courts.

The Court has not been called upon to consider the concept of defectiveness directly. In addition to the cases on maximal or minimum harmonisation discussed above, it has, for instance, decided that a hospital could be liable when a fluid caused a kidney destined for a transplant to become unusable.[28] However, its most relevant decision for our purposes is perhaps *Commission v United Kingdom*,[29] when it was called upon to determine whether the English version of the development risks defence, in s. 4(1)(e), Consumer Protection Act 1987 was too generous to the producers (by judging defendants in the light of producers of similar products and by introducing the notion of expectancy of discoverability rather than a test of mere discoverability).

The Court found that the Commission had not made out its case. One of its reasons for so holding perhaps indicates that the Court is not entirely *au fait* with the nature of personal injury litigation, at least in the United Kingdom. The Court considered it significant that there had not been a pattern of cases establishing that the English courts would interpret the provision at variance with the Directive. However, product liability cases are not so numerous that they trouble the courts on a regular basis and product liability cases raising the development risks defence are rarer still. Most product liability cases are settled by negotiation and the possibility that the defence will be generously construed will affect those

[28] *Henning Veedfald v Århus Amtskommune*, C-203/99, [2001] ECR I-3569 note G. Howells 6 (2002) *European Review of Private Law*: 847.

[29] C-300/95 [1997] ECR I-2649.

negotiations and thus should have been sufficient justification to support the Commission's decision to bring infringement actions.

Nevertheless, the judgment could be welcomed if it provides sufficient guidance on the scope of the defence to ensure that United Kingdom courts will indeed interpret the defence in line with the strict liability rationale which underpins the Directive and to which the development risks defence was intended to be a narrow exception, with the burden of proving the defence on the defendant. Here we have an irony, for whilst we shall see that the Court was not particularly demanding about when the defence could be invoked, this judgment was picked up by Mr Justice Burton and used as a reason for giving the defence a limited scope in *A v National Blood Authority*.[30]

Some of the language of Advocate General Tesauro in particular seemed to smack of negligence. For instance, he talked about the producer having to bear all *foreseeable* risks.[31] Whilst some aspects of the decision confirm the narrow scope of the defence – such as identifying the standard expected with the most advanced state of knowledge[32] – the Court also introduced the concept that for knowledge to defeat the use of the defence it must be accessible to the defendant.[33] Such an interpretation would make the defence available to every blameless producer, but seems to be an overly broad interpretation to the defence for which there is little support in the wording of the directive.

Advocate General Tesauro would have, for example, excluded findings in a Manchurian scientific journal.[34] In the English *National Blood* case Mr Justice Burton suggested that this might be a bad example in a case involving a product for which Manchuria was famous, but equally unpublished documents or research retained within the laboratory or research department of a particular company might be regarded as 'Manchurian'.[35] One might not like it but the case law does seem to have settled on a clear interpretation of the development risks defence to the extent that it excludes inaccessible information; even if some uncertainty still surrounds what is meant by inaccessible.

A further difficult issue is whether the development risks defence can apply to manufacturing defects or, as Mr Justice Burton preferred to refer to them, non-standard products.[36] The German Supreme Court decided that there was no need to refer to Luxembourg the question of whether

[30] [2001] 3 All ER 289. [31] Opinion para. 22.
[32] Judgment para. 26. [33] Judgment para. 29. [34] Opinion para. 23.
[35] *A & Others v NBA* [2001] 3 All ER 289, para. 49. [36] Para. 36.

the defence applied to a manufacturing defect, namely the undiscoverable crack in a mineral bottle. The failure to refer a matter which was far from obvious is regrettable.[37] Burton J agreed with the German court's conclusion that the defence should not apply on the basis that the risk was a known one. However, in such cases he would have allowed the defence potentially to apply on one occasion before the defect became known. If the issue had been referred, the European Court might have provided guidance and prevented the need for the point to be litigated across Europe with national courts all potentially producing their own slightly differing interpretations.

In his own case Burton J was faced with the argument that the defence should apply as it was impossible to detect the defect in the particular product given the lack of a test for the hepatitis C virus. He held that the defence did not apply once the risk was known, even if there was no possibility to detect it in individual products. This was a potentially viable defence, because the defence talked about the state of scientific and technical knowledge being such as 'to enable the existence of the defect to be discovered'; so it could be argued that it was not enough for the risk to be known, it must also have been possible to detect actual defects. Burton J noted that the Amsterdam County Court[38] had allowed such a defence in a case of HIV-infected blood, but he rejected that court's reasoning. He also distinguished an Australian case where the undiscoverability of contamination in individual oysters[39] allowed a similar defence to apply on the basis that the defence was differently worded in the Australian law. Instead the English judge relied on the opinion of Advocate-General Tesauro in *Commission v United Kingdom.* Earlier we criticised the Advocate General for talking in terms of foreseeable risks because this smacked of negligence, but in one respect it works to the claimants' advantage, for once risks are foreseeable it is clear that the defendant had the choice of stepping up experimentation or insuring. Burton found the development risks defence inapplicable to foreseeable risks.[40]

The reader will have noticed frequent references to the decision of Mr Justice Burton. This is not only an important decision on the particular issue of liability in England and Wales for infected blood, but is also

37 J. Stapleton describes the decision as extraordinary for merely asserting the defence did not apply: 'Restatement (Third) of Torts: Product Liability, an Anglo-Australian Perspective' 39 (2000) *Washburn LJ*: 363 at 383.

38 *Scholten v The Foundation Sanquin of Blood Supply*, 3 February 1999.

39 *Graham Barclay Oysters Pty v Ryan*, 102 FCR 307.

40 *A & Others v NBA* [2001] 3 All ER 289, para. 74.

significant because of the way the judge approached the case. For instance, he by-passed the English implementing statute and went straight to the Directive. Questionable as this may be, it shows he was open to the influence of European law. Equally, he referred to much academic writing, which is unusual for British judges and is obviously to be applauded. Moreover, he also relied on continental and US scholarly writing and as we have seen was well informed about and willing to learn from continental case law. Again this is a very healthy approach which should be emulated by all national judges faced with complex and ambiguous laws with an EC origin that have yet to be authoritatively determined by the European Court of Justice.

Indeed on the issue of defectiveness he adopted the approach of a German writer and treated the judge as the 'appointed representative of the public at large'.[41] What the public were entitled to expect could be more or less than what they actually did expect.[42] Avoidability was not a relevant circumstance in assessing defectiveness.[43] Standard products were differentiated from non-standard products.[44] On the facts the blood containing hepatitis C was treated as non-standard and defective because it was not sufficient that the medical profession knew of the risk. The public would not expect blood to be infected and would have expected to be informed of the risk and this had not been done. The impact any warnings, through the media or at the time of supply, might have had is not spelt out by the judge. It is certainly arguable that the case might not be so favourable to future claimants where warnings are supplied.[45]

Without going into detail in assessing the judgment one can at least see that this judgment should be widely read across Europe. One might also think the judgment throws up issues that only the European Court can settle for the whole of Europe. Thus we need to consider (i) the relationship between national case law and European case law, and also, (ii) the use of comparative jurisprudence. The former is a constitutional issue, which raises broader questions about access to the European Courts. The latter can perhaps be addressed by the development of a database on European product liability law drawing on the experience of the CLAB database in unfair terms. The Commission in the Green Paper had proposed the establishment of an expert group,[46] but that does not seem to

[41] H. Bartl, *Produkthafting nach neuem EG-Recht* (1989).

[42] *A & Others v NBA* [2001] 3 All ER 289, para. 31 (vii). [43] Para. 63. [44] Para. 80.

[45] See G. Howells and M. Mildred, 'Infected Blood: Defect and Discoverability: a First Exposition of the EC Product Liability Directive' 65 (2002) *Modern Law Review*: 95–105.

[46] Ibid. at p. 29.

have materialised and a database would in any event seem a more useful and openly available tool.

There is also some evidence of different practices emerging about how courts determine the issue of defectiveness. An important question is whether the fact a product when used as intended causes unexpected harm should be seen without more ado as evidence of a defect. In the United Kingdom this is certainly not the case. For instance, in a case involving a condom that broke it was not enough that the condom ripped as people should know condoms are not 100 per cent safe.[47] That may be a fair decision on its facts. Less easy to accept is a decision that a breast implant that leaks cannot be held to be defective until the claimant shows what caused the defect.[48] That risks taking us back to the dark days of negligence and the evidential difficulties that strict liability was intended to address. It is to be hoped that such a result would not be reached after the *National Blood* case, as the public would not expect breast implants to leak unless they were defective. By contrast, the French courts seem to take a different approach. For instance, the Court of Appeal in Toulouse presumed that tyres that exploded were defective[49] and equally the *Tribunal de grande instance* in Aix-en-Provence found liability when a glass window in a fireplace exploded without having to determine the exact cause.[50] Similarly the Green Paper cites a Belgian case in which the defect was inferred from the abnormal behaviour of an aerated beverage bottle that exploded.[51] Of course these can be viewed as simply instances of one or other of the courts getting things wrong, but they do perhaps suggest a different approach between jurisdictions. The issue of burden of proof is an issue the Commission has mentioned in the Green Paper and follow up report.[52] However, there is much more work that needs to be done in unpicking the relationship between burden of proof in establishing defectiveness and the related issue of proving a causal relationship between defects and damage.[53]

Conclusion

The Product Liability Directive has undoubtedly been a good thing from the consumer perspective. Without the Directive it is unlikely that all

[47] *Richardson v LRC Products Ltd.*, unreported decision of Mr Justice Kennedy 2 Feb. 2002.
[48] *Foster v Biosil*, 59 BMLR 178. [49] 7 November 2000. [50] 2 October 2001.
[51] OM (1999) 396 at p. 21. [52] Ibid. at pp. 21–2 and 13–16 respectively.
[53] See my paper 'Defect in English Law – Lessons for the Harmonisation of European Product Liability' at chapter 8.

Member States would have introduced strict liability and certainly it would not have arrived in so coherent a form. Yet doubts still remain about the degree to which product liability needs to be harmonised. Does the internal market demand uniformity, equivalence or merely that laws be harmonised to within broad bands of compatibility? The law looks silly at present by demanding that the first 500 Euros of property damage should not be recovered in any state, whilst leaving recovery of non-material damage to national law. This question of the extent of harmonisation is one which needs to be addressed in relation to all forms of internal market law. Within the private law field, the indirect impact private law rules have on traders might suggest a fairly relaxed regime as regards harmonisation is justified.

However, the tendency seems towards increased harmonisation and, within the field of product liability, increased competence of the European legislator at the expense of the national legislator. That places greater emphasis on the need to ensure the European laws are of a good quality and that efficient mechanisms exist for modernising them. Modernisation of EC product liability law to date has been restricted to the inclusion of primary agricultural products and game. The reasons for the lack of reform may indeed lie in the acceptance by all parties that the system is working well and not causing major problems. It may also be partly a result of the long lead-time for such actions (although this point becomes less significant as the Directive ages). The lack of litigation in the field may indeed mean that not enough experience has been gained to support calls for major reforms. One difficulty is that consumer groups in particular may simply not have had the time to devote to assessing the impact of the Directive. Indeed whilst it is easy to spot victims whose claims fail, the more difficult task may be to detect where people are failing to bring their claims to court. The problem may simply be that consumer groups have diverted their attention to other more immediately pressing topics. Although the Commission has investigated the area thoroughly, after the promptings of the European Parliament, one cannot help but feel that rather than rely on the initiative coming from the Commission alone there should still be room for national initiatives.[54]

Finally, we have noted that some of the core terms – defect and development risks – remain ambiguous. Guidance in the form of further legislative initiative or case law of the European Court of Justice might be

[54] See T. Wilhelmsson, 'Private Law in the EU: Harmonised or Fragmented Europeanisation?' 6 (2002) *European Review of Private Law*: 77.

welcomed, but cannot be guaranteed. It is likely that national case law will remain sporadic and so national courts may well be willing to engage in cross-border dialogues if there are easy means of doing so. In order to assist this process the Commission should set up the necessary communication structures, such as the development of case law databases. Indeed out of such necessity might actually come some of the most constructive practical moves towards the integration of European private law.

PART III

Comparing systems

13

Harmonisation or divergence? A comparison of French and English product liability rules

SIMON TAYLOR*

On the 19 May 1998, ten years after the deadline for transposition, France finally enacted legislation incorporating the 1985 Product Liability Directive into national law.[1] These provisions have been added to the *Code Civil* as articles 1386–1 to 1386–18.[2] The aim of this chapter is to consider to what extent French and English product liability laws have been harmonised by the incorporation of the Directive, but it will restrict itself to examining one aspect of this question, namely whether incorporation has had the effect of harmonising the rules relating to the acts generating liability in the two systems.[3]

The preamble to the Directive declares that harmonisation of national rules is necessary in view of the fact that disparities are liable to distort competition, to affect the free movement of goods and lead to differences in the level of protection offered to consumers against physical injury and

* This is an updated and expanded version of an article published in the *ICLQ*, 'The Harmonisation of European Product Liability Rules: French and English Law' 48 (1999) *ICLQ*: 419.

1 Loi n° 98–389 du 19 mai 1998. In 1993 France was judged by the European Court of Justice to be in non-compliance with its Treaty obligations (C291/91, 15 January 1993). The further delay by the legislator led to the threat of enforcement procedures by the Court with a fine of up to four million francs per day. It was the threat of this fine that finally led the government to push for the transposition of the Directive (see, for example, Mme Guigou, garde des sceaux, justice minister, débats Assemblée Nationale 25 mars 1998, *compte rendu analytique officiel*, p. 21).

2 I will consequently refer throughout to the numbering of the provisions in the *Code Civil*.

3 There are a considerable number of other actual or potential differences between English and French law. Many of the key concepts used in the Directive are left without precise definition. Notions such as 'product', 'put into circulation' and 'defect' leave scope for differences in interpretation at national level. Other areas, such as causation, recourse actions, calculation of damages and access to justice, are not dealt with by the Directive and thus provide obvious potential for divergence in approach. See S. Taylor, *L'Harmonisation communautaire de la responsabilité du fait des produits défectueux. Une étude comparative du droit anglais et du droit français* (Paris: LGDJ, 1999).

damage to goods caused by a defective product.[4] The Directive also aims to find 'a fair apportionment of the risks inherent in modern technological production'.[5] It is the difficulty in reconciling differences at national level in the conception of the apportionment of the risks between industry and the victim which led to the final version of the Directive being a compromise measure that includes a number of opportunities for divergence between national laws. Such differences in conception are clearly revealed in a comparison between French and English product liability laws.

This difference of views on the balance between the interests of defendant (industry) and consumer (victim) is in part reflected by certain provisions in the French enactment designed to offer the victim a more favourable position than under the Directive. However, in the recent decision *Commission v France*,[6] the European Court of Justice found France to be in breach of its obligations under the Directive on a number of points. The French parliament will have to introduce amending legislation to comply with the ECJ's judgement.

However, of more significance is the effect of the European Court of Justice's ruling in *Commission v France* and in *Sánchez v Medicina Asturiana*[7] on the interpretation of article 13 of the Directive. As part of the compromise inherent in the Community legislation, article 13 provides that 'this Directive shall not affect any rights which an injured person may have according to the rules of the law of contractual or non-contractual liability or a special liability system existing at the moment when this Directive is notified.'[8] The Directive therefore permits the coexistence of parallel contractual and non-contractual actions. According to European reformers, since the Directive would ensure a more favourable position for the victim than existing rules, it would finish in practice by replacing alternative actions.[9] However, as we shall see, the new French law in fact represents in many respects a less advantageous option than the contractual and delictual actions and the victim will often prefer to sue the defendant on the basis of these rules. Since the parallel French rules are more favourable to the victim than their equivalents in English law, the degree of harmonisation will depend greatly on to what extent these

4 Preamble, para. 1. 5 Ibid., para. 2.

6 *Commission v France*, 25 April 2002, C52/00 [2002] ECR I-3827.

7 25 April 2002, C-183/00 [2002] ECR I-3901. That judgment was a preliminary ruling on the question whether a claimant infected by hepatitis C following a blood transfusion could rely on the more advantageous Spanish Product Liability legislation dating from 1984.

8 Section 2(6) Consumer Protection Act; article 1386–18 *Code Civil*.

9 EC Bulletin n°11/76, n° 30, p. 20.

more favourable rules can continue to be applied by the courts. Whilst the recent decisions of the European Court of Justice appear to impose significant restrictions on the use of parallel regimes to by-pass the Directive, there still remains a clear potential for divergence here.

I will begin by comparing the liability of the manufacturer and supplier according to the legislative regimes in the two Member States before considering the parallel contractual and extra-contractual liability rules.

Liability according to the legislative rules

There is little difference between the English and French legislative provisions concerning the standard of liability of the manufacturer. Important differences that existed between the two Member States with regard to the liability of the supplier should now disappear following the ruling of the European Court of Justice in *Commission v France* on 25 April 2002.

The liability of the manufacturer

Neither the Consumer Protection Act nor the French law of 19 May 1998 imposes purely strict liability on the manufacturer of defective goods. This is due to the adoption by both national laws of the most controversial provision of the Directive, the so-called 'development risks defence'. Article 7(e) of the Directive allows the producer of defective goods to avoid liability by showing 'that the state of scientific and technical knowledge at the time when he put the product into circulation was not such as to enable the existence of the defect to be discovered'. The defence represents therefore an important protection for businesses since it allows them to avoid liability for unforeseeable defects. Article 15(1)(b) of the Directive, however, allows derogation from article 7(e) and thus permits Member States to opt to retain liability for development risks.

The Consumer Protection Act incorporates the defence but uses different wording from that employed in the Directive. Section 4(1)(e) states that it shall be a defence for the person proceeded against to show 'that the state of scientific and technical knowledge at the relevant time was not such that a producer of products of the same description as the product in question might be expected to have discovered the defect if it had existed in his products while they were under his control'.

The validity of the wording of section 4(1)(e) was contested by the European Commission, who brought an action before the European Court of Justice. The 1997 judgment of the Court provides some clarification as to the appropriate interpretation of article 7(e).[10] The Court found that there was nothing to indicate that English judges would not apply section 4(1)(e) in conformity with the objectives of the Directive.[11] For the Court, article 7(e) refers to the most advanced state of scientific and technical knowledge existing at the date the product is put into circulation.[12] However, according to the Court it is necessarily implied that 'that knowledge must have been accessible at the time when the product in question was put into circulation'.[13] As the Court noted, the notion of 'accessibility' will invite difficulties of interpretation.[14] Contrary to what was initially thought by certain French writers[15] the judgment of a national court would seem inevitably to involve deciding whether the producer has acted reasonably from an objective viewpoint.[16] A very high standard of behaviour will however be expected, and this is reflected in the recent English decisions in *Abouzaid v Mothercare*[17] and *A v National Blood Authority*.[18]

The debate over whether to allow the development risks defence provides the principal explanation for the ten-year delay in the incorporation of the Directive in French law.[19] In finally adopting the defence, the French

[10] *Commission of the European Communities v United Kingdom of Great Britain and Northern Ireland* C-300/95, 29 May 1997.

[11] Ibid., paras. 38–9. [12] Ibid., para. 26. [13] Ibid., para. 28.

[14] Ibid., para. 29. For the Advocate General Tesauro, there is a considerable difference between research published by an American academic in an English language periodical with a world-wide circulation, and a study published by a Manchurian researcher in Chinese. Whilst the first would in his view be 'accessible', the second would not (Opinion delivered 23 January 1997, paras. 23–4). Burton J in *A v National Blood Authority* [2001] 3 All ER 289 preferred the example of results which had not been published and were being kept in the research department of a company, para. 49.

[15] Y. Markovits, *La Directive CEE du 25 juillet 1985 sur la responsabilité du fait des produits défectueux* (Paris: LGDJ, 1990) p. 350; C. Larroumet 'La Convention européenne et la proposition d'une directive des communautés européennes en matière de responsabilité du fait des produits', *Droit et pratique du commerce international* (May 1978), 4(1), 29.

[16] C. Newdick, 'Risk, Uncertainty and "Knowledge" in the Development Risk Defence' (1991) *AALR*: 309, 314.

[17] [2000] All ER 2436. [18] [2001] 3 All ER 289.

[19] The initial *projet de loi* presented by the government in 1990 included a development risks defence, but it was rejected by the *Sénat* on their second reading in 1992. The clause was once again included in a new *proposition de loi* laid before the *Assemblée Nationale* in 1993 and was adopted by it in March 1997. However, things were again delayed when the new socialist government came to power in May 1997. The new government favoured excluding the development risks defence for all health products, in view of the great risks presented by these products, and for elements of the human body, due to the tragedy of the contamination of patients with the HIV virus through the transfusion of infected blood. This was opposed by the *Sénat* who preferred to allow the development risks defence for all products. The law finally passed is a compromise, producers of health products being

legislator follows the wording of the Directive, but creates an exception in its article 1386–12 which states that 'the producer cannot rely on [the development risks defence] where the damage has been caused by an element of the human body or by products extracted from it'. This clause was introduced to reflect public concern over the much-publicised tragedy of the transfusion of HIV-contaminated blood. Hence, blood transfusion centres, which will be considered as producers, will be liable for damage caused by infected blood even though the defect was not detectable at the time of supply. In contrast, other producers will be able to avoid liability for undiscoverable defects.

As a supposed counterbalance to the development risks defence, article 1386–12 of the *Code Civil* also provides that a producer will be unable to invoke the defence where the defect in the product was discovered within ten years of putting the product into circulation, and during that period the producer did not take the appropriate measures to avoid the damaging consequences. This provision thus places on the producer an additional post-circulation obligation to warn consumers of the dangers and to take appropriate evasive action (presumably such as recalling products) once the defect is revealed. The validity of this provision was contested by the Commission in their action brought against France for failure to fulfil their obligations under the Directive. The European Court of Justice, in its ruling of 25 April 2002, held that France was in breach of its obligations on this point. The Court stressed that the legal basis for the Directive was article 100 of the EC Treaty (now article 94 EC).[20] This basis did not give the Member States the possibility to introduce provisions departing from the harmonising legislation. The directive thus aimed at maximum rather than minimum harmonisation. The court rejected the French government's arguments that the Directive should be interpreted in the light of the growing importance of consumer protection within the Community.[21] Amending legislation will therefore be required to remove the post-circulation warning requirement from the French law. This change should not however be of any great significance for consumers. Manufacturers will indeed continue to be liable in contract and delict for failure to warn.[22]

able to rely on the defence, while the defence is not available where the damage is caused by an element of the human body or a product extracted from it.

[20] Concerning the approximation of such laws, regulations or administrative provisions of the Member States directly affecting the establishment or functioning of the common market.

[21] As reflected in article 153 EC.

[22] C. Larroumet, 'Les Transpositions française et espagnole de la directive sur la responsabilité du fait des produits défectueux devant la Cour de justice des communautés européennes' *Dalloz* 2002. *Jurisprudence* 2462, 2465.

The English manufacturer is subject to a similar duty in the tort of negligence to warn the public of defects and to take appropriate action to avoid damage. In *Wright v Dunlop Rubber Co.*,[23] the Court of Appeal observed that the duty of the manufacturer is not necessarily limited to the period preceding the date that the product is first put on the market. He must keep up to date with scientific developments and react if he learns that his product represents a danger.[24] In *Walton v British Leyland UK Ltd*,[25] Willis J expressed the view, *obiter*, that a manufacturer should recall products when the defect represents a danger. In *Hobbs (Farms) v Baxendale Chemicals Ltd*[26] the judge found a manufacturer of fire insulation liable to buyers when he failed to warn them subsequent to putting the product on the market that the product supplied provided less protection than intended.

The liability of the supplier

The difference in the nature of the liability of the defendant was more significant in relation to the liability of the supplier, although the position should again change following the decision of the European Court of Justice in *Commission v France*.

Article 3 of the Directive states that the importer into the EC of the defective product and 'any person who, by putting his name, trademark or other distinguishing feature on the product presents himself as its producer' are liable in the same conditions as the producer.[27] According to article 3(3) other suppliers will be able to avoid liability by identifying the producer or the person who supplied them with the product. Liability is thus channelled to the producer of the defective product who is in theory the best placed to prevent defects and to distribute loss. The Consumer Protection Act adopts the same approach.[28] In contrast, article 1386–7 of the *Code Civil* currently provides that the professional supplier 'is liable for the defect in the product on the same terms as the producer'. Thus, the supplier will be unable to avoid liability by identifying the producer

[23] [1972] 13 KIR 255.

[24] However, the case does not specify if the duty is simply to include warnings with products put into circulation after the discovery of the danger or if the producer must also warn buyers of products already in circulation.

[25] (1978) unreported. [26] [1992] 1 Lloyds Rep. 54.

[27] Shops such as Marks & Spencers and Sainsburys would fall within this category when the product is sold under their brand name.

[28] Section 2(3).

or his own supplier. This provides a significant advantage for the victim, who will often prefer the convenience of suing a local supplier than a foreign producer. The French provision also reduces the risk of the Plaintiff remaining without indemnity due to the insolvency of the producer. However, once again this provision will have to be amended following the judgment of the European Court of Justice of 25 April 2002 where the French rules were again held to be in breach of France's obligations under the Directive.

The decision of the European Court thus removes a particularly favourable element of the legislative regime for the consumer. The few cases which have been heard by the French courts to date under the new legislative regime in fact often concern the liability of the supplier rather than the producer.

French court decisions under the new regime

There are very few decisions of the French courts under the new legislation. This is not surprising given that the new regime only applies to products put into circulation after the law came into force on 21 May 1998.

The Toulouse Appeal Court found a butcher liable as a supplier of infected horse meat under the new legislation.[29] The risk of the existence of trichinae bacteria in horse meat had been known since 1975 and a 1994 Community directive[30] provides that tests for this infection should be performed by veterinary laboratories on horse meat samples. In this particular case the test had been incorrectly performed by the laboratory and the infection was not detected. The butcher tried to argue that since the infection had not been detected by the laboratory he could rely on the development risks defence. Not surprisingly, the Appeal Court upheld the decision of the first instance court and rejected this argument. It confirmed that the level of knowledge of the particular defendant was of no importance, what mattered was whether the risk was known objectively, and that knowledge was to be assessed, in line with the decision of the Court of Justice in *Commission v UK*, on the basis of the most advanced state of scientific and technical knowledge existing at the date the product

[29] CA Toulouse, 3e chambre, 1re sect., 22 February 2000, JCP 2000.II.10429, note Le Tourneau. The supplier of a defective tyre which burst causing an accident was also found liable in the same court: CA Toulouse, 7 November 2000, Resp. civ. et assurance 2001, n° 199, note Grynbaum.

[30] 94/59/EC.

is put into circulation. Since the risk and the techniques to detect the defect had been known since 1975, the defence was not available here.

In a decision of the *Tribunal de Grande Instance* in Aix-en-Provence[31] the supplier and manufacturer of a glass screen for a fireplace were held liable for the injuries incurred by the householder when she was injured by flying glass when the screen exploded. The defect and the causal link between the defect and the accident were inferred from the fact of the explosion, even though the manufacturer had indicated a number of other possible causes.

The Versailles Court of Appeal[32] applied the Directive rather than the new national legislation[33] in a case of a victim who had contracted multiple sclerosis three months after being vaccinated against hepatitis B. The new law could not be used since the vaccination was carried out in 1995. In finding the laboratory liable, the court was prepared to accept the defective nature of the product without discussion, based on the damage caused. The case is especially notable for its rather flexible view of the causal link between the vaccination and the claimant's disease.

It is difficult to take any view on the extent to which the legislative regimes will be applied in a harmonised manner by the domestic courts due to the limited available case law. However, what the cases do perhaps begin to indicate is a certain readiness to presume the defect in the product by the fact of the damage caused, and even a readiness to presume a causal link. Other decisions based not on the new law but on the parallel regimes mirror this approach (although this is certainly not always the case). We can therefore wonder to what extent there may prove to be a difference in approach to the notion of 'defect' between English and French law, since certain English cases have tended to less readily accept the existence of a defect.[34] This point will be mentioned further when I consider the application of the parallel regimes.

The contractual and extra-contractual actions

I will begin with a review of the English liability rules, before comparing them with the French contractual and delictual actions.

[31] TGI Aix-en-Provence, 2 Oct 2001, D.2001.IR. 3092.

[32] Versailles, 2 May 2001, D.2001. Somm. 1592. RTD civ. 2001.891, note P. Jourdain.

[33] Although the Directive would not seem to have direct effect in these circumstances, the clinic concerned being a private institution.

[34] *Richardson v LRC* [2001] LLR Med. 280; *Foster v Biosil*, 18 April 2000, 59 BMLR 178.

The English law

The business seller is strictly liable to his immediate buyer. Section 14(1) of the Sale of Goods Act 1979, as modified by the Sale and Supply of Goods Act 1994, provides that goods sold by a professional must be of 'satisfactory quality'. According to section 14(2)(A), goods are of satisfactory quality when they are of a quality which a reasonable person would consider as satisfactory, taking into account the price, the description of the goods and all other relevant circumstances. Section 14(2)(B) lists a number of relevant circumstances, which include specifically the safety of the goods.[35]

However, due to the strict application by the English courts of the principle of privity of contract, the victim, who will rarely have a contract directly with the manufacturer, will normally be obliged to sue the manufacturer and any intermediate supplier in the tort of negligence.[36]

In order to assess the standard of liability expected of a manufacturer in the tort of negligence, it is necessary to distinguish between defects caused by the manufacturing process and defects in the design of the product.[37]

For damage caused by manufacturing defects the victim will be able to discharge his burden of proof in English law by proving that the product was defective and that, on the balance of probabilities, the defect arose during the manufacturing process.[38] Even if the defendant shows that his quality control procedure complies with approved practice, the fact that a defect was present at the time that the item was put into circulation will be seen as evidence that a negligent act was committed by one of the defendant's servants.[39] The approach to the liability of the manufacturer in these circumstances therefore resembles the imposition of strict liability.

However, when we turn to consider the question of design defects, English law does not impose on the manufacturer liability for

35 Section 14(2)(B)(d).

36 The Court occasionally allows the buyer to sue the manufacturer on a collateral contract on the basis of representations made to the Plaintiff: *Shanklin Pier Ltd v Detel Products Ltd* [1951] 2 KB 854; *Wells v Buckland Sand* [1965] QB 170. See also *Carlill v Carbolic Smoke Ball Co.* [1893] 1 QB 256, and more recently *Bowerman v Association of British Travel Agents* [1996] CLC 451.

37 In *A v National Blood Association*, Burton J preferred to distinguish non-standard and standard products.

38 *Carroll v Fearon* (1998) *The Times*, January 26 1998 (CA); *Mason v Williams & Williams* [1955] 1 WLR 549; *Davie v New Merton Board Mills Ltd* [1957] 2 QB 368.

39 *Grant v Australian Knitting Mills Ltd* [1936] 1 All ER 283.

development risks in the tort of negligence. This is not to say that a very high level of care is not expected of the manufacturer.[40] He is expected to take reasonable precautions to discover the dangers of the product. In cases of a particular complexity, he must not solely rely on his own knowledge, but must consult experts in the area.[41] He must keep up to date with the major developments in scientific knowledge.[42] However, where it cannot be reasonably expected of a manufacturer of products of the type in question to discover the defect, the Defendant's liability will not be engaged.[43] Therefore, in circumstances such as those concerning the drug thalidomide, the victim in English law will fail in his action against the manufacturer since he is unable to establish negligence.

The mere seller of a defective product will only be liable to the third party victim on proof of his negligence. His liability will be engaged if the defect is due to the way the product has been conserved by him, by his maintenance work or in his assembly of the product, or if he has failed to transmit a warning to his buyer.[44] In certain situations, he will be under an obligation to examine the product before sale and to repair defects or at least indicate them to the buyer.[45]

The French law

Despite the fact that the *Code Civil* does not specifically provide for an action for damages in contract to compensate the buyer for physical injury and damage to goods, the French courts have been able to adapt certain articles of the *Code Civil* in order to create a contractual action. Judges first attached an '*obligation de sécurité*' to the '*garantie contre les vices cachés*' in articles 1641–8 of the *Code Civil.* Article 1641 provides that the seller guarantees the goods sold against hidden defects ('*vices cachés*') which render the goods unsuitable for the use for which they were destined. However, according to article 1645 the seller is only liable in damages to the purchaser if it can be established that he was aware of the defect at the time the product was sold. From the 1920s the French courts began to recognise a presumption that all professional sellers were

[40] C. Newdick, 'The Future of Negligence in Product Liability' (1987) *LQR*: 289, 294.
[41] *Lambert v Lewis* [1978] 1 Lloyd's LR 610.
[42] *Stokes v GKN (Bolts and Nuts) Ltd* [1968] 1 WLR 1776.
[43] *Thompson v Smiths Ship Repairers Ltd* [1984] 1 All ER 88.
[44] *Kubach v Holland* [1937] 3 All ER 907.
[45] *Andrews v Hopkinson* [1957] 1 QB 229; *Watson v Buckley, Osborne, Garrett & Co.* [1940] 1 All ER 174.

aware of the defect at the time of sale, thus enabling victims to recover damages.[46] The presumption has in time been transformed into a substantive rule: professional sellers are strictly liable to the buyer for damage caused by hidden defects in the goods.[47]

However, the action based on articles 1641–8 presents certain difficulties for the victim. According to article 1648 his action must be started within a '*bref délai*' ('within a short period') of the discovery of the defect by the buyer.[48] The defect must also have been 'hidden' at the time of the sale, and the buyer will not succeed if the defect is one that someone with average diligence ought to have discovered.[49] In view of these obstacles, the judges began to turn to other articles of the *Code Civil* to provide the victim with an action in contract. French courts have therefore recognised an '*obligation de sécurité*' independent of articles 1641–8 on the basis of article 1135, which allows the Court to imply terms in a contract. The *Cour de Cassation* recognises on this basis that 'the professional seller is obliged to deliver products free from all vice or manufacturing defect which is susceptible to create a danger for persons or goods'.[50] Damages can then be awarded under article 1147, which provides for the award of damages in the event of the nonexecution of a contract. The liability is, as in the Sale of Goods Act, strict. This has been clearly confirmed by the *Cour de Cassation* in its decisions relating to the liability of blood transfusion centres for contaminations with blood infected by the HIV virus. The Court confirmed the contractual liability of the transfusion centres to the victims despite the fact that it was impossible to discover the defect in the blood at the time of its supply.[51]

46 Cass. civ. 1re, 21 Oct. 1925, D.P. 1926, 1, rapport du conseiller CELICE, note L. Josserand; Cass. civ. 1re, 24 Nov. 1954, J.C.P. 1955, II, 8565, note HB; Rennes 25 Nov. 1955, Gaz. Pal. 1956, I, 137.

47 Cass. com. 17 April 1971, JCP 1972.II.17280, note Boitard & Rabut; Cass. civ. 1re, 21 Nov. 1972, Bull. civ. I, p. 224, no.257.

48 Cass. com. 22 Nov. 1965, Bull. civ. III, n°593; Cass. com.18 February 1992, Bull. civ. IV, n°82.

49 J. Huet, 'Traité de droit civil. Les principaux contrats spéciaux' (Paris: LGDJ, 1996), p. 263, n°111328; Trib. Civ. Seine 21 Dec. 1956, D. 1957, p. 47; Req. 18 March 1924, DH. 1924, p. 261.

50 Cass. civ. 1re, 20 March 1989, D. 1989, p. 581, note P. Malaurie; Cass. civ. 1re, 22 June 1991, RTD civ. 1991, p. 539; Cass. civ. 1re, 11 June 1991, Bull. civ. I, n°201; Cass. civ. 1re, 17 January 1995, Bull. civ. I, n°43, D. 1995, p. 350, note P. Jourdain; Cass. civ. 1re, 14 Nov. 1995, Bull. civ. I, n°414; Cass. civ. 1re, 9 juillet 1996, J.C.P. 1996, I, 3985, note G. Viney; Cass. civ. 1re, 28 April 1998, JCP 1998.II.10088, rapp. P. Sargos.

51 Cass. civ. 1re, 12 April 1995 (2 decisions) JCP 1995.I.3893, note G. Viney; Cass. civ. 1re, 9 July 1996, D. 1996 jur., note Y. Lambert-Faivre.

In contrast to English law, in France it is the contractual action that has traditionally provided the main means of compensation for the victim. With the initial intention of improving the protection of the victim by offering him a strict liability claim,[52] French judges have got round the principle of '*la relativité des conventions*' (the equivalent of our privity of contract) by various techniques in order to allow buyers to jump the links in the supply chain to sue in contract the manufacturer of the goods or any intermediate supplier. The principal technique employed in the case of a buyer suing a supplier higher in the supply chain is that of the '*action directe*'.[53] A contractual '*obligation de sécurité*' is considered to be 'attached' to the product and to be transferred along with it from buyer to buyer.[54]

Hence, due to the 'discovery' by the courts of an '*obligation de sécurité*' and the use of the '*action directe*' manufacturers and intermediate distributors are strictly liable in contract to all buyer victims. French law therefore offers more protection to the buyer and places a greater burden on the manufacturer and seller than English law, where in the vast majority of cases the victim will have to rely on an action in the tort of negligence.

However, the advantages offered to the victim by French law do not stop here. In fact, parallel to the development of a strict liability contractual action, the judges also recognise an extra-contractual strict liability claim.

Article 1384.1 of the *Code Civil* has been used by French judges as the principal tool in the introduction of strict liability in delict. Article 1384.1 states that 'a person is responsible not only for the damage caused by his own actions, but also for that caused . . . by the things over which he exercises control'.[55] The courts use this formula to impose liability on the sole basis of the 'use, direction and control'[56] by the defendant of the

[52] P. Remy, 'La Responsabilité contractuelle: histoire d'un faux concept' *RTD* civ. 1997.323.

[53] Cass. com. 27 April 1971, JCP 1972.II.17280, 1re espèce, note Boitard & Rabut; Cass. com. 15 May 1972, Bull. civ. IV, p. 143, n°144; Cass. civ. 1re, 9 March 1983, Bull. civ. I, n°92, p. 81; Ass. Plén. 7 February 1986, D. 1986, p. 293, note A. Bernabent; G. Viney, *Traité de droit civil. Introduction à la responsabilité* (Paris: LGDJ, 1995), p. 339, n°189–1; J. Ghestin and B. Desche, *Traité des contrats. La vente* (Paris: LDGJ, 1990) 1036, n°1015.

[54] This interpretation seems to be confirmed by the case *Besse c. Protois*, JCP 1991.II.21743, note G. Viney; *Dalloz* 1991, p. 549, note J. Ghestin; P. Jourdain, 'La Nature de la responsabilité civile dans les chaînes de contrats après l'arrêt de l'assemblée plénière du 12 juillet 1991' *Dalloz* 1992, chron. 149.

[55] 'On est responsable non seulement du dommage que l'on cause par son propre fait, mais encore de celui qui est causé par . . . des choses que l'on a sous sa garde.'

[56] According to the formula established by the *Chambre réunie* of the *Cour de Cassation* in the case *Franck*, 2 December 1941, D.C. 1942, 25, note Ripert; S. 1942, I, 217, note H. Mazeaud.

'thing' which caused the damage. The causal link between the 'thing' and the damage is presumed when it was moving at the time of the accident. However, where the 'thing' was inert the Plaintiff will have to show that it was in an abnormal position or in bad condition.[57] The only defence will be on the basis of a '*cause étrangère*'.

The courts have on occasions used article 1384.1 to impose strict liability on the manufacturer in delict. Despite the fact that the manufacturer does not have the genuine 'use, direction and control' of the product when he has supplied it to another, where the product 'has its own dynamism which is liable to create a danger' the courts have drawn a distinction between the '*garde de la structure*' ('control of the structure') of the product and the '*garde du comportement*' ('the control of its behaviour').[58] Though the manufacturer, on supplying the product, loses control over its behaviour, he retains control over its structure. French courts have thus been able to impose strict liability on the manufacturer of defective goods. The manufacturer has often been found liable on this basis where an explosion is caused by a gas appliance[59] or a product containing gas.[60] The action on the basis of article 1384.1 is also of considerable interest for the victim in actions against other categories of defendants. Hence, a child becomes '*gardien*' of an abandoned bottle which he kicks,[61] a climber is the '*gardien*' of the ropes he uses and is liable when the ropes dislodge rocks which cause damage,[62] a pedestrian is the '*gardien*' of his raincoat when the handlebar of a passing cyclist gets lodged in the pocket causing the cyclist to fall![63]

[57] Cass. civ. 2e, 11 January 1995, Bull. civ. II, n° 18. (a plate covering a roof light which broke under the weight of a person who had climbed on the roof to carry out an official inspection was held not to be the cause of the damage since it was in its normal position and was in good condition). See also Cass. civ. 2e, 29 May 1964, JCP 1965.II.14248, note Boré. This requirement seems to have been confirmed recently after some doubt, in Cass. civ. 2e, 7 May 2002, Cass. civ. 1re, 9 July 2002, Cass. civ. 2e, 11 July 2002; *Dalloz* 2003, sommaires commentés, 462, P. Jourdain.

[58] Cass. civ. 1re, 12 Nov. 1975, JCP 1976.II.18479 (1re espèce), note G. Viney; Cass. civ. 2e, 4 June 1984, Gaz. Pal. 1984.2.634, note F. Chabas; V. H., L., J. Mazeaud, *Traité de la responsabilité civile*, II, 6e édition, n° 1160–2 et s.; G. Viney, *La Responsabilité: conditions* n° 691 et seq.

[59] Paris, 27 Nov. 1978, *E.L.M. Leblanc c. Leroy* (unreported); Cass. civ. 2e, 3 October 1979, JCP 1980.IV.360; Cass. civ. 1re, 2 February 1982, D. 1982, IR, p. 330. G. Viney, 'L'Indemnisation des atteintes à la sécurité des consommateurs en droit français', in *Sécurité des consommateurs et responsabilité du fait des produits défectueux* (Paris: LGDJ, 1987) 71, 82.

[60] Cass. civ. 2e, 5 June 1971, Bull. civ. II, n° 204, p. 145 (fizzy drink); Cass. civ. 2e, 29 April 1982, Gaz. Pal. 1982, 2e sem., p. 331, note F. C. (aerosol can).

[61] Cass. civ. 2e, 10 February 1982, JCP 1983.II.20069, note Coeuret.

[62] Aix-en-Provence, 8 May 1981, JCP 1982.II.19819, note Sarraz-Bournet.

[63] Rennes, 20 June 1975, D. 1976, 351, note Tunc.

However, due to the difficulties encountered in the interpretation of the concepts of 'control of the structure', 'control of the behaviour' and 'own dynamism', the courts have often preferred to base the liability of the manufacturer on article 1382.

Article 1382 of the *Code Civil* provides that 'loss caused to a person by another's behaviour must be compensated by the person whose fault caused the loss'.[64] The *Cour de Cassation* considers that 'the putting on the market of a defective product constitutes in itself a delictual fault which engages the liability of the manufacturer towards third parties on the basis of article 1382 of the *Code Civil*'.[65] By defining the manufacturer's fault as the placing of the product on the market, the courts have extended the strict liability regime to third party victims who have no contractual link with any member of the chain of distribution.

In an important decision on 17 January 1995[66] the *Cour de Cassation* went even further and declared the supplier also to be strictly liable to the third-party victim. In the case, a young girl was injured in the eye when a plastic hoop with which she was playing in the school playground snapped. The intermediate seller and the manufacturer of the hoop were found liable in an action brought by the parents of the child. Since there was no contractual link between the plaintiffs and the manufacturer and supplier, the action had to be brought on the basis of article 1382 of the *Code Civil*. The *Cour de Cassation* stated that 'the professional seller is under an obligation to deliver products exempt from vice or manufacturing defects which are susceptible to create a danger to persons or goods; and he is liable in the same way to third parties and to purchasers'.

This was the first clear confirmation by the courts that the same strict '*obligation de sécurité*' applied to manufacturers and suppliers irrespective of whether the victim is a buyer or a third party and this was confirmed by two important decisions in 1998.[67] What became clear was that, from 1989 when the Courts had first discarded the *garantie des vices cachés* to confirm an autonomous *obligation de sécurité* based on article 1147, the French judges had been developing an independent action, which now clearly applied equally to buyers and third-party victims, either simply in

[64] 'Tout fait quelconque de l'homme, qui cause à autrui un dommage, oblige celui par la faute duquel il est arrivé, à le réparer.'

[65] Cass. civ. 1re, 21 March 1962, Bull. civ. I, 155; Cass. civ. 1re, 5 May 1964, Bull. civ. I, 181.

[66] *Planet Wattohm c. CPAM du Morbihan et s.*, D. 1995, inf. Rap. P.67; JCP 1995.IV.702; JCP 1995.I.3853, obs. G. Viney; *RTD civ.* 1995, p. 631, note P. Jourdain.

[67] Cass. civ. 1re, 3 March 1998, JCP G 1998.II.10049, rapp. P. Sargos; Cass. civ. 1re, 28 April 1998, JCP G 1998.II.10088, rapp. P. Sargos.

anticipation of the incorporation of the Directive, or perhaps to exist in parallel, as appeared to be authorised by article 13.[68] Thus, in the first of the important 1998 decisions, the *Cour de Cassation* closely followed the wording of the Directive in stating that 'the manufacturer must deliver a product free of any defect liable to present a danger to persons or goods, that is to say a product providing the safety which people are entitled to expect'. Although the action is nominally based on articles in the *Code Civil*,[69] it uses the liability rules established by the Directive and thus centres liability on the notion of 'defect', but does not allow a development risks defence.

The majority of cases decided since 1998 concern products put into circulation before the French legislation came into force. In these decisions, the courts have continued to follow the same line in confirming the existence of this autonomous action. Hence a blood transfusion centre was held liable to a claimant who had contracted hepatitis C following a blood transfusion.[70] Notably, the *Cour de Cassation* declared as a substantive rule that, where the victim does not belong to a category of the population at risk, it was for the transfusion centre to prove that the blood products supplied were not defective. Thus there is a reversal here of the burden of proof of defect and causal link: a solution which is certainly much more generous to the victim than the Directive, but which is limited to the specific question of blood transfusions. However, it does clearly indicate a willingness by the *Cour de Cassation* to find solutions favourable to the victim.[71]

A private clinic was held strictly liable by the *Cour de Cassation* on the basis of article 1147 *Code Civil* when a patient suffered burns following the application of skin disinfectant.[72] The court again adopted a rather victim-friendly approach to the notion of 'defect': damage which would not have been expected in normal circumstances was sufficient to presume a defect.[73]

[68] J. Calais Auloy, 'Menace européenne sur la jurisprudence française concernant l'obligation de sécurité du vendeur professionnel' 2002 *Dalloz* 2458, 2459; G. Viney and P. Jourdain *Traité de droit civil. Les conditions de la responsabilité* (Paris: LGDJ, 1998), 788.

[69] Articles 1147 for buyers, articles 1382 and 1384.1 for third parties. Sometimes also now article 221–1 of the *Code de la consommation*, on product safety.

[70] Cass. civ. 1re, 9 May 2001, *Dalloz* 2001 2149, note P. Sargos.

[71] Calais Auloy, 'Menace européenne'.

[72] Cass. civ. 1re, 7 Nov. 2000, Bull. civ. I, n°272, *RTD civ.* 201, p. 151, obs. P. Jourdain.

[73] In another case, a motorcyclist was injured in the eye when his goggles smashed when he was hit by a bird. Again, the court was prepared to presume the goggles defective: Cass. civ. 1re, 15 Oct. 1996, Bull. civ. I, n°354; *Dalloz* 1997, 287 obs. Jourdain. See also Cass 1re

The *Cour de Cassation* held that breach of the strict contractual '*obligation de sécurité*' by a private clinic to their patient constituted a fault under article 1382 where the action was brought by the daughter of a victim who had contracted the HIV virus following the transfusion of defective blood.[74] The *Tribunal de Grande Instance* in Montpellier found the suppliers of a growth hormone strictly liable to the victim of Creutzfeld-Jacob disease on the basis of article 1147[75] and the *Tribunal de Grande Instance* in Nanterre found the manufacturer of *distiblène*, a product used in the prevention of miscarriages, liable for the vaginal and uteral cancer caused to the daughter whose mother had used the product.[76] The last two cases cited illustrate the importance of the existence of the parallel regimes, since both products had been put into circulation well before the ten-year cut-off date introduced by the directive.

The future of liability rules in France following the incorporation of the Directive

The contractual and extra-contractual regimes therefore provide actions that are more favourable to the victim than the new French statutory provisions. The responsibility of the manufacturer, the supplier and the '*gardien*' under the parallel regimes is on the basis of strict liability, and the defendant cannot avoid liability by establishing a development risk.

Added to this, there are a number of other significant advantages presented to the plaintiff by a contractual or delictual action. The limitation period for an action in *responsabilité contractuelle* is thirty years from the date of the damage or the date that the Plaintiff became aware of the damage,[77] and for the delictual action ten years from the same date.[78] The French statute, like the Directive and the Consumer Protection Act, includes a cut-off date for actions at ten years from the date the product

3 March 1998, *Dalloz* 1999, 36, note G. Pignarre and P. Brun (*contra* P. Jourdain 1998 *RTD civ.* 683). However, it should not be thought that French courts systematically equate damage with a defect, since some cases have denied liability despite a clear causal link between the product and the damage because no defect has been established on the facts. See, for example, Cass. civ 1re, 22 Jan. 1991, *RTD civ.* 1991.539.

74 Cass. civ. 1re, 12 Feb. 2001, Bull. civ. I, n°35.

75 TGI Montpellier, 9 July 2002, *Fachin c Institut Pasteur*, JCP 2002.II.158, note F. Vialla.

76 TGI Nanterre, 1re chambre, 24 May 2002, *Bobet c UCB Pharma*, 2002. Somm. 1885, *RTD civ.* 2002, p. 527, obs. P. Jourdain. This time, the court based liability on article 221–1 of the Consumer Code.

77 Article 2262 *Code Civil.* Cass. soc. 18 April 1991, Bull. civ. V, n°598.

78 Article 2270–1 *Code Civil.*

was put into circulation.[79] The contractual and delictual actions are subject to no such cut-off. The new legislative regime does not apply to damage occurring before the product was put into circulation.[80] Victims of such damage will therefore rely on the pre-existing rules.

The extent to which victims may continue to use the parallel regimes as an alternative to an action under the new law is thus of great significance for European harmonisation. The decisions of the European Court of Justice dated in *Commission v France* and in *González Sánchez v Medicina Asturiana SA*[81] are of considerable importance here. In finding France to be in breach of its obligations, the European Court of Justice emphasised that the Directive was adopted under article 100 (now article 94) of the EC Treaty and that that legal basis 'provides no possibility for the Member State to maintain or establish provisions departing from Community harmonising measures'.[82] The degree of discretion available to the Member State must therefore be determined exclusively by the provisions of the Directive itself. The Court continued: 'as is clear from the first recital . . . , the purpose of the directive is to ensure undistorted competition between traders, to facilitate the free movement of goods and to avoid differences in levels of consumer protection'.[83] In addition: 'The directive contains no provision expressly authorising the Member States to adopt or maintain more stringent provisions . . . in order to secure a higher level of consumer protection'.[84]

It follows that 'article 13 of the directive cannot be interpreted as giving the Member States the possibility of maintaining a general system of product liability different from that provided for in the directive'.[85] However, 'the reference in article 13 . . . to the rights which an injured person may rely on under the rules of the law of contractual or non-contractual liability must be interpreted as meaning that the system of rules put in place by the directive . . . *does not preclude the application of other systems of contractual or non-contractual liability based on other grounds, such as fault or a warranty in respect of latent defects*'.[86] The reference in article 13

[79] Article 1386–16 *Code Civil*; Schedule 1 Consumer Protection Act introducing a new section 11A in the Limitation Act 1980; article 11 of the Directive.

[80] Article 7(a).

[81] Quotations throughout are from *Commission v France* (see footnote 6 above). The same wording is employed in *Sánchez v Medicina Asturiana SA* (see footnote 7 above), paras. 23–32.

[82] I quote here from *Commission v France*, para. 14.

[83] Ibid., para. 17. [84] Ibid., para. 18. [85] Ibid., para. 21.

[86] Ibid., para. 22 (emphasis in the original).

to the rights which an injured person may rely on under a special liability system existing at the time the Directive was notified 'must be construed . . . as referring to a specific scheme limited to a given sector of production'.[87]

Much therefore depends on what the European Court of Justice means by 'other grounds'. If the 'grounds' for the action under the Directive are article 100 (new article 94 EC), then clearly this would not prevent claimants relying on the '*obligation de sécurité*' developed by the French courts from 1989. However, the European Court's meaning here would appear not to be so restrictive, since it specifically cites actions based on fault or on warranties in respect of latent defects as being 'on other grounds', thus implying that other actions could be on the same grounds.[88] It would therefore seem that the European Court means that an action is on the same grounds when it is based on liability for loss caused by putting a defective product into circulation, which would seem to be the case for the action based on an independent '*obligation de sécurité*'. The annual report of the *Cour de Cassation* for 1995 indeed specifically recognised that this autonomous '*obligation de sécurité*' followed the same line taken by the Directive, and, as explained, this link was expressly confirmed by two judgments dated 3 March 1998 and 28 April 1998, the latter stating that articles 1147 and 1384 of the *Code Civil* were being interpreted in the light of the Directive to impose liability on producers for product defects.[89] It therefore follows that this action should logically disappear with the transposition of the Directive in 1998.[90]

[87] Ibid., para. 23.

[88] G. Viney, 'L'Interprétation par la CJCE de la directive du 25 juillet 1985 sur la responsabilité du fait des produits défectueux' 2002 *JCP. G.* 1945, 1947.

[89] 3 March 1998, *JCP. G.* 1998, II, 10049, rapp. P. Sargos; 28 April, *JCP. G.* 1998, II, 10088, rapp. P. Sargos.

[90] This is certainly the view of French academic commentators: Calais-Auloy, 'Menace européenne'; D. Mazeaud, 'Rapports entre le régime mis en place par la directive du 25 juillet 1985 sur la responsabilité des produits défectueux et les autres régimes de responsabilité' *Dalloz* 2003, sommaires commentés, 463; Larroumet, 'Les Transpositions française et espagnole'; P. Jourdain, note, RTD civ. 2002.523, 526; Viney, 'L'Interprétation' (with a little less certainty). The difficulty in maintaining the independent common law action following the transposition of the directive had already been anticipated by certain commentators back in 1998 (cf Jacques Ghestin, 'Le nouveau titre IV bis du Livre III du Code Civil "De la responsabilité du fait des produits défectueux". L'application en France de la directive sur la responsabilité du fait des produits défectueux après l'adoption de la loi n°98–389 du 19 mai 1998' 1998 *JCP. G.* I 148; Larroumet, 'La Responsabilité du fait des produits défectueux' p. 311.

Presuming that the French courts will be forced to abandon their use of an independent '*obligation de sécurité*', this could certainly have the effect of achieving increased harmonisation by ensuring that more French actions are brought under the new law. In this case, French consumers would seem to be the losers. However, the ruling of the European Court of Justice will not necessarily have as significant an effect on harmonisation as it might first appear. Indeed, other parallel actions would still seem to be open to the victim since the European Court of Justice specifically states that 'the application of other systems of contractual or non-contractual liability based on other grounds, such as fault or a warranty in respect of latent defects' is not precluded.[91] Logically victims should therefore still be able to rely on contractual and delictual actions which existed prior to the courts anticipating the transposition of the Directive in 1989, even if these do not offer ideal solutions.[92] There may therefore be a return to reliance on articles 1641–1 to 1641–8 and 1384–1 of the *Code Civil*, and the courts may continue to find that breach by the manufacturer or supplier of his '*obligation de sécurité*' constitutes a fault.[93] If this is the case, the European Court of Justice's ruling of 25 April may well prove to be counterproductive by encouraging divergence rather than harmonisation: the French courts accepting the old actions with their various particular rules rather than an action which, since 1989, was at least based on the Directive. In addition, the ECJ's ruling on the liability of suppliers and the duty to warn would seem to push victims to rely on the parallel regimes if they wish to sue a home supplier rather than a foreign producer, or to rely on a duty to warn rather than risk falling foul of the development risks defence.

However, the use of these solutions would clearly be artificial in many cases and may consequently be contested by the European Court of Justice as simply being disguises for an action on the same grounds as the Directive.[94] They would certainly seem to go against the aim of the ECJ in *Sánchez* and *Commission v France* of maximising the effectiveness of harmonisation. Even if the French courts do apply these parallel rules, the consumer will still see a reduction in his protection with the disappearance of the autonomous '*obligation de sécurité*'. The traditional

[91] *Commission v France*, para. 22. [92] Calais-Auloy, 'Menace européenne'.

[93] Viney, 'L'Interprétation'.

[94] J. Calais-Auloy, 'Menace européenne sur la jurisprudence française concernant l'obligation de sécurité du vendeur professionnel' 2002 *Dalloz*. 2458, 2460; Patrice Jourdain, note, *RTD civ*. 2002, p. 523 at 527.

contractual action under article 1641 is designed to sanction breach of a contractual obligation and not a failure to offer the security which the consumer is entitled to expect, and thus may not provide a remedy for the consumer in all situations.[95] A return to these actions also has the disadvantage of applying different rules to buyers and third-party victims. But the French system will also face particular difficulties if the victim is unable to rely on these parallel actions since the French liability system will appear extremely inconsistent if it continues to impose strict liability, under article 1384.1, on those with control of an object which causes damage in a wide variety of situations if it has to allow the manufacturer of a product to avoid liability for development risks. The European Court of Justice's judgment could thus have implications outside the area of product liability.

In cases where the new action *is* relied on, it is possible that French judges might adopt an extensive interpretation of the knowledge that is 'accessible' to a producer, given the favourable approach of French courts towards the liability of manufacturers in contractual and delictual actions. As the Court of Justice indicated in its recent judgment in *Commission v UK*, the notion of 'accessibility' will lead to difficulties in interpretation and it would certainly be possible for the French courts to take the approach that practically all knowledge is accessible. However, such an interpretation would obviously also risk being the subject of challenge by the European Court of Justice in a reference under the preliminary rulings procedure, although given the enormous variety of potential factual situations, it would seem extremely difficult for the Court to produce a normative ruling on the interpretation of the notion of accessibility.

Also, it must be remembered that the presence of a parallel strict liability action and the duty to warn were presented during French Parliamentary debates as important counterbalances to the development risks defence. During the Parliamentary debates on the development risks defence, the French government was constantly at pains to stress that the inclusion of the defence did not signify a reduction in the protection of the victim, since he would still be able to bring his action on the basis of the contractual or delictual rules.[96] If consumers want to blame someone for the apparent reduction in their level of protection, their target should perhaps be the

95 Calais-Auloy, 'Menace européenne', 2460.

96 As Mme Guigou, Justice Minister, stated: 'it is not possible to state that the defence penalises victims, since they can rely on our case law, which establishes a strict "*obligation de sécurité*"

French parliament for agreeing to include the development risks defence if they saw it as so important the consumers should be able to avoid it![97] It may be that, following the ECJ's ruling, calls will be made to review the inclusion of the development risks defence in the French statute, although an amendment would seem unlikely under the present centre-right government.

There is also a risk that the notion of 'defect' will be interpreted differently in the two systems, and as noted, recent French case law seems often to presume a defect when damage occurs, without further consideration.

What does seem clear is that the European Court of Justice's decision risks sacrificing a higher level of consumer protection in France in the interests of greater harmonisation, although the true effect of the decision on both consumer protection and harmonisation remains to be seen.

Conclusion

Five years after the transposition of the Product Liability Directive in France, it is difficult to draw any firm conclusions on the extent to which the Directive has contributed to harmonising French and English law. There does, however, still appear to be a considerable potential for divergence. In addition to the scope for different interpretations offered by key notions such as the development risks defence and the defect requirement, article 13 continues to offer the potential for varying levels of liability despite the decisions of the European Court of Justice in *Commission v France* and *Sánchez.* Much will depend on the reactions to the rulings by the French courts.[98]

In any event, this is only one element of the divergence between national rules, and differences in particular in rules relating to causation and access to justice will continue to limit harmonisation. Hence, if, as the preamble to the Directive suggests, competition within the Community is distorted and the free movement of goods affected by divergences in national product liability laws, this will continue to be the case. Differences

even in the case of non-detectable defects' (Débats Sénat, 5 fév. 1998, compte rendu analytique officiel, n°4).

[97] D. Mazeaud, 'Rapports entre le régime mis en place par la directive du 25 juillet 1985 sur la responsabilité des produits défectueux et les autres régimes de responsabilité' *Dalloz* 2003, sommaires commentés, 463, 464.

[98] P. Jourdain, for example, argues for open defiance of the ECJ's rulings by the French legislator and courts. *RTD civ.*, 2002, p. 527.

in the levels of protection will also encourage forum shopping by victims who hope to ensure the application of the most favourable national rules.

In its 2001 Report,[99] which followed a Consultation document,[100] the European Commission stated that the information available on the functioning of the Directive was not yet sufficient to draw any firm conclusions and that it was premature to envisage any changes to the current liability system.[101] The replies to its Consultation Document had shown that 'most of the observations are opposed to the Directive becoming the common and sole system of liability for defective products, but in favour of maintaining the present situation under article 13'.[102]

Claimants continue to use parallel regimes for a variety of reasons. Many claims still concern products put into circulation before national legislation came into force. This is certainly the case in France, where the legislation is only applicable to products put into circulation from May 1998. There may of course be a certain reluctance by some lawyers to rely on the new action rather than traditional contract and tort claims with which they are more familiar. Actions under the new legislation should therefore increase in time, as the regime becomes more familiar. It is however clear that, at least between the two systems studied, article 13 still potentially constitutes an obstacle to effective harmonisation.

Such a conclusion would seem to lend support to the idea of removing the article 13 provision as a means of ensuring greater harmonisation. In its recent report the Commission stated that in the medium term a study was needed to analyse and compare the practical effects of the different systems applicable, and specifically whether a uniform product liability system could be introduced, which would imply the removal of the availability of parallel regimes. The law firm Lovells has been appointed by the Commission to undertake this study.[103] In France, such a choice would be seen as highly undesirable by many, since, unless this was accompanied by other changes, it would clearly lead to a further reduction in the level of protection of victims in that country. Economic efficiency and consumer protection could however be reconciled by accompanying the imposition of a single regime with other changes favourable to the victim, such as removing the development risks defence and facilitating the proof of

[99] COM (2000) 893 final. [100] Green Paper, COM (1999) 396 final of 28.7.1999.
[101] Commission Report, p. 28. [102] Ibid., p. 9.
[103] Press release Lovells, 13 February 2002.

defect.[104] Given the perceived importance of finding 'a fair apportionment of the risks inherent in technological production' any proposed changes to the main provisions of the Directive are unlikely to be adopted without extremely delicate and protracted negotiations.

[104] The possibility was aired in the Commission Green Paper 1999. Calais Auloy suggests changes to remove the development risks defence and to facilitate the proof of defect to compensate for the effect of the ECJ's rulings in *Sánchez* and *Commission v France* (2002 *Dalloz* 2458, 2461).

14

Product liability law in Central Europe and the true impact of the Product Liability Directive

MAGDALENA SENGAYEN

Introduction

This study investigates the process of evolution of Central European[1] product liability regimes, with particular attention to the effect of the implementation of the Product Liability Directive[2] in the context of the 2004 Enlargement of the European Union. Central Europe has been chosen as an example of a region which, although remaining under a strong Socialist influence until 1989, has had a long and relatively close relationship with the West. This relationship placed the Central Europeans in a position described by Alan Mayhew as 'floating dangerously between East and West'.[3] David and Brierley,[4] in 1985, classified the Central European countries, together with Slovenia and Croatia, as the 'countries of western tradition' among the Socialist jurisdictions.[5] They pointed out the common historical development of the 'western tradition' with Germany,

[1] Central Europe, for the purposes of this study, includes Poland, the Czech Republic and Hungary. These three countries formed the 'Visegrad Three' when their presidents met in Visegrad, Hungary, in 1990. The Visegrad Three subsequently became 'Visegrad Four' when the division of Czechoslovakia took place in 1993. The study does not extend its scope to Slovakia, but continues observing the Czech Republic after the division. Therefore, depending on the historical period referred to, the study refers to Czechoslovakia or the Czech Republic.

[2] The Council Directive of 25 May 1985 *on the approximation of laws, regulations and administrative provisions of the Member States concerning liability for defective products*, hereinafter referred to as 'the Directive', or 'the Product Liability Directive'.

[3] A. Mayhew, *Recreating Europe: the European Union's Policy towards Central and Eastern Europe* (Cambridge: Cambridge University Press, 1988), at p. viii.

[4] R. David and J. Brierley, *Major Legal Systems in the World Today: an Introduction to the Comparative Study of Law* (3rd edn, London: Stevens, 1985) at p. 167.

[5] This paper uses the notions 'Socialist', and on occasion also 'Communist' and 'post-Communist', to describe the Central and Eastern European states (the two latter terms are rather only used when quoting other authors). The reader should not be misled by the term 'post-Communist', as none of those countries was ever a Communist entity (Communism assumes the abolishment of the state).

Austria and France – the tradition of Romano-Germanic law.[6] Central European countries seemed to have been too highly developed for a direct implementation of the Communist concepts from Soviet Russia. They were the first nations to break free from the Socialist grip, and the first post-Socialist nations to have concluded Association Agreements with the European Union.[7] The region, so distinct from the West but also so deeply linked to it,[8] is a particularly fertile ground upon which analyses of the post-Socialist transformations can be carried out.

Product liability law, like every other new, specialised discipline of law, has created some confusion within legal science more generally. Its interrelationship with the fields of law from which it has derived, as well as its place within the entire legal system, is as yet uncertain, both in Western and in Eastern Europe. The changing conditions of the markets throughout the world brought about the need for legal intervention in the sphere of damages caused by unsafe products, and the bond between the markets and the product liability laws has remained very important. It is this very bond, and particularly the effect the product liability laws may have on markets, that renders it so difficult to establish the conceptual framework of these laws. The European Community,[9] which has, by its mere existence, organisation and operation, created a new, complex system of law, has decided to harmonise the product liability laws of its Member States. Yet, even here the link of product liability laws with markets, although triggering the need for regulation, rendered this regulation an enormously troublesome task. The problems have been greater still because of the existing divergences in the approach of various Member States to the substantive and procedural dimensions of product regulation. These fundamental problems are very likely to increase with the enlargement of the European Union into the territories previously under a strong Socialist influence – such as Central Europe. Surprisingly,

[6] See their book for the exploration of the theory of 'legal traditions' and 'legal families'.

[7] See below.

[8] See the part of the study devoted to the characteristics of the Central European legal systems for the most fundamental of these distinctions and links.

[9] For the nature and history of the European Community examined in further detail see for instance: C. Rhodes and S. Mazey (eds.), *The State of the European Union. Vol. 3. Building a European Polity?* (Oxford: Lynne Rienner Publishers, Longman, 1995); W. Sandholtz and A. Stone Sweet, *European Integration and Supranational Governance* (Oxford: Oxford University Press, 1998); P. Craig, 'The Nature of the Community: Integration, Democracy and Legitimacy', in P. Craig and G. de Búrca, *The Evolution of EU Law* (Oxford; New York: Oxford University Press, 1999); P. Craig and G. de Búrca, *EU Law. Text, Cases and Materials* (3rd edn, Oxford: Oxford University Press, 2000); and the literature referred to there.

however, the major raison d'être of these problems is not an entirely different substantial law of product liability in Central Europe. In its substantive dimension, the development of product liability law in this region resembled the development of the law in Western Europe. On the other hand, the link of product liability laws with markets created a very peculiar climate around the product liability laws of Central Europe. Wide-ranging transformations have been taking place throughout the region; transformations prompted on the one hand by the demise of Socialism, and on the other by the hopes for and, at the moment, also the obligations of the membership in the European Union.

Methodology and structure of the study

The study aims to depict the true characteristics of the Central European product liability regimes. Such an ambitious endeavour entails a wide outlook on the relevant issues, reaching beyond the Product Liability Directive and its implementation by the analysed jurisdictions. The changes occurring within the post-Socialist states are so profound and wide-ranging that their comprehensive analysis reaches beyond the scope of any discipline. Scholars attempting to explore the framework of these transformations rarely succeed in providing more than a case study illustrating the proceedings of reform following the demise of Socialism (for instance Dupré,[10] Łętowska,[11] or Harmathy).[12] This paper is another case study of this kind, seeking to portray the product liability regimes in a wider context of the accompanying transformations. While revealing the context in which the product liability laws operate the author illustrates the true nature of reform taking place in the region. The Central European states have already implemented the Product Liability Directive, and, apart from certain inconsistencies which will be dealt with in the paper, the newly adopted laws of product liability now resemble the Directive. After introducing the rationale behind the implementation of the Product Liability Directive, and the proceedings of this implementation, the study assesses the main characteristic features of the consumer

[10] C. Dupré, *Importing the Law in Post-Communist Transitions. The Hungarian Constitutional Court and the Right to Human Dignity* (Oxford; Portland, OR: Hart Publishing, 2003).

[11] E. Łętowska, *Prawo umów konsumenckich* (The Law of Consumer Contracts) (C. H. Beck, 1999).

[12] A. Harmathy, *Introduction to Hungarian Law* (The Hague; Boston: Kluwer Law International, 1998).

policy[13] and the market conditions within Central Europe during Socialism and after the transformation into democracy and market economy. The author argues that it is in this sphere that the most profound changes have appeared and are still likely to appear. It is submitted that consumer policies and the position of consumers[14] in the market play a crucial role in the development and operation of product liability laws. The chapter also describes the main features of the Central European legal systems which have affected the development and the shape of the product liability regimes. The second part of the chapter is devoted to the substantive law of product liability. Alongside the account of the manner in which the Directive has been implemented, it is also deemed necessary to introduce the product liability regimes as they functioned before its implementation. Such an exercise has been undertaken for two reasons: first of all, in order to support the key contention of the paper – product liability laws of Central Europe have not differed significantly from Western European laws. Further, it is common knowledge that the regime introduced by the Directive does not apply to all the possible cases of damages and injuries caused by defective products.[15] There are those who hope the Directive can provide an additional, if not the main, very attractive avenue of redress for the victims of defective products. With its 'strict' liability standard[16] it seems the Act is capable of generating trust in its effectiveness and encouraging consumers to use the remedies it offers.[17] However, those

[13] Consumer policy can be defined for the needs of the study as covering 'safety, economic and legal issues relevant to consumers in the market place, consumer information and education, the promotion of consumer organisations and their contribution with other stakeholders to consumer policy development' (Communication from the Commission *Consumer Policy Strategy 2002–2006*, C/137/2). The issue is further analysed below.

[14] For an elaboration on the notion 'consumers' see for instance: K. Mortelmans and S. Watson, 'The Notion of Consumer in Community Law: a Lottery?', in J. Lonbay, *Enhancing the Legal Position of the European Consumer* (London: British Institute of International and Comparative Law, 1996) at pp. 36–57.

[15] Article 13 of the Directive.

[16] In fact, serious doubts as to the true nature of liability introduced by the Directive have been articulated in the literature. The views of Jane Stapleton should be distinguished as particularly critical: J. Stapleton, *Product Liability* (London: Butterworths, 1994) at p. 228.

[17] See for instance the EEC Directive on Liability for Defective Products, Explanatory Memorandum of September 1976; COM (1976) 372 final. Professor Hans Claudius Taschner expressed a similar opinion during the seminar on 'Basic Problems of Product Liability Law from a Comparative Perspective' at the British Institute of International and Comparative Law, 22 October 2003. Central European legal writers and civil servants seem to share the optimism of the Directive (E. Łętowska, 1999; M. Maczonkai, *Hungarian Product Liability Case Law under Civil Code and the New Product Liability Regime*, in

less optimistic, such as Jane Stapleton, provide a very extensive proof of why the Directive cannot and will not be of much benefit to those involved in product liability claims.[18] According to her, 'far from harmonising laws within the EC, the Directive has added a further layer of liability'.[19] She concludes that consumers will still use national contract or tort of negligence remedies, along with the new regime.[20] However optimistic one may be regarding the value of the Product Liability Directive, it seems that, generally, writers on the topic agree on the continuous value of the laws of contract and tort of negligence for product claims (Howells,[21] Hodges).[22] This study follows this tendency.

Only after having examined both the evolution of the substantive rules of product liability and the context in which these rules operated can one truly see the picture of the Central European product liability regimes. The exact impact of the Product Liability Directive is thus clearly visible.

The political momentum for the implementation of the Directive – Central Europe striving to join the European Union

The obligation to implement the Product Liability Directive, and indeed the process of transformation of the Socialist political and economic conditions, was prompted by the growing hopes for membership of the European Union, additionally enforced by the Association Agreements (Europe Agreements)[23] which the Central European states signed with the Union.

Hungary – From Europe Agreements to a Member Status in the EU (ECSA Europe, 1996); M. Dobiasova, Introductory part on the Czech product liability law prepared for the BIICL Product Liability Database, see: www.biicl.org).

18 *Product Liability*, p. 355.

19 Ibid., p. 355. This contention might have lost some of its strength due to the recent jurisprudence of the European Court of Justice declaring that the Directive is a maximum harmonisation measure – judgments: *Commission of the European Communities v French Republic* C-52/00, *González Sánchez v Medicina Asturiana* C-183/00, *Commission of the European Communities v Hellenic Republic* C-154/00.

20 Stapleton, *Product Liability*, p. 355.

21 G. Howells, *Comparative Product Liability* (Aldershot; Dartmouth: Ashgate, 1993).

22 C. Hodges (ed.), *Product Liability. European Laws and Practice* (London: Sweet and Maxwell, 1993).

23 The Europe Agreements 'provide the framework for bilateral relations between the European Communities and their Member States on the one hand and the partner countries on the other. The . . . Agreements cover trade-related issues, political dialogue, legal approximation and other areas of cooperation . . .' (www.europa.eu.int/comm/enlargement/pas/europe˙agr.htm).

In a short time after the demise of Socialism in Central and Eastern Europe, post-Socialist states undertook significant reforms of their political, economic and social systems.[24] In recognition of these transformations, the European Community commenced the process of strengthening the relations with the newly freed countries. The European Commission was thus asked to draw up proposals for association agreements in order to establish a 'special type of relationship reflecting geographic proximity, shared values and increased independence'.[25] The Europe Agreements were not very explicit about the future chances for membership of the European Union, only referring to the membership as the 'final objective' of the post-Socialist states.[26] Nevertheless, it was clear that the process of 'merging the CEECs back into the Western part of Europe, and re-establishing a sense of belonging that they have always claimed' had begun.[27] Article 69 of the Hungarian Agreement[28] and Articles 68 of the Polish[29] and Czech[30] Agreements stipulated the obligation to approximate the national law to the *acquis communautaire*,[31] the following provisions of the Agreements containing the most crucial areas of law to be dealt with, and among those, consumer protection laws. The relations

24 P. G. Lewis, *Central Europe since 1945* (London and New York: Longman, 1994).

25 Commission of the European Communities, *Association Agreements with Poland, Czechoslovakia and Hungary*, Background Brief (Brussels, February 1992); J. Gower, 'EU Policy to Central and Eastern Europe', in K. Henderson (ed.), *Back to Europe. Central and Eastern Europe and the European Union* (London; Philadelphia: University College London Press, Taylor and Francis Group, 1999).

26 Gower, 'EU Policy', p. 5.

27 V. Curzon Price, A. Landau and R. G. Whitman (eds.), *The Enlargement of the European Union, Issues and Strategies* (London and New York: Routledge, Routledge Studies in European Economy, 1999) at p. 13; Gower, 'EU Policy', referred to the 'major shift in EU policy' (at p. 7).

28 The Europe Agreement concluded between Hungary and the European Union contains Article 67 requiring Hungary to approximate their laws to the laws of the European Union (*Official Journal L 347*, 31/12/1993 pp. 2–266). In Article 68 specific fields of interest are listed, and among them consumer protection including product liability.

29 The Association Agreement of the European Union with the Republic of Poland contains Article 68 obliging Poland to approximate its laws to the laws of the European Union (*Official Journal L 348*, 31/12/1993 pp. 2–180).

30 The Czech Association Agreement, renegotiated after the division of Czechoslovakia, contains similar provisions to those included in the Hungarian and Polish Agreements. The necessity of approximating consumer protection laws has been expressly stipulated in Article 69 (*Official Journal L 360*, 31/12/1994 pp. 2–210).

31 The *acquis communautaire* are 'all the rights and obligations, actual and potential, arising from the Treaties, EC law and the jurisdiction of the Court of Justice plus declarations, resolutions and international agreements adopted within the Community framework' (Gower, 'EU Policy', 18).

between the Union and the post-Socialist countries have evolved further as a result of the Essen European Council, where the Commission was asked to prepare 'concrete proposals to draw together all the various EU policy instruments into a coherent strategy to prepare the countries of CEE for accession'.[32] During the meeting of the Council the Commission was invited to draft a White Paper to be presented at the Cannes European Council the following year.[33] While the White Paper was welcomed by the post-Socialist states as an implicitly drafted 'action plan' for them, it also stressed the areas which the Commission considered as being of particular significance, including the 'legal approximation' of economic laws of the associated states.[34] The 'legal approximation' was to involve, apart from adopting a significant volume of legal instruments,[35] also ensuring their practical operation, through establishing relevant enforcement and administrative procedures.[36] The impact of this, however obvious, requirement on regimes such as product liability is clear. Although the author does not attempt to comprehensively examine what enforcement procedures have been in place with regard to product-related injuries (access to justice, and in particular the procedural framework or the system of legal aid), the issue is no doubt of paramount significance and begs further analysis. The study, illustrating the context in which the regimes have operated, may well constitute a valuable basis for such enquiries.

Following the encouragement from the European Community, Poland and Hungary formally applied for membership in the structure in 1994 and the Czech Republic did the same in 1996.[37] In 2001 in Gothenburg the leaders of the EU concluded that enlargement negotiations would be completed by 2002 and the enlargement would take place in 2004.[38] In 2002 the European Commission confirmed that the ten applicant countries[39] would join the Union in 2004, and the Copenhagen European Council

[32] Gower, ibid., p. 9; see Commission of the European Communities, *The Europe Agreements and Beyond: a Strategy to Prepare the Countries of Central and Eastern Europe for Accession* COM (94) 320 final, and *Follow up to Commission Communication* COM (94) 361 final, 1994.

[33] Commission of the European Communities, *White Paper: Preparation of the Associated Countries of Central and Eastern Europe for Integration into the Internal Market of the Union* COM (95) 163 final.

[34] Gower, 'EU Policy', p. 9.

[35] '80,000 pages of EU law' (www.europa.eu.int/pol/enlarg/overview_en.htm).

[36] Gower, 'EU Policy', p. 9. [37] Ibid., pp. 10, 18.

[38] www.europa.eu.int/pol/enlarg/overview_en.htm.

[39] These countries are: Hungary, Poland, the Czech Republic, Lithuania, Latvia, Slovakia, Slovenia, Estonia, Cyprus and Malta.

formally welcomed the new Member States.[40] The Treaty of Accession[41] was signed on 16 April 2003. With the moment of joining the Union (1 May 2004), the obligation to implement all the *acquis communautaire* becomes legally binding, and the new Member States can be subject to an Article 226 action by the European Commission for failing to implement the Directive correctly; the action which can find its conclusion in the European Court of Justice.[42]

Implementation of the Directive

Hungary and the Czech Republic decided to implement the Directive by enacting separate Acts instead of incorporating the provisions into their Civil Codes. The decisions were taken for technical reasons (possibility of updating the Act quicker) and greater 'transparency' for consumers.[43]

Hungary implemented the Directive the earliest – Act I of 1993 came into force on 1 January 1994.[44] It was later amended by Act XXXVI of 2002 *amending Act IV of 1959 on the Civil Code of the Republic of Hungary and other Acts for the harmonisation of consumer protection*, passed by the Parliament on 5 November 2002.[45]

The Czech Republic implemented the Directive by Act No. 59/1998 *on Liability for Damage caused by a Defective Product*. The Act came into force on 1 June 1998. It was amended by Act No 209/2000, reflecting the amendments of the Directive in 1999.[46]

Poland has adopted the Act of 2 March 2000 *on the protection of certain rights of consumers and liability for damage caused by an unsafe product* in order to implement the Product Liability Directive. The Act inserted Articles 449.1 to 449.11 into the Polish Civil Code of 1964 (title VI.1 introduced into Book III 'Obligations' of the Code). It came into force

[40] www.europa.eu.int/pol/enlarg/overview_en.htm.

[41] http://www.europa.eu.int/comm/enlargement/negotiations/treaty_of_accession_2003/table_of_content_en.htm.

[42] Not all the provisions of the Central European product liability legislation actually follow the Directive – thus such a situation is possible (see below).

[43] Maczonkai, 'Hungarian Product Liability Case Law'.

[44] The Hungarian Act on Product Liability of 1993 contains a short Preamble which elaborates upon the motives for the adoption of the Act. What is unique is the reference of the Preamble to the existing achievements of the case law, and the need for their consolidation in a written piece of legislation (E. Kalman, V. Lelkes, M. Domonkos, (2003) BIICL Database report on the Hungarian Product Liability Law, at 4).

[45] Personal communication, Judit Bartfai – Hungarian Ministry of Justice.

[46] Personal communication, Monika Dobiasova – Czech Ministry of Trade and Industry.

on 1 January 2001. An interesting fact is that the place in which the new regulation is situated in the Code does not indicate tortious liability (the latter covered by Title VII). This has already raised questions of some prominent representatives of the doctrine of law as to the true nature of this new category of liability.[47]

The internal momentum for change – Central Europeans striving for strict liability and beyond

Throughout Central Europe the legal profession and academia observed the need for reform of the product liability regimes long before the implementation of the Directive actually became a political necessity, and even before the demise of Socialism. Following this movement, the development of product liability regimes in Central Europe was quite impressive; particularly so in Hungary, but also in Poland. Even the Czechoslovak regime, although not sufficiently developed because of the very peculiar characteristics of the law and legal doctrine in this country (explored below), started evolving in the direction of stricter liability. Yet, in spite of these significant developments, several academics and politicians argued for even more wide-ranging reforms in the area of product liability and, more generally, consumer protection law.

In the early 1980s Hungary made considerable progress in establishing a strict product liability regime, stricter than the liability established by the Product Liability Directive. It is therefore intriguing that one of the members of the Hungarian Parliament who initiated reforms of consumer protection laws, including the product liability law, in the early 1990s postulated the 'defencelessness' of the Hungarian consumers against the manufacturers of defective products.[48] Putting aside the possible political motives of such a statement, it appears to imply that regime which already reached the level of protection offered by the Product Liability Directive was considered somehow inadequate. It is by no means submitted that the politician considered the regime of the Directive unsatisfactory. Rather he concluded that the sum total of protection provided to Hungarian consumers was insufficient.

[47] E. Łętowska (2001), *Ochrona Niektórych Praw Konsumentów. Komentarz* (3rd edn, Warsaw: Wydawnictwo C. H. Beck) at p. 122.

[48] L. Kecskés (1994), *Termékfelelõsség a Magyar Jogban* (Budapest: Pécs) pp. 68–101 – records of parliamentary debate on product liability.

The Polish doctrine of law used examples of the United States of America or the existing Member States of the European Union as a rationale for reform of the existing regime, which was considered unacceptable by many.[49] The regime based on fault, although as a result of some groundbreaking judgments facilitated with the concepts of anonymous fault, *res ipsa loquitur* or evidence *prima facie*, was seen by many as inadequate and far from the achievements of American and Western European regimes.[50]

The Czechoslovak academics stressed the importance of reform of their product liability regime as well.[51] Here the need was most pressing, as the development of liability into a stricter standard was slow and not well articulated in the very insignificant number of judgments.

The politicians and academics postulating reforms often emphasised crucial factors lying outside the scope of the substantive liability regime. Maczonkai concluded that it was indeed impossible to ascertain the true position of the Hungarian consumer by analysing decided cases.[52] How often did cases such as those analysed below find their way to court? Or, even more importantly, how consistent were the courts in following the breakthrough judgements? Unfortunately the data on these issues is unavailable. Maczonkai conducted quite a comprehensive analysis of the existing case law on product liability in Hungary, but his conclusion that Hungarian consumers were not, or rather not so, 'defenceless' seems incomplete, as he himself acknowledges.[53] On the one hand, the mere nature of product liability litigation, involving very rare cases with considerable damages and significant costs, does not allow the establishment of the true situation by looking at the decided cases. The number of cases reported in the literature is small, and it would be an overstatement to claim that either the Hungarian, Polish or, especially, the Czech product liability regime was satisfactory based upon only this insignificant number of judgments. On the other hand, the circumstances surrounding the

[49] M. Nesterowicz, *Odpowiedzialnosc za szkody wyrzadzone wprowadzeniem do obrotu rzeczy niebezpiecznych z wadami* (1979) Pal Nr 11; E. Łętowska, 'Ksztaltowanie sięodrębności obrotu mieszanego', in *Tendencje rozwoju prawa cywilnego* (1983, Ossolineum).

[50] B. Gnela, *Odpowiedzialnosc za szkode wyrzadzona przez produkt niebezpieczny (tzw. odpowiedzialnosc za product)* (Krakow: Zakamycze, 2000).

[51] J. Svestka, 'Damage Caused by the Sale of a Defective Product by a Trading Corporation to a Citizen as Buyer under the Czechoslovak Civil Code' in T. Wilhelmsson and J. Svestka (eds.), *Consumer Protection in Czechoslovakia and Finland* (Helsinki: Helsingin Yliopisto, 1989) at p. 107.

[52] Maczonkai, 'Hungarian Product Liability Case Law', 115.

[53] Ibid.

operation of product liability laws – political attitudes, economic conditions, attitudes of the legal profession, and consumer awareness – are all of extreme relevance for ensuring adequate defences for consumers. The implementation of the Product Liability Directive, which in the case of Hungary should have entailed no more than, in most aspects, condensing or simply summarising in a written document the already existing principles, is therefore not likely to combat the said 'defencelessness'.[54] Although in Poland and the Czech Republic a more significant legislative effort was needed, the same can be concluded regarding the position of consumers. It is the transformation of all the issues mentioned above, accompanied by the reform within the entire area of consumer protection laws, which should benefit consumers.

The context of product liability laws in Europe – consumer policies, consumer position and consumer law – differences between the East and the West

Let us now examine the sources of this dissatisfaction with the reality of the product liability regimes. Essentially, product liability law centres upon the manner in which risk inherent in products may be most efficiently apportioned. The group very clearly affected by any decisions regarding this issue are consumers. Thus, in spite of doubts expressed in the contemporary literature on the subject,[55] the link between product liability law and consumer protection policies is crucial. It seems clear, in particular from reading the Preamble and the text of the Product Liability Directive, that consumers are in fact at least the main subjects of focus of the contemporary product liability laws. Thus any comprehensive analysis of product liability laws must necessarily refer to the consumer protection policy of the discussed jurisdictions. It is this policy that has been so unsatisfactory indeed in the Socialist and post-Socialist states.

What exactly is consumer protection policy and how does it translate into consumer protection laws? Where can one locate the failures of

[54] In some cases the implementation of the Directive by Hungary actually means a less stringent liability standard (see below).

[55] In Poland: Gnela, *Odpowiedzialność*; one of the most extreme views, dismissing the need to consider consumers as those to whom product liability laws relate, is M. Jagielska, *Odpowiedzialność za produkt* (Product Liability, 1999), also S. Simitis, 'Products Liability: the West-German Approach', in C. J. Miller (ed.), *Comparative Product Liability* (London: The United Kingdom National Committee of Comparative Law, 1986) at pp. 118, 119.

Socialism and how have they affected product liability regimes? Trubek defined consumer protection policy as a policy of government intervention in 'market place transactions', including intervention by law; and consumer protection law as 'the sum total of the ways in which a state constitutes, defines, and intervenes in markets for the purpose of protecting the ultimate consumer of goods and services'.[56] Consumer protection law thus becomes, according to Trubek, 'a series of relationships, direct or indirect, between state institutions . . . on the one hand and private economic actors on the other'.[57] As Roper and Snowdon point out, in a perfect market 'it is competition which acts as the key regulator ensuring that individual greed does not lead to exploitation'.[58] However, the markets in reality do not correspond to the free market ideals and therefore economists developed a concept of 'market failure'. Thus, the need for state intervention arises. In recognition of these failures, Lipsey and Chrystal wrote that, in practice, every economy is a mixed economy.[59] The prevailing market system characterises capitalist countries, and the centrally planned system prevails in socialist countries. Consumer protection laws, as a form of intervention of states in the market, remain different in these two systems. According to Bourgoignie, the evolution of consumer protection policies and laws of the existing Member States of the European Union commenced with the recognition that the traditional, liberal legal approaches to the governance of market relations were unsatisfactory, for they created only 'myths of rights' for consumers.[60] Such tendencies could also be noticed in the Socialist countries of Central and Eastern Europe. The 'modern political economy of consumer protection' devised by Trubek is a vision of consumer protection law as it stands at present. In contrast to the traditional or 'classical' vision, the modern approach, not convinced of the perfectibility of markets, favours state action as 'supplementing if not supplanting market determination'.[61] While in capitalist states the supplementary function is primary, in Socialist

[56] T. Bourgoignie, D. Trubek, L. Trubek and D. Stingl, *Consumer Law, Common Markets and Federalism in Europe and the United States*, vol. 3 of *Integration Through Law, Europe and American Federal Experience*, A Series under the General Editorship of M. Cappelletti, M. Seccombe, J. Weiler (Berlin: Walter de Gruyter, 1987) at pp. 1, 6.

[57] Ibid., at p. 6.

[58] B. Roper and B. Snowdon (eds.), *Markets, Intervention and Planning* (London and New York: Longman, 1987) at p. 11.

[59] R. G. Lipsey and K. A. Chrystal, *Positive Economics* (8th edn, Oxford: Oxford University Press, 1995) at p. 11.

[60] Bourgoignie *et al.*, at p. 90.

[61] Bourgoignie *et al.*, at p. 7.

states the state rather supplants the market.[62] The laws of consumer protection, being a form of governmental intervention in the market, may assume various roles and character – for instance regulation of private transactions and their legal consequences, or providing for products of specified safety standards to enter the markets.[63] Product liability laws clearly can be counted among those rules. Such laws have been introduced both in Western and Eastern Europe, based upon similar policy considerations mentioned above, since the second half of the twentieth century.[64] Significant differences between the two parts of the continent were, however, related to the internal mechanism of evolution of product liability regimes, the latter manifestly linked to the evolution of the entire body of consumer protection laws. These remained under the influence of the political and economic environment.

First of all, in Western Europe the courts commenced the development of product regimes early in the twentieth century in recognition of the rights of buyers, and subsequently of non-buyer victims of defective products. Consumer awareness arrived later, when the regimes were already relatively well developed. In the Central European countries no significant attempt to create a regime of liability for products was made until the second half of the twentieth century – and at the time the region was under Socialist domination. Apart from Hungary the dealings between 'socialist organisations'[65] were excluded from the civil codes or the jurisdiction of the civil courts.[66] The civil courts were focussed on consumer relations, as these were the relations they mainly dealt with. The full impact of such consumer focus was however suppressed by the

[62] The intervention of the Socialist states in the markets, although more intense than in capitalist countries, was by no means more effective in providing sufficient level of protection for consumers (see below).

[63] Svetsa 'Damage', at p. 9.

[64] A particular difficulty related to regulation of consumer issues is that several, often conflicting, interests are involved. The area of product liability is no exception in this respect. One must remember that the reason behind the introduction of consumer protection laws was in the first place the will to offset the 'gross disparities of effective economic power' between the professionals and consumers (Bourgoignie et al., at p. 10).

[65] These were state-owned undertakings and cooperatives – the main form of economic presence in the Socialist markets.

[66] In Poland relations between 'socialist organisations', although regulated mostly by the Civil Code, were excluded from the jurisdiction of the civil courts, and special arbitration tribunals resolved disputes between them. In Czechoslovakia they were entirely separated from the Civil Code and regulated by the Economic Code. In fact, the regimes of product liability between the socialist organisations were more stringent than the ordinary regimes of liability for defective products (Gnela, *Odpowiedzialność*, 175–9).

workings of the Socialist economic and social policy which are explored below.

Further, Western European consumer protection laws in general have significantly changed their focus over the last thirty years – a change which can only recently be observed in Central Europe. In order to appreciate these contemporary developments, one needs to understand what actually happens in the process of consumers acquiring goods or services. For this purpose the method adopted by Morris can be used.[67] According to him, there are three distinct stages in this process: 'shopping', 'buying' and 'consuming'. It seems essential that consumers should be protected during all three stages, but different kinds of protection are required during each one. Morris suggests that in the 'shopping' stage, when the consumer searches for the right product, adequate information, protection against misleading practices, and safety of goods and services must be ensured. During the 'buying' stage the transaction is being concluded. The law must safeguard fairness and the binding effect of the contracts. The 'consuming stage' Morris understood as 'using, eating, displaying, or consuming in other ways'.[68] Products and services should not be harmful to the consumers or their property and ought to satisfy their needs in accordance with their reasonable expectations. Product liability laws feature rules protecting buyers in the last 'consuming' stage. At the moment, however, the focus of protection for consumers has generally shifted to the stage of 'shopping'. With the significant influence of the European Union, and in the climate of increased economic efficiency and healthy competition, laws aimed at providing consumers with adequate information on products and services are being gradually introduced in Europe. Furthermore, safety became a very important issue, and laws ensuring that only safe goods enter the market are in operation (General Product Safety Directive).[69] As far as the 'buying' stage is concerned, extensive legislation has been adopted, safeguarding fairness of consumer contracts and their terms. The law also shifted from blind enforcement of contracts to granting the consumer the time to think (*tempus ad deliberandum*), change his mind, as well as making the binding effect dependent on the

[67] D. Morris (ed.), *Economics of Consumer Protection* (London: Heinemann Educational Books, 1980) at p. ix.

[68] Ibid., at p. x.

[69] The Council Directive 92/59/EEC of 29 June 1992 on general product safety (OJ L 228 of 11.08.1992) has now been replaced by the Directive 2001/95/EC of the European Parliament and the Council of 3 December 2001 on general product safety (OJ L 11 of 15.01.2002), with effect from 15 January 2004.

fairness of the contract (the Unfair Contract Terms Directive 1993).[70] Steps are being taken to ensure that the traditional product liability laws (relating to the 'consuming' stage) are treated as a 'last resort' measure by the consumers. Further, the European Union has been developing other ways of satisfying consumer claims, without the use of courts and legal rules.[71]

What transpires from the above analysis is that product liability law, being only a small part of a consumer protection system, should be accompanied by a significant number of other legal regimes. The latter, together with the relevant political and economic conditions, as well as the specific types of attitudes of the legal profession mentioned below, form an undivided whole. The crucial fact is that this complex system of laws and policies which normally ought to accompany product liability laws did not fully exist and operate in Central Europe. This issue is explored in the following part of the study.

Central Europe and consumers – particular sources of divergences

The position of Central European consumers has been affected by the changing historical, political and economic circumstances. Below the author depicts the evolution of this position, describing the developments within the consumer protection policies and laws and their effect upon the product liability regimes.

When consumer protection ideas started exerting influence upon the European policymakers, Central Europe was still under the rule of Socialism. Consumer protection policy was not a notion which has been entirely absent from the Socialist policies, laws and markets. Yet, in spite of product safety and quality being the most significant problems faced by the consumers of the epoch, in the light of the political and market conditions of Socialism the consumers' position could not be improved.[72] Below is an analysis of the reasons for this situation.

[70] Council Directive 93/13/EEC of 5 April 1993 *on unfair terms in consumer contracts* (OJ 1993 L 95, p. 29).

[71] 'Most consumer disputes are characterised by the disparity between the economic value at stake and the cost and duration of its judicial settlement. To remedy the specific problems of consumer disputes, several Member States have opted for out-of-court mechanisms whose flexibility may be more attuned to the needs of both consumers and professionals' (European Commission DG Health and Consumer Protection; see www.europa.eu.int/comm/dg24/policy/developments/acce_just/acce_just04_en.html).

[72] Łętowska , *Prawo umów konsumenckich*, p. 5.

First of all, significant consumer protection laws, especially those aimed at product safety or unfair contractual terms, were simply not in existence. The populist vision of social interest being more significant than the individual interest, and the holist ideology of what is good for the state is good for each citizen[73] did not prompt the governments to enact consumer protection legislation. The focus remained upon industry, mostly state owned, the performance of which was regulated by administrative instruments. Consumers were obviously prevented from taking direct action in case a breach of such an instrument occurred, although they frequently suffered the ill consequences of such breaches.

Further, even those consumer protection provisions which were in fact enacted were ineffective for a number of reasons. Lack of competition was the major contributor to the lack of incentive to produce safe goods. In this situation, the mere existence of an administrative instrument or a legislative provision obliging an undertaking to take safety precautions was insufficient. Furthermore, the façade character of the Socialist consumer protection laws was reflected in the attitudes of the legal profession,[74] which were the result of the workings of the Socialist doctrine. The doctrine of Socialism rendered many claims against state-owned undertakings futile, as such claims were understood as, at least to a certain extent, claims against the state. It is also not difficult to understand that because the representatives of the legal profession, who after all are also consumers, were abused by organisations, they did not feel the need to assist others who found themselves in the same position.[75] It is clear that in the light of these factors consumer knowledge of remedies offered by law and their confidence in the law were very poor.[76]

[73] Ibid., p. 2.

[74] 'Legal profession' can be defined as consisting of those bearing the power of lawmaking ('the lawmakers'), those in a position of delivering judgments based upon the law established by the lawmakers ('the adjudicators'), and those with the authority to advise ordinary citizens on the importance and the exact meaning of the laws adopted by the lawmakers ('the legal advisers'). Such classification of the legal profession has been adopted by the author for the needs of the study, for it is considered comprehensive enough to include all the members of this profession who may have had an influence on consumer protection laws and policies, including the product liability regimes.

[75] Łętowska wrote about the very popular proverbs during the times of Socialism: 'One cannot win with the railway company/ bank/ social insurance company' – proverbs undoubtedly related to the fact that these were owned by the state (Łętowska, *Prawo umów konsumenckich*, pp. 2, 7).

[76] For a further elaboration upon the attitudes of the legal profession, and the political and economic conditions affecting these attitudes, see the article published by the author of this study (M. Sengayen, 'Consumer Sales Law in Poland: Changing the Law, Changing Attitudes' (2002) 25 *Journal of Consumer Policy*: 427).

In these circumstances product liability laws were developing quite steadily. In the market where incentives for safety and quality improvements in production did not exist, all the legal system could have done was provide remedies for damages caused by these, then unavoidable, dangerous products. Very solid bases for the further development of product liability regimes were laid down by the Central European courts. Still, following the idiosyncrasies of the legal profession mentioned above, the number of cases reaching the courts was insufficient, and many cases were never settled, either in or out of court.

During the 1970s and 1980s the efforts of the Central European courts aiming at improving the product liability regimes gradually intensified and resulted in the establishment of quite comprehensive and notably progressive rules (probably with the exception of Czechoslovakia).[77] Along with the gradual movement towards greater appreciation of market philosophy, accompanying the abandoning of the strict Socialist doctrine, throughout Central Europe the attitudes of the legal profession were gradually changing towards greater recognition of the fact that the interests of undertakings were not necessarily similar to the interests of society. Especially in the 1980s the contention that the consumers' interests ought to be protected to a greater extent gained strength among the lawmakers, the adjudicators and the legal advisers. Svestka explicitly elaborated upon the 'reconstruction of the direction of the national economy taking place in the socialist countries'.[78] This reconstruction was concerned with the spirit of initiative and enterprise, free competition and commencement of liquidation of monopolies.[79] Administrative means of regulating national economy started giving way to economic means.[80] The changes placed new requirements upon the legal profession, with the lawmakers challenged to amend the unsatisfactory legal provisions, and the judges having to interpret the existing legal provisions in a manner consistent with the new tendencies. The specific time when the ideas of consumerism became popular depended upon the level of economic and social development of a particular jurisdiction, this development remaining under the influence of the political circumstances. Hungary was the first country to change its political philosophy into a much more free-market-focussed one. The

[77] See below for the reasons for the poor development of the Czech product liability regime.

[78] J. Svestka, 'Damage Caused by the Sale of a Defective Product by a Trading Corporation to a Citizen as Buyer under the Czechoslovak Civil Code', in T. Wilhelmsson and J. Svestka (eds.), *Consumer Protection in Czechoslovakia and Finland* (Helsinki: Helsingin Yliopisto, 1989) pp. 92, 93.

[79] Ibid. [80] Ibid.

first true recognition of the needs of the markets, and the needs of consumers, took place directly after the economic reforms in Hungary in the 1970s. The Civil Code was amended in 1977 towards a greater control of contracts by courts,[81] and administrative planning was no longer treated as an effective means to ensure the evolution of the market in the desired direction.[82] In terms of the product liability regime, this was also the time when the courts started realising that the existing solutions were unsatisfactory, and searched among the rules available to them to provide more effective remedies. Czechoslovakia followed shortly, although its changes to the Socialist ideals and their effect upon consumers were narrower in scale and scope. There is, however, no doubt that the need for consumer protection was recognised there, at least in the 1980s. Czechoslovak scholarly writers elaborated upon the situation of consumers[83] ('the so-called non-professional contractual party', a party 'lacking experience and professional product knowledge') as being in the 'weakest economic position'.[84] In the 1980s the problems of consumers were widely recognised in Czechoslovak law, both in the Civil Code and in other regulations, especially in the field of administrative law (regulating product quality, technical standards or prices).[85] The contention that 'protection of the interests of citizens as buyers, e.g. consumers in general, is not resolved by the very act of taking over of the means of production and planning' became very popular.[86] Among other measures, Svestka mentioned control of common trade conditions, instalment and credit sales, obligatory statutory guarantees, and also remedies provided to those who sustained damages caused by defective products.[87] In fact, the issue of liability for defective products received some attention in the Czechoslovak doctrine of law. The doctrine postulated preventive measures aimed at securing quality, but also distribution of risks through compensation of losses caused by defective products.[88] Compensation was to cover the losses and, even more important, be easily obtainable. Polish consumer protection policy suffered for a long time from lack of attention caused by serious

[81] Harmathy, *Introduction to Hungarian Law*, p. 98.

[82] Harmathy, when referring to the Hungarian market after the 1970s' reforms, spoke clearly of the 'economy in transition to a special kind of mixed market and planned economy' (ibid., p. 98).

[83] Svestka refers to them rather as 'citizens as buyers' and 'third parties', or simply 'citizens' (1989: 90, 92). He also, sporadically, uses the notion 'consumers' (1989: 92). Knappowa (M. Knappowa and T. Wilhelmsson, in T. Wilhelmsson and J. Svestka (eds.), *Consumer Protection in Czechoslovakia and Finland* (Helsinki: Helsingin Yliopisto, 1989) concentrates on 'the citizen as consumer' (at p. 131).

[84] Ibid., p. 91. [85] Ibid., p. 92. [86] Ibid. [87] Ibid. [88] Ibid., p. 94.

political and economic crises, and hence in Poland the change took place latest. Łętowska wrote in the early 1980s of the necessity to accept the need for greater protection of consumers and thus to abandon the Socialist ideals in this sphere.[89] The scholarly writings on the issue of consumer protection were numerous even before this point, but they seemed to have focussed solely upon the matters of liability for defective products.[90] It will be seen from the analysis below that, although there were no written provisions regulating this area, Polish courts were relatively active in interpreting the general liability rules towards gradually greater protection for the victims of the defective products which constantly flooded the Polish market. In terms of other issues concerning consumers, the Polish legal and economic system was truly unsatisfactory.[91] Enacted regulations aimed at securing the desired quality of products were never fully applied in practice.

The tendencies which could be observed throughout Central Europe in the 1980s led to significant improvements in the position of consumers, although they were obviously limited by the still existing Socialist political and economic reality. The demise of Socialism also did not give rise to an immediate improvement of this position. In 1989 the peaceful revolution broke down Socialism and transformed it into a totally different reality. The consumers of the entire post-Socialist Europe were faced with new challenges, not very often perceived as such by the legal profession.[92] In Socialist systems the state was falsely proclaimed as being able to protect the citizens' interests, and among the protective activities those aimed at the consumers were distinguished. Because such belief was fundamentally false and even detrimental to consumer interests, the legal profession was disillusioned with state intervention in the market.[93] They welcomed free-market ideas as an infusion of healthy, fair competition, hoping that,

[89] Letowska, *Kształtowanie*, p. 401. See also C. Żuławska 'Ochrona konsumenta w reformowanej gospodarce' (1985) 3 *Spółdzielczy Kwartalnik Naukowy*: No. 41, at 41–9, or C. Żuławska (1987) *Obrót z udziałem konsumenta – ochrona prawna*, Wrocław; 41–9.

[90] S. Sołtysiński (1970) *Odpowiedzialność producenta wobec konsumenta za szkody wyrządzone wprowadzeniem do obrotu rzeczy z wadami* (Krakow: Studia Cywilistyczne, vol. XV, p. 172) – a study postulating introduction of the contractual liability of the producers for defective products; liability based upon the 'guarantee promise'; or Nesterowicz, 'Odpowiedzialność za szkody wyrzadzone wprowadzeniem do obrotu rzeczy niebezpiecznych z wadami' 11/4 *Paletstra*: 4–19.

[91] M. Sengayen 'Consumer Sales Law in Poland: Changing the Law, Changing Attitudes' (2002) 25 *Journal of Consumer Policy*, Special Issue on Law, Information and Product Quality, No. 3/4 403, at 425.

[92] Łętowska, *Prawo umów konsumenckich*, pp. 3, 4.

[93] Ibid.

on its own, the free market would be capable of curing the ills of the post-Socialist markets and provide the consumers with an adequate level of protection. Thus, yet again, the system of consumer laws and policies was incomplete and did not operate successfully. This situation was however gradually changing, owing partly to internal movements within academia and the legal profession, but also largely to the pressures from the European Union. With a view to membership, Central Europeans began to introduce a comprehensive consumer protection system following the laws and policies of the European Union. In 1998 Hungary adopted the Act on the Protection of Health and Consumers. It provided basic consumer rights in accordance with the expectations of the European Union *acquis*.[94] Subsequently, further pieces of Community legislation were implemented, and the process advanced so significantly indeed that this chapter of negotiations was provisionally closed in 2002.[95] In spite of significant delays in implementing the consumer *acquis* Poland ultimately sped up the development and also provisionally closed the chapter in 2002.[96] No consumer protection Act was adopted in Poland, which rather focussed upon separate regulation of specific issues. The progress of the Czech Republic was also noted as unsatisfactory by the Commission, although the chapter was closed in 2002.[97] In 1992 the Czech Republic adopted the Consumer Protection Act[98] creating various rights for consumers. Apart from establishing substantive legal provisions Central European states also focussed upon building an organisational framework for protection of consumers. Various state institutions and bodies were set up, both within the consumer protection Acts and outside their scope, in order to adequately secure enforcement of consumer rights. More powers were given to consumer organisations, which commenced active lobbying

[94] www.europa.eu.int/scadplus/leg/en/lvb/e16103.htm.

[95] Ibid. See Commission Reports on the progress of Hungary: COM (1997) 2001 final, COM (1998) 700 final, COM (1999) 505 final, COM (2000) 705 final, SEC (2001) 1748 final, COM (2002) 700.

[96] www.europa.eu.int/scadplus/leg/en/lvb/e16106.htm. See the Commission Reports: COM (1997) 2002 final, COM (1998) 701 final, COM (1999) 509 final, COM (2000) 709 final, SEC (2001) 1752, COM (2002) 700 final.

[97] www.europa.eu.int/scadplus/leg/en/lvb/e16107.htm. See the Commission Reports: COM (1997) 2009 final, COM (1998) 708 final, COM (1999) 503 final, COM (2000) 703 final, SEC (2001) 1746, COM (2002) 700 final.

[98] Act No. 634/1992 Coll., as amended by Acts No. 217/1993 Coll., No. 40/1995 Coll., No. 104/1995 Coll., and as promulgated in Act No. 34/1996 Coll. Subsequently amended by Acts No. 110/1997, No. 356/1999, No. 64/2000 (www.spotrebitele.cz/legislativa/zakochrspot-000710.html).

of the governments and parliaments. In fact, the importance of the process of implementation of the *acquis* rests with, apart from the weight of the newly adopted black-letter legislation, the emphasis upon mechanisms of enforcement virtually unknown before. The European Union considers the enforcement of laws, establishment of the pertinent administrative and judicial structures and coordination of institutions involved in the enforcement procedures, of paramount importance, and imposes such an approach on the aspiring Member States.[99] The approach is a novelty in the post-Socialist states where exactly this issue of enforcement of law, especially with regard to consumer protection law, did not receive adequate attention. Thus, considerable change follows the implementation of the entire body of the, widely understood, consumer protection laws, and the policies and attitudes accompanying them. The latter are the result of the heritage of the Western European Member States of the European Union, consolidated and harmonised in a regime unknown to the post-Socialist jurisdictions.

At the present moment economic incentives are much greater and product safety laws, other laws regulating products (such as legal and commercial guarantees) and the entire regime of consumer protection laws are operating more effectively in compliance with the EU expectations. In fact, the balance among these provisions is being restored. Product liability laws are therefore hoped to become the 'last resort' measure, with greater emphasis upon damage prevention by product safety laws. Such is the true impact of the body of laws, including the Product Liability Directive, policies and attitudes deriving from the European Union.

Central European legal systems and their effect upon the product liability regimes

There is no doubt that the nature and shape of the Central European civil codes also affect the shape and operation of the product liability regimes. Here also further sources of fundamental divergences from and similarities to Western laws can be observed.

[99] See *Communication from the Commission to the European Parliament, the Council, the Economic and Social Committee and the Committee of the Regions: Consumer Policy Strategy 2002–2006* 2002/C 137/02, COM (2002) 208 final: 'There is no good law if it is not properly enforced. As the degree of economic integration in the internal market steadily increases and more opportunities are open for consumers, consumers should be given in practice the same protection throughout the EU, and even more so in an enlarged EU' (at C 137/06).

Central Europe has always had very strong ties with the Western European legal systems, with its laws being modelled on the French, Austrian and German laws. There is no doubt that the Central European jurisdictions have traditionally belonged to the civil law family.[100] Civil Codes of Central Europe were, however, enacted during the times of Socialism (Hungary in 1959, Czechoslovakia and Poland in 1964), and its philosophy had an impact upon the shape of the Codes. In Socialist legal systems, law was perceived as merely a tool assisting the governing party in shaping the desired social order. Central European Civil Codes, although retaining many of the civil law features, reflected such a tendency. Black-letter law was to be of a general nature, capable of being interpreted and re-interpreted for the needs of the system. The role of the courts, therefore, was quite significant in the Socialist jurisdictions. This could be seen in the product liability case law, which in Poland and in Hungary was substantial in amount and scope. Czech law and legal doctrine have suffered from a very peculiar handicap which caused a lack of a consistent approach to basic legal issues. Frequent very significant changes of the main sources of civil law (amendments of the civil code, or introduction of new civil codes) had a different character than the legal changes in other jurisdictions, even other Socialist jurisdictions. 'The new' entirely replaced 'the old', and hence the case law and the doctrine of law established under the operation of 'the old' kept losing their value.[101] Because of the lack of valuable sources of reference in case law and writings of the doctrine, the legal profession (the judges and the lawyers) were forced to have recourse only to the written law. The positivism and formalism so created manifested themselves through lack of creativity of the legal profession and this, in the opinion of Tichy, led almost to the denial of law (*denegatio justitiae*).[102] Tichy refers directly to the regime of manufacturers' liability for defective products as the area suffering from the passive attitude of the legal profession, not willing to interpret the available legal provisions creatively. Tichy criticises both sides of the Czech legal profession – the lawmakers for the unavailability of a continuous basis for forming opinions and judgments, and the judges and legal writers for lack of thorough research and lack of any inspirational conceptions.[103] He goes as far as

[100] K. Zweigert and H. Kotz, *An Introduction to Comparative Law* (3rd rev. edn, Oxford: Clarendon Press, 1998).

[101] L. Tichy, *Czech Republic. Development of Czech Law of Tort*, in H. Koziol and B. C. Steininger (eds.), *European Tort Law 2001* (Tort and Insurance Law Yearbook, Vienna, New York: Springer) at p. 106.

[102] Ibid. [103] Ibid.

referring to the 'impotence of the Czech legal community'.[104] This very peculiar state of affairs is the reason why the analysis of the Czechoslovak and Czech product liability doctrine and case law in this chapter is far from comprehensive.

Central European product liability regime – before the implementation of the Directive and the new regulation

Introductory remarks

As explained above, the position of the law of product liability in the Central European countries was very peculiar, especially in the times of Socialism. And yet, many crucial similarities in the development of the substantive product liability laws between the West and Central Europe may be observed. The Central European product liability regimes were developed by courts, since an express provision regarding liability for defective products in general did not exist in these legal systems. The development commenced from the contractual liability of the sellers. In Central Europe it was possible to declare the seller liable in tort even though his conduct amounted also to a breach of contract (although the Czech courts did not attempt to do this). Because of significant advantages of tortious over contractual liability (such as no restraints of privity – both in the horizontal and vertical dimension; the possibility, not available in contractual liability, of recovering non-pecuniary damages, recovery of *lucrum cessans*; longer (resembling the regulation of the Directive) periods for bringing an action) contract was very nearly abandoned as a possible avenue of action for victims of defective products in Poland and Hungary. In Czechoslovakia and the Czech Republic it still very much remains a crucial basis for seeking redress if there was a contract between the seller and the victim. The implemented Product Liability Directive added a new basis for liability; for the first time in Central Europe it is a written legal basis.

While analysing Central European product liability rules the author makes references to the laws before and after the implementation of the Directive. Thus the vital elements of the framework of the Central European product liability regimes are provided by the study.

Contractual liability

Contractual liability has been the primary form of product liability, both in Western and in Central Europe. It is at times considered more

104 Ibid.

advantageous for victims of defective products, mostly because it allows recovery of pure economic loss (particularly the damage or loss of the defective product itself). However, while in the United Kingdom liability in contract has been strict, in the continental legal systems it has traditionally been based upon fault. In Central Europe fault is presumed, hence it is for the defendant to exonerate herself if the exercise of due care in fulfilling the contractual obligations can be shown.

The Polish Civil Code of 1964 regulates contractual liability in Book 3 'Obligations'.[105] Article 471 stipulates:

> The debtor is required to repair the loss resulting from the non-performance, or incorrect performance, of an obligation, unless the non-performance or the incorrect performance of the obligation is a result of factors for which the debtor is not responsible.[106]

In Poland it was made clear by the courts that, although the level of care required of professionals was the 'maximum level of care', sellers were not held liable for damages which occurred beyond their control (the *Fiat Multipla* case).[107]

A similar approach of the courts could be observed in Czechoslovakia and the Czech Republic. An interesting fact is that the Czech Civil Code, following its Austrian counterpart, does not distinguish between contractual and non-contractual liability. It contains one provision regulating all (contractual and non-contractual) types of liability in general. Before the significant amendment of the Czechoslovak Civil Code in 1991,[108] the Code contained Sections 420 and 421, which separately regulated liability of legal and physical persons (the latter referred to in the Code as 'citizens', the former as 'organisations'). Section 420 used to read:

> 1. A citizen is liable for damage which he has caused by infringement of a legal duty.
> 2. A citizen is exonerated from liability if he proves he was not at fault in causing the damage.[109]

[105] Title 7 'Performance of Obligations and the Effects of their Non-Performance', Division 2 'The Effects of Non-Performance of Obligations'.

[106] The provision had remained unchanged since it was first inserted into the Code in 1964. Translated by this author.

[107] Judgment of the Supreme Court of 6 February 1963, 2 CR 96/62, OSN (*Jurisprudence of the Supreme Court*) 1964/95.

[108] Act no. 509/1991 Coll. came into effect on 1 January 1992.

[109] From the commentary on the Code by T. J. Vondracek, *Commentary on the Czechoslovak Civil Code* (Dordrecht; Boston; Lancaster: Martinus Nijhoff Publishers, 1988) at p. 375.

Section 421 used to read:

> 1. An organisation is liable to a citizen for damage which it has caused by infringement of a legal duty.
> 3. An organisation is exonerated from liability if it can prove that it could not have prevented the damage even by the exertion of every effort which can be required from it. An organisation, however, cannot be exonerated from its liability by pleading that it was following the orders of superior organs.[110]

The Code was amended in 1991 and now Section 420 refers to all types of persons. It reads:

> 1. Everyone shall be liable for damage caused by violating a legal duty.
> 3. A person who proves not to have caused the damage shall relieve himself of the liability for it.[111]

The defendant has been able to avoid liability if he proved he was unable to prevent the damage 'with his utmost effort (care) which could have been required of him in the particular situation'.[112] It also must be added that it has been relatively easier for a 'trade corporation' (seller) to adduce satisfactory evidence of proper conduct than it has been for the manufacturer.[113] Svestka offered a number of examples where the 'trade corporation' was held liable: breach of an obligation concerning the quality acceptance of products, or failure to employ adequate practices concerning sales of products (such as unsuitable storage of products, neglect in inspections and tests of products, failure to monitor products introduced into circulation and remove defective products from circulation, selling expired products).[114]

The Hungarian Civil Code gives no definition of a breach of contract.[115] Normally the party in breach of contract will only then be required to compensate the other party for the breach if he was at fault.[116] Thus the defendant must prove he has taken all the necessary steps which would be expected in the circumstances of the case.[117] However, the case law

[110] Ibid., at p. 378.
[111] From the new version of the Code sent by Dobiasova, personal communication.
[112] Svestka, 'Damage Caused by the Sale of a Defective Product', p. 98.
[113] Ibid., p. 101. The manufacturer who is liable in tort – see below.
[114] Ibid. [115] Harmathy, *Introduction to Hungarian Law*, p. 111.
[116] Article 339 (in conjunction with Article 318) – applies to contractual and tortious liability (ibid., p. 113).
[117] Harmathy, *Introduction to Hungarian Law*, p. 113.

of the Hungarian courts in the area of product liability shows that it has not been easy for the seller to prove he was not at fault in providing defective products to the buyer.[118] Harmathy even suggested that not much importance had actually been attached to the behaviour of the seller, and a much more crucial factor in determining liability had been 'the fact of the defect of the good'.[119] In the 'paint case' the seller was held liable for a breach of contract irrespective of the fact that he had no opportunity to control the contents of the tins of paint.[120] The same approach was pursued in the 'chickens case' – the seller of chickens had no influence over the fact that the breeder handled the chickens in such a manner that they started dying after being bought by the farmer.[121] The Hungarian courts have thus developed a mechanism similar to the French *obligation de garantie*.[122]

Contractual liability seemed relatively advantageous for victims of defective products, especially in Hungary. However, it was still hindered by one very crucial obstacle – privity of contract. Privity was fought only in Hungary, where the seller was treated as an *assistant in performance* of the producer; and hence the producer could be liable in contract ('turnip cabbage seed case').[123] Poland headed rather for tortious liability in response to this weakness of contract liability rules (privity). The Czech Republic combined contractual liability where there was a contract with tortious liability where there was no contract.

Contractual liability is clearly unlikely to be directly affected by the Product Liability Directive. It is, however, essential to present its characteristics, in order to show the patterns of development within the product liability regimes have not been at all different in the analysed region of

118 Ibid., p. 114. 119 Ibid.

120 Maczonkai, *Hungarian Product Liability Case Law*, p. 110. Also: Benedek-Világhy, *A polgári Törvénykönyv a gyakorlatban* (Budapest, 1965) at pp. 301–6. The paint bought by a house painter had different qualities to those specified on the tin, causing damage to the painter.

121 Cited by T. Tercsák (1993) *A termékfelelősség jogintézményének alakulása az Európai Közösség irányelvének nyomán – különös tekintettel a küszöbönálló hazai szabályozásra* (The Development of Product Liability due to the Directive of European Communities – with Special Attention to Hungarian Regulation in progress), in *Polgári jogi dolgozatok* (Papers on Civil Law) MTA Államés Jogtudományi Intézet, ELTE Állam- és Jogtudományi Kar, Budapest, at 224. See also Maczonkai, *Hungarian Product Liability Case Law*, p. 110.

122 Maczonkai, *Hungarian Product Liability Case Law*, p. 110. A party in breach of contract cannot defend herself by claiming that the breach was beyond her control.

123 Cited in ibid., p. 111 and Tercsák, footnote 121 above, 224. Such liability would be joint and several; see below on the issue of joint and several liability.

Europe, and in order to show a still valid legal basis for redress in product liability claims.

Tortious liability

Legal bases of tortious liability regimes

No specific legal bases for tortious product liability existed in Central European law until the implementation of the Product Liability Directive. By default, general provisions concerning tortious liability, or, in case of the Czech Republic, and essentially also Hungary, both contractual and tortious liability, were used.

Article 339 of the Hungarian Civil Code of 1959[124] stipulates:

> (1) Whoever unlawfully causes damage to another shall be bound to compensate the same. He shall be relieved of such responsibility if he can prove that he has been acting in such a way as might, as a rule, reasonably be expected in the given situation.
> (2) The Court, having regard to the circumstances of the case deserving special appreciation, may partly relieve the person, responsible for the damage, of his responsibility.[125]

The Czech tortious liability has been based upon the provisions quoted in the part of the study devoted to contractual liability.

By virtue of Article 415 of the Polish Civil Code of 1964:

> Whoever by his fault caused a damage to another person shall be obliged to redress it.[126]

Tortious liability has been dependent upon the existence of the fault of the defendant, presumed in Hungary and the Czech Republic, and it was generally understood by the doctrine and practice of law that the 'fault' ought to include the objective element (unlawfulness – breach of certain

[124] It is the first article in Title II – 'Responsibility for Damages Caused out of Contract and for Unjust Enrichment', chapter 29 – 'General Rules Referring to Compensation of Damages'.

[125] Civil Code of the Hungarian People's Republic. Polgari Torvenykonyv English, translated by P. Lamberg (Budapest: Corvina, 1960).

[126] This is the first article in Title VI 'Czyny niedozwolone' (Torts) Book III 'Zobowiazania' (Obligations) of the Code. Translated by O. A. Wojtasiewicz (O. A. Wojtasiewicz (2000) *The Polish Civil Code* (ed.) Joanna Miler. Warszawa: TEPIS Publishing House of the Polish Society of Economic, Legal and Court Translators, 2000). The Polish codification of tortious liability resembles the French and the Swiss codifications (Article 1382 of French *Code Civil*, Article 41 of Swiss Code of Obligations).

provisions of safety laws, or the 'principles of community life'),[127] and the subjective element (the fault proper). The fault proper has been defined as a subjective, improper character of a person's conduct, improperness of the behaviour concerning the moment of foreseeability, and the moment of will,[128] or a substantial, concrete claim of improper conduct.[129] The particular defendant is held to be at fault because in the particular circumstances he failed to behave in a way he should have, and could have, behaved. Two main theories of fault have been put forward in the theory of civil law. These are: the psychological theory and the normative theory.[130] According to the psychological theory the improperness of the defendant's behaviour ought to be judged considering his mental attitude towards the behaviour or towards the consequences of this behaviour. Normative theory focusses upon the manner in which this mental attitude can be judged by an outside observer and the courts in particular.[131] The Polish legal doctrine seems to have favoured the normative theory, but the Czech and Hungarian doctrines rather favoured the psychological theory. For the needs of the product liability regime the requisites of liability were held to include: the tortious conduct – introduction of a defective product into circulation (bearing the characteristics of fault),[132] the damage suffered by the victim, and the causal link between the two. The burden of proof of the requisites of liability and fault in Poland rested upon the victim, while in Hungary and the Czech Republic the fault rather had to be disproved by the defendant.

The Product Liability Directive obviously introduced the 'strict' liability standard, limited by the notion of defect, into the Central European product liability regimes. However, it will be seen below that in many respects even this seemingly profound transformation of the basis of liability (fault – strict liability) did not mean many changes in the manner in which product liability cases were handled in Central Europe. In the case

[127] The principles were a general clause very popular during Socialism, enabling the Central European courts to interpret the legal provisions in the spirit of the era. At present they have either been abandoned (Hungary and the Czech Republic) or given an entirely different meaning – closer to Western European concepts such as 'good faith' (Poland).

[128] W. Czachórski, *Zobowiązania. Zarys wykładu* (Warsaw: Wydawnictwo Prawnicze Lexis Nexis, 2002) at p. 203.

[129] Łętowska, *Prawo umów konsumenckich*, p. 98.

[130] Czachórski, *Zobowiązania. Zarys wykładu*, p. 204. See also J. Dąbrowa, *Wina jako przesłanka odpowiedzialności cywilnej* (Wrocław, 1968).

[131] Czachórski, *Zobowiązania*, p. 204.

[132] Fault, therefore, was considered to be an attribute of the defendant's conduct and not another requisite of his liability.

law of the Central European courts, increasing focus upon the objective element of fault, and even abandoning the dogmatics of fault altogether, could be seen before the implementation of the Directive.

The possible defendants – from the seller to the manufacturer and the importer

All the Central European states implemented Article 3 of the Directive, identifying the 'producer' (including the 'quasi-producer' and the importer) as the primary defendant and other suppliers as subsidiary defendants. Sections 1 and 3 of the Hungarian Product Liability Act contain regulation of the manufacturers' and importers' liability. The liability of other participants in the distribution chain ('distributors') is, following the intentions of the Directive, of subsidiary character, being set in motion only if the manufacturer cannot be identified by the distributor within thirty days from the day of the 'written request of the injured party' (Section 4). The distributor can also relieve herself of liability having revealed the identity of another distributor from whom the product was obtained within the same time period (§4.1). The Hungarian Act clearly attempted to introduce an element of certainty to the notion of 'reasonable time' contained in Article 3.3 of the Directive. This provision concerning possible defendants has been interpreted by the Hungarian Supreme Court in Decision 2000/350 – at the time of writing this study, the only decision based upon the provisions of the implemented Directive in Central Europe. The case revealed the inadequacies in the Hungarian implementation of the Directive and following the decision the Act was amended. The primary version of the Act did not contain the unequivocal possibility of the defendant escaping liability upon the identification of the importer (if the product had been imported).[133] The case involved a defective angle grinder imported from Germany. The claimant – an insurance company with whom the victim of the product had an insurance contract – took proceedings against two vendors. The first vendor purchased the angle grinder from the second vendor, and the claimant demanded their joint and several liability. Neither of the defendants indicated the manufacturer or the importer, and thus their liability

[133] The version of the Act provided by Judit Fazekas, personal communication, also mentioned by Kalman, Lelkes and Domokos, footnote 44 above.

was declared, pursuant to the Hungarian Product Liability Act 1993.[134] Following the judgment in this case, the Act was amended in 2002 (Act XXXVI of 2002) and at present Section 4.1 'shall also apply to imported products where the manufacturer is indicated but the importer cannot be identified'. Section 2 of the Czech Act simply repeats the wording of the Directive, although the time period for the identification of the producer by the distributor has been set to be one month. Article 449.5 of the Polish Civil Code contains a similar regulation.

The situation before implementation was not very different. The Polish Supreme Court judgments of 6 February 1963[135] and of 28 April 1963,[136] based on the Code of Obligations of 1933,[137] introduced the idea of the seller being liable in tort to the buyers injured by the cars. The Polish Supreme Court found that selling a motor vehicle with technical defects capable of causing an accident, if fault could be proven, was not only a breach of contractual obligations, but also a breach of the general duty not to put human life and health in danger. Unfortunately fault had not been found in these cases, hence the sellers avoided liability.[138] The case introducing the idea of liability in tort for defective products in Hungary – the 'motorcycle accident' case[139] (loose handles of the motorcycle led to an accident) – focussed upon the seller and his obligations to those coming in contact with the products he sells. There was no privity of contract between the victim (the person riding the motorcycle) and the seller; hence the difficulty for the court to award damages using contract liability rules. It held that selling defective products in the market gave rise

[134] The details of the judgment provided by E. Kalman, V. Lelkes, M. Domokos, ibid.

[135] Fiat 'Multipla' – the mechanism keeping the wheels in place was not properly welded to the floor of the car – defect only discoverable on taking the paint off the relevant place underneath the car. The judgment of the Supreme Court of 6 February 1963, 2 CR 96/62, OSN 1964/95.

[136] A defective 'P-70' car – a hidden defect of the steering system. The judgment of the Supreme Court of 28 April 1964, II CR 540/63, OSN 1965/32.

[137] The Code of Obligations preceded the Civil Code of 1964; the regulation of tortious liability was similar to the Civil Code.

[138] The cars were imported, and the sellers had no opportunity to find the defects. Although under the regime introduced by the Directive the sellers could also avoid liability, by pointing to another, from the point of view of a consumer these were very unsatisfactory judgments. They are examples of the early tendencies in the development of the product liability regime in Poland. With its further development, as the focus shifted onto manufacturers and importers, the consumers' position became increasingly advantageous.

[139] Bírósági Határozatok (Court Decisions) 1973/1, No. 19, quoted by Maczonkai, *Hungarian Product Liability Case Law*, p. 111.

to the retailer's liability in tort. Czechoslovak and Czech courts usually attempted to render the seller liable in contract if there was a contract between him and the victim (the case of poor quality cement).[140]

Soon, however, the focus of the courts and doctrine of law was on the manufacturers and even importers. The Polish Supreme Court found the manufacturer of a cake containing a pin at fault and hence liable for injuries suffered by the claimant.[141] The Hungarian case of the chemical spray (1977) introduced the idea of manufacturers' liability in tort (here for inadequate information about the product),[142] and the cases of the colour television sets (Hungary – 1984,[143] Poland – 1981)[144] confirmed the tendency of focussing upon the manufacturer, both in Poland and Hungary. Czechoslovak and Czech courts normally rendered the manufacturers liable in tort (the case of poor quality cement).[145]

In Poland the importers were, with some initial hesitation, considered liable to the same extent as the manufacturers. In the already mentioned cases of the Fiat 'Multipla' and the 'P-70' car the Polish Supreme Court refused to impose on the importers liability similar to the manufacturers' liability (if with the exercise of reasonable care in checking the car the defect could not have been discovered the importer could escape liability); but the judgment of the Supreme Court of 26 March 1984 (defective Wartburg)[146] changed this attitude, confirmed in the judgment of the district court of Rzeszów of 18 April 2001 (sudden release of an airbag in a stationary Ford Mondeo).[147] Although the topic was not explored in depth by the Hungarian and Czech courts, theoretically there is no obstacle to tortious liability of other actors taking part in the distribution chain, such as importers.

[140] Judgment of the Supreme Court of the Slovak Socialist Republic Cz 29/75. From the contribution to the product liability database. Personal communication, Monika Dobiasova – Czech Ministry of Trade and Industry.

[141] The judgment of the Supreme Court of 6 VIII 1981, I CR 219/81, OSPiKA 1982/7–8, p. 144.

[142] Birósági Határozatok (Court Decisions) 1977/1 No 31, quoted by Maczonkai, *Hungarian Product Liability Case Law*, p. 112.

[143] Legfelsõbb Bíróság Gf. III. (Supreme Court. Economic Affairs College) 31. 208/1984, quoted by Maczonkai, *Hungarian Product Liability Case Law*, p. 113.

[144] The judgment of the Supreme Court of 24 July 1981, IV CR 252/81, OSN 1982/84.

[145] Judgment of the Supreme Court of the Slovak Socialist Republic Cz 29/75.

[146] Judgment of the Supreme Court of 26 III 1984, II CR 57/84; OSN 1984/186.

[147] Judgment of the District Court of Rzeszów of 18 April 2001, *Rzeczpospolita* 19 April 2001.

In common with the implemented Directive,[148] there was a possibility of joint and several liability of a number of persons. It was of no importance in the Czech litigation that the basis of the liability of the seller was contract and the liability of the manufacturer tort.[149]

The beneficiaries of the product liability regime – possible claimants

Although the scope of protection provided by the Directive is considerable, the limits related to the type of property for which recovery is possible constitute a significant restriction. Such a restriction has not been present in the Central European product liability regimes. Since the regime was placed in the area of tort, any victim of a defective product, subject to the requirements of the regime being met, was able to make a claim, unhindered by privity constraints. Although consumers have usually been the victims in need of redress, protection was also provided to small businesses and entrepreneurs, even in respect of damages to property used for business purposes. The Polish Supreme Court provided protection to an owner of a poultry farm (Supreme Court, 3 June 1986, II CR 131/86), an owner of a sugar beet plantation (Supreme Court, 21 June 1985, I CR 127/85), or a person renting a farm for business purposes (Supreme Court, 28 June 1972, II CR 218/72). Similar tendencies could be noticed in Hungary. Certain Hungarian cases based upon tort law provided protection for small entrepreneurs.[150] It is not clear from the jurisprudence and the writings of the Czech doctrine what approach to this issue has been adopted there. Czechoslovak case law and doctrine rather focussed upon the 'citizen' as a victim of a tort.[151]

Products within the scope of application of product liability laws

Article 2 of the Directive has been implemented by the Central European states without any reservations, including the recent amendments. Both

[148] Article 5 of the Directive, implemented by Article 449.5.3 of the Polish Civil Code, Section 5 of the Hungarian Act on Product Liability, and Section 7a of the Czech Act. The Polish Civil Code also contains a general provision on joint and several liability in Article 441. Article 344 of the Hungarian Civil Code describes this type of liability. The Czech Civil Code envisages the possibility of joint and several liability in Section 438.

[149] Svestka, 'Damage Caused by the Sale of a Defective Product', p. 100.

[150] The 'chemical spray case' and the 'bee case' – Maczonkai, *Hungarian Product Liability Case Law*, p. 110.

[151] The concept of 'citizen' has now disappeared from the regulation of liability in the Civil Code.

the Hungarian and the Czech product liability Acts initially excluded primary agricultural products and game from the scope of their applicability. The Polish Act was adopted after the amendment of the Directive and hence included the new version of the definition of 'products'. The Hungarian and Czech Acts have been amended[152] following the amendment of the Directive,[153] and at present 'products' include: in Hungary: 'any movable property, even if it subsequently becomes a component or part of another movable or real property, as well as electrical energy';[154] in the Czech Republic: 'any movable goods which were produced, extracted or otherwise gained irrespective of the degree of their processing and which are intended for placing on the market' as well as 'parts and accessories to movable goods and fixtures and fittings to immovable goods';[155] and in Poland: 'a movable thing, even if it has been connected with another thing' as well as 'animals and electrical energy'.[156]

The concept of 'products' was not recognised in the Civil Codes before the implementation of the Directive. The product liability regime was based upon the traditional civil notion of 'things'.[157] Things were only material goods. No division between processed and unprocessed goods existed. However, only a movable could be the subject matter of product liability litigation. No significant transformation has therefore taken place after the implementation of the Directive in the understanding of the subjects of product liability cases.

One significant difference, however, concerns component parts, which according to the Directive are treated as independent products, and according to the traditional tortious liability regimes of Central Europe

[152] In Hungary – Act XXXVI of 2002, in the Czech Republic – Act no. 209/2000.

[153] Directive 99/34 of 10.05.1999, OJ L 14/20.

[154] Section 1.1 of the Act on Product Liability. Kalman, Lelkes and Domokos point to the failed attempt to regulate product liability together with other areas of consumer protection laws, where 'products' were defined as 'movables and things regarded by the same criteria', which could potentially lead to declaring strict liability for damages caused by water, steam or gas (BIICL Database report on Hungarian Product Liability Law).

[155] Section 3 of the Act 59/1998. [156] Article 449.1 para.2 of the Civil Code.

[157] The concept of 'things' was utilised by, for instance, laws on legal and commercial guarantees – in Articles 556–82 of the Polish Civil Code. The Czechoslovak and Czech Civil Codes were largely inconsistent in their terminology relating to 'things': Sections referring to contracts of sale (§§590–611) use the notion 'object of sale', Sections referring to special provisions on sale of goods in shops (§§612–18) – 'goods' or 'things', Sections referring to liability for defects – 'things' (§§619–27). The Hungarian Civil Code did not specifically deal with the concept of things, although it used the notion (Article 95.2). 'Things' were rather taken for granted and referred to in terms of subjects of property (Articles 92–5).

did not have such status. The Polish Civil Code has defined component parts of a 'thing' as 'everything that cannot be separated from it without damaging or without causing a crucial alteration of the whole, or without damaging or causing a crucial alteration of the separated thing' (Article 47.2).[158] Things connected with other things only for some temporary use are not to be treated as their components (Article 47.3). The legal effect of classifying a thing as a component of another is the loss of its independence as a separate thing, or as a separate subject of property or other rights (Article 47.1). The Hungarian Civil Code avoids defining 'things', but it is possible to find a regulation concerning components among the provisions referring to property. According to Article 95.1 'the right of ownership comprises all that is permanently united with the thing in such a way that separation would produce the destruction of the thing, or a considerable decrease in the value or utility of the thing or of the separated part thereof (component part)'. The Czechoslovak and Czech Civil Code defines components of a thing as 'all that appertains to the thing according to its nature and cannot be separated from the thing without devaluation of the thing' (Section 120).[159] It also seems clear that components cannot be subjects of separate property rights: according to Section 135a 'Accessions of the thing, even if they were separated from the main thing, shall belong to the owner of the thing.'[160] Thus, although in fault liability systems it would be feasible that manufacturers of component parts of things, when these components and not the final products actually caused damage to others, were liable, such a possibility was not developed in the case law. The exception has been the jurisprudence of Hungarian courts, where, in the case of 'turnip cabbage seed', the possibility of suing every producer, also the producers of component parts, together with the sellers, was established.[161] From the point of view of the Directive such a situation would be unsatisfactory for the victims of defective products. Were the Central European rules indeed disadvantageous for them? It seems that on a great many occasions the victim is unaware of which particular part of the product exactly caused the damage. In these cases being able to sue the end producer facilitates his position.

[158] Translated by the author. [159] Version sent by Dobiasova, personal communication.

[160] Quoted from the text of the Code sent by Dobiasova, personal communication.

[161] Cited by Łętowska and Maczonkai, *Hungarian Product Liability Case Law*, p. 111. This was in fact a judgment based on the law of contract and the already analysed concept of assistant in performance.

The requisites of tortious product liability:

The requisites of product liability must be shown by the victims of defective products. The existence of the possibility of redress is conditional upon their presence.

Introduction into circulation of a defective product

1. Introduction into circulation

The concept of introduction into circulation, upon which the Directive has been based, existed in Central Europe ever since the first product liability cases appeared in courts. It was not defined in the Civil Codes, but was mentioned frequently in court judgments.[162] The doctrine of law attempted to define it, referring to the moment when the product enters the market,[163] or when the producer loses control over it.[164] The notion extended to all the actors in the distribution chain and was not solely focussed upon the manufacturer.

The requirement of a product actually being introduced into circulation suggests that victims of products not yet introduced into circulation (persons such as employees of the manufacturer or his family) would be unable to use the regime of the Directive in order to recover compensation for their injuries.[165] Such an approach to the product liability regime has not been unfamiliar to the Central European jurisdictions, where the courts clearly delimited the scope of applicability of the regimes using the moment of introduction of a product into circulation.[166]

2. Defective product

It seems clear from the text of the Directive that it did not endorse the division, or 'boxing',[167] of three types of defects (design, manufacturing and failure to warn defects) so popular in the American and also European

[162] The judgment of the Polish Supreme Court of 21 November 1980, III CZP 50/80, OSN 1981/205 (defective Fiat 125 engine); in Hungary – Birósági Határozatok (Court Decisions) 1973/1 no. 19 (quoted by Maczonkai); Hungary – 'motorcycle accident' case.

[163] W. Czachórski, *Zobowiązania. Zarys wykładu* (Warsaw: Wydawnictwo Prawnicze Lexis Nexis, 2002) 230.

[164] Łętowska, *Prawo umów konsumenckich*, p. 95.

[165] Ibid.

[166] The victims so excluded could therefore use the ordinary regime of liability – normally tortious, but in case of employees of the producer also possibly contractual and other regimes.

[167] The notion 'boxing' was used by Burton J in *A v National Blood Authority* [2001] 3 All ER 289.

product regimes.[168] It seems justified to some extent to abandon the classification into types of defects in a strict liability regime, for considering which type of defect has caused the damage – especially in case of the design and the failure to warn types of defects – involves an analysis of the defendant's behaviour. The latter analysis surely ought to be abandoned in a strict liability regime. It is a notable fact that, as will be seen from the analysis of the Central European product liability in tort, fault liability systems endorsed these 'boxes', in terms of classifying both the types of defects and the types of negligent behaviour of the defendants. The unfortunate fact is that the Directive provides the vague test of social expectations instead. The 'circumstances' listed in Article 6 do not assist in a better understanding and application of the standard to complex cases which without a doubt should appear before European courts.

Section 2 of the Hungarian Act on Product Liability reads: 'A product shall be regarded as defective if it fails to provide a level of safety generally expected, with special regard to the purpose of the product and the way in which it can be reasonably be expected to be used, the information provided in connection with the product, the date of the sale of the product, and the current state of scientific and technological achievements.' Section 4 of the Czech Act defines a defective product as a product which 'in terms of safety of its use . . . fails to guarantee the properties as may rightly be expected to pertain to the product, particularly with reference to: (a) the presentation of the product, including the information provided, or (b) the purpose which the product is expected to serve, or (c) the time at which the product was placed on the market'. Interestingly, the Polish regulation abandoned the notion of 'defect', considered necessary by the Directive, for the notion of 'lack of safety' (thus a 'defective product' is referred to as an 'unsafe product').[169] The rationale behind this approach was the need to distinguish defects of quality, regulated in the provisions concerning legal and commercial guarantees,[170] from

[168] Some authors, however, disregard this dismissal by the Directive to refer to the 'boxes', and simply treat their existence as obvious according to the 'general legal principles' (C. W. Hoffman and S. Hill-Arning, *Guide to Product Liability in Europe. The New Strict Product Liability Laws, Pre-existing Remedies, Procedure and Costs in the European Union and the European Free Trade Association* (Deventer: Kluwer Law and Taxation Publishers, 1994) at p. 6).

[169] *Produkt niebezpieczny.*

[170] See M. Sengayen, 'Consumer Sales Law in Poland: Changing the Law, Changing Attitudes' 25 *Journal of Consumer Policy*, Special Issue on Law, Information and Product Quality, No. 3/4 403.

lack of safety.[171] The concept of 'defect' has, however, been considered by many commentators[172] as wide-ranging and all-accommodating, and the use of another, possibly narrower, notion by Poland is likely to upset the delicate relations within the regime. It is very likely that the Commission may consider this discrepancy with the text of the Directive serious enough to commence Article 226 proceedings against Poland. However, it is worth noting that, apart from this difference, the description of the notion follows the text of the Directive carefully. Article 449.1.3 of the Polish Civil Code stipulates that a product shall be considered 'unsafe' if it does not provide the safety which can be expected taking into account normal use of the product. Circumstances from the time of its introduction into circulation are said to determine the safety, and in particular the presentation on the market and the information about the qualities of the product provided to consumers.[173] All the Central European regulations on product liability contain the 'state of the art' element stating that the product cannot be deemed defective ('unsafe') merely because a safer product has later been put into circulation.

In spite of the fact that the ordinary tortious liability regimes utilised the 'boxes' system with regard to defects, the emphasis upon safety and not merely the quality of products has been a significant factor which the case law of Central Europe and the Directive have had in common.[174] A number of types of defects were recognised by the Central European product liability regime. Defects which had their origin in the design of products (design defects) were discussed in the Polish and Hungarian 'television sets cases'.[175] Manufacturing defects were established by the courts in the Polish 'pin in the cake case',[176] the Hungarian 'motorcycle accident case'[177] and the Czech 'poor quality cement case'.[178] Instruction

[171] E. Łętowska, *Ochrona Niektórych Praw Konsumentów. Komentarz* (3rd edn, Warsaw: Wydawnictwo C. H. Beck, 2001) at p. 135.

[172] See for instance Stapleton, *Product Liability.*

[173] Translated by the author of the study.

[174] Central European courts and doctrine of law expressed the view that a merely defective product could not give rise to product liability and that the product must have had some dangerous features rendering it unsafe for use (decision of the Polish Supreme Court of 21 November 1980, III CZP 50/80, OSN 1981/205 – (Sengayen, 'Consumer Sales')).

[175] The judgment of the Polish Supreme Court of 24 July 1981, IV CR 252/81, OSN 1982/84. Legfelsõbb Biróság Gf. III (Supreme Court of Hungary. Economic Affairs College) 31. 208/1984, quoted by Maczonkai, *Hungarian Product Liability Case Law*, p. 113.

[176] The judgment of the Supreme Court of 6 August 1981, I CR 219/81, OSPiKA 1982/7–8, p. 144.

[177] Birósági Határozatok (Court Decisions) 1973/1, No. 19, quoted by Maczonkai, *Hungarian Product Liability Case Law*, p. 111.

[178] Judgment of the Supreme Court of the Slovak Socialist Republic Cz 29/75.

or information defects were common indeed. The Polish judgment in the case of a chemical mousse is a classic example – the case involved a chemical mousse for use in the bathroom, equipped with inadequate warnings as to the danger of explosion.[179] A similar case took place in Hungary.[180] The Polish and Hungarian 'television sets cases'[181] and the Polish 'airbag case'[182] were other examples. Further, another type of defect was recognised in Poland, directly related to the information defect. In the chemical spray case it was held that the fact the manufacturer and the seller of the chemical did not supply protective equipment, the use of which was according to them necessary for safe use of the product, rendered the chemical defective.[183] Finally, 'observation defects' – the professionals' failure to fulfil the obligation to monitor products introduced by them into circulation for possible defects and dangers not known before – were also recognised. 'Television sets cases' in Poland and Hungary illustrate this issue.

It seems that, in spite of the 'boxing' apparently not desired by the Directive, the Central European courts continued their work in the direction set by this instrument. Products were supposed not to present dangers to those using them and their property, and those which caused damage could be the subject of product liability litigation. In a strict liability regime the notion of 'defect' is obviously likely to gain even more importance,

179 The Judgment of the Polish Court of Appeal of Białystok of 30 November 2000 (I ACa 340/00, 43–9). The instructions on the packaging informed the users of the necessity of holding the can in the desired manner, and warned that one should not use the mousse in closed spaces and should not heat the can, without however indicating the consequences of not following the warnings.

180 Łętowska and Maczonkai, *Hungarian Product Liability Case Law*, p. 110.

181 Here the producers were shown to have known of the danger of sudden explosion of the TV sets (from previous accidents), and failed to pass this information on to the buyers, or withdraw the sets from the market.

182 Judgment of the District Court of Rzeszów of 18 April 2001, *Rzeczpospolita* 19 April 2001. The case involved a Fiat Mondeo in which the airbag suddenly inflated (while the car was parked), injuring the claimant. The judgment focussed upon the fact that the dealers were aware of the danger of sudden inflation of the airbag, but failed to inform the buyer (the father of the claimant) about it.

183 The Judgment of the Supreme Court of 28 June 1972, II CR 218/72, OSN 1972/228, 67–74. This was an example of a tragic set of events (leading to the deaths of two people) caused by the lack of appropriate warnings and protective equipment. The information contained on the packaging of the spray included instructions for proper use – in closed spaces a gas mask capable of protecting from contact with benzol ought to be worn. Unfortunately masks of this sort were not available on the market at the time. The Court indicated that the manufacturer's and the seller's fault had been demonstrated in their failure to provide such gas masks (it seems that producing them would be a good solution for the manufacturer). Another aspect of the case were inappropriate warnings on the can of the spray – warning of the danger of poisoning, not of death.

but it appears that the previous experience of the Central European courts in the area can serve them better than the elusive guidelines established by the Directive through the concept of 'defect'.[184]

3. Fault – the attribute of the defendant's conduct

The requirement of fault in the Central European tortious liability regimes does not find a counterpart in the Directive. Yet, one ought to focus upon the position of claimants in product litigation and seek an answer to the question, does the implementation of the Directive mean an improvement of this position? In principle, liability based upon fault puts an onus of proof of fault upon the claimant. Such a burden may constitute a significant impediment to both the commencement of litigation and a favourable conclusion of the case. The principal advantage of strict liability is that it relieves the claimant of this burden. Therefore, again in principle, the regime introduced by the Directive ought to be much more advantageous for the claimants in Central Europe than the traditional tortious liability regime. Is that truly so?

The standard of liability introduced by the Directive has been described by its most consistent critic – Jane Stapleton – as uncertain, owing to the multitude of defences available to the 'producer', and the development risk defence in particular.[185] In contrast, Central European states attempted to facilitate the task of the claimant in product liability litigation. In Hungary fault was presumed, and in the evolution of the product regime strict liability was developed by the courts. The Czech Civil Code also introduced presumption of fault, but here development did not reach as far as introducing strict liability. In Poland there was no presumption of fault, hence the position of the victims was more challenging. The Polish courts, however, introduced a number of legal constructs aimed at facilitating this position.

As mentioned above, the concept of fault in Central Europe was considered to include the objective element of unlawfulness and the subjective element of will. In the process of development of the product liability regimes a gradual defeat of the subjective in favour of the objective element can be observed, the defeat so significant indeed that liability very close to a strict standard was established. The emphasis upon the objective element of unlawfulness was so strong that Central European courts

[184] Another constant source of inspiration should obviously be the jurisprudence of courts of other Member States of the European Union.

[185] *Product Liability*, p. 228.

gradually disallowed the defence of compliance with existing safety provisions. The Directive introduces such a defence for producers in showing that the 'defect is due to compliance of the product with mandatory regulations issued by the public authorities' (Article 7(d)). Central European courts, on the other hand, increasingly attempted to defend the argument that compliance with mandatory provisions did not automatically mean safety of the product.[186] This situation seemed more advantageous for victims of defective products, but it was not really so. In the European Union the safety regulations are numerous and usually strictly adhered to. In the Socialist countries safety regulations were not as comprehensive, and compliance with them did not automatically mean that the products were safe to use. While the implementation of the Directive means an incorporation of the defence of compliance into the product liability regimes, the implementation of the product safety laws deriving from the European Union by Central Europe is likely to improve the safety level of products present on the markets.

The particularly progressive attitude of the Central European courts may be seen in the manner in which they dealt with the subjective element of fault. The Polish product liability regime obviously required the existence of fault, and certain suggestions to establish a strict liability regime were not accepted by courts. Yet, in order to facilitate the victim's task in proving fault, the concept of *anonymous, organisational fault*, widely accepted by the representatives of the doctrine of law and the courts, has been devised. As long as the victim was able to point to the fact of the defendant legal person as a whole not having acted in an expected manner, there was no need to search for a particular person within the structure of the latter who had been the cause of the defect. A further concept introduced to facilitate the role of the victim was the rule of *res ipsa loquitur*. These concepts were used in the 'pin in a cake case'.[187] After having established the facts, the lower instance court assumed that

[186] The Polish Supreme Court in the judgment of 4 December 1981 confirmed this view. In this case of self-igniting television sets the conformity with the 'Polish Norm' was no defence for the producer who used cheap 'replacement materials', unsuitable for proper isolation of flammable objects inside the television sets. Similar judgments could be found in Hungary (the 'television sets case' – the producer unsuccessfully claimed compliance with the standards of the Commercial Quality Control Institute – Legfelsõbb Bíróság Gf. III (Supreme Court of Hungary. Economic Affairs College) 31. 208/1984. Quoted by, *Hungarian Product Liability Case Law*, p. 113 and the Czech Republic.

[187] The Judgment of the Supreme Court of 6 August 1981, I CR 219/81, OSN 1982, item 37.

the pin must have been inside the cake.[188] An interesting phenomenon which could be observed in the judgment is that the plaintiff – the person who was unfortunate enough to have swallowed the pin which then injured his throat – did not have to prove the fault of the manufacturer. The mere presence of the pin in the cake was held to have demonstrated the weaknesses in the production and supervision processes.[189] The use of *res ipsa loquitur* can also be seen in the 'self-igniting television sets' case.[190] Not only the use of cheap 'replacement materials' in the production process, held the Court, but also the knowledge of the danger and failure to warn the users of the television sets of the imminent danger to their life, health and property, determined the existence of fault. Crucially, the Court of Appeal of Katowice in the judgment of 10 October 1996 indicated that all products, if used according to their ordinary purposes, ought to be safe and no accidents should occur.[191] Such an accident (in this case the cap of a bottle of Pepsi-Cola detached and hit the plaintiff's eye), argued the court using the *res ipsa loquitur* rule, demonstrated either a defective technological process or some other defect in production.

The Hungarian courts have been determined to render the manufacturer's liability for damage caused by the product strict. In the 'chemical spray case' the court has paved the way for strict liability by holding the manufacturer liable for failure to supply adequate information about the product and refusing him the opportunity to claim that his conduct was otherwise proper.[192] The landmark 'colour television sets case' introduced strict liability into the Hungarian product liability litigation.[193] Here the television set exploded causing property damage to the claimant. The

[188] Having excluded all other possibilities, such as the pin being for some reason left on the plate on which the cake was served, the court went on to hold that the person liable for the presence of the pin in the cake was the producer (no need to point to a particular employee of the producer).

[189] Łętowska, *Prawo umów konsumenckich*, p. 99. The manufacturer did not succeed in defending itself against this *res ipsa loquitur* presumption, and this was so especially in the light of the statement of one of its employees, who pointed out that sugar used in production was not being properly tested.

[190] The judgment of the Supreme Court of 24 July 1981, IV CR 252/81, OSN 1982/84.

[191] I Acr 500/96, Wokanda 2/1998, 40–3.

[192] Birósági Határozatok (Court Decisions) 1977/1 No 31 quoted by Maczonkai, *Hungarian Product Liability Case Law*, p. 112.

[193] Legfelsõbb Biróság Gf. III (Supreme Court of Hungary. Economic Affairs College) 31. 208/1984, quoted by Maczonkai, *Hungarian Product Liability Case Law*, p. 113.

court abandoned the requirement of fault only to hold that all the claimant needed to prove was that the conduct of the defendant was unlawful, that the damage occurred, and that there was a causal link between the two. It established the test of 'social expectations' and stated that if the product did not comply with them, the fact that the producer behaved properly in the given circumstances was irrelevant. It seems that even *force majeure* did not exempt the defendant in this regime of liability.[194]

For the reasons mentioned above, the case law of the Czech Republic was not as comprehensive as Polish or Hungarian case law. However, it remains clear that according to the Czech courts the manufacturer was required to prove that throughout the manufacturing process he had exerted due care.[195] If he managed to show this, he would be able to avoid liability. A very interesting phenomenon was the amendment of the Civil Code in 1991 which seems to have removed the subjective requirement of fault from the list of requisites of liability (the new Section 420, quoted above).[196] The commentary to the Civil Code by Trade Links suggests that the features of liability are now: a breach of a legal obligation, damage caused, a causal link between the damage and the breach.[197] Trade Links also point out that liability for damage has become liability of an 'objective' character.[198] It may be contended that this point goes too far, and that the wording of Section 420 is still relatively ambiguous.[199] To support the latter argument the comparison ought to be drawn between the new Section 420 and the old Section 421, this one undoubtedly based upon fault. Tichy points out very clearly that, 'in addition to the general principle of liability for fault (Section 420), the Civil Code was in 1991 supplemented by a principle of strict liability as a second pillar' (Section 420a, not analysed in the study).[200] It is indeed extremely difficult to establish the authoritative opinion of the Czech courts or doctrine of law, as the number of written analyses of tort law and cases since the amendment of the Civil Code has been truly insignificant.[201]

194 Maczonkai, *Hungarian Product Liability Case Law*, p. 113.

195 Svestka, 'Damage Caused by the Sale of a Defective Product', p. 102.

196 Act no. 509/1991 Coll.

197 *Obcansky zakonnik English. Civil Code, Criminal Code*, translated by Trade Links (Prague: Trade Links, 1996).

198 Ibid.

199 In an internet interview with the author of this study Dobiasova pointed out that according to her the regime is still based upon 'presumed culpability'.

200 Tichy, *Czech Republic*, p. 118.

201 Ibid., 120–3.

Even after having analysed these developments within the Central European concept of fault, and having mentioned the ambiguity of the standard of liability required by the Directive, it still remains difficult to formulate definite conclusions regarding the differences or similarities in the liability standards. The ultimate question whether the claimant's position in product liability litigation in Central Europe became less demanding with the implementation of the Directive thus remains unanswered. A further factor affecting this issue are the defences available to the defendant – these should enable the author to throw more light upon the claimant's position. They are analysed below.

4. Defences in a 'fault' liability system of Central European tort law and in the 'strict' liability system of the Directive

In a fault liability system the main defence is obviously the lack of fault. However, in certain cases, especially those involving manufacturing or instruction defects, it was difficult for the manufacturer or another person to defend themselves in Central Europe. Mere showing that all due care had been taken in organisation and control of production did not suffice. Maximum care had to be shown to have been exercised by all those taking part in the distribution chain. Further, in Hungary and in some cases also in Poland, even maximum care was insufficient to relieve the defendant of liability. In Poland and the Czech Republic the argument of *force majeure* was acceptable, but the manner in which the concept itself was understood by the courts rendered proof a difficult task. In the Polish case of the Pepsi-Cola bottle, the manufacturer of the bottle attempted a defence by claiming *force majeure*.[202] His arguments were rejected by the Court of Appeal. According to the court, a *force majeure* is an 'unusual, external, impossible to prevent event, which is not an ordinary accident (*casus*). These are phenomena such as natural catastrophes (*vis naturalis*), the acts of public authorities which an individual cannot oppose (*vis imperii*), and military acts (*vis armata*).'[203]

At the moment the defences prescribed by Article 7 of the Directive, including the development risk defence,[204] have been duly implemented by the Central European states. The only discrepancies between the Directive and the implemented texts are the Polish and Hungarian regulations of the defence of the defect not existing at the time the product was put

[202] I Acr 500/96, Wokanda 2/1998, 40–3. [203] Translated by the author of the study.

[204] The latter regulated by Article 7(e) of the Directive, Section 7(d) of the Hungarian Act, Section 5.1(e) of the Czech Act, and Article 449.3.2 of the Polish Civil Code.

into circulation (Article 7(b) of the Directive). While the Directive is satisfied with a mere probability that the defect did not exist at this point, both the Hungarian and Polish Acts (Article 449.3.2 of the Polish Civil Code and Section 7(c) of the Hungarian Act) require absolute certainty, and do not seem to be satisfied with the probability of non-existence of the defect. Whereas it is likely that such a difference has been conditioned by the divergences in the rules and requirements of procedure, and in particular the burden of proof and the necessity to prove a fact without doubt, not on the balance of probabilities, it may still lead to controversies. Considering the, already mentioned, maximum character of harmonisation provided by the Directive, stressed in the recent judgments of the European Court of Justice, this discrepancy may lead to an action being taken against these two states under Article 226 of the Treaty of Rome. Putting this lack of compliance with the Directive aside, however, has the position of the claimant improved with implementation, or has it become more difficult?

The defence of regulatory compliance was obviously unavailable throughout Central Europe. However, as explained above, this did not in any way improve the position of consumers – for the regulatory coverage of safety and quality of products within Central Europe during Socialism and a few years after was truly unsatisfactory.

In the regimes based upon fault a certain standard of care required of the defendants should not be a novelty; nevertheless it must be submitted that, at least in Hungary, the existence of the development risk defence introduces a standard of product liability less stringent than the one which the courts so bravely put forward. In fact, it can be said following the opinion of Maczonkai that 'considering the doctrines and assuming the coherence of doctrine . . . only the defences of the producer who had never supplied the product and the product was not delivered with a view to profit could have prevailed' in the traditional tortious liability regime established by the Hungarian courts.[205] Could the defences prescribed by the Directive also be used in the traditional tortious liability regimes of Czechoslovakia, the Czech Republic and Poland? In contrast to Hungary, the development risk defence would be very likely to exonerate the defendant in these legal systems. The notion of 'introduction into circulation', as mentioned above, was popular in the product liability case law of Central Europe,

[205] *Hungarian Product Liability Case Law under Civil Code and the New Product Liability Regime*, in *Hungary – From Europe Agreements to a Member Status in the EU* (ECSA Europe, 1996) 117.

and therefore the defence of the product not having been put into circulation by the defendant was available even before the implementation of the Directive. Further, the defence of the product not having been introduced into circulation for business purposes could be used in these two jurisdictions. The entire movement within the Central European doctrine of law towards introduction of strict product liability was indeed rooted in the increasingly perceived need for stricter liability of professionals. Central Europe, in common with other post-Socialist states, only recently started to understand the concepts of 'business' and 'business activity' in the manner in which these concepts are understood in the West.[206]

A very interesting change appeared in the Central European laws with the introduction of the specific defence for manufacturers of spare parts (Article 7(f) of the Directive). In principle, the independent liability of the manufacturers of component parts did not exist in the Central European product liability regimes before the implementation of the Directive, as the component parts were not considered independent 'things' by virtue of the Civil Codes. Hence, apart from Hungary, where such a possibility was confirmed,[207] there seemed to have been no prospect of suing the manufacturer of the component which caused loss. At present, in Hungary 'the producer of raw material or a component shall be exempt from liability upon providing proof that: (a) the defect was caused by the structure or composition of the final product, or (b) the defect was the consequence of instructions given by the producer of the final product'; the Czech Act in Section 5.2 stipulates that 'the producer of any constituent part of the product shall be exempted from his responsibility if such a producer is able to prove that the defect was caused by the construction of the product in which the constituent part was incorporated or that the defect was caused by the instructions for the use of the product', and the Polish Civil Code in Article 449.5 stipulates that the producer of a raw material or a spare part should be free of liability if the sole cause of damage was defective construction of the product or the instructions provided by the producer of the final product. Although independent liability of the

[206] For instance the Polish Act on Economic Activity of 19 November 1999. See also Sengayen, 'Consumer Sales': 403.

[207] The case of 'turnip cabbage seed' opened the possibility of suing every producer, also the producers of component parts, together with the sellers. Maczonkai considered the development of the concept of *assistant in performance* as a particular advantage of the Hungarian contractual liability system over the Product Liability Directive and the Hungarian Product Liability Act.

manufacturers of spare parts did not formally exist in the Central European product liability regimes before the implementation of the Directive, this provision could be said to refer to the fault liability system – the said manufacturer cannot be held liable for defects which were not caused by him. Thus, it appears that while the implementation of the Directive means a less stringent liability standard in Hungary, no very significant change of the developed liability standards is likely in Poland and the Czech Republic (at least as far as substantive law is concerned).

Damages

The existence of a loss or damage caused by the tortious act of introducing a defective product into circulation has been another crucial requisite of product liability. Here the rules have not differed from the general principles of ordinary tortious liability. Generally damage has been defined as 'every wrong inflicted upon an interest protected by law, be it property, dignity, freedom, limb or life'.[208] Not all suffered damages could be recovered under the rules of tort, however. Normally the damage recoverable must be measurable in money.[209] Law distinguishes between damages to property and damages to person. The latter can, but need not, be measured in money, and their consequences may be emotional distress and pain (non-pecuniary damages), as well as the costs of treatment or rehabilitation, temporary or permanent loss of employment capabilities, or loss of earnings (pecuniary damages).[210] Damages of a pecuniary nature can be classified either as direct pecuniary loss to the victim (*damnum emergens*), or loss of profits which would have been achieved by the victim if the tort had not been committed (*lucrum cessans*).[211] In contrast to the general tendency, for instance, in English law,[212] tort laws of certain Central European countries have normally permitted recovery of both latter types of losses.

[208] W. J. Wagner, *Polish Civil Law.* Volume II. *Obligations in Polish Law*, in Z. Szirmai, *Law in Eastern Europe* (Leiden: A. W. Sijthoff, 1974) at p. 147. This definition, provided with reference to Polish law, is no doubt applicable throughout Central Europe.

[209] Ibid. [210] Ibid.

[211] Ibid. Such a classification can also be seen in other legal systems, for instance in French law: *perte – profit*, or German law: *wirklicher Schaden – Entgang des Gewinnes* (ibid., p. 98).

[212] *Spartan Steel Alloys v Martin* [1972] QB 27, with the exception of *Junior Books v Veitchi* [1982] AC 520.

In terms of damages product liability law presents certain interesting problems and demands to be treated differently from the general tortious liability regime. The manner in which they have developed in the product liability context in Central Europe is examined below.

Generally the damage capable of setting the 'product liability machine' in motion has not been merely, any but a particular type of damage. As explained above, the most crucial delimitation of the scope of product liability concerned the common contention in Central Europe, following the world trend on the subject, that it only involved damages caused *by*, and not *within*, the defective products.[213] The latter damages have traditionally been attributed to contractual liability. How have the Central European legal systems dealt with the issue of damages in product liability cases? It must be remembered that even the Product Liability Directive does not allow recovery of all the sustained damages, and leaves the regulation of recovery of non-pecuniary damages to the national law. Therefore the manner in which the legal systems in question have approached the issue of damages remains significant even after the implementation of the Directive. It seems that especially recovery of non-pecuniary damages and *lucrum cessans* caused some problems within Central Europe. In Hungary, from the introduction of the Civil Code of 1959, the tortious regime did not distinguish between the protected objects, be it property or a person.[214] It was, however, clearly stated in the Civil Code that in case of personal injuries caused by a tortious act only pecuniary damages were to be recovered.[215] Hence, although the courts were willing to award compensation for non-pecuniary damages caused by injury to a person, they were unable to do so openly in the light of the regulation of the Code.[216] However, after the amendment of the Civil Code in 1977, an exception was inserted into the chapter of the Code concerning liability: in cases of serious injuries or serious infringements of personal rights it has since been possible to recover non-pecuniary damages.[217] The courts' decisions followed this amendment, but still, according to Harmathy, there has been a lack of 'clear principles of the obligation to pay non-pecuniary damages' in the Hungarian legal system.[218] This lack of clarity remains until today. In contrast to the Hungarian Civil Code, the Czechoslovak and then the Czech Code unequivocally ensured recovery of both pecuniary and non-pecuniary damages. Injuries to the health and body were separated from

[213] Łętowska , *Prawo umów konsumenckich*, p. 103.
[214] Harmathy, *Introduction to Hungarian Law*, p. 117.
[215] Ibid. [216] Ibid. [217] Ibid. [218] Ibid.

other kinds of damages. The former were regulated in the part of the Civil Code concerning 'protection of personhood' (Sections 11–17).[219] Apart from demanding that the violation of the particular right be stopped, its 'consequences be removed and that adequate satisfaction be given to him or her' the victim could also have the right to 'pecuniary satisfaction of the immaterial detriment' in case of 'considerable reduction of dignity or honour' (Section 13). Generally, however, the rules of recovery of damages to personhood were the same rules governing all other kinds of damages. These were regulated in Sections 442–50 of the Code. The former version of the Czechoslovak Civil Code, in Section 442 referring both to tortious and contractual liability, generally only allowed for *damnum emergens* to be recovered.[220] Further, greater emphasis was placed by the Article upon *restitutio in integrum* or *restitutio in natura* than on compensation (the more ideologically proper and cheaper solution always to be given priority unless 'impossible' or 'inefficient' (Section 442.1)),[221] although in practice most cases did see compensation paid to the victim.[222] *Lucrum cessans*, which Vondracek refers to as an 'ideologically tainted notion', was not usually recoverable.[223] However, as an exception from this rule the Code introduced, in Section 422.2, the notion of 'other damage', recoverable on the court's discretion determined by the principles of 'socialist community life'[224] if the damage was caused deliberately. Vondracek pointed out, however, that it was unlikely for loss of earnings to be compensated,[225] although it was still possible under exceptional

[219] By virtue of Section 11: 'An individual shall have the right to protection of his or her personhood, in particular of his or her life or health, civic honour and human dignity as well as of the privacy, name and expressions of personal nature' (translation sent by Dobiasova).

[220] Section 442.1 reads: 'Only real damage is compensated . . .' (Vondracek, *Commentary on the Czechoslovak Civil Code* (Dordrecht, Boston, Lancaster: Martinus Nijhoff Publishers, 1988) 394).

[221] Also some representatives of the doctrine of law were in favour of this solution.

[222] Vondracek, *Commentary*, p. 395; V. Knapp and J. Pauly, 'Zamyšleni nad novelo u občanského zákoníku' *Pravnik*: 717–33, at 730–3. For example cases: R 1971, No 55 c.c., 339 et seq.; R 1977, No 27 c.c., 312. Vondracek, however, mentions the case where the Provincial Court in Bratislava held that the builder who caused damage to the neighbouring house by explosives used in his work ought to repair the building himself instead of paying the compensation (R 1984, No 21 c.c., 175 et seq.; Vondracek, *Commentary*, p. 395).

[223] Vondracek, *Commentary*.

[224] The principles of Socialist community life in the Czechoslovak Civil Code were a general clause which resembled the Polish 'rules of social cooperation'.

[225] Vondracek, *Commentary*, p. 396.

circumstances. The Code was amended in 1991 and now Section 442 puts greater emphasis upon compensation than *restitutio in integrum*, and the compensation is held to include 'compensation of the real damages as well as what the damaged party lost (lost profit)'.[226] Similarly with the jurisdictions analysed above, basing product liability on the general tortious liability provision of the Polish Civil Code determined that damages recoverable in product liability cases were damages which could normally be recovered under the general tortious liability regime.[227] In Poland damages to the person have been governed mainly by Article 444 of the Civil Code. The provision stipulates that in cases of injury to person (damage to body and health) the victim can recover all the costs, such as the cost of treatment, and, if the damage involves permanent incapacity to perform the existing profession, also the cost of retraining for a different profession. In cases where the victim is not, or is to a lesser extent, capable of working, or his needs have increased, or his prospects for the future have worsened, the person liable may also be required to pay an allowance (paid in instalments). In special circumstances the court can, instead of the allowance of a part of it, require the defendant to pay a lump sum (Article 447). Non-pecuniary damages can be recovered, and this, together with the possibility of recovering *lucrum cessans*, has normally been considered as the greatest benefit of tortious liability over contractual liability.[228]

On the one hand, the scope of damages recoverable in Central Europe was larger than the scope prescribed by the Product Liability Directive. For instance, there has been no minimum amount involved, and the property recoverable could also be used for purposes related to business. Such a large scope still remains and will undoubtedly be of use even after the implementation of the Directive in cases where, because of the particular damages involved, the latter does not apply. On the other hand, the specific practices governing award of damages contributed to the fact that on many occasions the damages awarded to victims of defective products were insignificant. The damages awarded in Poland were, in the words of Gnela, of moderate amounts.[229] In Hungary, Harmathy stressed that, particularly in the period of Socialism, awards were limited.[230] Again, here is where the need for a new approach in product liability litigation is particularly pressing.

[226] The translation of the Code sent by Dobiasova. [227] Gnela, *Odpowiedzialność*, p. 192.

[228] Although certain representatives of the doctrine of law pointed out that non-pecuniary damages should also be recovered in contract (ibid., p. 194).

[229] Ibid. [230] Harmathy, *Introduction to Hungarian Law*, p. 194.

Causal link between the defendant's act and the damage

Two main theories developed in Western Europe, the equivalence of the cause (*conditio sine qua non*) and the adequate causal connection, exerted a considerable influence upon the Central European approach in the area. Central European tortious liability law, conditioned by particular political and economic circumstances, offered its own theory of causal link, following the thoughts explored in Soviet Russia. The theory of necessary and accidental causal links reflected the common contention of Socialist legal writers that law ought to use the same concept of causal connection as other sciences, and especially social sciences. Accordingly, only necessary causal links (determined by science and experience) between the tortious act and the damage could give rise to liability. This theory was however described as only verbally different from the theory of adequate causal connection.[231] At the moment the adequate causal connection theory is used, as well as in product liability cases.

1. Time limits for bringing action

The Directive introduces changes into the Central European limitation provisions.[232] All the analysed states implemented the three- and ten-year periods,[233] although the regulation is more beneficial for the victims as regards the time limits for bringing claims in Poland: both the three- and the ten-year periods required by the Directive are in Poland not extinguishing periods, but limitation periods. A potential action by the European Commission can be envisaged with respect to this discrepancy.

Conclusion

Although the substantive provisions of the Directive are unlikely to cause a significant change within the Central European product liability regimes, it must be submitted that crucial transformation, also involving product

[231] Czachórski, *Zobowiązania*, p. 155.

[232] The Hungarian Civil Code does not differentiate between contract and tort law claims, establishing a period of five years for bringing all claims (Article 324.1). While in the Polish Civil Code, according to Article 118, the term for bringing all claims is ten years; under Article 554 claims which arise out of a sale conducted in the course of a seller's business must be brought within two years. In the Czechoslovak and Czech Civil Code no differences can be seen in the limitation periods between contractual and tortious claims. Section 106 refers to 'right to compensation of damage'. This right is limited to within 'two years from the day when the damaged person learnt of the damage and of the liable person'.

[233] Article 449.8 of the Polish Civil Code, Sections 9 and 9a of the Czech Product Liability Act, and Section 10 of the Hungarian Act.

liability law and practice, is on the way in the region. True reform lies not in the changes in the substantive product liability law, but in the transformation of other factors which have an undisputed influence upon the effectiveness of substantive laws of product liability, factors which can be placed within the broadly understood consumer policy. A very complex set of interacting issues, brought in mainly by the European Union, of legal and extra-legal nature, revolutionised not only the product liability regimes, but also the entire area of consumer protection law. Such transformation within all tiers of society and its political and economic life has been conducted in Central Europe after the demise of Socialism with a view to adapting states to the requirements of their future membership in the European Union. It is submitted rather that the entire process of enlargement of the European Union, the return of Central Europe to its civil law roots,[234] democracies and free market economies, the adoption of the consumer policies and attitudes deriving from Western Europe, various Western institutions, mechanisms and concepts relating to enforcement of the regimes of product liability, are likely to create a significant transformation in Central Europe.

[234] This statement refers to the fact that Central Europe, in common with the rest of the Eastern European bloc, firmly placed within the civil law family, for a brief period of time used to belong to the family of Socialist law as defined by comparative law: K. Zweigert and H. Kotz, *An Introduction to Comparative Law* (3rd rev. edn, Oxford: Clarendon Press); P. de Cruz, *Comparative Law in a Changing World* (2nd edn, London, Sydney: Cavendish Publishing Limited, 1999). For the definition of the notion 'legal family' see the above authors.

15

Bugs in Anglo-American products liability

JANE STAPLETON*

Introduction

The face of European products liability may be about to change considerably. The first places where change probably will occur are in the procedural and funding areas. Though the density of European products cases has been and probably will continue to be slight compared to that in the United States, it is of note that a growing trend within the European case law is a shift to multi-party actions. Proposed procedural rule changes are about to fuel this shift.[1] At the same time, fundamental changes in the way civil litigation is funded within European Union Member States have disproportionately encouraged group actions.[2] They have also shifted greater risk, responsibility and power to plaintiffs' lawyers.

On the legislative front, the reform of the separate European products liability doctrine, set out in the 1985 *European Directive on Product*

* This chapter was first printed in the *South Carolina Law Review*.

1 For an excellent study of this phenomenon see C. Hodges, *Multi-Party Actions* (2001); see also Lord Chancellor's Department, *Consultation Paper, Representative Claims* (Feb. 2001), at http://www.lcd.gov.uk/consult/general/repclaims.htm (last visited 10 September 2004); C. Hodges, 'Multi-Party Actions: A European Approach' 11 (2001) *Duke J. of Comp. & Int'l L.*: 321; C. Hodges, 'Factors Influencing the Incidence of Multiple Claims' 4 (1999) *J. Pers. Injury Litig.*: 289.

2 For example, the European Commission has published a proposal for a Directive establishing minimum common rules relating to legal aid and other financial aspects of civil proceedings in cross-border disputes at COM (2002)13 final. See *The Problems Confronting the Cross-Border Litigant: Green Paper from the Commission on Legal Aid in Civil Matters*, COM (2000) 51 final; *Access of Consumers to Justice and the Settlement of Consumer Disputes in the Single Market: Green Paper from the Commission*, COM (1993) 576 final. On the recent introduction in the United Kingdom of conditional fees, which are not contingency fees, but 'no-win no-fee' arrangements, see Lord Chancellor's Department, *Regulatory Impact Assessment: Improvement in the Availability and Use of Conditional Fees* (Nov. 1998).

Liability,[3] is on hold. Following both a Green Paper[4] and a White Paper,[5] the European Commission (the Commission) concluded that it had insufficient evidence to advise on the future of the Directive at present, and thus, it has both set up an expert advisory committee and funded two major research studies on products liability in Europe. These studies are to collect information, particularly on the costs that might result from any future repeal of the most controversial defence in the Directive. Very significantly, one of the commissioned studies has been set to the task of investigating the feasibility of introducing a uniform products liability system across the European Union (EU), replacing the divergent national rules (for example, in contract and under sales legislation) that co-exist with the Directive.[6] The parallel with the aim of the Reporters of the *Restatement (Third) of Torts: Products Liability* (*Restatement Third*) should not go unnoticed.[7]

My aim here is to sketch the contrasting state of products liability doctrine in Europe and those foreign jurisdictions that have adopted clones of the European Directive. But the focus I will use, the lens on our different

[3] See Council Directive 85/374, 1985 OJ (L 210) 29 (hereinafter Directive) (addressing approximation of the laws, regulations, and administrative provisions of the Member States concerning liability for defective products).

[4] *Liability for Defective Products: Green Paper from the European Commission*, COM (1999) 396 final; see José J. Izquierdo Peris, 'Liability for Defective Products in the European Union: Developments Since 1995 – The European Commission's Green Paper' 1999 *Consumer LJ*: 331.

[5] *Commission Report on the Application of Directive 85/374 on Liability for Defective Products*, COM (2000) 893 final; see Donna Lambert, 'European Strict Product Liability Laws' (March 2001) *European Prod. Liab. Rev.*: at 16. This was the second report; the first was *Commission Report on the Application of Directive 85/374*, COM (95) 617 final.

[6] John Meltzer *et al.*, 'European Commission Launches Major Product Liability Study' (Dec. 2001) *European Prod. Liab. Rev.*: at 4.

[7] *Restatement (Third) of Torts: Products Liability* (1998) [hereinafter *Restatement Third*]. In the *Restatement Third* §2 comment *n*, the Reporters sought, at the level of something they called 'functional requisites', to amalgamate causes of action which rely on identical facts. See also James A. Henderson, Jr and Aaron D. Twerski, 'Achieving Consensus on Defective Product Design' 83 (1998) *Cornell L. Rev.*: 867, 918 ('So long as the functional requisites of section 2 are satisfied, plaintiffs may couch their design claims in negligence, implied warranty, or strict liability in tort'). Whether this will succeed in producing a general simplification of products liability litigation is a matter of some controversy. The problem here lies not so much with the amalgamation of claims that might previously have been argued both under *Restatement (Second) of Torts* §402A (1965) (*Restatement Second*) and negligence theory, for the duplicative nature of many such claims is fairly well agreed. The difficulty lies in knowing where warranty claims fit in and whether the full extent of existing warranty entitlements is reflected in the *Restatement Third*. See J. Stapleton, 'Restatement (Third) of Torts: Products Liability, An Anglo-Australian Perspective' 39 (2000) *Washburn LJ*: 363.

experiences, will be how regimes are responding to the increasing challenge of pathogenically infected products – as the title of this chapter puts it, 'bugs' – in products liability. These range from well-known bacterial infections, such as salmonella, legionnella, and escherichia-coli 0157 (E coli),[8] to viral infections, such as the infection of blood by the Human Immuno-Virus (HIV)[9] and hepatitis C (Hep C),[10] to diseases, such as Bovine Spongiform Encephalopathy (BSE) and Creutzfeldt-Jakob Disease (CJD).[11]

Rough comparison of common law systems: form and substance of product regimes

The divergence of the US system from other common law systems is considerably more striking than that between those other common law systems and the civil law systems in the EU. This fact is easily set out in a rough comparison of substantive and legal system characteristics such as that in table 15.1.

In relation to the special products liability rule, the manifestation of this US divergence that is most obvious to students is length. In the United States, the seminal doctrinal treatment is the *Restatement Third*, published in 1998, which runs to 382 pages. Contrast this with the Directive, which occupies a little over four pages in the *Official Journal of the European Communities*, or compare reported case law.[12] One of the first cases to deal with the *Restatement Third* ran to only eight pages;[13] one of

[8] See also the following: campylobacter bacteria, cryptosporidium, listeria, botulism, psittacosis, and mycobacterium avium subspecies paratuberculosis.

[9] See, e.g., Simon Garfield, *The End of Innocence: Britain in the Time of AIDS* (1994).

[10] See also the following: the Ebola virus (it is now thought that the Black Death was caused by this virus being passed from person to person, not via infected rats. Robert Uhlig, 'Black Death Caused By "Ebola" Virus, not Rats' *Daily Telegraph* (London), 22 Nov. 2001); Q fever, rhizopus, the foot and mouth virus and the smallpox virus.

[11] See J. Cooke, *Cannibals, Cows and the CJD Catastrophe* (New York: Random House, 1998); D. Powell and William Leiss, *Mad Cows and Mother's Milk* (Montreal: McGill-Queens University Press, 1997); S. Rampton and J. Stauber, *Mad Cow USA* (1997); R. Rhodes, *Deeply Feasts: Tracking the Secrets of a Terrifying New Plague* (1997) (detailing the controversy as to the form of the infective agent in transmissible spongiform encephalopathies); Clive Martyr, 'BSE in Europe' (March 2001) *European Prod. Liab. Rev.*: at 4; Organic Consumers' Ass'n, *Mad Cow Disease*, available at http://www.OrganicConsumers.org/madcow.htm (last visited May 6, 2002).

[12] See footnote 3 above.

[13] *Delaney v Deere & Co.*, 985 F. Supp. 1009, 1017 (D. Kan. 1997) (concerning the grant of defendant's motion for summary judgment). For the appeal, see *Delaney v Deere & Co.*, 999 P.2d 930 (Kan. 2000).

Table 15.1. *Common law systems: what do they have in common?*

						Compare Non-Common Law Systems	
Substantive legal differences	**UK**	**Canada except Quebec**	**Australia**	**New Zealand**	**USA**	*EU itself*	*EU Member States, except Eire and UK*
Written Constitution?	**No**	**Yes**	**Yes**	**Yes**	**Yes**	*No*	*Yes*
Federal system that explicitly divides legislative competence on basis of subject matter?	**No**	**Yes**	**Yes**	**No**	**Yes**	*No*	*Yes/No*
Sub-national legislative capacity in private law?	**No**	**Yes**	**Yes**	**No**	**Yes**	*N/A*	*Yes/No*
Unitary (i.e. national) private common (i.e. judge-made) law?	**Yes**	**Yes**	**Yes**	**Yes**	**No**		
Does fact-finder give written reasons?	**Yes**	**Yes**	**Yes**	**Yes**	**No**	*Yes*	*Yes*
Level of judicial loyalty to precedent, consistency of outcome?	**High**	**High**	**High**	**High**	**Low**	*Relatively High*	*???*
Public law reform bodies?	**Yes**	**Yes**	**Yes**	**Yes**	**No**	*No*	*Yes/No?*

Legal system differences							
Adversarial?	**Yes**	**Yes**	**Yes**	**Yes**	**Yes**	*Yes*	*Yes/No?*
Are juries common in private law?	**No**	**No**	**No**	**No**	**Yes**	*No*	*No*
Are punitive damages very rare in private law?	**Yes**	**Yes**	**Yes**	**Yes**	**No**	*Yes*	*Yes*
Are contingency fee arrangements often used?	**No**	**No**	**No**	**No**	**Yes**	*No*	*No*
Loser pays winner's costs?	**Yes**	**Yes**	**Yes**	**Yes**	**No**	*Yes*	*Yes*
Are (many) judges elected?	**No**	**No**	**No**	**No**	**Yes**	*No*	*No*
Level of influence of the Legal Academy on the development of the common law?	**Not high**	**Not high**	**Not high**	**Not high**	**Very high**	*High W.R.T. A-G*	*High?*
Broad consensus for comprehensive social security/welfare support?	**Yes**	**Yes**	**Yes**	**Yes**	**No**	*N/A*	*Yes*
Is the quantum of damages subject to tight judicial control?	**Yes**	**Yes**	**Yes**	**Yes**	**No**	*N/A*	*Yes*

the first cases to apply the Directive in the United Kingdom ran to 113 pages.[14]

But there is no mystery here. A non-US jurisdiction, with a uniformly high-quality judiciary, single court of final appeal, tight system of precedent, and active legislature, can often 'make do' with a very sparse formulation of its binding legislative rules. Such foreign jurisdictions accomplish this task because the legal rules are definitively elaborated in a unitary appellate case law and because academic treatises serve broadly the same role as the Comments and Reporters' Notes of the *Restatement Third*. Similarly, in jury-free systems, the triers of fact must provide written reasons for their determinations, and this often produces very lengthy expositions of legal reasoning.

Orientation of United States products regimes

Section 402A of the *Restatement (Second) of Torts* (*Restatement Second*)[15] was a top-down law reform motivated, not by social or forensic pressures, but by the enthusiasm of a small group of Legal Realists that saw the opportunity to make what they saw as a small win–win change to legal entitlements. Out of, what I call 'classical' (because privity bounded) warranties,[16] a new cause of action had grown; under the tag of strict liability 'warranty' claims, plaintiffs were in fact being allowed to sue manufacturers with whom they had no contractual privity – what I call 'aclassical' warranty claims. If this were so, and if elsewhere, disguised as 'negligence' liability, courts were in fact covertly imposing strict liability for manufacturing errors in products, then it seemed to make sense to clarify this state of affairs by recognising a separate class of strict liability in tort for products defects. The apparent neatness, low impact and intellectual glamour of this move led its promoters to overlook major gaps in the theoretical foundations of the rule in the new §402A. Traditional incidents of the warranty claim, such as its limit to products and, further, to only those products that had been commercially supplied, were limits that were explicable in classical privity-based warranty claims. But these limits were then carried over holus-bolus into the *Restatement Second* with little or no attempt at justification. Little, if any, concern seems to have been raised

[14] *In re Hepatitis C Litig.* (*A v National Blood Authority*) [2001] 3 All ER 289.

[15] *Restatement Second*, footnote 7 above, §402A.

[16] J. Stapleton, *Product Liability* (London: Sweet and Maxwell, 1994), pp. 16–20 (describing classical warranties as those involving traditional contractual privity between the parties).

about the fresh anomalies that would be created by separate tort liability for commercially supplied products. Indeed, it was a revealing feature of the work of products liability theorists that most resorted to ignoring the destabilising phenomenon of bystander injuries before stating a theory of the law,[17] while the work of general tort theorists, such as Jules Coleman, abandoned any attempt to accommodate products liability within their scheme of 'core' tort law concepts.[18]

Given current product regimes and controversies, it is noteworthy that, in general, the *Restatement Second* contained no separate black-letter treatment of specific product types such as blood, had no separate treatment of types of product defect and gave no guidance on what might constitute a product defect.[19] These oversights may be explained by the fact that, although the *Restatement Second* was not explicitly limited to manufacturing errors, it was clearly intended as a reform focussed on products defects introduced by the manufacturing process. In such cases, the production line norm offered what seemed to be a simple benchmark for the requirement of a 'defect'. This unexpressed focus on manufacturing errors had a critical effect on the development of US tort law. Together with the lack of a domestic thalidomide tragedy in the United States, this focus led the drafters of the *Restatement Second* to overlook the legal dilemma posed by unforeseeable side effects of a product's intended design.

The 1998 *Restatement Third* is a considerable contrast to the *Restatement Second.* In constructing the *Restatement Third,* its Reporters were centrally concerned with perceived bottom-up pressure on the US products regime from 'classic design cases'.[20] The most common expression

[17] See ibid. at p. 127 and n. 13.

[18] See, e.g., Jules L. Coleman, *Risks and Wrongs* (Cambridge: Cambridge University Press, 1992) (defending and criticising economic analysis of tort concepts). In particular, see chapter 20 for Coleman's analysis of product liability theory at pp. 407–29.

[19] But see *Restatement Second,* footnote 7 above, §402A cmt. k; see also George W. Conk, 'Is There a Design Defect in the Restatement (Third) of Torts: Products Liability?' 109 (2000) *Yale LJ*: 1091–101, at 1087 (discussing the history of §402A and its application, through comment *k*, to 'unavoidably unsafe' products such as drugs, cigarettes and alcoholic beverages).

[20] So-called 'classic design cases' are ones that 'do not involve product malfunctions, violations of safety regulations, or egregiously dangerous products' (James A. Henderson, Jr. and Aaron D. Twerski, 'What Europe, Japan, and Other Countries Can Learn from the New American Restatement of Products Liability' 34 (1999) *Tex. Int'l LJ*: 1, 17 [hereinafter 'New American Restatement']. Yet, 'the plaintiffs nevertheless plausibly claim that the designs are unacceptably dangerous, and therefore, legally defective': Henderson and Twerski, 'Achieving Consensus', footnote 7 above, at pp. 876–7.

of these claims is where the plaintiff argues that the product did not perform its intended function sufficiently well: a chair or axle was 'not strong enough', the side-panels of a car were 'not strong enough' in a crash, and so on. While the *Restatement Third* gives separate treatment to classes of product claims according to certain proof shortcuts[21] and according to certain product classes such as food,[22] the main focus of the Reporters is on the residual class in §2 under which they accept that most classic design cases will fall.[23] Section 2 gives separate treatment to three classes of product defects: manufacturing defects, design defects and warning defects.[24]

Like the *Restatement Second*, the *Restatement Third* pays little attention to the defect issues on which Europeans focus so keenly – those posed by unforeseeable side effects of intended design. As a result, there is no black-letter treatment in the *Restatement Third* of how and why such cases should be treated.[25] However, the *Restatement Third* does try to give some guidance on the issue of defectiveness. For example, under §2(a), manufacturing errors are not only defined as ones that depart from their intended design but are, merely by satisfying that definition, classified as defective conditions.[26] In contrast, design and warning conditions that fall within this residual §2, such as most classic design cases, are to be judged by reasonableness criteria.[27] By implication then, this means that a product with an unforeseeable design condition that causes harm cannot, by definition, be defective. Finally, the *Restatement Third* pays no attention to the phenomenon of the waves of BSE, CJD, Hep C, and HIV infections that had been appearing since the 1980s and 90s. This oversight, as we will see, leaves such infection cases to be treated in a highly fractured manner by the *Restatement Third*.

[21] See *Restatement Third*, §3 ('Circumstantial Evidence Supporting Inference of Product Defect'; describing a sort of generously reinterpreted *res ipsa loquitur* class); see also §4 ('Non-compliance and Compliance with Product Safety Statutes or Regulations'); §2 cmt. e (dealing with 'manifestly unreasonable design', other terms for which are categorically defective design, generically defective design, and egregiously dangerous product type).

[22] See ibid. §7; see also §5 (components); §6 (prescription drugs and medical devices); §8 (used products).

[23] See generally Stapleton, 'Restatement (Third) of Torts' (discussing the odd positioning of the 'residual' section at the beginning of the Restatement and criticising other features of the *Restatement Third*).

[24] *Restatement Third*, §2.

[25] There are two passing mentions in the non-black-letter text. See *Restatement Third*, §2 cmt. l; §6 cmt. g (relating to prescription drugs and medical devices).

[26] Ibid., §2(a). [27] Ibid., §2(b), (c).

Orientation of the European Union Directive and its clones

The orientation of the *Restatement Third* is in marked contrast to that of the EU Directive and its clones in other countries such as Japan, Australia, Taiwan and Israel.[28] The Directive did not result from some perceived bottom-up forensic pressure from claims. Rather, the engine of this reform was social and political.[29] In particular, the concern of the public in these countries had been galvanised by the disaster caused by the unforeseen side effects of the thalidomide pregnancy drug.[30] Meanwhile, by the late 1970s, the European Commission was keen to promote consumer protection measures to show Europeans that the 'common market' was not there simply to serve big business. It proposed very pro-consumer draft Directives in 1976 and 1979.[31] Yet there remained intense concern within the European Parliament and the Council that substantial exculpatory provisions be included in any future Directive.[32]

As a result, the Directive is one of the high-water marks of Euro-fudge and textual vagueness.[33] It used a cryptic 'definition' of defect in Article 6:[34] 'A product is defective when it does not provide the safety

[28] See Jocelyn Kellam (ed.), *Product Liability in the Asia-Pacific* (2nd edn, St. Leonards, NSW: Kluwer Law International, 1999); Luke Nottage, 'The Present and Future of Product Liability Dispute Resolution in Japan', 27 (2000) *Wm. Mitchell L. Rev.*: 215.

[29] Stapleton, *Product Liability*, at pp. 37–65.

[30] Ibid., at pp. 39–43.

[31] See Commission Proposal for a Council Directive Relating to the Approximation of the Laws, Regulations, and Administrative Provisions of the Member States Concerning Liability for Defective Products, 1976 OJ (C241) 9 [hereinafter First Draft Directive]; Commission Amendment of the Proposal for a Council Directive Relating to the Approximation of the Laws, Regulations, and Administrative Provisions of the Member States Concerning Liability for Defective Products, 1979 OJ (C271) 3 (hereinafter Second Draft Directive).

[32] See, e.g., Economic and Social Committee (ECOSOC), *Report on Proposal for a Council Directive on Liability for Defective Products*, COM (1976) 372 final at pp. 41–5 (hereinafter ECOSOC Report) (stating that industry should not be made 'liable for products which could not have been made to a safer standard at the time when they were put into circulation'; 'it may be in the patients' interests to put into circulation products which are known to have side-effects when taken by some or indeed all persons. . . .'; also note early concern about the uncertainty of the concept of undiscoverability in the comment 'scientists might be far less willing than lawyers to define what at the present level of technological and scientific development is ("undiscoverable") as opposed to undiscovered. Undiscoverability is itself very doubtful from a scientific point of view'; note the view of the Section for Industry, Commerce, Crafts, and Services against inclusion of liability for development risks, emphasising that their inclusion 'could have an inhibiting effect on innovation' at pp. 44–5.

[33] See footnote 117 below and accompanying text.

[34] It was at the initiation of the Legal Affairs Committee of the European Parliament that the definition of defect included this statement that the Court should be required to 'take

which a person is entitled to expect, taking all circumstances into account. . . .'[35] It also allows a Member State discretion on a number of critical matters including the exculpatory Article 7(e), which became known as the 'development risk defence'; Article 7(e) would allow a manufacturer to escape liability if it can prove that 'the state of scientific and technical knowledge at the time when it put the product into circulation was not such as to enable the existence of the defect to be discovered'.[36] Article 15 allows a Member State to implement the Directive in domestic legislation without that defence.[37] The final legislative body, the Council of Ministers, even allowed individual Member State delegations to append Unilateral Declarations to the Directive to expound their local interpretations of its provisions. The point is that the Directive tries to square a circle: it uses the rhetoric of 'strict liability', and yet, in Articles 6(2) and 7(e), it seems to provide solid protection for reasonable businesses, a compromise demanded by the UK Government of Margaret Thatcher.[38]

Textually, the Directive is in certain respects quite like the *Restatement Second*. It gives no separate treatment to product types or defect types, and the definition of defectiveness in Article 6 is, at best, circular. On the other hand, just as the focus of the *Restatement Second* had been manufacturing errors and the focus of the *Restatement Third* is on classic design cases, the Directive also reflects its historical trigger: the thalidomide disaster. Unlike the Restatements, the Directive attempts to grapple explicitly with unforeseen side-effects of a product's intended design by giving product suppliers the crucial exculpatory defence in Article 7(e). However, the Directive has its own gaps; failure to reflect on the US experience leaves the Directive with no provision as to how to treat classic design cases – the 'how strong should a chair be' cases. Needless to say, just as the Restatements give no guide as to how infection cases should be handled, nor does the Directive address these issues.

into account all the circumstances' of the particular case ((1979) *Eur. Parl. Doc.* (COM 1971) 18). Specifically, there should be a reference to time to make 'it clear that the user of an old product cannot expect the same degree of safety from such a product as from a product which has just been put into circulation'. Ibid. Characteristically, the pro-plaintiff Commission refused to include this amendment in its second draft Directive (Second Draft Directive, footnote 31 above, at 3).

35 Directive, footnote 3 above, art. 6. Such circumstances include foreseeable use and therefore must extend to misuse.

36 Ibid., art. 7(e). 37 Ibid., art. 15. 38 Ibid., arts. 6(2), 7(c).

Pre-manufacture generic infection cases

The Reporters of the *Restatement Third* have attacked the Directive.[39] One of their principal complaints seems to be that it does not distinguish between types of defect.[40] This omission then blocks the Directive from adopting what the Reporters say is 'the [o]nly [s]ensible [s]tandard for [d]efect in [c]lassic *[d]esign* [c]ases'.[41] This is, they argue, the requirement of convincing proof of a reasonable alternative design, a requirement the *Restatement Third* does not impose on plaintiffs in manufacturing error cases.[42] But what if the case in favour of separating out types of defect is itself dubious? This has always been one of the core dilemmas in modern products liability and yet again, it is being neatly exposed, this time by premanufacture generic infection cases.

Pre-manufacture generic infection cases are a discrete type of case, distinct from cases of chemical contamination, such as when a worker carelessly puts the wrong chemical into the water storage pond of a water supply company,[43] or a delivery person incorrectly mixes fire retardant chemical with stock feed.[44] Unlike chemical contamination cases, in premanufacture generic infection cases, the danger lies in the presence of a transmissible pathogen. By definition, *pre-manufacture* generic infection cases are distinct from cases where a product is contaminated or infected during the production process. They are cases where the infection in a product was present in the raw materials and, therefore, before manufacture of the product.[45] Pathogenic infections can be isolated events; take, for example, a local outbreak of 'wool-sorter's disease'

[39] 'New American Restatement', footnote 20 above.

[40] Ibid., at 13–14. [41] Ibid., at 19 (emphasis added).

[42] Ibid. [43] *AB v SW Water Services Ltd* [1993] QB 507.

[44] In 1973, toxic chemicals were accidentally fed to dairy cattle in the State of Michigan with the result that virtually all nine million in the state's human population became permanently contaminated by the hazardous chemical polybrominated biphenyl. See Joyce Egginton, *Bitter Harvest* (1980) 14, 275, 281. Scientists estimated 'that only about 10 per cent of the body burden of PBB contamination being carried by nine million people would be excreted in their lifetimes' (at 307); see also *Mich Chem Corp v American Home Assurance Co.*, 728 F.2d 373, 376 (6th Cir. 1984) (involving negligent shipment of toxic-flame retardant as livestock feed additive); *Oscoda Chapter of PBB Action Commission Inc v Dep't of Natural Res.*, 268 N.W.2d 240 (Mich. 1978) (involving suit to prevent burial of contaminated cattle in clay-lined pit).

[45] See J. Stapleton, 'BSE, CJD, Mass Infections and the 3rd US Restatement', in C. Rickett and T. Telfer (eds), *International Perspectives on Consumers' Access to Justice* (Cambridge: Cambridge University Press, forthcoming).

caused by one anthrax-infected sheep,[46] Legionnaire's disease contracted from one infected piece of machinery,[47] or the sort of E-coli 0157 infection from one contaminated batch of food that killed twenty-one people in Lanarkshire in 1996.[48] But the sharpest lessons from infection cases come from those where it is feared that the infection is *generic* to a product class as in the case of BSE, foot-and-mouth disease and other recent epidemics.[49]

To sum up the characteristics I have used to define pre-manufacture generic infection cases:

(1) The infection is not part of the condition of the product which the supplier 'intended' in the sense of 'desired'
(2) The infection was present before any artificial 'manufacturing' process occurred
(3) The infection is, however, known or suspected to be 'generic' in the sense that it has affected an entire product sector such as the beef industry, the blood product sector, or the water supply
(4) This sector is an 'essential' product sector, such as milk or blood, in the sense that it does not have realistic substitutes
(5) The infection in the product type is not present in each item of the product but testing each item for that infection is impossible/impractical etc. and
(6) The infection is not necessarily limited to one generation of products or victims but may be transmissible to following generations.[50]

[46] The scientific name is *Bacillus anthracis*. See also the *meningococcus* infection.

[47] See, e.g., *Brennen v Mogul Corp.*, 557 A.2d 870 (Vt. 1988) (addressing a case where a plumber sued the manufacturer of water treatment equipment when he allegedly contracted Legionnaire's disease while working on a cooling tower because the manufacturer's equipment and chemicals did not prevent growth of legionella bacteria).

[48] J. Leake, 'New Health Alert as Coli Hits Half of Cattle Herds', *Sunday Times* (London), 9 September 2001, at 5G (reporting that as a result of raw meat coming in contact with cooked meat, 500 other people became ill).

[49] See also V. Elliott, 'Dairies Told to Improve Hygiene to Beat Milk Bug', *Times* (London), 7 December 2001, at 20 (writing that some scientists fear that a significant but unknown proportion of the UK milk supply is infected with *Mycobacterium avium* subspecies *paratuberculosis*, from which each year 90,000 people in Britain contract Crohn's disease).

[50] See, e.g., Robert Uhlig, 'BSE Cannot Be Inherited by Calves, Study Finds', *Daily Telegraph* (London), 26 February 2002. It is currently thought that BSE is transmitted between cattle by giving them food contaminated with the remains of infected animals (but not from infected mother to offspring). But see footnote 65 below.

Pre-manufacture generic infections: some United Kingdom statistics

Before we compare the responses of the different products liability regimes to these cases, let me sketch some of the socio-economic contexts in which Western European lawyers will be setting these claims. By far the most high-profile recent disaster concerning pre-manufacture generic infection cases is the UK mad cow (BSE) epidemic. Some statistics may help sketch the magnitude of the problem.

By March 2002, BSE cases in the UK cattle population numbered 191,000,[51] and 5.5 million cattle had been slaughtered in an attempt to contain the plague.[52] However, scientists fear that BSE may have become endemic in British cattle because young cattle are being raised in fields that have been contaminated by the dung of BSE-infected cattle.[53] The infection has spread abroad: it is currently believed that BSE spread from the United Kingdom across Europe and further afield by infected proteins used in animal feed.[54] In late 2001, two cows in Japan were found to have BSE; a limited cull of cattle is now underway in that country.[55]

The magnitude of the public health problem in the United Kingdom is reflected in the fact that between 1980 and 1996, the number of BSE-infected animals eaten by the UK population is estimated to have been one million.[56] By January 2002, 113 people in the United Kingdom had died from Creutzfeldt-Jakob disease (CJD), the human form of BSE.[57] Currently, the worst-case estimate of people who are or will be infected by CJD stemming from the current outbreak of BSE in cattle is 136,000, of whom 40,000 will die of the disease despite its long incubation period because they were sufficiently young when infected.[58] Faced with civil

[51] Department for Environment, Food and Rural Affairs (DEFRA), BSE Statistics, at http://www.defra.gov.uk/animalh/bse/index.html (last updated 1 March 2002).

[52] Ibid., DEFRA at http://www.defra.gov.uk/animalh/bse/bse-statistics/level-3-scheme.html (last visited 6 May 2002).

[53] James Meikle, 'Infected Fields Could Spread BSE, Scientists Say', *Guardian* (London), 13 September 2001.

[54] 'USA's Mad Cow Risk is Low, Study Finds', *USA Today*, 3 December 2001, at 6D.

[55] James Brooke, 'Potentially Mad Cows to Die', *New York Times*, 27 November 2001, at A6.

[56] Roger Highfield, 'Epidemic of Human BSE May Be at Its Peak', *Daily Telegraph* (London) 26 October 2001.

[57] Lorraine Fraser, 'Charles Backs Controversial CJD Research', *Daily Telegraph* (London), 13 January 2002.

[58] Mark Henderson, 'Number of vCJD Cases "Will Not Exceed 40,000"', *Times* (London), 26 October 2001.

claims from families affected by CJD,[59] the UK Department of Health set up a £55 million compensation trust fund.[60] This amount is likely to be grossly inadequate if BSE has infected the national sheep herd. If such is the case, the UK government has announced that the entire flock of 40 million sheep will be culled.[61] Even with such a cull, the worst-case estimate of future vCJD deaths if sheep have been infected with BSE is around 150,000.[62] Also, it is already known that CJD has been contracted through infected products from human bodies, such as dura mater, transplant tissue, human growth hormone, and fertility products.[63] It is feared that human CJD infection may occur through the possible *generic* infection of a number of product sectors (that is, where it is suspected that there is a risk of infection but no way of screening and isolating all particular cases of infection) such as vaccines (and other blood products such as plasma),[64] meat,[65] gelatin,[66] dairy products,[67] human

[59] The civil cases, known as the *Creutzfeldt-Jakob Disease Litig.*, may be found at the following: 54 BMLR 1 (QB 1995) (No. 1); 54 BMLR 8 (QB 1996) (Nos. 2, 4); 54 BMLR 79 (QB 1996) (No. 3); 54 BMLR 85 (QB CA 1997) (Nos. 2, 4); 54 BMLR 92 (QB 1997) (No. 5); 54 BMLR 95 (QB 1998) (No. 6); 54 BMLR 100 (QB 1998) (No. 7); 54 BMLR 104 (QB 1998) (No. 8); 54 BMLR 111 (QB 1998) (No. 9).

[60] '£155,000 for vCJD Victim An Insult' *Times* (London), 17 November 2001, at Scotland 6.

[61] 'Plan to Cull All Sheep if BSE is Found', *Daily Telegraph* (London), 28 September 2001.

[62] Mark Henderson, 'Sheep Meat May Pose Massive CJD Risk', *Times* (London), 10 January 2002, at 8; Roger Highfield, 'Scientists Refuse to Rule Out Epidemic of vCJD from Sheep', *Daily Telegraph* (London), 10 January 2002.

[63] See Cooke, *Cannibals*, footnote 11 above; Rampton and Stauber, *Mad Cow* footnote 11 above, at p. 71; Rhodes, *Deeply Feasts*, footnote 11 above, at pp. 131–51.

[64] The UK government concedes that blood products including vaccines may be at risk of contamination by CJD. L. Rogers and B. Christie, 'Scientists Warn of CJD Risk in Child Vaccines', *Sunday Times* (London), 22 February 1998, at 7. Thenceforward, the Department of Health advised (a) that the CJD risk with current blood supplies was 'theoretical', but (b) that experts agree that there is no way of guaranteeing this. See House of Lords Debates, 590 Hansard 680 (5 June 1998) available at http://www.publications.parliament.uk/pa/ld/ldhansard.htm (last visited 6 May 2002); House of Lords Debates, 611 Hansard 985 (30 March 2000); House of Commons Debates, 345 Hansard 124 NH (7 March 2000), available at http://www.publications.parliament.uk/pa/cm/cmhansard.htm (last visited 6 May 2002).

[65] Continuing uncertainty on this issue is reflected in the fact that the UK government is funding the research of minority-view scientists who suspect beef is not the cause of CJD. Valerie Elliott, 'Scientists to Test if Beef is the Cause of CJD', *Times* (London), 18 May 1999, at 15; *Metro* (London) 12 October 2001. Some postulate a key role for divalent cations such as manganese, which is found in many manufacturing processes and in pesticides. George Monbiot, 'Mad Cows, Bretons and Manganese: the French Cases of BSE May Not Have Been Spread from Britain', *Guardian* (London), 23 November 2000.

[66] Rhodes, *Deeply Feasts*, footnote 11 above, at p. 257.

[67] David Brown, 'Food Agency Urges Mass Screenings of Sheep for BSE', *Daily Telegraph* (London), 1 November 2000.

blood,[68] human tissue,[69] leather or woollen clothing,[70] and the water supply.[71] In July 1996, Carleton Gajdusek, who won the 1976 Nobel Prize in Medicine for his work on transmissible spongiform encephalopathies in humans, noted that in the United Kingdom:

> [A]ny species could be carrying it – dairy cows, beef cattle, pigs, chickens... All the pigs in England [were] fed on this meat-and-bone meal... Probably all the pigs in England are infected. And that means not only pork. It means your pigskin wallet. It means catgut surgical suture, because that's made of pig tissue. All the chickens fed on meat-and-bone meal; they're probably infected. You put that stuff in a chicken and it goes right through. A vegetarian could get it from chicken-shit that they put on the vegetables. It could be in the tallow, in butter . . . These people who've come down with CJD have given blood. It's undoubtedly in the blood supply. . . . And by the way, it could be in the milk...'[72]

The BSE/CJD crisis and its poor handling by Member State governments and central EU authorities has had a dramatic impact on the issue of food safety in the EU, which is now recognised as a core issue in European

[68] Early suspicions among a minority of scientists that CJD could be spread by blood donations is reported by Nicholas Schoon, 'CJD Could Be Spread by Blood Transfusions', *Independent* (London), 8 October 1997, at 1. Plans were made to ban plasma made from pooled donations of UK blood donors because of CJD risk. Nigel Hawkes, 'British Blood Products Banned as Too Risky', *Sunday Times* (London), 27 February 1998, at 1. This ban was put in place in May 1998. Joanna Blythman, 'Blood on the Boil', *Guardian* (London), 14 May 1998. It was reported that 'Britain's blood supplies are almost certainly infected with the human form of mad cow disease, the Government has been told', *Daily Mail* (London), 6 July 1998, at 20. The NHS has been reported as considering banning all transfusion recipients from donating blood, which would eliminate ten per cent of donations. James Meikle, 'CJD Fears Could Lead to Blood Donor Ban', *Guardian* (London), 21 November 2000. It is feared that half the UK blood donors will refuse to donate from fear that the CJD screening process will reveal they are infected. James Meikle, 'Blood Supplies "Could Be Halved" as Donors Fear Results of vCJD Tests', *Guardian* (London), 2 October 2001.

[69] For an early report of suspicions of the possibility of CJD infection from donated implanted tissue, see J. Laurance, 'Transplant Patients Risk CJD After Receiving Tissue from Infected Woman', *Independent* (London), 1 December 1997, at 3.

[70] In a 1998 study, researchers found a startling and confusing link between CJD and 'exposure to leather, including wearing it'. Celia Hall, 'Research Fails to Find Link Between Beef and CJD', *Daily Telegraph* (London), 10 April 1998, at 13.

[71] On suspicions that part of the UK water supply is contaminated with BSE/CJD, see Charles Arthur, 'Animals Raise New Fear on Spread of CJD', *Independent* (London), 30 August 1997, at 8; Anthony Mitchell *et al.*, 'Don't Drink the Water', *Daily Express* (London), 25 May 2001. Similar fears exist in Ireland where a high proportion of water is contaminated with animal slurry. Lorna Siggins, 'Report Attempts to Put Public's Fears in Context', *Irish Times*, 12 December 2000, at 7.

[72] Rhodes, *Deeply Feasts*, footnote 11 above, at 220–1.

Community policy.[73] In response to this crisis, the EU amended the Directive in 1999 to remove the possibility that a Member State could bar claims concerning unprocessed primary products.[74]

The scientific uncertainty concerning the nature and transmission routes of these infectious diseases makes it of considerable concern that some captive and free-range deer and elk in Colorado, Montana, Nebraska, Oklahoma, South Dakota, and Wyoming suffer from Chronic Wasting Disease (CWD), a member of the transmissible spongiform encephalopathies (TSE) group of diseases which also includes BSE and CJD.[75] Indeed, an estimated 15 per cent of wild deer in the United States are already infected, making CWD a 'front-burner' public-health concern.[76] Culls of thousands of US deer and elk are under way.[77] It is significant that three hunters in America have already died of CJD.[78] Finally, transmissible mink encephalopathy has broken out in at least eleven US milk farms.[79]

The *general* state of infection in human food in the United Kingdom has become a matter of grave national importance. There are between 4.5 and 5.5 million cases of food poisoning per year.[80] Poisonous bacteria have been found in half of all chickens sold,[81] while it has been reported that

73 Martyr, 'BSE in Europe' footnote 11 above. See also the withering report by the European Parliament on the BSE fiasco at the EU level, Resolution on the Results of the Temporary Committee of Inquiry into BSE, 1997 OJ (C 85) 61. At the UK level see the Phillips inquiry: Report to an Order of the Honourable the House of Commons for the Report Evidence and Supporting Papers of the Inquiry into the Emergence and Identification of Bovine Spongiform Encephalopathy (BSE) and variant Creutzfeldt-Jakob Disease (vCJD) and the Action Taken in Response (Oct. 2000), available at http://www.bse.org.uk/report/index.htm (last visited 6 May 2002).

74 Council Directive 1999/34/EC, 1999 OJ (L 141) 20–1. On the exemption, see Stapleton, *Product Liability*, footnote 16 above, at 303–5.

75 'Mad Cow-Like Disease Spreads Rapidly in Wild Deer', *Environmental News Network*, 1 October 2001; David Usborne, 'Elk Get Blame as US is Hit by CJD Scare', *Independent* (London), 21 January 2001.

76 Joseph B. Verrengia, 'Disease Prompts Slaughter of Elk, Deer Herds', *Seattle Times*, 17 March 2002, at A7.

77 Ibid.

78 Charles Clover, 'Vets to Test Wild Animals for "Mad Deer Disease"', *Daily Telegraph* (London), 3 May 2001.

79 David Usborne, '"Mad Cows" May Have Reached Midwest', *Independent* (London), 15 January 2001.

80 'Danger of Eating Out', *Daily Express* (London), 10 January 2002; 'Rise in Food Poisoning Cases', *Daily Telegraph* (London), 12 February 2002.

81 Richard Alleyne, 'Poisonous Bacteria Found in Half of All Chickens Sold', *Daily Telegraph* (London), 17 August 2001.

E-coli has been discovered in half of Britain's cattle herds.[82] The concern over British food was compounded by the 2001 outbreak of foot-and-mouth disease. The number of animals affected was around 3,500,[83] and ten million animals (17 per cent of all UK livestock) were slaughtered in the subsequent preventative cull.[84]

Finally, the national supply of blood products in the United Kingdom is suspected of being generically infected. The first high-profile wave of infection was by the HIV virus. This was followed by a wave of Hep C infection. The impact of these disasters on the UK haemophiliac population of 5,000 is illustrative: their use of infected blood products during the 1980s resulted in 1,200 contracting HIV of whom 800 have died,[85] and 4,800 contracting Hep C of whom more than 110 have died.[86] In the United Kingdom, virtually all haemophiliacs who are presently over the age of fifteen are infected with HIV, Hep C or both.[87] To date, Australia, Belgium, Canada, Germany, Hong Kong, New Zealand, Switzerland, and the United States have banned blood donations by people who had lived in the United Kingdom during the BSE/CJD outbreak.[88] Of course, the United Kingdom cannot impose a similar ban on its domestic donors.

[82] Leake, 'New Health Alert', footnote 48 above, at 5G.

[83] C. Clover and S. Barwick, 'Foot and Mouth Epidemic is World's Worst', *Daily Telegraph* (London), 4 September 2001.

[84] R. Uhlig, '10 Million Animals Were Slaughtered in Foot and Mouth Cull', *Daily Telegraph* (London), 23 January 2002. It is of interest that while the cost of the foot-and-mouth outbreak was £2 billion, £1.2 billion of this is being claimed from the EU. See Melissa Kite, *Times* (London), 23 November 2001, at 1.

[85] *Daily Telegraph* (London), 11 November 2001.

[86] H. Studd, 'Hepatitis Cases Land NHS With £10m Bill', *Times* (London), 27 March 2001, at 5L. In the United States, half the haemophiliac population contracted HIV or Hep C from blood products. Conk, 'Is there a Design Defect?', footnote 19 above, at 1090.

[87] See footnote 64 above. Compare the UK experience with the Hep C disaster in Canada. According to Michael Trebilcock, R. Howse and R. Daniels, 'Do Institutions Matter? A Comparative Pathology of the HIV-Infected Blood Tragedy', 82 (1996) *Va. L.Rev.*: 1407, 1485–6, it was conservatively estimated in 1996 that there are 100,000 people in Canada infected with Hep C, the current per unit risk of blood for Hep C is one in 40,000, as many as 12,000 people may have been infected with Hep C between 1986 and mid-1990 when screening began in Canada, and that 70 per cent of Canadian haemophiliacs over the age of seven are infected with Hep C. In Canada, class actions related to infection with Hep C from blood precipitated a settlement of $1.5 billion (Canadian) (Garry D. Watson, 'Class Actions: The Canadian Experience', 11 (2001) *Duke J. Comp. & Int'l L.*: 269, 282–3.

[88] See Patrick Barkham, 'Australia Bans Blood of Travellers to UK', *Guardian* (Australia), 22 September 2000; 'Blood Ban', *Sunday Times* (Canada), 18 July 1999, at 26; J. Carroll, 'Tighter Blood-Donor Rules Are Backed to Fight Spread of Mad-Cow Disease', *Wall Street Journal*, 5 June 2001, at B4. The bans apply to those who spent more than six months in the United Kingdom between 1980 and 1996.

Response of the *Restatement Third*

By omitting any substantive discussion in its text, the *Restatement Third* suggests that, apart from blood infection cases, the United States has had no significant case law experience with generic infection cases formulated as products liability claims. In addition, in the blood infection cases, the consensus seemed to be that it was too difficult to accommodate them coherently within the US products liability rule.[89] In other words, the US rule could not both extend to such cases and accommodate an adequately convincing explication of the policy and moral issues at stake. These cases had, after all, led to the widespread adoption of 'blood shield' statutes in most states.[90] But, if we were to speculate upon what approach to pathogenic infection cases would be taken under the *Restatement Third*, we would find it highly fractured according to the type of product:

(1) If the infection was contracted from human blood or human tissue, the *Restatement Third* provides no redress;[91]
(2) If the infection was contracted from a vaccine, the case would be decided under §6, which provides special protection to defendants;[92]
(3) If the infection was contracted from food, the case would be decided under §7, which would only provide recovery on the basis of the consumer expectations test, namely if a reasonable consumer would not expect the food to contain that infection. Even within this class, as we will see, the case law divides incoherently between sub-classes;[93]

[89] Even under a negligence theory, plaintiffs have typically failed. See Christopher DeMayo, 'Malpractice: Alaska Supreme Court Limits Duty of Hospitals to Disclose Risks of Blood Transfusions' 26 (1998) *J.L. Med. & Ethics*: 252, 252 (discussing a holding that there existed no duty to warn of risk of Hep C from transfusion); George W. Conk, 'The True Test: Alternative Safer Designs for Drugs and Medical Devices in a Patent-Constrained Market' 49 (2002) *UCLAL. Rev.* 737, 773–4 [hereinafter 'The True Test'].

[90] See Dan B. Dobbs, *The Law of Torts* (2000) 979–80. But see Conk, 'Is there a Design Defect?', footnote 19 above, at 1091–101 (staging a bracing attack on the protective attitude of blood shield statutes). For cases that succeeded despite these laws, see R. Jo Reser and Barbara A. Radnofsky, 'New Wave of Tainted Blood Litigation: Hepatitis C Liability Issues' 67 (2000) *Def. Couns. J.*: 306. Interestingly, the blood shield statutes followed an epidemic of transfusion-associated hepatitis in the mid-1960s. See Conk, 'Is there a Design Defect?', footnote 19 above, at 1098–9 (arguing that statutes' enactment led to the continuing transfusion infections in the decades that followed). 'The blood shield laws thus allowed the blood industry to continue to make blood products that were *avoidably* unsafe' at 1100.

[91] *Restatement Third*, footnote 7 above, §19(c).

[92] Ibid. §6. See also James A. Henderson, Jr. and Aaron D. Twerski, 'Drug Designs Different', 111 (2001) *Yale L.J.*: 151 (hereinafter 'Drug Designs') (rebutting Conk's criticism of the *Restatement Third*).

[93] See footnote 94 below and accompanying text.

(4) If the infection was contracted from other products, such as leather or woollen clothing, the case would be decided under §2. Even here, the treatment is explicitly fractured according to how we classify the product condition:
   (a) If the product condition is classified as a 'manufacturing defect' case, just as infected raw material cases are currently classed (on the basis that the condition of such infected products departs from their intended easily known design), recovery would be possible without further proof of defect, a 'reasonable alternative design' (RAD) or fault.
   (b) If the product condition is classified as a design/warning case (on the basis that the artificial manufacturing process did not introduce the problem), defectiveness would be determined by the cost-benefit/reasonableness principle and the RAD requirement.

Of course, this odd fragmentation prompts the question of why the *Restatement Third* differentiates between product types at all.[94] Perhaps, when a new legal rule emerges without a well-conceived theoretical basis, as was the case with the *Restatement Second*, courts are tempted to give the rule 'structure' by compartmentalising fact situations. In theory, if not in practice, it is very easy to distinguish cases of infection from eating meat and cases of infection from wearing infected clothing. The problem is that the law has no compelling reason to make the distinction – quite the contrary.

Consider the position of five different people who have contracted CJD from five different classes of BSE-infected products. Whatever the product vehicle for the infection, there is a very strong argument that the moral, deterrence, and other socio-legal concerns, which are common across all five cases, swamp any special factor relating to a particular product type. This is also true within a product class. For example, the incoherence of the treatment of infected food cases in the United States already highlights this flaw in the structure of the US regime; food which happened to be classed as 'adulterated' by infection is treated under a manufacturing errors framework, but food which happened to be classed as 'inherently infected' is treated more like a design case.[95]

Infection cases also illuminate the central absence of a rationale for the *Restatement Third* regime – namely, its attempt to treat manufacturing errors separately. Why are manufacturing errors treated differently from

[94] See Conk, 'Is there a Design Defect?', footnote 19 above, at 1088–90 (attacking the 'special, protective standard' given to prescription drugs and medical devices in §6).

[95] See Stapleton, 'BSE', footnote 45 above.

other product conditions in *Restatement Third*? The origin of the special regime for products liability is traditionally recognised as having drawn its features from both warranty and tort. However, warranty does not provide a foundation for the special treatment of manufacturing errors in our modern separate product regimes.

It is true that, for more than a century before the *Restatement Second*, courts allowed plaintiff-buyers to succeed in warranty claims against a product supplier even though the relevant product condition, such as infection in milk, was undiscoverable.[96] This warranty liability was, therefore, clearly strict. Moreover, these 'classical' warranty claims were just as available in relation to a product design and were just as strict. The reason that this strict-liability-for-design norm did not prove unworkable was that a warranty claim only succeeded if the product failed in one of its intended uses. In other words, classical warranty cases were effectively ring-fenced by the requirement that the plaintiff prove the product had 'failed in its intended use'. This was a requirement a plaintiff could rarely meet in a *design* case because, in virtually every case, the manufacturer would have at least tested his design to ensure it did what it was supposed to do. This meant that there was no need or rationale for warranty law to distinguish manufacturing from design cases. Both could be kept within bounds. Strict liability could be imposed on both.

Rather, it was from the negligence side that the special treatment of manufacturing errors originated. To many observers, negligence courts seemed to have ratcheted up the standard of care in manufacturing error claims, though the requirement of fault was never explicitly abandoned.[97] In time, this treatment led to the widespread conclusion that the law, in effect, imposed covert strict liability for manufacturing errors, albeit under the guise of the tort of negligence. In the United States, recognition of a separate products rule in tort in the 1965 *Restatement Second* aimed to regularise this perceived masking of a pocket of strict liability. So, what we now have in the *Restatement Third* is a regime where a product with a manufacturing error, *even if the error is unforeseeable*, by definition is defective. This is real strict liability for manufacturing errors. In contrast, a

[96] See *Frost v Aylesbury Dairy Co.* [1905] 1 KB 608, 610.

[97] I have yet to find a case based on a claim in the tort of negligence where the imposition of strict liability could be the only explanation for the result. For example, I have been unable to find a case where liability was imposed even though all parties agreed that the relevant risk was completely unforeseeable. Of course, if such a case did exist, it could only be explained on the basis of strict liability, because it is not possible to be careless in relation to a risk that is unforeseeable.

product with a dangerous design condition, if the danger is unforeseeable, cannot, *by definition*, be defective. Liability for design is not strict, but is based on and bounded by reasonableness.

As table 15.2 shows, pre-manufacture generic infection cases share factual characteristics with both the traditional classification of manufacturing defects cases and the traditional classification of design cases. This means that, before we can successfully classify pre-manufacture generic infection cases as one or the other, we need to be clear about what factual characteristics we have used to distinguish types of product condition and to be clear about the normative basis for drawing distinctions based on those characteristics. The Reporters define 'manufacturing defect' as the product departing from its intended design.[98] Infected products certainly depart from what the manufacturer *hoped* the product condition would be, but the manufacturing process did not *introduce* the danger. It follows that if the reason we subject manufacturing errors to strict liability is embedded in the idea that the danger was introduced into the product by the artificial process of manufacture, pre-manufacture generically infected products would fall outside the classification of 'manufacturing errors' and therefore outside strict liability treatment. The absence of an agreed-upon rationale for the imposition of strict liability on manufacturing error conditions is reflected in the incoherence of US case law on isolated infected products. Remarkably, this theoretical void exists even though these were the product conditions that were at the very heart of the new tort rule set out in the *Restatement Second*.[99]

We still have no principled explanation of why, for example, it is fair to hold a manufacturer strictly liable for some product flaws he could not discover (for example, some manufacturing errors), but not fair to do so in relation to a different set of product flaws he could not discover (namely, unforeseeable design dangers).[100] We have never clarified whether the normative motive for a harsher attitude to manufacturing errors stems from a *specific*, albeit unexpressed, rationale concerning the distribution

[98] *Restatement Third*, footnote 7 above, §2(a).

[99] See Stapleton, 'BSE', footnote 45 above.

[100] Of course, even in negligence, we tolerate significant pockets of liability that is strict – the objective standard of care, recovery for 'unforeseeable' consequences of breach, and unforeseeable eggshell skulls. There can be reasons for strict liability – for example, technology-forcing, loss spreading, superior information of the defendant, proof problems – but what we do not have is a reason substantial enough to delineate and defend the boundaries of this special pocket of strict liability for products from the general law of negligence.

Table 15.2. *How pre-manufacture generic infection (P-M GI) conditions straddle pro and con arguments concerning strict liability. 3R = Restatement Third*

Manufacturing error: arguments for strict liability	*P-M GI cases: favouring strict Liability*	*Pre-manufacture generic infection cases: characteristics*	*P-M GI cases: not favouring strict liability*	*Design conditions: arguments against strict liability*
Risk of unavoidable failure of manufacturing system should be on the manufacturer	*Hep C 2001*	*Danger not introduced by manufacturing system . . . militates against imposition of strict liability*	*Scholten 1999* *Korn 1995* *Ryan 1999*	*Risk of unavoidable inadequacy of scientific knowledge should not be on the manufacturer*
Fair to defendant to impose liability for unforeseeable product conditions	*Treatment under 3R, of raw materials*	*Risk is foreseeable in the generic class; but unforeseeable in the individual product . . .*	*Blood shield statutes*	*Unfair to defendant to impose liability for unforeseeable product conditions*
The pragmatic convenience of the production-line norm supports imposition of strict liability	*Treatment under 3R, of food seen as 'adulterated' by infection*	*The existence of the intended/hoped for production-line norm lends pragmatic support to imposition of strict liability*	*Treatment under 3R, of food seen as 'inherently' infected*	*The absence of a convenient norm militates against imposition of strict liability*

of risks associated with dangerous conditions introduced into products by artificial manufacturing processes. Additionally, we have never clarified whether the pragmatic argument in favour of strict liability for manufacturing errors, namely the availability of the production line norm, requires that departure from that norm *be due to* the failure of the production system. Case law experience on both sides of the Atlantic, even in cases of isolated infected products, gives little conceptual or pragmatic guidance on these crucial questions. This gap means it is not possible to determine from first principles how and why we should classify pre-manufacture generic infection cases.

In short, infection cases highlight both the absence of any fundamental rationale for the traditional tri-fold classification of product defects and suggest that it is unlikely for there to be any agreement on where and why such lines should be drawn before a full debate on the issue has occurred. A recent high-profile academic debate has unwittingly confirmed these points. In 2000, George Conk launched a scathing attack on how the *Restatement Third* had, under §6, given especially protective treatment to prescription drugs and medical devices.[101] As an exemplar of the problems he argued would be created by §6, Conk referred to the alleged 'design defect' in blood infected with Hep C.[102] In their response article, the Reporters attempted to rebut this classification by merely asserting that '[t]he plaintiffs in the blood cases did not claim that the blood products that harmed them were defectively designed . . . Instead, the contaminants that caused their harm constituted manufacturing defects.'[103] Conk's otherwise powerful reply seems just as ad hoc on the classification point:

> The basic distinction between a manufacturing defect and a design defect is that the former departs from the manufacturer's specifications and intentions for the product. A claim of design defect attacks the manufacturer-designer's product concept or its failure to adopt specific safety measures. . . .
>
> This 'departure from its intended design' definition of a manufacturing defect underlies my categorization of the defect in [the blood product] as one of design. . . . [V]iral contamination was not a flaw, a departure from design expectations, or even from consumer expectations, but rather was considered an 'acceptable risk', one left by the manufacturers to their customers' physicians to manage medically. Decisions on

[101] Conk, 'Is there a Design Defect?', footnote 19 above, *passim*.
[102] Ibid. at 1112.
[103] Henderson and Twerski, 'Drug Designs', footnote 92 above, at 160.

> whether . . . to flameproof fabrics are considered product design choices. . . . The defect in [the blood product] was neither an unintended departure from manufacturer's specifications, nor a disappointed consumer expectation defect like botulism in improperly canned food, but rather one of design. . . .
>
> Every batch of the concentrated blood proteins was made without departure from its intended design. The hemophiliacs' product liability claims, therefore, were not for manufacturing defects. Rather, the hemophiliacs . . . correctly alleged design defects, citing failure to market a practical and feasible alternative safer design.[104]

Response of the Directive and its clones: the problem of the European Commission and the 'official' record

Does the Directive provide a clearer resolution of the anomalous treatment of manufacturing errors that pre-manufacture generic infection cases expose? Certainly the Directive has no confusing fracturing around the classification of the product type. There is also no explicit classification based on type of product defect. Moreover, in the general law of the EU and its Member States, there are no laws shielding certain entities, such as blood banks, no equivalent doctrine of federal pre-emption under which so many US infection claims can be held to be barred, and no general tort immunity for state entities.[105] On the other hand, unlike in the US regimes,[106] under the Directive, a party cannot sue for physical loss to its commercial property.[107] This means, for example, that the claims against cattle feed producers currently being made by French farmers whose stock has allegedly contracted BSE from the feed cannot be brought under the Directive.[108]

[104] Conk, 'The True Test', footnote 89 above, at 772–3 (citations omitted).

[105] See, e.g., *Boulahanis v Prevo's Family Mkt, Inc.*, 583 N.W.2d 509, 509 (Mich. Ct. App. 1998) (holding the claims of consumers who were made sick (one died) by beef infected with E-Coli 0157 were pre-empted by the Federal Meat Inspection Act); cf. *Smith v Secretary of State for Health* (QB 15 February 2002) (Morland J), available at http://www.lexis.com (concerning a negligence claim against the government agency which regulates medicines by a child whose Reye's Syndrome was triggered by aspirin).

[106] David A. Fischer and William Powers, Jr, *Products Liability: Cases and Materials* (2nd edn 1994), p. 567; *Restatement Third*, footnote 7 above, §21 cmt. e.

[107] Directive footnote 3 above, art. 9.

[108] See Martyr, 'BSE in Europe', footnote 11 above, at 14. The UK exported potentially contaminated feed to sixty-nine countries. 'French Ministries are Raided in BSE Inquiry', *Independent* (London), 18 January 2001.

Finally, it is significant that under the Directive a product condition may qualify as a defect under Article 6, but not attract liability because it was undiscoverable at the time of circulation and so triggers the development risk defence in Article 7(e). In contrast, under §2(b) of the *Restatement Third* the undiscoverability of a design flaw prevents the product from even qualifying as defective.

Thus far, products case law under the Directive and its clones is very thin. Importantly, European case law concerning infected products is just as incoherent as infected product case law in the United States, though for different reasons. The principal case, at least of those available in English, is In Re *Hepatitis C Litigation (A v National Blood Authority)*.[109] Here 114 British claimants sued the National Blood Authority (NBA) over Hep C infection from blood products.[110] When the trial judge, Justice Michael Burton, looked at the idea of defect in Article 6 of the Directive, he rightly noted that the words in 'all relevant circumstances' must be read in the light of the statutory purpose.[111] But, as we have seen, there was no coherent and consistent statutory purpose behind the Directive. It was a political fudge that tried to square a circle. It used the rhetoric of strict liability and yet seemed to protect reasonable businesses in Article 6(2) and 7(e).[112]

An added problem for the trial judge was that a large proportion of the historical record available to the court consisted of papers from the European Commission, which, unlike conventional Westminster-style bureaucracies, is not obliged to provide neutral advice to the EU institutions. In particular, it could well be argued that the role of the European Commission prior to the Final Directive of 1985 was highly partisan.

[109] [2001] 3 All ER 289. The author of this chapter acted as Consultant to the defendants in this case.

[110] Ibid. Though this was a group action, it was also a 'test' case for the 3,000–5,000 people in the United Kingdom who have contracted Hep C from transfused blood and blood products. In the United States, there are about 2.7 million persons chronically infected with HCV. Miriam J. Alter, Deanna Kruszon-Moran and Omana V. Nainan, 'The Prevalence of Hepatitis C Virus Infection in the United States, 1988 Through 1994' 341 (1999) *New Eng. J. Med.*: 556, 556. Before 1990, 300,000 people received blood products and are therefore at risk of having been infected with hepatitis C. Reser and Radnofsky, 'New Wave', footnote 90 above, at 317. In the United Kingdom, most health care is delivered under the National Health System (NHS). The supply of goods and services under the NHS is free at the point of delivery, and there is no contractual relationship between the patient and any party within the delivery system.

[111] *In re Hepatitis C Litig*, 3 All ER at 290.

[112] Directive, footnote 3 above, arts. 6(2), 7(e).

It is well known that the thalidomide tragedy focussed, and perhaps unduly mesmerised, European attention on cases of generic product conditions. But it is inaccurate to conclude that all European countries wanted strict liability imposed on manufacturers, even if it was limited to cases of personal injuries. No Member State ratified the 1977 Convention of the Council of Europe,[113] which contained just such a regime. Another reason Member States failed to ratify the (non-EC) Convention was that, as we have seen,[114] within the European Communities political concern arose in the late 1970s to give the European Communities a 'human face', to show, for example, that it had consumers' interests at heart as well as being concerned with the facilitation of a level playing field for business.[115] However, Member States were firmly divided on the substantive content of any new Directive on products liability.

The result of the protracted and often grossly secretive negotiations,[116] a result not achieved until 1985, was a Directive with a cryptic text that even the European Court of Justice, the highest court in the EU, has attacked as hard to interpret.[117] A major danger when approaching the interpretation of the text is the past attitude of the Commission. Throughout the 1970s, the Commission embraced a strong preference for an unqualified strict liability being imposed on manufacturers for injuries due to the condition of their product. This is reflected in the fact that neither of the Commission's draft Directives (1976 and 1979)[118] mention any exculpatory ideas couched in terms of 'state of the art' or 'development risks'. Yet, there was intense concern within the European Parliament and the Council that substantial exculpatory provisions should be included.[119] For example, the official Economic and Social Committee (ECOSOC), that represents

[113] Council of Europe, *European Convention on Products Liability in Regard to Personal Injury and Death* (Strasbourg, 27 January 1977) available at http://conventions.coe.int/treaty/en/Treaties/Html/091.htm (last visited 6 May 2002).

[114] See footnote 29 above and accompanying text.

[115] Stapleton, *Product Liability*, footnote 16 above, at 47–8; Frank A. Orban, III, *Product Liability: a Comparative Legal Restatement – Foreign National Law and the EEC Directive* 8 (1978) *Ga. J.Int'l & Comp. L.*: 342, 374.

[116] On the secrecy of the Council's deliberations, see Commission's Written Answer to Question No. 1152/84.

[117] Case C-300/95, *Commission v United Kingdom* 1997 ECR I-2649, [1997] All ER 481 (providing a report which includes both the judgment of the European Court of Justice (ECJ) and the advice given to the Court in the previous Opinion of the Advocate General (23 Jan. 1997) (G. Tesauro) that reached the same conclusion via a somewhat different route).

[118] See First Draft Directive, footnote 31 above, at 9; Second Draft Directive, footnote 31 above, at 3.

[119] See footnote 31 above.

sectional interests (mostly workers)[120] and advises the Commission and the Council, maintained that industry should not be made 'liable for products which could not have been made to a safer standard at the time when they were put into circulation' and specifically noted that 'it may be in the patients' interests to put into circulation products which are known to have side-effects when taken by some or indeed all persons'.[121] The same concern prompted other EU institutions to make two critical exculpatory changes to the Commission's proposed text. One was the inclusion in the Article 6[122]definition of defect, not merely of the time qualification that a relevant factor was 'the time when the product was put into circulation', but the statement that 'a product shall not be considered defective for the sole reason that a better product is subsequently put into circulation'; the second was the inclusion of the development risk defence in Article 7(e) with an option for an individual Member State to exclude that defence.[123] The Commission's continued opposition to such pro-defendant amendments was deeply resented by some Members of the European Parliament. For example, in debate one Member accused the Commission of misleading the European Parliament in order to get the Commission's pro-plaintiff product liability proposals accepted while another complained that the European Parliament's proposals were 'arbitrarily changed by the Commission'.[124]

[120] Paul Craig and Gráinne de Búrca, *EC Law* (Oxford: Oxford University Press, 1995), pp. 89–90.

[121] ECOSOC Report, footnote 32 above, at 41–5.

[122] See footnote 34 above and accompanying text.

[123] Directive, footnote 3 above, at 29–33. See Kathleen M. Nilles, 'Note, Defining the Limits of Liability: a Legal and Political Analysis of the European Community Products Liability Directive', 25 (1985) *Va. J. Int'l L.*: 729, 754 (describing how it was the Council's Permanent Representatives Committee (COREPER) in February 1982 and not the Commission that formulated the route to the final 'options' compromise, abandoning the absolute position on development risks adhered to by the Commission); see also Amended Proposal from Presidency of Council (26 Apr. 1985), which sought to accommodate the position of six delegations opposed to liability for development risks. These were not the only points on which the Commission was defeated. For example, there was an insertion of an option concerning an exemption for unprocessed agricultural products.

[124] See *Eur. Parl. Deb.*, 1980–1981 OJ (Annex 1–256) 261, 293 (1980), quoted in the excellent study of the Directive's history by Nilles, 'Note', footnote 123 above, at 753, n. 143, 754, n. 146; see also Nilles, 'Note', footnote 123 above, at 757–8 (blaming the slow progress on the agreement of a Final Directive on, *inter alia*, the intransigence and the lack of rigour by the Commission that polarised interested parties); The Lord Griffiths *et al.*, 'Developments in English Product Liability Law: a Comparison with the American System', 62 (1988) *Tul. L. Rev.*: 353, 389 (concerning the strong opposition of the European Parliament to the inclusion of liability for development risks in the Commission's drafts).

The Commission's attitude seemed to be the result of three factors. First, at the outset, the Commission asserted, at least in public, that Member States genuinely were willing and committed to providing a legal entitlement to compensation to those in the future who found themselves in the equivalent position of the thalidomide children. This necessitated the imposition of genuine strict liability, at least for unforeseeable generic design conditions. Secondly, the Commission shared a common crude misconception, circulating in Europe in the 1970s, that the common law in the United States had successfully adopted genuine strict liability for products merely by making producers liable on proof that the plaintiff had been injured by a 'defect' in the product.[125] Of course, the actual position was very different and less impressive. The reformists behind §402A of the *Restatement Second*[126] were centrally concerned only with manufacturing errors. Here the notion of 'defect' seemed unproblematic because it could be, it was thought, conveniently determined by the production line norm. Later events revealed that §402A failed to address the sort of claims that were to trouble the legal regimes in the United States (classic design cases) and Europe (allegedly unforeseeable generic conditions). Thirdly, the Commission seemed to think that the notion of defect could be deployed independently of an evaluation of the 'appropriate' or 'reasonable' level of safety to be required of a product. This crudely sanguine attitude cannot withstand the most elementary consideration of classic design cases such as a claim that a chair or axle was 'not strong enough'.[127]

By the time of the adoption of the Final 1985 Directive, it was clear that the UK Government would only agree to a Directive that gave industry the capacity to answer a claim on the basis that it had done all it realistically could and should have done to make the product safe in all the circumstances.[128] Other demands by Member States ensured the final

[125] See, e.g., Hans Claudius Taschner, 'Product Liability in Europe: Future Prospects' in *EEC Strict Liability in 1992* (New York: Practising Law Institute, 1989) 81, 89: ('[T]he concept of defect has not caused any practical difficulties for courts throughout the world').

[126] *Restatement Second*, footnote 7 above, §402A.

[127] See footnotes 20–4 above and accompanying text.

[128] The British Minister for Consumer Affairs noted the United Kingdom's insistence on 'the incorporation of the "state of the art" defence'. See 991 *Parl. Deb., H.C.* (5th Ser.) col. 1107 (1980); see also at cols. 1106–200; Department of Trade and Industry Explanatory Memorandum of European Community Legislation (1985). '[The 1979 Commission draft Directive] was not acceptable. One of the most important changes to be sought was the incorporation of a "state of the art" defence. This is now incorporated in the proposed [Final] Directive' para. 11. 'The standard [of defectiveness] should be determined objectively having regard to all the circumstances in which the product was put into

text of the Directive was a political 'fudge' that tried to square the circle of disagreement between Member States by use of ambiguous terms and a cryptic text. Most importantly, other Member States acquiesced in the attachment – to the Council's decision on the Directive – of a number of Unilateral Statements by individual delegations, including a *Unilateral Statement by the United Kingdom Delegation on Article 7(e)* which stated:

> This provision should be interpreted in the sense that the producer shall not be liable if he proves that, given the state of scientific knowledge at the time the product was put into circulation, no producer of a product of that kind could have been expected to have perceived that it was defective in design.[129]

The whole purpose of the insertion, against the wishes of the Commission, of the exculpatory defence in Article 7(e), as well as the time dimension introduced into the notion of defect in Article 6, was to give a substantial protection to industry, particularly new and innovative industries. Yet, even after the adoption of the 1985 Directive with these provisions, Hans Claudius Taschner,[130] a principal member of the Commission's products liability team, maintained that the correct interpretation of the Directive was one that gave little, if any, room for defendants to exculpate themselves from liability.[131]

circulation . . . [and] a product shall not be considered defective for the sole reason that a better product is subsequently put into circulation' para. 13. 'Both the House of Commons and industry consider [the development risks] defence as a *sine qua non* for their agreement to the Directive. It is now included in the proposed [Final] Directive.'

[129] *Note Point 'A' au Conseil (8205/85): Statements to be Entered in the Council Minutes* para. 7 (23 July 1985).

[130] Sometime Head of Division, Directorate General for Internal Market and Industrial Affairs, European Commission; Adviser to the Hep C claimants.

[131] Concerning the risk in the thalidomide case, Taschner claims it was not 'absolutely unforeseeable' and so was not a true example of a development risk for which liability was removed by Article 7(e). Hans Claudius Taschner, 'European Initiatives: The European Communities', in C. J. Miller (ed.) *Comparative Product Liability* (1986) 1, 6 (claiming that the opposite was 'wrongly considered by the two British Law Commissions'). Since, he asserts, the criterion for development risk is that the 'existing defect could not be discovered by anyone', Taschner's view is that Article 7(e) would not protect the producer in a new thalidomide-like disaster (at 11); see also Hans Claudius Taschner, 'Harmonization of Products Liability Law in the European Community', 34 (1999) *Tex. Int'l L.J.*: 21, 32 [hereinafter 'Harmonization of Products Liability Law']. In contrast to Taschner, most commentators consider that Article 7(e) would protect the defendant in such cases. See Aubrey L. Diamond, 'Product Liability and Pharmaceuticals in the United Kingdom', in G. F. Woodroffe (ed.), *Consumer Law in the EEC* (London: Sweet and Maxwell, 1984) 129, 135 (citing the view of the Pearson Commission

The political reality is that the Thatcher Government used its EU legislative veto to insist on protection for a producer who had done all it realistically could and should have done to make the product safe in all circumstances. More generally, the literature on the status of Unilateral Statements from Member State delegations is thin. This is odd given that their existence exposes the political controversies to which they bear witness. It is also odd given the potential political storm that may flow by any crude enforcement of a rule that Unilateral Statements should not be considered in determining the appropriate interpretation of the EU instrument.[132] Certainly, an argument can be made that unless the European Court of Justice is willing to imply that the other Member States acted in bad faith in acquiescing to the UK's Unilateral Statement, the Directive should be read, at least by UK courts, in the light of the UK's Unilateral Statement and the clear demands of the United Kingdom for a substantial defence for industry. This was, after all, a Directive that *explicitly* gave considerable latitude to Member States to achieve local variations in the regime it sets up. Indeed, this political reality seems to be what lay behind the fairly cryptic European Court of Justice judgment in favour of the United Kingdom in *European Commission v United Kingdom*,[133] which Taschner has attacked as 'misunderstanding' the Directive.[134] The European Court of Justice held that the development risk defence in Article 7(e) would succeed if the knowledge of the defect existed but was not 'accessible'.[135] The liability regime demanded by the United Kingdom would also require

at para. 1259); Christopher Newdick, 'Strict Liability for Defective Drugs in the Pharmaceutical Industry' 101 (1985) *LQR*: 405, 408; M. Griffiths, 'Defectiveness in EEC Product Liability' 1987 *JBL*: 222, 227; *Parl. Deb.* (H.L.) col.1455 (1980) (Lord McKay of Clashfern).

[132] See, e.g., Joined Cases C-283/94, C-291/94 & C-292/94, *Denkavit Int'l BV, VITIC Amsterdam BV, Voormeer BV v Bundesamt fur Finanzen*, 1996 ECR I-5063 at para. 28 (acknowledging that a substantial group of Member States had believed that 'when the Directive was being adopted by the Council, it was agreed that relatively vague terms should be used in order to allow for differing interpretations according to the requirements of the domestic legal systems'); see also Jan Klabbers, 'Informal Instruments Before the European Court of Justice' 31 (1994) *CMLRev.*: 997, 1008–9 (discussing reliance on Member States' Declarations in legislation minutes); Sir William Nicoll, 'Note the Hour – and File the Minute' 31 (1993) *J. Common Mkt. Studs.*: 559, 561 (stating that '[d]eclarations have no legal value, but they offer some insight into the intentions of the parties').

[133] Case C-300/95, *Commission v United Kingdom*, 1997 ECR I-2649, [1997] All ER 481.

[134] 'Harmonization of Products Liability Law', footnote 131 above, at 34.

[135] Case C-300/95, *Commission v United Kingdom*, 1997 ECR I-2649, [1997] All ER 481. See Taschner, 'Harmonization of Products Liability Law', footnote 131 above, at 34.

similar 'reasonableness' glosses on other issues such as whose ideas were relevant to 'knowledge'.[136]

In short, official EU papers describing the Commission's pre-1985, pro-plaintiff vision for the content of a products directive and later comments by Taschner do not in any way capture the true compromise finally adopted in the text of the Directive. They fail to address the profound implications for the defect notion of the insertion of the time clause in Article 6 and the dilemma of how to determine defectiveness in design or warning, such as the classic design cases of the chair and axle, without the consideration of notions of behaviour and reasonableness. Commission documents also afford Article 7(e) a width so narrow and nugatory that they could suggest the United Kingdom was deceived by the other Member States in the meaning of the alleged agreement to the Final Directive. Yet it seems that Commission documents available to the court in the Hepatitis C case far outnumbered any official papers opposed to Commission proposals. These are critical points for addressing the dilemma of what is to be taken as the statutory purpose of any EU Directive.

Response of the Directive and its clones: the Hepatitis C judgment

In the Hepatitis C case, the court noted that the Directive 'must be construed by reference to its recitals and indeed to its legislative purpose, insofar as it can be gleaned otherwise than from the recitals'.[137] The court asserted in a number of places that 'the purpose of the Directive is to achieve a higher and consistent level of consumer protection throughout the Community and render recovery of compensation easier, and uncomplicated by the need for proof of negligence'.[138] Yet the court gives little if any weight to Recital 7, which states a purpose of the Directive was to vindicate the notion that a 'fair apportionment of risk between the injured person and the producer implies that the producer should be able to free himself from liability if he furnishes proof as to the existence of certain exonerating circumstances'.[139]

[136] J. Stapleton, 'Products Liability in the United Kingdom: the Myths of Reform' 34 (1999) *Tex. Int'l L.J.*: 45, 59.

[137] *In re Hepatitis C Litig.*, [2001] 3 All ER 289, 305.

[138] Ibid. at 310–11; see also ibid. at 328 (stating that the purpose of the Directive was 'consumer protection and ease of recovery of compensation'); ibid. at 342 (stating purpose was 'to prevent injury and facilitate compensation for injury'); ibid. at 341 (explaining analysis of Article 7(e) to achieve underlying purpose).

[139] Ibid. at 304 (quoting Recital 7).

Similarly, the court neglects two important political facts: the United Kingdom's Unilateral Statement and the fact that the European Parliament and Member States successfully insisted, against the opposition of the Commission, on the inclusion of exculpatory provisions to achieve that 'fair apportionment'. Moreover, the court marginalises the important legal fact that, when in *European Commission* v *United Kingdom*,[140] the European Court of Justice read into the Directive extra concerns, they were ones that provided exculpation for defendants. Finally, the court ignored the phenomenon well known among comparative lawyers that – in contrast to the 'candour' of pragmatic regimes such as those in England, Scotland and the Netherlands – courts in certain continental legal systems use 'hidden and indirect means of controlling' liability arising from the formal statement of broad entitlements.[141] This phenomenon is obviously relevant to properly 'domesticating' an EU provision couched in vague terms.

In short, the court in the Hepatitis C case was determined to give the Directive 'work to do' in the United Kingdom;[142] that is to give it a wider ambit of entitlement than existed elsewhere in the English law of obligations. It was eager to avoid a construction that would 'not only be toothless but pointless'.[143] The trial judge seems to have thought this required an adoption of the construction urged by the claimants. In my view, this was mistaken. For example, it would still be consistent with the pro-consumer purpose of the Directive, as selected by the judge, that the Directive was aimed merely at levelling up other Member States to the level of consumer protection already in place in the United Kingdom. In any case, the Directive *did* unequivocally make a number of improvements to the position of the UK consumer that did not require the court to adopt the claimants' construction.[144]

In my view, the 'reformist zeal'[145] of the trial judge in the Hepatitis C case simply preferred the heroic rhetoric of the claimants' cause.[146] His decision has already faced academic criticism,[147] and there are certainly

[140] 1997 ECR I-2649, [1997] All ER 481.

[141] M. Bussani and V. Palmer, *The Frontiers of Tort Liability: Pure Economic Loss in Europe* (2002), pp. 71, 152–3.

[142] *In re Hepatitis C Litig.* [2001] 3 All ER 289. [143] Ibid. at 340.

[144] Stapleton, 'Products Liability', footnote 136 above, at 61–2.

[145] Geraint Howells and Mark Mildred, 'Infected Blood: Defect and Discoverability. A First Exposition of the EC Product Liability Directive' 65 (2002) *MLR*: 95, 98.

[146] *In re Hepatitis C Litig.* [2001] 3 All ER 289.

[147] See C. Hodges, 'Compensating Patients' 117 (2001) *LQR*: 528; Howells and Mildred, 'Infected Blood', footnote 145 above, at 96–8; Simon Pearl, 'Damaging Goods' *Solicitor's Journal*, 11 May 2001, at 424.

some very strange factual holdings and pieces of legal reasoning in it – most of which are not directly pertinent to the topic of this chapter. However, one core aspect of his approach is relevant here. To find in the claimants' favour, the trial judge created a new set of central concepts and then implied them into the Directive. Specifically, while he concludes that 'there is no place . . . in the Directive' for the 'American terms' of manufacturing defects, design defects and instruction defects,[148] the trial judge himself read into the Directive distinctions based on a type of product defect. Indeed, he constructed a whole new class of product conditions called 'non-standard products' which covers not only manufacturing error cases but also covers pre-manufacture infection cases.[149] By then asserting that a non-standard product was to be compared with the 'standard' (that is intended, and hoped for) state of the product (namely one that was not infected), the judge arrived at the conclusion that the infected batches of blood had been defective.[150] The classification as 'non-standard' seems inexorably to lead to a finding of defect, at least if there has been no warning.

Though the defect provision, Article 6, stresses that 'all the circumstances' are to be taken into account, the judge reformulates this as all the circumstances relevant to the purpose of the Directive. By this device and his focus only on the pro-consumer goals of the Directive as set out in its recitals, he excludes, as irrelevant to defectiveness, issues such as the avoidability of the dangerous condition,[151] the utility of the product line, whether safer substitutes were feasible and the cost of seeking to limit the risk, even if these factors are judged with hindsight. It goes without saying the judge also ignored the sort of public-policy concerns about the special importance of a blood supply that led to the blood shield laws in the United States.[152]

[148] *In re Hepatitis C Litig.* [2001] 3 All ER 289, 318.

[149] Ibid., at 319. And product conditions classified 'as a design defect resulting from a way in which the producer's system was designed'.

[150] Ibid.

[151] In my view, avoidability is not *necessarily* relevant, but can be when it is combined with the absence of available substitutes and high utility. For instance, what if a vaccine is developed that can immediately and permanently clear the HIV virus from the system of an infected foetus? The vaccine involves a risk of slight hearing loss to 1 to 3 per cent of affected foetuses but there is no test to pre-screen which foetus will have its hearing damaged. The foetus cannot be warned, the utility of the vaccine is high (because there are no substitutes), and the cost risk is low. Yet according to the trial judge, these factors are not relevant to defect. Ibid. at 290.

[152] Hodges, 'Compensating Patients', footnote 147 above, at 530. The trial judge went on to hold, in relation to the defence in Article 7(e), that once risk of infection in a product sector was 'known', the development risk defence was no longer available even if the dangerous

However, consider how this approach to the Directive would apply to 'standard' products such as aspirin, an issue that is of immediate concern to the public. Even consumer advocates regard aspirin as non-defective despite the risk it poses to some users and the consumers' unawareness of the risk.[153] On the one hand, the Hepatitis C court chose consistency and stated that utility should be ignored here just as it asserts it should be ignored when judging the defectiveness of non-standard products.[154] But if we ignore the overall social utility of the standard product, which in the case of aspirin is universally acknowledged to be massive, how can aspirin's non-defectiveness be established given that, from the perspective of the victim, its cost outweighed its benefit? The court's attempt to bridge this gap in its approach is the mere assertion that 'standard products, if compared at all, will be compared with other products on the market'.[155] But this is, of course, itself a *utility* measure: a product's defectiveness being measured by any available substitutes on the market that have more successfully avoided the risk![156]

What the Hepatitis C court seems to have done is extend the former class of 'manufacturing errors' to include pre-manufacture infection cases, naming this new class 'non-standard' products. This extension does not avoid the unprincipled and anomalous treatment of a class of product conditions simply on the basis that they can be cheaply compared with a product condition that the producer hoped to produce, the so-called 'standard' product. If aspirin can be judged non-defective even though it cannot be made safe for all users, why should non-standard products that cannot be made safe for all users, but which have equivalent massive social benefits and low risk not also be judged non-defective? This point is not academic but one of real practical importance.

Say a product is developed that immediately clears HIV infection from an infected foetus's system but causes mild hearing loss in a percentage of those treated, and the state of scientific knowledge is such that this can neither be avoided nor the cases where this injury will occur be identified

condition was not discoverable in an individual product. *In re Hepatitis C Litig.* [2001] 3 All ER 289 at 305. This means that after the first victim's claim, non-standard products cannot attract the defence.

153 Howells and Mildred, 'Infected Blood', footnote 145 above, at 101.

154 *In re Hepatitis C Litig.* [2001] 3 All ER 289, at 339.

155 Ibid., at 319.

156 Directive, footnote 3 above, art. 6. Article 6 of the Directive, with its emphasis on time frame, strongly suggests that the existence or non-existence of feasible substitutes was intended as relevant to the notion of 'defect' (ibid.).

in advance. When the defectiveness of the product is being determined under the Directive, why should it matter if the product is a pure chemical preparation (like aspirin, a 'standard' product) to which an undetectable percentage of users is prone, or a vaccine derived from blood which has an undetectable infection in some percentage of doses (like Factor VIII, a 'non-standard' product)?[157] If, as the Community has said, one of its major aims is to promote competition and innovation, and if, as it has also said, 'effective legal protection is a vital incentive for innovation',[158] there seems to be some room for the argument that innovation leading to the development of one form of a HIV product should not be disproportionately inhibited. Yet this is exactly what is threatened by the approach taken by the Hepatitis C court.

My general point here is not that the decision in the Hepatitis C case was necessarily wrong.[159] It is to show that, like the *Restatement Third*, the Directive does not accommodate pre-manufacture infection cases at all clearly because the entire regime lacks a coherent rationale. But whereas the failings of the *Restatement Third* stem from the over-compartmentalisation of doctrine and the neglect of discoverability issues, in Europe it was the incoherent political purpose of the Directive and its fudged terminology that has presented EU courts with the job of choosing the central norms on which it is to be read. Whichever side of the normative line one might choose, it is impossible to be

[157] The approach of the court in the Hepatitis C case seems to dictate that the vaccine is defective (*In re Hepatitis C Litig.* [2001] 3 All ER 289, at 339). But how odd, then, that such a lifesaving product with no substitutes is defective but a non-lifesaving standard product with many safer substitutes, such as a car, may be judged non-defective!

[158] *Green Paper on Innovation from the European Commission*, COM (95) 688 final at 19. See C. Hodges, 'Development Risks: Unanswered Questions' 61 (1998) *MLR*: 560, 561–2. This was also the concern of ECOSOC when it advised the Directive that it should not inhibit innovation (see footnote 32 above). But see Mark Mildred and Geraint Howells, 'Comment on Development Risks: Unanswered Questions' 61 (1998) *MLR*: 570 (a critique of Hodges's article).

[159] In my view, the text of the Directive clearly failed to achieve the imposition of strict liability on product manufacturers. Unless those who hoped that it would do so accept that it failed to do so and act to ensure that the Directive is reformed carefully and precisely to achieve this imposition, continued confusion is likely as courts are forced 'to make it up as they go along'. The Hepatitis C case also raises an interesting issue concerning the feasibility of a contribution action by the National Blood Authority (NBA) against any pharmaceutical company who had supplied the NBA with infected blood products. In some other jurisdictions such companies are required to contribute substantial sums to the state compensation schemes for hepatitis C victims of infected blood products. Ina Brock, 'State Compensation for HCV Infections in the Federal Republic of Germany' (December 2000) *European Prod. Liab. Rev.*: at 16.

confident that the text of the Directive delivers a clear vindication of that position.

Other responses to pre-manufacture generic infection cases

Three cases show that a court dealing with the Directive or its clones might simply opt to use norms opposite to those chosen by the Hepatitis C court.[160] In *Scholten v The Foundation Sanquin of Blood Supply*,[161] a Dutch court held that while the HIV-infected blood was defective, it was protected by the development risk defence in the Directive. Similarly, a Canadian judgment, albeit not a case on the Directive, reflected the same normative impulse as that at work in *Scholten*. In *Ter Neuzen v Korn*,[162] the Canadian Supreme Court refused to imply a warranty of merchantability in a case involving HIV infection from an artificial insemination procedure, noting in dictum that 'it must be recognized that biological products such as blood and semen, *unlike manufactured products*, carry certain inherent risks'.[163] The court held that at most the standard should be one of reasonableness.[164]

Thirdly, we have *Ryan v Great Lakes Council*, an Australian case of food poisoning from hepatitis-infected oysters.[165] The plaintiffs failed in their claim under a clone of the Directive. Though the judge found the product was defective, he held that the development risk defence protected if the defect *in the individual product* was not capable of discovery and this was the case with the oysters.[166] In terms of our conflicting norms, the judge agreed with the impulse in *Scholten* and *Ter Neuzen* – that the risk of scientific unavoidability should not rest on the oyster-growers.[167] He refused to distinguish between the unfairness in holding manufacturers

160 Certainly it is not unusual for common law courts dealing with strict liabilities to embrace this opposite norm. For example, when addressing the strict liability provision against misleading and deceptive conduct in §52 of the Trade Practices Act 1974 (Austl.), a court recently stated that 'it cannot reasonably be expected that the supplier is to inform the public of every possible risk . . . in the ordinary course of human affairs things go wrong in connection with the supply of products and services and . . . nobody could reasonably assume, absent disclosure, that such supply will be risk free' (*Johnson Tiles Pty v Esso Austl. Ltd* [2000] 104 FCR 564, 592, para. 67).

161 *Scholten/The Foundation Sanquin of Blood Supply*, Rb., Amsterdam, 3 Feb. 1999, NJ 621 (ann. DJV).

162 *Ter Neuzen v Korn* [1995] 3 SCR 674. 163 Ibid., at para. 108. 164 Ibid.

165 *Ryan v Great Lakes Council* [1999] 78 FCR 309, *on appeal sub nom., Graham Barclay Oysters Pty v Ryan* [2000] 102 FCR 307.

166 *Graham Barclay Oysters Pty*, 102 FCR at 462. 167 Ibid.

liable for *design flaws* they could not discover as in thalidomide and the unfairness in holding them liable for pre-manufacturing infections that they could not discover.

More fundamentally, the *Ryan* case, like most infection cases, highlights the artificiality of any product/service distinction in our law of obligations and the incoherence of the idea that products liability can sensibly look at the product and not the human behaviour surrounding its production and handling. In *Ryan*, the hepatitis infection of the oysters could have been prevented by reasonable surveillance of the quality of the water supply; thus, although the claim under the clone of the Directive failed, parallel claims in negligence succeeded.[168] This vitality of negligence,[169] a vitality rooted in its focus on human behaviour and the platform it provides in each case for the examination of the complex moral and economic dilemmas that can characterise product cases, prompts one to ask why we have a separate regime for product injuries at all.

But infection cases also prompt us to ask why such a regime is limited to products that have been commercially supplied. It is certainly tough to justify why we have a separate liability rule that only covers cases of infection by contact with infected products that have been commercially supplied, but not cases of, say, the American hunters infected by deer suffering from CWD, or neighbours infected by the wind from pyres burning stock slaughtered in a foot-and-mouth epidemic,[170] or farmers, abattoir workers, and slaughtermen infected by diseased animals?[171]

168 In this regard, it is interesting to note two recent Italian decisions (not dealing with the Directive) in which the Italian Ministry of Health was found to have been careless in relation to the risks of infections in blood, including the risk of Hep C infection during the same years at issue in *In re Hepatitis C Litig.* See Roberto Marengo, 'Court of Rome Rules on Liability for HIV, HBV and HCV Infections' (September 2001) *European Prod. Liab. Rev.*: 28 (discussing Court of Appeal of Rome decision (October 2000) and Court of Rome decision (June 2001)).

169 See Gary T. Schwartz, 'The Vitality of Negligence and the Ethics of Strict Liability' 15 (1981) *Ga. L.Rev.*: 963.

170 See *Daily Express* (London), 25 May 2001 (discussing atmospheric and water supply risk of CJD infection from burning of cattle in the foot-and-mouth cull); see also Nigel Hawkes, 'Animal Pyres Linked to Cancer Risk in Milk', *Times* (London), 26 May 2001, at 10. (Discussing chemical contamination by this route. More than six million of the animals slaughtered in the 2001 foot-and-mouth outbreak in the United Kingdom were burned on massive funeral pyres. Yet this process itself increased the atmospheric dioxin level by an average of 18 per cent over the nation, and there is now major concern about the contamination of milk from nearby herds!)

171 See D. Brown, 'Worst of the Epidemic Over by Election Day', *Daily Telegraph* (London), 26 April 2001, at 15; Sally Leany, 'We're Not Safe Yet', *Daily Telegraph* (London), 23 April 2001.

Certainly we now see from the *Restatement Third* that the experiment has been abandoned in the United States in the case of product conditions classed as design or warning conditions. In these cases, the US courts now recognise that you cannot coherently detach the concept of defect from behaviour. Perhaps it will be the infection cases that finally convince jurisdictions on both sides of the Atlantic and beyond that the treatment of imposing true strict liability only for manufacturing defects is not only anomalous and normatively unacceptable, but unworkable. If we are to treat infection cases as harshly as manufacturing error cases, which is what the English court chose to do in the Hepatitis C case, we will have to explain why transfusion recipients get a strict liability remedy while it is refused to those who, for example, collected the blood from infected donors or were otherwise environmentally infected.[172]

Conclusion

When we look through the dramatic lens of pre-manufacture generic infection product cases, we see that neither the *Restatement Third* nor the Directive coherently cope with the challenges they throw out. These cases force us to confront the question of whether it was wise, either as a matter of theory or pragmatism, for the *Restatement Third* to carve out for 'special' treatment classes of product claims according to proof shortcuts and according to product classes such as food. They also prompt us to ask whether it was wise to give separate treatment to manufacturing errors on the one hand from that given to design and warning conditions on the other. Even more fundamentally, the infection cases also force us to question why in the *Restatement Third* and the Directive we tolerate a special tort rule for injuries that happened to have been caused by commercially supplied products.

From the perspective of many decades of experience, there does not seem to be any particular moral, economic or social reason why the victims of such injuries should have been accorded any more special treatment than the victims of medical misadventures or environmental disasters – both areas in which plaintiffs typically find it hard to establish liability under traditional causes of action. The concern I share with other commentators is that the creation of special rules for injuries associated with

[172] Each year in the United States 5,600 health-care workers acquire Hep C through accidental needle sticks. See K. Elieson, 'Legal Standards Applicable to Transmission of HIV and Other Communicable Diseases' 61 (1998) *Tex. B.J.*: 938, 944.

commercially supplied products warps our laws of obligation for little if any benefit and blinkers us to important common themes that run through all personal injury cases generally.

Though neither the *Restatement Third* nor the Directive provides a clear accommodation for pre-manufacture generic infected product cases, we have seen that the reasons for their failure differ. Both regimes have developed through the particular, accidental and necessarily limited local experience.[173] Both have gaps. Both sides have lessons to learn from the experience of the other. The world's legal systems are not in competition. We simply do not confront the same advantages and disadvantages. But there are also limits on the fruitful lessons we can learn from other systems. Comparative law can be illuminating, but it has many limitations, not the least of which are the language barriers and prejudices most of us labour under when seeking to learn from the experience of other systems. It is a valuable corrective to the more ambitious claims of comparative law scholarship to remember that, even among most comparativists, deep expertise is limited to a few systems.

173 Eric A. Feldman, 'Blood Justice: Courts, Conflict, and Compensation in Japan, France, and the United States' 34 (2000) *Law & Society Rev.*: 651.

16

Comparing product safety and liability law in Japan: from Minamata to mad cows – and Mitsubishi

LUKE NOTTAGE

Mitsubishi, mad cows and Minamata

One of Japan's premier brand names, Mitsubishi, has come under severe pressure. On 24 March 2004, the Mainichi newspaper reported that Mitsubishi Fuso Truck and Bus Corporation ('Fuso', until recently part of Mitsubishi Motors Corporation or 'MMC') had announced the recall of an astonishing 113,000 large vehicles, admitting that defective hubs were the cause of wheels coming off and dozens of accidents. Over June, Fuso revealed that it had failed to report 159 cases of vehicle defects, causing 24 accidents resulting in injuries, 63 resulting in property damage, and 101 fires. On 6 May, seven former and current senior MMC executives were arrested on charges of false reporting to regulatory authorities, and professional negligence causing a death and injuries in Yokohama. On 10 June, moreover, other former MMC executives (including former president Katsuhiko Kawasoe) were arrested for professional negligence, involving another fatal truck accident in Yamaguchi Prefecture. Several, including Kawasoe, maintain their innocence, but Japanese prosecutors select their cases very carefully and therefore almost always succeed. Also in June, MMC announced a recall of another 170,000 smaller vehicles, involving seventeen passenger car models.[1] MMC was reported to have confessed that it 'hid twenty-six defects in its cars from regulators – in addition to four problems it publicised in 2000 – to avoid issuing recalls for the vehicles'.[2] Déjà vu?

[1] These events are documented in the news archives searchable at http://mdn.mainichi.co.jp (copies on file with the author). For a detailed analysis of prosecutions in Japan, see D. T. Johnson, *The Japanese Way of Justice: Prosecuting Crime in Japan* (Oxford: Oxford University Press, 2002).

[2] 'Mitsubishi Motors Hid 26 Other Defects In Cars – Report', *Dow Jones International News*, 2 June 2004.

Pressure had actually been building on MMC from July 2000 when, after an insider tip-off, Japan's Transport Ministry conducted a spot inspection. Officials uncovered evidence suggesting that for decades the company had hidden claims regarding its automobiles, and had conducted clandestine recalls of automobiles claimed or found to be defective. The Ministry passed on information for prosecutors to bring charges regarding the former breach of the Road Transportation Vehicles Law (fines of 0.4 million yen against the company, and 0.1 million yen against four company officers), and for the Tokyo District to enforce fines regarding the latter (totalling 4 million yen). Although the amounts were small, these actions confirmed already a reconfiguration in the cosy relationships between the automobile industry and its main regulator. This had begun with warnings given to Daihatsu in late 1998, followed by fines amounting to 1.4 million yen against Fuji Heavy Industry in March 2000. From mid-2000, MMC recalled 620,000 vehicles, losing significant market share. In addition, no doubt in the shadow of warranties or representations by Mitsubishi when agreeing that month to take a 34 per cent shareholding for US$2.1 billion, DaimlerChrysler announced in September 2000 that it would only pay US$1.9 billion, and appointed a key executive to the number-two position in Mitsubishi after its president resigned.[3]

In the wake of the further recalls and arrests in 2004, the Kyodo news service reported that the Japan Business Federation (Nippon Keidanren), Japan's most powerful business lobby, had barred MMC from its activities and may impose further sanctions.[4] A month later, Governor Shintaro Ishihara announced that the Tokyo Metropolitan Government would suspend purchases from MMC and Fuso, which had supplied about an eighth of its fleet. Even before these unusual events, a proposed reconstruction of MMC had been put into disarray. Despite being the largest shareholder now with 37 per cent, DaimlerChrysler announced on 24 March 2004 that it would not inject funds into the loss-making firm. Other shareholders

[3] L. R. Nottage, *Product Safety and Liability Law in Japan: From Minamata to Mad Cows* (London: RoutledgeCurzon, 2004), pp. 2–3.

[4] 'Keidanren Bars Scandal-Tainted M'bishi Motors from Group Activities', reported at http://home.kyodo.co.jp/all/news.jsp?news=business&an 10 May 2004. Summaries of a press conference that day published by the Federation state instead that 'Mitsubishi Motors Corporation informed Keidanren today that for the time being it wishes to abstain from membership activities and withhold from the post of a member of the Board of Directors as well as the Board of Executive Directors', and that this 'request' was met (http://www.keidanren.or.jp/english/speech/press/2004/0510.html).

within the Mitsubishi group (notably Mitsubishi Heavy Industries, general trading company Mitsubishi Corporation and the Bank of Tokyo-Mitsubishi) have reiterated their continued support for the automaker's reconstruction.[5] But throwing (increasingly scarce) 'good money after bad' risks severely affecting the entire group, in an increasingly cut-throat Japanese market.

How should we assess these disastrous events afflicting some of Japan's most well-known companies, beginning with 'the summers of living dangerously' in 2000 and 2001, when Mitsubishi Electric also had to withdraw thousands of television sets and the first case of mad cow disease ('BSE') was discovered? Is Japan still a 'producers' paradise', as in the 1950s and 1960s when economic growth was the top priority for the re-industrialising nation, even at the expense of large-scale injuries caused by defective products or environmental pollution in places like Minamata? Or do recent events point to more awareness and willingness to complain about and resolve these sorts of problems? A recent comprehensive study tends towards the latter interpretation.[6] Events such as the ongoing Mitsubishi saga should still be seen in a cautiously positive light, as a significant 're-orientation' of Japanese law and society towards a more appropriate balance between producer and consumer interests for the twenty-first century.

Comparing product liability and safety in Japan

Chapter 2 of the study compares the historical trajectory of product liability ('PL') law in Japan. From the perspective of more 'pro-consumer' substantive PL law (legislation and case law), Japan's path can be depicted as in figure 16.1

Thus, despite early mass-torts litigation especially over the 1960s, PL in Japan experienced more of a 'still-birth' from the early 1970s, compared to Australia, the EU and, especially, the US. Judicial innovation slowed. This may have been due to more general conservative reactions both within judicial administration, as well as a society afflicted by the Oil Shocks. But the slowdown also came about because legislators and bureaucrats did strengthen some product safety regulation, while industries introduced

[5] See the news archives searchable at http://mdn.mainichi.co.jp (copies on file with the author).

[6] See L. R. Nottage, *Product Safety and Liability Law in Japan: From Minamata to Mad Cows* (London: RoutledgeCurzon, 2004).

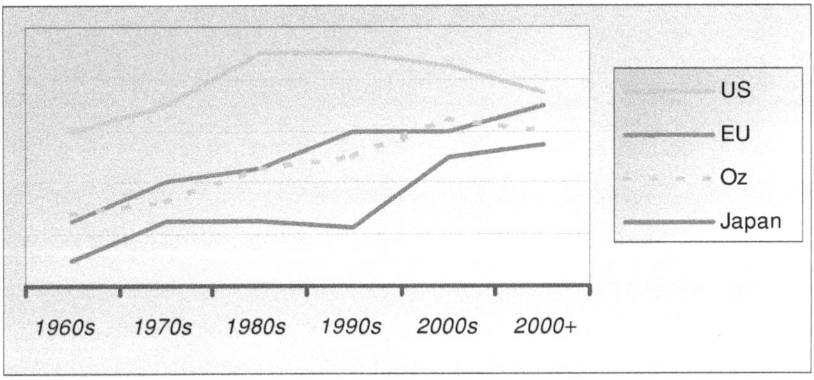

Figure 16.1 Comparative PL law trajectories

better product safety mechanisms. From the late 1980s, however, PL went through a 're-birth'. Reports of product defects emerged, and in 1993 the conservative Liberal Democratic Party lost its virtual monopoly on political power since 1950. These developments coincided with external pressures. Trade liberalisation accelerated, and the European Community's PL Directive of 1985 proved popular even beyond Europe (e.g. in Australia, when Part VA was added to the Trade Practices Act 1974 (Cth) in 1992), despite PL's retrenchment in the US (reflected and further cemented by the *Restatement Third*, promulgated in 1998). On 22 June 1994, Japan enacted its Product Liability Law ('PL Law'), modelled on the Directive and adding a new strict liability cause of action to the tort regime in the venerable Civil Code.

Chapter 3 compares the PL Law primarily with the (more or less) strict liability regimes in Europe, Australia and the US. The scope of liability under the PL Law is quite broad. Sometimes, this is true even relative to the US, especially as further reined in by 'tort reforms' through state legislation – a more general phenomenon also in Australia, since 2002. Japan's expansive tendency has been advanced by most judgments there since 1999, rendered quite quickly compared to the 'lead-in' time for the Directive in Europe or Part VA in Australia. No litigation explosion is evident or expected, given the constraints of Japan's broader civil justice system. However, those constraints are often shared especially by continental European legal systems, which continue to influence civil dispute resolution in Japan. Anyway, barriers to suit are being reduced following the recommendations of the blue-ribbon Judicial Reform Council presented to the Prime Minister in 2001. Recent measures to improve access to justice

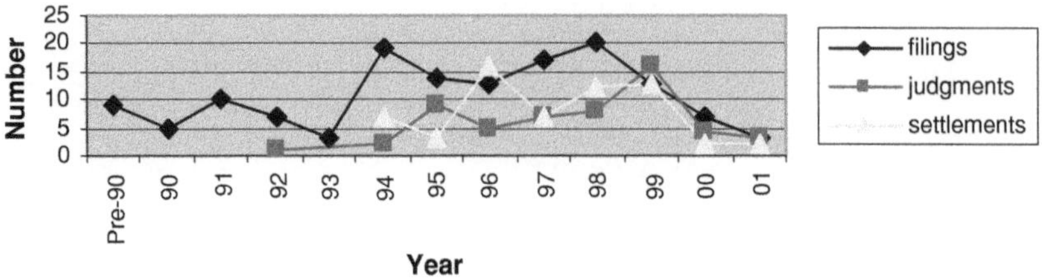

Figure 16.2 PL litigation in Japan over the 1990s

include the establishment of graduate 'law school' programmes aimed at more 'professional' legal education; significant increases in the numbers of judges, lawyers and prosecutors; more competition from 'quasi-lawyers', like patent attorneys; another round of civil procedure reforms; parallel strengthening of Alternative Dispute Resolution ('ADR' processes, such as enactment of a new Arbitration Law, in force from April 2004); and reintroduction of a 'lay assessor' scheme in serious criminal cases.[7]

Chapter 4 turns to the 'PL Law in action' at various levels. As well as somewhat more judgments annually, the data summarised in figure 16.2 show significantly more suits filed from the mid-1990s, and settlements seemingly more in favour of plaintiffs. This comes off a low base compared to the US, but the patterns are similar in Europe and Australia.

In addition, Japan has seen considerable activity in ADR. Rather than formal mediation services, PL ADR centres established by industry associations have mainly provided a further avenue to obtain legal and technical advice for those with possible claims about product safety, including borderline situations involving just quality of the goods themselves or related services. Local government funded consumer counselling services showed parallel growth. The net result, unsurprisingly, is widespread survey and more anecdotal evidence of a considerable ratcheting up of product safety activities on the part of Japan's manufacturers since the mid-1990s.

Chapter 5 of the study concludes with some questions and challenges for the 'Future of PL in Japan', particularly relevant in light of the ongoing sagas involving Mitsubishi and mad cows, and Japan's still-shaky economic recovery. No doubt there will be further calls to reform Japan's

[7] See also e.g. L. Nottage, 'Japan's New Arbitration Law: Domestication Reinforcing Internationalisation' (2004) *International Arbitration Law Review*: 54; L. Nottage, 'Civil Procedure Reforms in Japan: The Latest Round', (2004) 18 *Zeitschrift für Japanisches Recht / Journal of Japanese Law*: 2004; T. Ginsburg, 'Transforming Legal Education in Japan and Korea' 22(3) (2004) *Penn State International Law Review*: 433; and K. Anderson & E. Saint, 'Japan's Quasi-Jury (Saiban-in) Law' (2005) 6 *Asian Pacific Law & Policy Journal*: 233.

PL Law itself, for example by extending coverage to primary (unprocessed) agricultural produce, as occurred in 1999 with the EC Directive in the wake of Europe's much more extensive BSE epidemic. As in Europe, however, most focus will instead be directed on broader reforms in access to civil justice. Those reforms will provide additional scope for judges and commentators to restate or reformulate a growing corpus of PL law. Already, however, there has been and will be significant re-regulation, bolstering the substantive requirements and enforcement mechanisms in product safety regulation. So far, this has occurred on a product- or industry-specific basis in Japan. However, a new regulatory framework on product safety generally can be expected, probably again along EU lines, namely its recently revised Product Safety Directive. Such regulatory schemes offer considerable potential for synergy with – not just substitution for – private law liability regimes, to address appropriately the increasingly complex problems thrown up by the likes of BSE.

Americanisation, Europeanisation or globalisation?

Despite significant advances in understanding about BSE, the disease and its links to variant Creuzfeldt-Jakob Disease (fatal to humans) continue to generate scientific uncertainty and public controversy. In Japan, a twelfth mad cow was confirmed on 9 September 2004, the first in the Kyushu region. The news came just after the government's new Food Safety Commission moved to relax requirements that all cows be tested in Japan, limiting tests to those aged twenty months or older.[8] This should still help resolve an impasse with the US, created by Japan's ban on imports of US beef following the discovery there of its first mad cow in December 2003, because Japan had insisted that the US test all its cows. However, negotiations will be needed on the age below which untested US beef can be sent to Japan, as testing in the US (and the EU) is limited to cows aged 30 months or older. The US also does not track birth dates precisely, and wants to persuade Japan to accept some statistical sampling.[9] Thus, BSE

[8] Of the mad cows detected so far in Japan, one was 21 months old and another was 23 months old. All others were more than 30 months old, the norm in other countries. Meanwhile, it was reported on 1 June 2004 that Kirin Brewery Co. and a US biotechnology firm have succeeded in genetically engineering a cow to make it immune to BSE, but that the cow's cells will only be used to develop medicines for humans; it will not be used as a food source. See the news archives searchable at http://mdn.mainichi.co.jp (copies on file with the author).

[9] 'An End to Japan's Ban on American Beef May Be in Sight', *The Economist*, 11 September 2004, 75.

remains a major issue in global trade and diplomacy, as well as domestic law and politics. Yet the governance regime established by the World Trade Organisation retains serious enforcement and legitimacy problems. On the other hand, the experience first in the United Kingdom, then in Japan, and perhaps now in North America, suggests how powerful domestic interests may dominate or divert the norm-settling and enforcement potential of national regulators. Although the EU governance regime had its own difficulties in dealing with BSE, those prompted many reforms, now linked to a raft of broader governance changes for the EU. At least for some sectors, therefore, there seems to be considerable scope for Japan to develop a 'regional' governance regime. One pragmatic way to advance this agenda may be to add an explicit harmonisation agenda, with EU-like institutions, to its growing set of bilateral free-trade agreements.[10]

Even without injecting such a novel EU-like element into Japanese law and policy-making, it is clear that Japan has been heavily influenced by the European model in generating and implementing its strict liability PL regime. The model gained even more kudos from its adoption beyond Europe, as in Australia and other parts of the Asia-Pacific region. That process demonstrates that globalisation still does not equate to Americanisation, at least where – as in PL law and (especially) practice – the US maintains many idiosyncrasies.[11] Certainly, it is misleading to provide PL as an example of the 'Americanisation of Japanese law', even though Japan over the 1990s has indeed been subjected to political fragmentation, economic deregulation and growth in legal services markets.[12] Japanese private law's ongoing 'Europeanisation' also underpins the likelihood of Japan 're-regulating' product safety more on EU models. However, the extent and timing is likely to vary depending on the sectors involved, and the models that happen to be available. Coupling legal reform in Japan to rapidly evolving EU law therefore places growing demands on Japan's policymakers, including the academic community more generally.

[10] L. Nottage, with M. Trezise, 'Mad Cows and Japanese Consumers' 14(9) (2003) *Australian Product Liability Reporter*: 125; L. Nottage, 'Redirecting Japan's Multi-level Governance', paper presented at the symposium on 'Changes of Governance in Europe, Japan, and the US: Corporations, State, Markets, and Intermediaries', Japan-German Center Berlin, 9–11 September 2004 (forthcoming in proceedings co-edited by Harald Baum and Klaus Hopt).

[11] M. Reimann, 'Liability for Defective Products at the Beginning of the Twenty-First Century: Emergence of a World-Wide Standard?' 51 (2003) *American Journal of Comparative Law*: 751.

[12] D. Kelemen and E. C. Sibbitt, 'The Americanization of Japanese Law' 23 (2002) *University of Pennsylvania Journal of International Economic Law*: 269.

Appendix: Council Directive of 25 July 1985 on the approximation of the law, regulations and administrative provisions of the Member States concering liability for defective products (85/374/EEC)

THE COUNCIL OF THE EUROPEAN COMMUNITIES

Having regard to the Treaty establishing the European Economic Community, and in particular Article 100 thereof,

Having regard to the proposal from the Commission,[1]
Having regard to the opinion of the European Parliament,[2]
Having regard to the opinion of the Economic and Social Committee,[3]

Whereas approximation of the laws of the Member States concerning the liability of the producer for damage caused by the defectiveness of his products is necessary because the existing divergences may distort competition and affect the movement of goods within the common market and entail a differing degree of protection of the consumer against damage caused by a defective product to his health or property;

Whereas liability without fault on the part of the producer is the sole means of adequately solving the problem, peculiar to our age of increasing technicality, of a fair apportionment of the risks inherent in modern technological production;

Whereas liability without fault should apply only to movables which have been industrially produced; whereas, as a result, it is appropriate to exclude liability for agricultural products and game, except where they have undergone a processing of an industrial nature which could cause a defect in these products; whereas the liability provided for in this Directive should also apply to movables which are used in the construction of immovables or are installed in immovables;

Whereas protection of the consumer requires that all producers involved in the production process should be made liable, in so far as their finished product, component part or any raw material supplied by

[1] OJ No. C 241, 14. 10. 1976, p. 9 and OJ No. C 271, 26. 10. 1979, p. 3.
[2] OJ No. C 127, 21. 5. 1979, p. 61. [3] OJ No. C 114, 7. 5. 1979, p. 15.

them was defective; whereas, for the same reason, liability should extend to importers of products into the Community and to persons who present themselves as producers by affixing their name, trade mark or other distinguishing feature or who supply a product the producer of which cannot be identified;

Whereas, in situations where several persons are liable for the same damage, the protection of the consumer requires that the injured person should be able to claim full compensation for the damage from any one of them;

Whereas, to protect the physical well-being and property of the consumer, the defectiveness of the product should be determined by reference not to its fitness for use but to the lack of the safety which the public at large is entitled to expect; whereas the safety is assessed by excluding any misuse of the product not reasonable under the circumstances;

Whereas a fair apportionment of risk between the injured person and the producer implies that the producer should be able to free himself from liability if he furnishes proof as to the existence of certain exonerating circumstances;

Whereas the protection of the consumer requires that the liability of the producer remains unaffected by acts or omissions of other persons having contributed to cause the damage; whereas, however, the contributory negligence of the injured person may be taken into account to reduce or disallow such liability;

Whereas the protection of the consumer requires compensation for death and personal injury as well as compensation for damage to property; whereas the latter should nevertheless be limited to goods for private use or consumption and be subject to a deduction of a lower threshold of a fixed amount in order to avoid litigation in an excessive number of cases; whereas this Directive should not prejudice compensation for pain and suffering and other non-material damages payable, where appropriate, under the law applicable to the case;

Whereas a uniform period of limitation for the bringing of action for compensation is in the interests both of the injured person and of the producer;

Whereas products age in the course of time, higher safety standards are developed and the state of science and technology progresses; whereas, therefore, it would not be reasonable to make the producer liable for an unlimited period for the defectiveness of his product; whereas, therefore, liability should expire after a reasonable length of time, without prejudice to claims pending at law;

Whereas, to achieve effective protection of consumers, no contractual derogation should be permitted as regards the liability of the producer in relation to the injured person;

Whereas under the legal systems of the Member States an injured party may have a claim for damages based on grounds of contractual liability or on grounds of non-contractual liability other than that provided for in this Directive; in so far as these provisions also serve to attain the objective of effective protection of consumers, they should remain unaffected by this Directive; whereas, in so far as effective protection of consumers in the sector of pharmaceutical products is already also attained in a Member State under a special liability system, claims based on this system should similarly remain possible;

Whereas, to the extent that liability for nuclear injury or damage is already covered in all Member States by adequate special rules, it has been possible to exclude damage of this type from the scope of this Directive;

Whereas, since the exclusion of primary agricultural products and game from the scope of this Directive may be felt, in certain Member States, in view of what is expected for the protection of consumers, to restrict unduly such protection, it should be possible for a Member State to extend liability to such products;

Whereas, for similar reasons, the possibility offered to a producer to free himself from liability if he proves that the state of scientific and technical knowledge at the time when he put the product into circulation was not such as to enable the existence of a defect to be discovered may be felt in certain Member States to restrict unduly the protection of the consumer; whereas it should therefore be possible for a Member State to maintain in its legislation or to provide by new legislation that this exonerating circumstance is not admitted; whereas, in the case of new legislation, making use of this derogation should, however, be subject to a Community stand-still procedure, in order to raise, if possible, the level of protection in a uniform manner throughout the Community;

Whereas, taking into account the legal traditions in most of the Member States, it is inappropriate to set any financial ceiling on the producer's liability without fault; whereas, in so far as there are, however, differing traditions, it seems possible to admit that a Member State may derogate from the principle of unlimited liability by providing a limit for the total liability of the producer for damage resulting from a death or personal injury and caused by identical items with the same defect, provided that this limit is established at a level sufficiently high to guarantee adequate protection of the consumer and the correct functioning of the common market;

Whereas the harmonization resulting from this cannot be total at the present stage, but opens the way towards greater harmonization; whereas it is therefore necessary that the Council receive at regular intervals reports from the Commission on the application of this Directive, accompanied, as the case may be, by appropriate proposals;

Whereas it is particularly important in this respect that a re-examination be carried out of those parts of the Directive relating to the derogations open to the Member States, at the expiry of a period of sufficient length to gather practical experience on the effects of these derogations on the protection of consumers and on the functioning of the common market,

HAS ADOPTED THIS DIRECTIVE

Article 1

The producer shall be liable for damage caused by a defect in his product.

Article 2

For the purpose of this Directive, 'product' means all movables even if incorporated into another movable or into an immovable. 'Product' includes electricity.

Article 3

1. 'Producer' means the manufacturer of a finished product, the producer of any raw material or the manufacturer of a component part and any person who, by putting his name, trade mark or other distinguishing feature on the product, presents himself as its producer.
2. Without prejudice to the liability of the producer, any person who imports into the Community a product for sale, hire, leasing or any form of distribution in the course of his business shall be deemed to be a producer within the meaning of this Directive and shall be responsible as a producer.
3. Where the producer of the product cannot be identified, each supplier of the product shall be treated as its producer unless he informs the injured person, within a reasonable time, of the identity of the producer or of the person who supplied him with the product. The same shall apply, in the case of an imported product, if this product does not

indicate the identity of the importer referred to in paragraph 2, even if the name of the producer is indicated.

Article 4

The injured person shall be required to prove the damage, the defect and the causal relationship between defect and damage.

Article 5

Where, as a result of the provisions of this Directive, two or more persons are liable for the same damage, they shall be liable jointly and severally, without prejudice to the provisions of national law concerning the rights of contribution or recourse.

Article 6

1. A product is defective when it does not provide the safety which a person is entitled to expect, taking all circumstances into account, including:
   (a) the presentation of the product;
   (b) the use to which it could reasonably be expected that the product would be put;
   (c) the time when the product was put into circulation.
2. A product shall not be considered defective for the sole reason that a better product is subsequently put into circulation.

Article 7

The producer shall not be liable as a result of this Directive if he proves:

(a) that he did not put the product into circulation; or
(b) that, having regard to the circumstances, it is probable that the defect which caused the damage did not exist at the time when the product was put into circulation by him or that this defect came into being afterwards; or
(c) that the product was neither manufactured by him for sale or any form of distribution for economic purpose nor manufactured or distributed by him in the course of his business; or
(d) that the defect is due to compliance of the product with mandatory regulations issued by the public authorities; or

(e) that the state of scientific and technical knowledge at the time when he put the product into circulation was not such as to enable the existence of the defect to be discovered; or
(f) in the case of a manufacturer of a component, that the defect is attributable to the design of the product in which the component has been fitted or to the instructions given by the manufacturer of the product.

Article 8

1. Without prejudice to the provisions of national law concerning the right of contribution or recourse, the liability of the producer shall not be reduced when the damage is caused both by a defect in product and by the act or omission of a third party.
2. The liability of the producer may be reduced or disallowed when, having regard to all the circumstances, the damage is caused both by a defect in the product and by the fault of the injured person or any person for whom the injured person is responsible.

Article 9

For the purpose of Article 1, 'damage' means:

(a) damage caused by death or by personal injuries;
(b) damage to, or destruction of, any item of property other than the defective product itself, with a lower threshold of 500 ECU, provided that the item of property:
   (i) is of a type ordinarily intended for private use or consumption, and
   (ii) was used by the injured person mainly for his own private use or consumption.

This Article shall be without prejudice to national provisions relating to non-material damage.

Article 10

1. Member States shall provide in their legislation that a limitation period of three years shall apply to proceedings for the recovery of damages as provided for in this Directive. The limitation period shall begin to run from the day on which the plaintiff became aware, or should reasonably

have become aware, of the damage, the defect and the identity of the producer.

2. The laws of Member States regulating suspension or interruption of the limitation period shall not be affected by this Directive.

Article 11

Member States shall provide in their legislation that the rights conferred upon the injured person pursuant to this Directive shall be extinguished upon the expiry of a period of ten years from the date on which the producer put into circulation the actual product which caused the damage, unless the injured person has in the meantime instituted proceedings against the producer.

Article 12

The liability of the producer arising from this Directive may not, in relation to the injured person, be limited or excluded by a provision limiting his liability or exempting him from liability.

Article 13

This Directive shall not affect any rights which an injured person may have according to the rules of the law of contractual or non-contractual liability or a special liability system existing at the moment when this Directive is notified.

Article 14

This Directive shall not apply to injury or damage arising from nuclear accidents and covered by international conventions ratified by the Member States.

Article 15

1. Each Member State may:
   by way of derogation from Article 7 (e), maintain or, subject to the procedure set out in paragraph 2 of this Article, provide in this legislation that the producer shall be liable even if he proves that the state of scientific and technical knowledge at the time when he put the product into circulation was not such as to enable the existence of a defect to be discovered.

2. A Member State wishing to introduce the measure specified in paragraph 1 (b) shall communicate the text of the proposed measure to the Commission. The Commission shall inform the other Member States thereof.

   The Member State concerned shall hold the proposed measure in abeyance for nine months after the Commission is informed and provided that in the meantime the Commission has not submitted to the Council a proposal amending this Directive on the relevant matter. However, if within three months of receiving the said information, the Commission does not advise the Member State concerned that it intends submitting such a proposal to the Council, the Member State may take the proposed measure immediately.

   If the Commission does submit to the Council such a proposal amending this Directive within the aforementioned nine months, the Member State concerned shall hold the proposed measure in abeyance for a further period of eighteen months from the date on which the proposal is submitted.
3. Ten years after the date of notification of this Directive, the Commission shall submit to the Council a report on the effect that rulings by the courts as to the application of Article 7 (e) and of paragraph 1 (b) of this Article have on consumer protection and the functioning of the common market. In the light of this report the Council, acting on a proposal from the Commission and pursuant to the terms of Article 100 of the Treaty, shall decide whether to repeal Article 7 (e).

Article 16

1. Any Member State may provide that a producer's total liability for damage resulting from a death or personal injury and caused by identical items with the same defect shall be limited to an amount which may not be less than 70 million ECU.
2. Ten years after the date of notification of this Directive, the Commission shall submit to the Council a report on the effect on consumer protection and the functioning of the common market of the implementation of the financial limit on liability by those Member States which have used the option provided for in paragraph 1. In the light of this report the Council, acting on a proposal from the Commission and pursuant to the terms of Article 100 of the Treaty, shall decide whether to repeal paragraph 1.

Article 17

This Directive shall not apply to products put into circulation before the date on which the provisions referred to in Article 19 enter into force.

Article 18

1. For the purposes of this Directive, the ECU shall be that defined by Regulation (EEC) No. 3180/78,[4] as amended by Regulation (EEC) No. 2626/84.[5] The equivalent in national currency shall initially be calculated at the rate obtaining on the date of adoption of this Directive.
2. Every five years the Council, acting on a proposal from the Commission, shall examine and, if need be, revise the amounts in this Directive, in the light of economic and monetary trends in the Community.

Article 19

1. Member States shall bring into force, not later than three years from the date of notification of this Directive, the laws, regulations and administrative provisions necessary to comply with this Directive. They shall forthwith inform the Commission thereof.[6]
2. The procedure set out in Article 15 (2) shall apply from the date of notification of this Directive.

Article 20

Member States shall communicate to the Commission the texts of the main provisions of national law which they subsequently adopt in the field governed by this Directive.

Article 21

Every five years the Commission shall present a report to the Council on the application of this Directive and, if necessary, shall submit appropriate proposals to it.

Article 22

This Directive is addressed to the Member States.

[4] OJ No. L 379, 30. 12. 1978, p. 1. [5] OJ No. L 247, 16. 9. 1984, p. 1.
[6] This Directive was notified to the Member States on 30 July 1985.

INDEX

For EU product safety concerns, contact us at Calle de José Abascal, 56–1°,
28003 Madrid, Spain or eugpsr@cambridge.org.

www.ingramcontent.com/pod-product-compliance
Ingram Content Group UK Ltd.
Pitfield, Milton Keynes, MK11 3LW, UK
UKHW011326060825
461487UK00005B/373

* 9 7 8 0 5 2 1 8 4 7 2 3 0 *